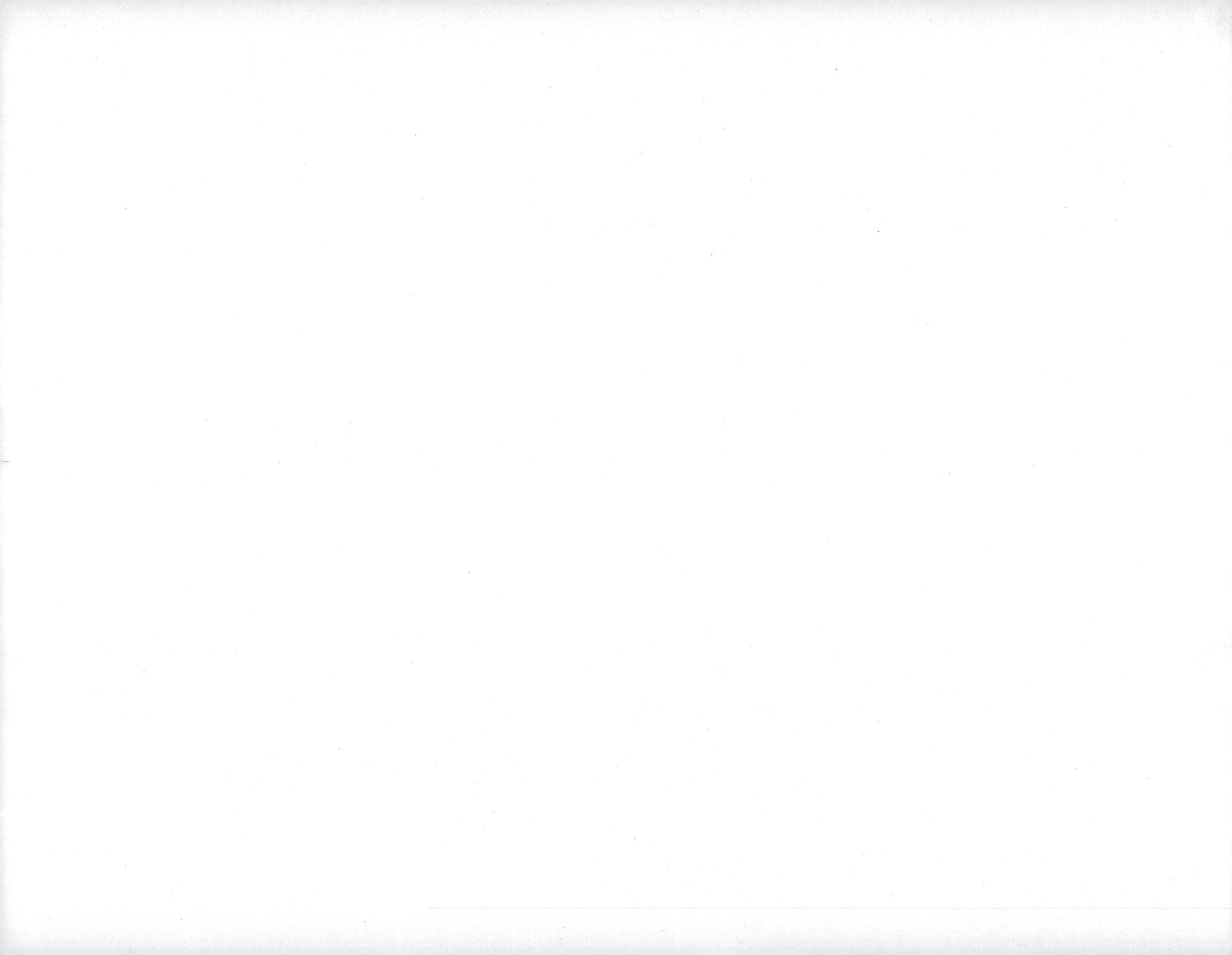

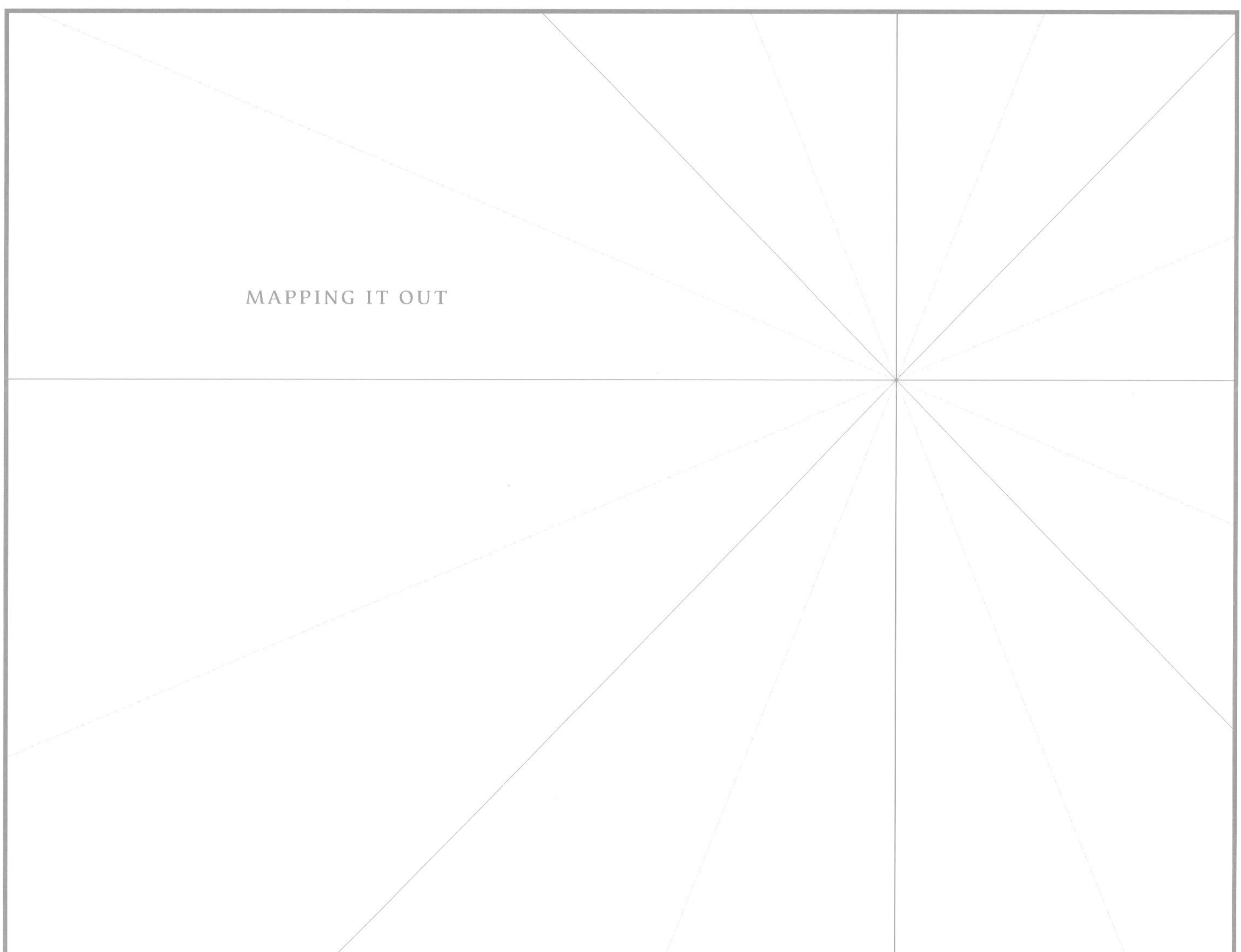

MAPPING IT OUT

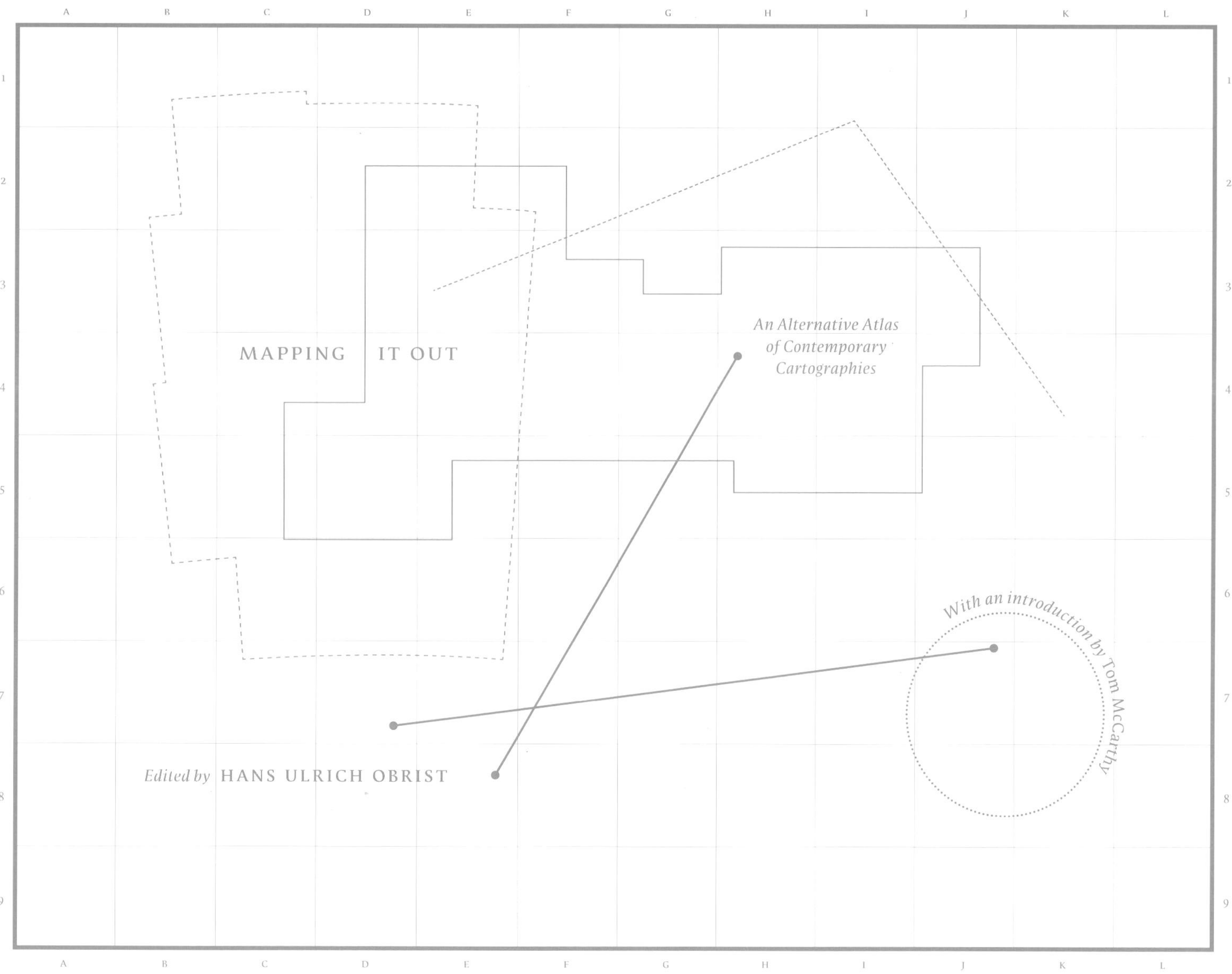

Thames & Hudson

KEY

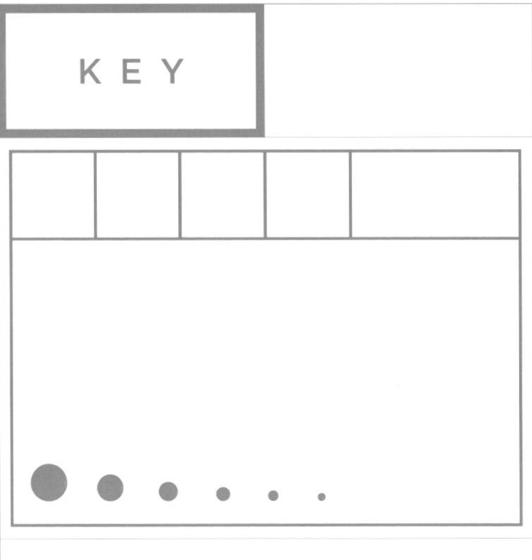

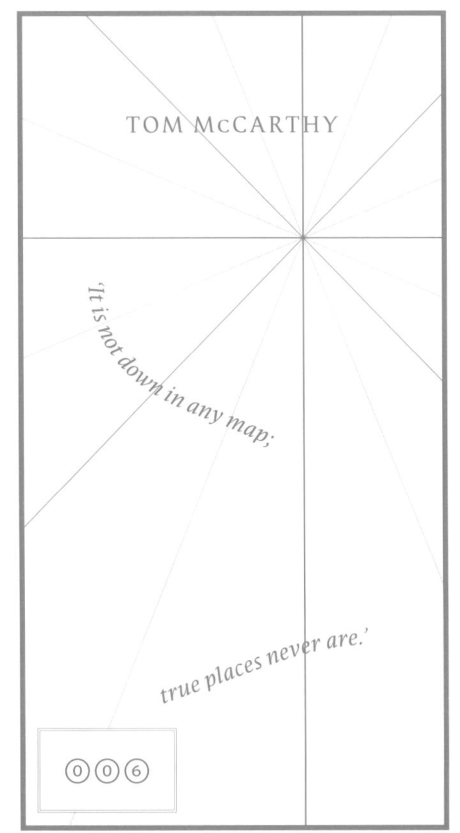
TOM McCARTHY
'It is not down in any map;
true places never are.'
006

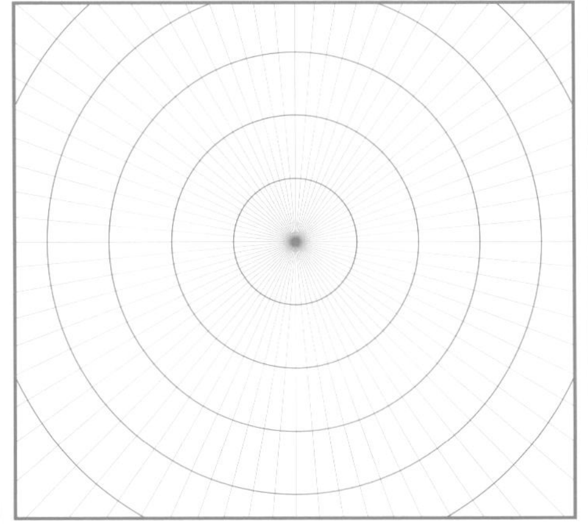

Scientia Naturalis
THREE 124

Invented Worlds
FOUR 152

1 2 3 4 5 6 7

A B C D E F G H I J K

1 2 3 4 5 6 7

The Unmappable
FIVE 190

You are here ... and now

> ‘It is not down in any map; true places never are.’

HERMAN MELVILLE
Moby-Dick

TOM McCARTHY

A few years back, when Google’s various cartographic apps became ubiquitous, discussion groups were flooded with accounts of strange anomalies. Buildings, streets or, on occasion, entire cities disappeared; coastlines and mountain ranges warped; highways kinked and buckled; giant lacunae sprung up, sinkholes yawning from innocuous fields and deserts. The cause, of course, was glitch-ridden software and faulty collating techniques. But to dismiss this as a uniquely twenty-first-century phenomenon, a digital quirk, would be to overlook an essential feature of all maps: namely, that they don’t work, and never have. Pick up any textbook on cartography, and the very first paragraph will invariably remind you that the Earth is spherical but paper is flat; and, as J. A. Steers points out in his 1927 *Introduction to the Study of Map Projections*, just ‘as it is impossible to make a sheet of paper rest smoothly on a sphere, so it is impossible to make a correct map on a sheet of paper’. Maps are not *copies*; they are *projections*, ‘means’ (Steers again) ‘of representing the lines of latitude and longitude of the globe on a flat sheet of paper’.

Now, this is where the problems start. Projections are not neutral, natural or ‘given’: they are constructed, configured, underpinned by various – and quite arbitrary – conventions. When drawing up a map, a cartographer must choose between zenithal, gnomonic, stereographic, orthographic, globular, conical, cylindrical or sinusoidal modes of projection – each of which brings with it as many disadvantages as benefits. In world maps drawn using Mercator’s projection, the one that served as the standard in atlases for centuries, the equatorial areas pan out fine, but the map starts to distend enormously as it nears the polar regions, stretching Greenland out until it looks bigger than Africa. The poles themselves cannot be represented at all: to depict these you must rotate the image round through ninety degrees – the Transverse Mercator projection does this – but then another pair of points (on the equator) undergo infinite distortion and become invisible. Another option is to replace Mercator’s projection with a polar gnomonic one – but this merely makes the rest of the world distend and drop off the horizon.

No wonder, then, that artists from Leonardo and Dürer to Boetti and Ruscha have been fascinated by maps: the cartographer’s problem is the draughtsman’s problem, the problem of perspective. Holbein understood this perfectly. In his famous painting *The Ambassadors*, two statesmen stand surrounded by cartographic paraphernalia: globes, a torquetum, a quadrant and so on. Yet occupying the space between the two men on the carpet is a proto-Googlish blur, an anamorphic zone in which the entire image goes all ‘wrong’. As visitors to London’s National Gallery discover, when they move round to the painting’s side, this zone resolves itself into the image of a skull, which looms into focus at the very moment the men and their instruments melt away into an imbroglio of random marks. Thus Holbein confronts us with the futility not only of wealth and status, but also of perspective itself: beyond a certain limit, both are doomed to formlessness, to vanishing – to the skull and, by extension, to death.

Melville's Polynesian harpoonist Queequeg seems to understand this too. Already covered in a cosmic tribal map (his entire body is tattooed with curves and lines that form 'a complete theory of the heavens and the earth'), he copies this same map onto a coffin lid – or rather, since his body is curved, lanky and generally three-dimensional while the coffin lid is flat, he *projects* it. Once more, it's death, or its marker, that provides the surface across which this map-projection finds its form. Readers of *Moby-Dick* will recall that the coffin makes a comeback at the novel's end, when, after the *Pequod*'s wreck, it provides Ishmael with a life raft upon which to float, effectively conveying the text of *Moby-Dick* to us (had Ishmael, our narrator, not survived, there'd be no narrative to hear, no book to read). This harks back to the novel's opening vignette, a short description of an archivist who, with a handkerchief 'mockingly embellished with all the gay flags of all the known nations of the world ... loved to dust his old grammars; it somehow mildly reminded him of his mortality'. Once more, a global cartographic motif (flags and nations) joins one of death (dust and mortality); and, just as Queequeg's tattoo-map is also a synecdoche for knowledge in its entirety – it is, Melville informs us, 'a mystical treatise on the art of attaining truth' – so this man's dusty action, the purveying of lexicons and dictionaries, stands in for the bearing of all archives, of all books. The entire domain of literature, it seems, is tied up in the question of the map.

ABOVE

Hans Holbein the Younger,
The Ambassadors, 1533

Moby-Dick is, of course, a political novel, concerned as it is with the trajectories of global commerce, zones and strata of dominion and power. And, to state the even more obvious, *The Ambassadors* is a political painting: what are Holbein's figures doing if not carving up the continents and oceans into dominions, empires? Mapping always, at some level, involves violence. The recent work of Eyal Weizman on Israeli military strategy gives countless examples of Arab territories being bulldozed, ploughed through and reshaped until they conform to the occupier's cartographic vision. Brian Friel's 1980 play *Translations* paints the Maps Section of the British Army as the real villains of the Irish occupation, since in anglicizing local names they voided the landscape of its history and legends. Yet if maps serve the oppressor, they can also play a role in the armoury of the oppressed. For every 'official' map, there are two, five, twenty possible counter-maps. In the Surrealist world map of 1929, countries are reallotted sizes concomitant with their importance to the overall Surrealist project. England, consequently, disappears, as does America (with the exception of Alaska), while Mexico, Peru and Easter Island assume giant proportions. The Situationists, for their part, redrew the map of France, replacing French names with Algerian ones. In instances like these, map-making, far from fixing a reality, becomes a wild proliferation of alternative ones, of possible worlds each one as faulty and fantastic as the next ...

And yet, explicitly or not, all maps carry with them a certain claim: that *this* one is somehow *truer* than the others with which it competes; that it depicts a territory in a more subtle, penetrative, intimate or nuanced way. The fantasy that lies behind cartography is that of seeing space deeply, totally and *really* – either from its outside or else from some buried, hidden inner vantage point that commands all sightlines and allows no enclave, pocket or aporia to elude its visual field and slink away into the dark. This is the fantasy of Kafka's molelike creature in *The Burrow*, who, having charted every chamber, passageway and trapdoor of his large and sprawling subterranean territory, realizes that even this is not enough: he has to go *outside* the burrow, and observe this entire world from just beyond its borders (which, of course, lays him vulnerable to the very predators he built the burrow to avoid). This is also the pathology that afflicts Fred Madison in David Lynch's masterpiece *Lost Highway*, leading him to break into and film his home and, ultimately, himself, from beyond the boundary line of both of these – an act, of course, that is both physically and ontologically impossible, that can, and does, lead only to psychosis.

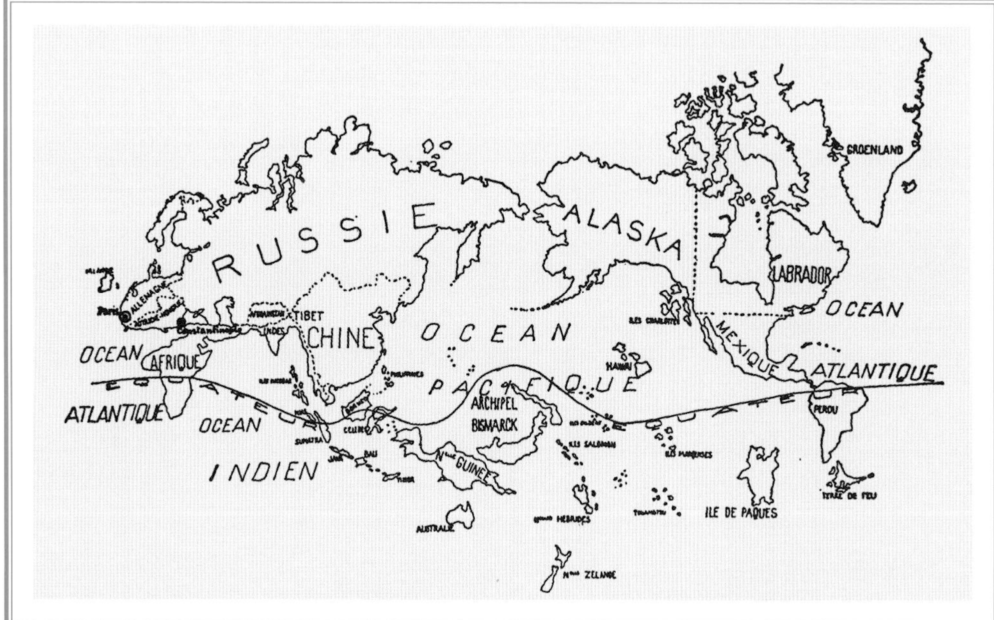

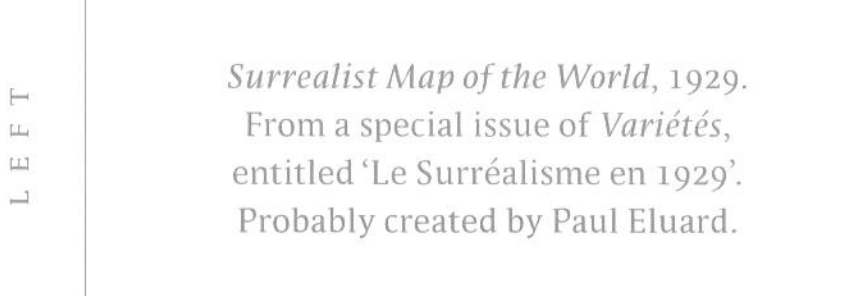

LEFT

Surrealist Map of the World, 1929.
From a special issue of *Variétés*, entitled 'Le Surréalisme en 1929'.
Probably created by Paul Eluard.

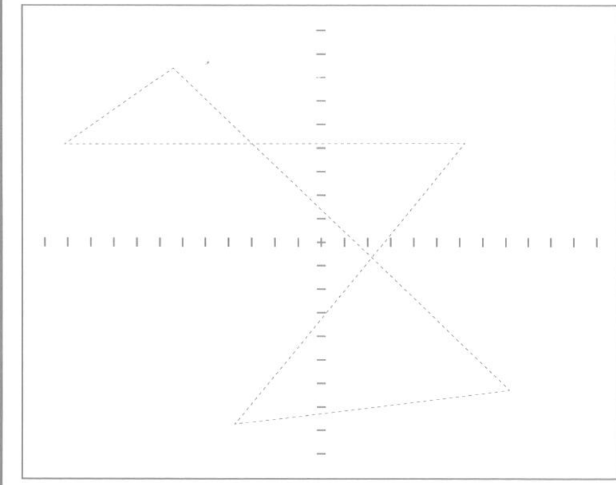

Cartopsychosis: I propose that this is the truth not only of geography but also of identity *tout court* – that is, of Being. We live in the gaps: the oblique, morphing interzones between perspectival regimes that themselves are anything but stable; the mangled and unkeystoned buckle-fields where grids unravel into random strings; regions whose real capitals and landmarks are Novaya Zemlya, Fata Morgana, Hillingar and Castles-in-the-Air; a territory whose true north, or degree zero, if it could be shown (which it can't), would take the form of a kind of pregnant invisibility. Which is why, for me, the only *genuinely* accurate map ever drawn is the one Lewis Carroll gives us in *The Hunting of the Snark*. Addressing his crew (all of whose titles, as though to emphasize their status as Beings, start with the letter B), the vessel's Bellman rhetorically – and brilliantly – asks:

> What's the good of Mercator's North
> Poles and Equators, Tropics, Zones,
> and Meridian Lines?' So the Bellman
> would cry: and the crew would reply,
> 'They are merely conventional signs!'

The Bellman then pulls out – four whole decades before Malevich, it should be noted – a piece of paper, white as an albino whale, on which precisely Nothing is depicted. And the crew erupts in jubilation: no cartographic fools, they understand the huge importance of the document they've just been gifted:

> 'Other maps are such shapes,
> with their islands and capes!
> But we've got our brave captain to thank'
> (So the crew would protest)
> 'that he's bought *us* the best –
> A perfect and absolute blank!'

R I G H T

'The Bellman's Ocean-Chart', from Lewis Carroll's *The Hunting of the Snark: An Agony in Eight Fits*, 1876

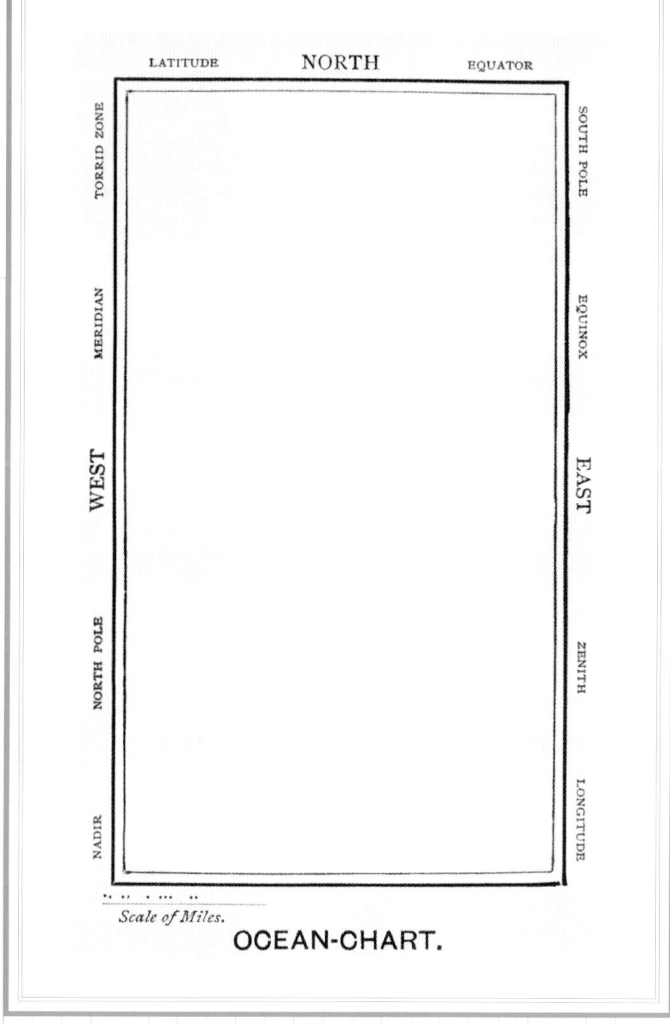

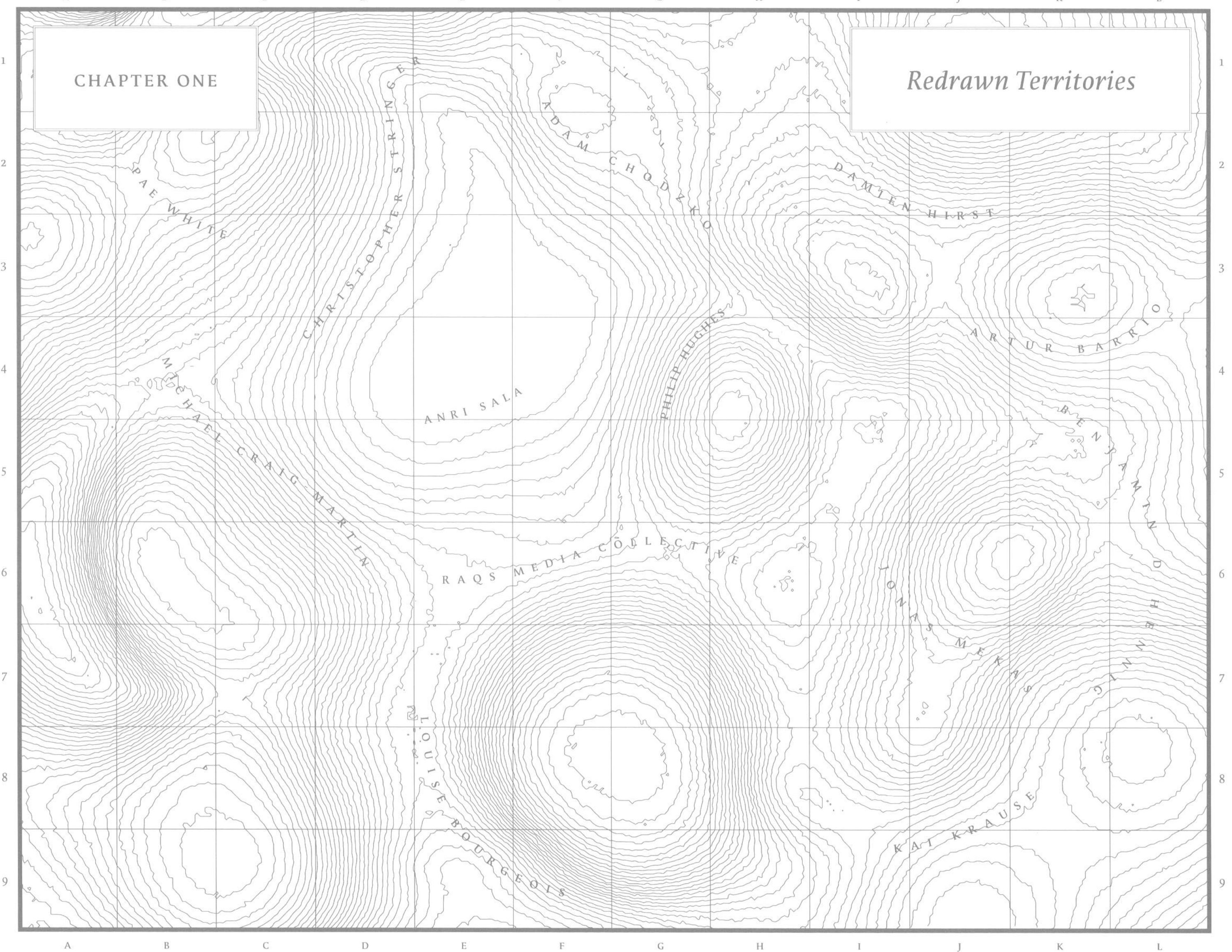

CHAPTER ONE
Redrawn Territories
PAE WHITE
CHRISTOPHER STRINGER
ADAM CHODZKO
DAMIEN HIRST
ARTUR BARRIO
PHILIP HUGHES
ANRI SALA
MICHAEL CRAIG MARTIN
BENJAMIN HENNIG
RAQS MEDIA COLLECTIVE
JONAS MEKAS
LOUISE BOURGEOIS
KAI KRAUSE

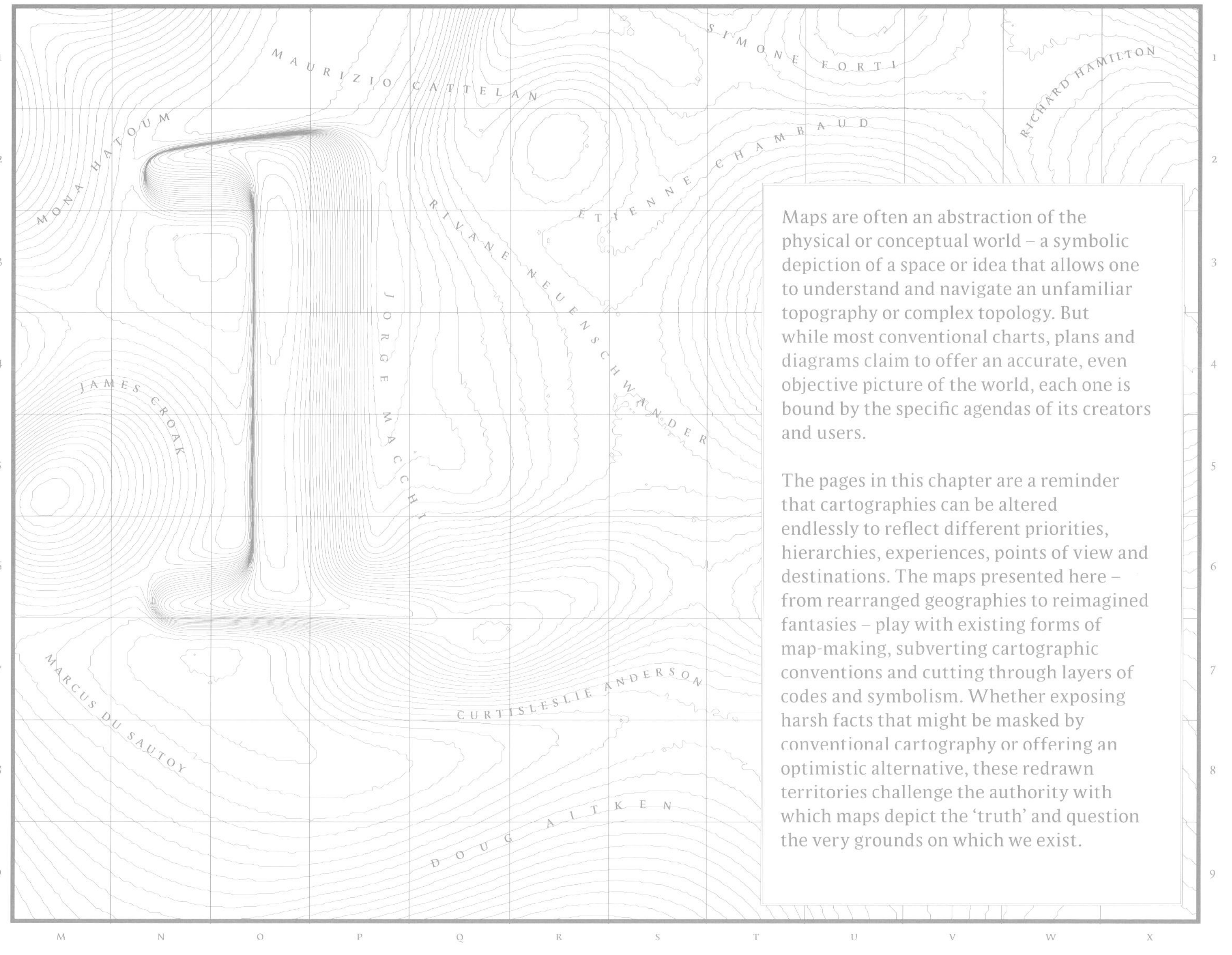

Maps are often an abstraction of the physical or conceptual world – a symbolic depiction of a space or idea that allows one to understand and navigate an unfamiliar topography or complex topology. But while most conventional charts, plans and diagrams claim to offer an accurate, even objective picture of the world, each one is bound by the specific agendas of its creators and users.

The pages in this chapter are a reminder that cartographies can be altered endlessly to reflect different priorities, hierarchies, experiences, points of view and destinations. The maps presented here – from rearranged geographies to reimagined fantasies – play with existing forms of map-making, subverting cartographic conventions and cutting through layers of codes and symbolism. Whether exposing harsh facts that might be masked by conventional cartography or offering an optimistic alternative, these redrawn territories challenge the authority with which maps depict the ‘truth’ and question the very grounds on which we exist.

LOUISE BOURGEOIS
A—R—T—I—S—T

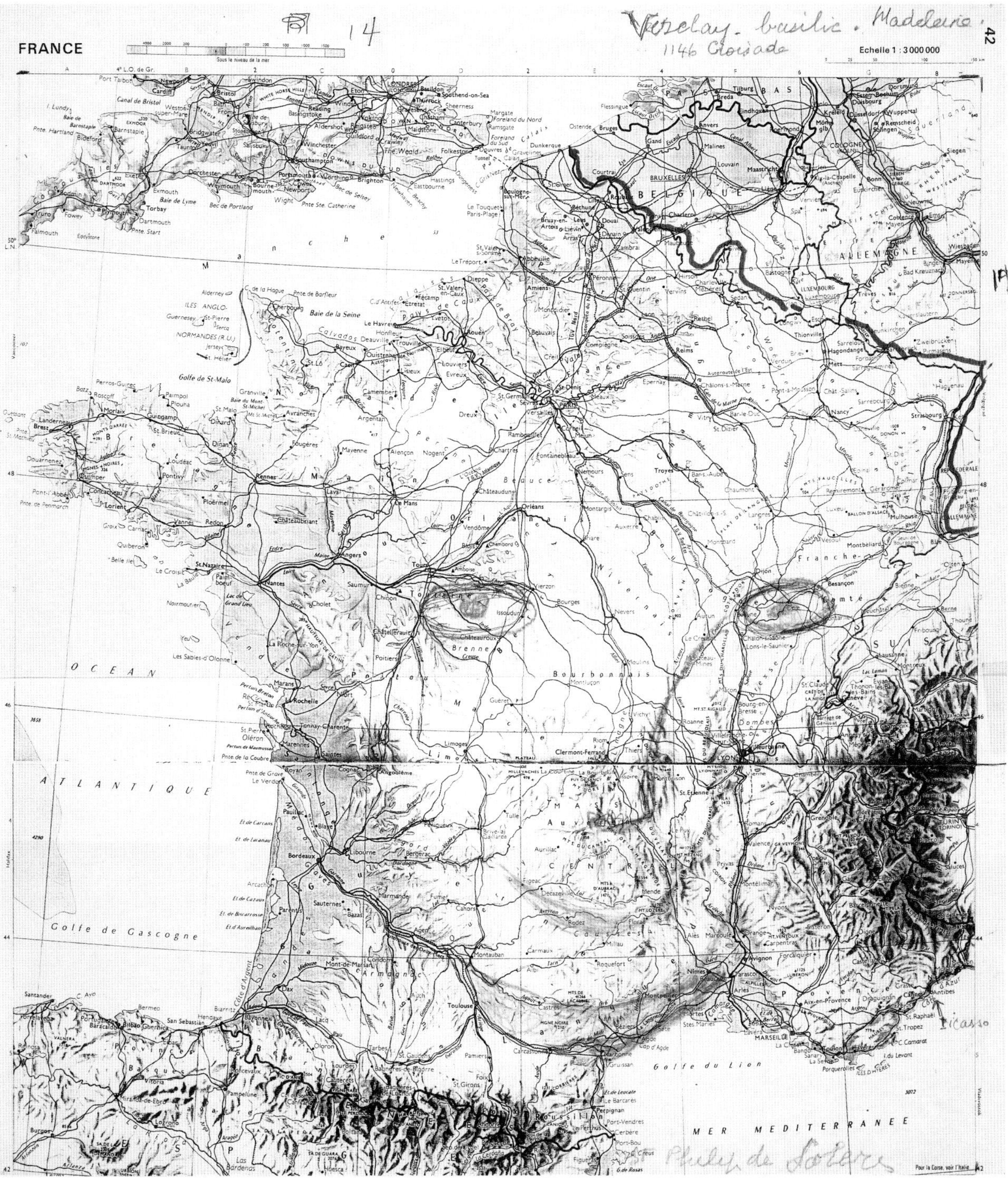
FRANCE
Echelle 1 : 3 000 000
42
14
1146 Croisade
Picasso
Manche
OCEAN
ATLANTIQUE
Golfe de Gascogne
Golfe du Lion
MER MEDITERRANEE
BELGIQUE
ALLEMAGNE
LUXEMBOURG
PARIS
LYON
MARSEILLE
Bordeaux
Toulouse
Orléans
Limoges
Clermont-Ferrand
Nantes
Rennes
Le Mans
Tours
Angers
Dijon
Besançon
Strasbourg
Reims
Amiens
Rouen
Le Havre
Cherbourg
Brest
Lorient
Poitiers
La Rochelle
Avignon
Nîmes
Montpellier
Perpignan
Grenoble
Nice
Toulon
Bretagne
Normandie
Beauce
Bourbonnais
Auvergne
Provence
Pays de Caux
Brenne
Golfe de St-Malo
Baie de la Seine
ILES ANGLO-NORMANDES (R.U.)
Pour la Corse, voir l'Italie

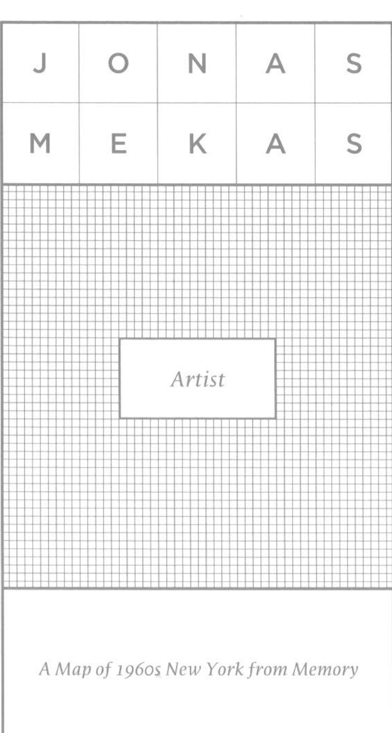

A Map of 1960s New York from Memory

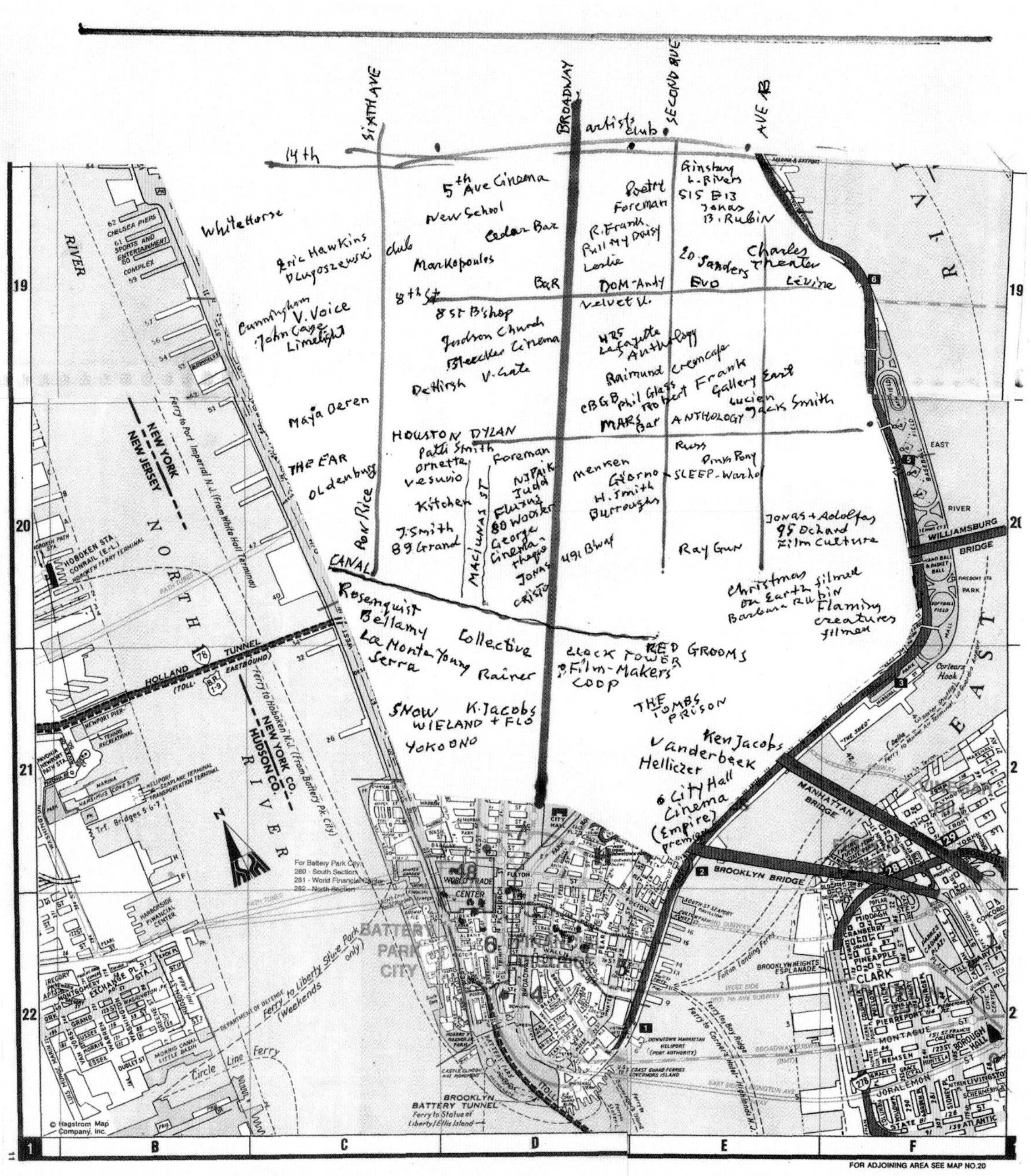

Bleec

DeHirsh V. Gate

Raimund Creme

Robert Frank

Gallery East

CBGB Phil Glass

Lucien

Jack Smith

Maya Deren

MARS Bar ANTHOLOGY

HOUSTON DYLAN

Patti Smith

Ornette

Foreman

Russ

Pinks Pony

THE EAR

Oldenburg

Vesuvio

NJPAIK

Menken

Giorno - SLEEP - Warhol

Judd

H. Smith

Burroughs

Ron Rice

Kitchen

MACIUNAS ST

Fluxus

80 Wooster

J. Smith

89 Grand

George Cinematheque

JONAS

491 Bway

Ray Gun

JONAS + Adolfas

95 Orchard

Film Culture

CANAL

CRISTO

Christmas on Earth filmed

Barbara Rubin

Flaming creatures filmed

Rosenquist

Bellamy

Collective

La Monte Young

Serra

Rainer

CLOCK TOWER

Film-Makers COOP

RED GROOMS

SNOW

K. Jacobs

WIELAND + FLO

YOKO ONO

THE TOMBS PRISON

Ken Jacobs

Vanderbeek

Helliczer

City Hall Cinema (Empire) premiere

CITY HALL

WORLD TRADE CENTER

MANHATTAN BRIDGE

BROOKLYN BRIDGE

"THE SHED"

NEW YORK CO.

Hoboken N.J. (from Battery Pk. City)

BATTERY PARK

For Battery Park City:
280 - South Section
281 - World Financial Center
282 - North Section

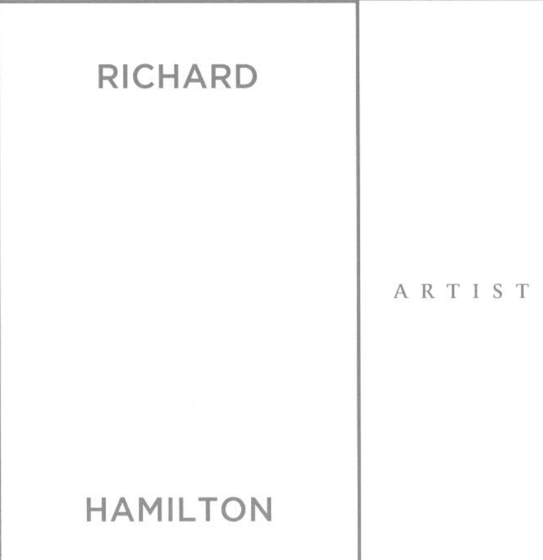
RICHARD
HAMILTON
ARTIST

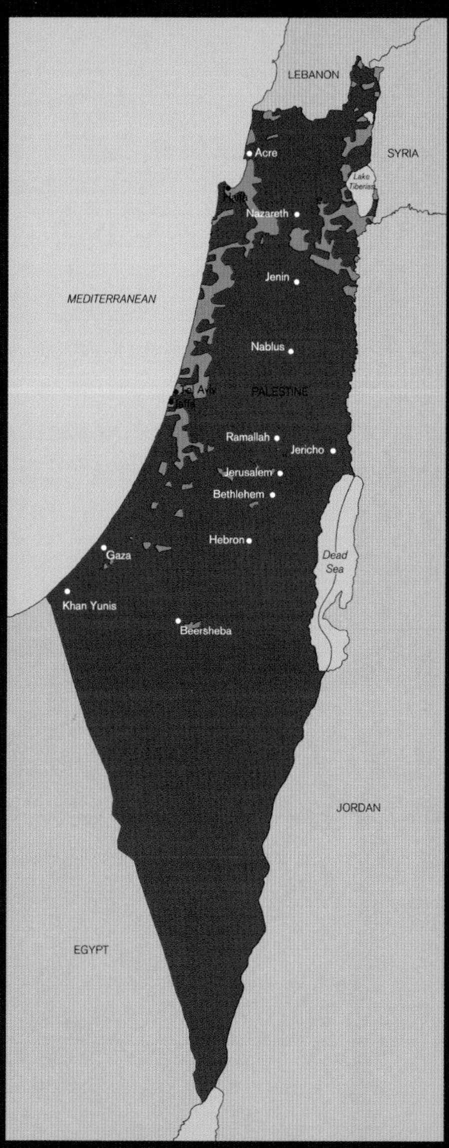

Palestine prior to partition

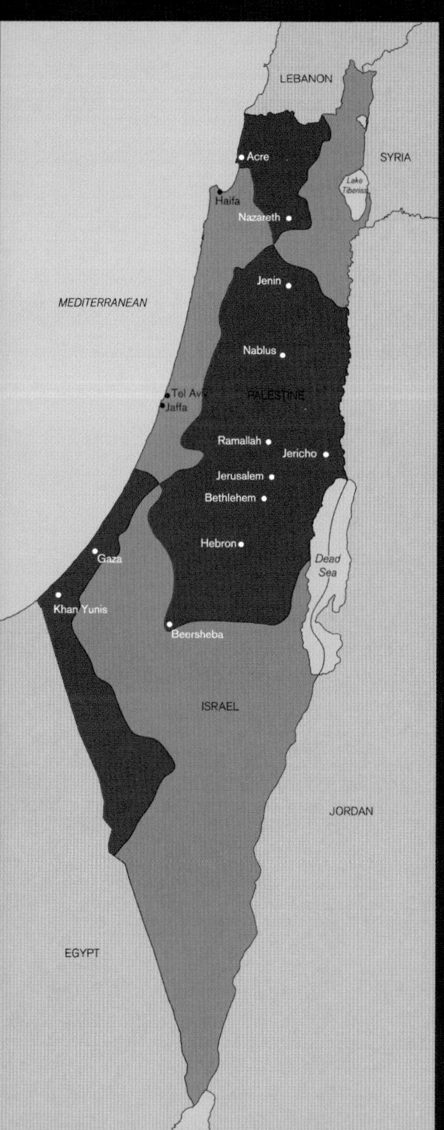

1947 UN partition plan

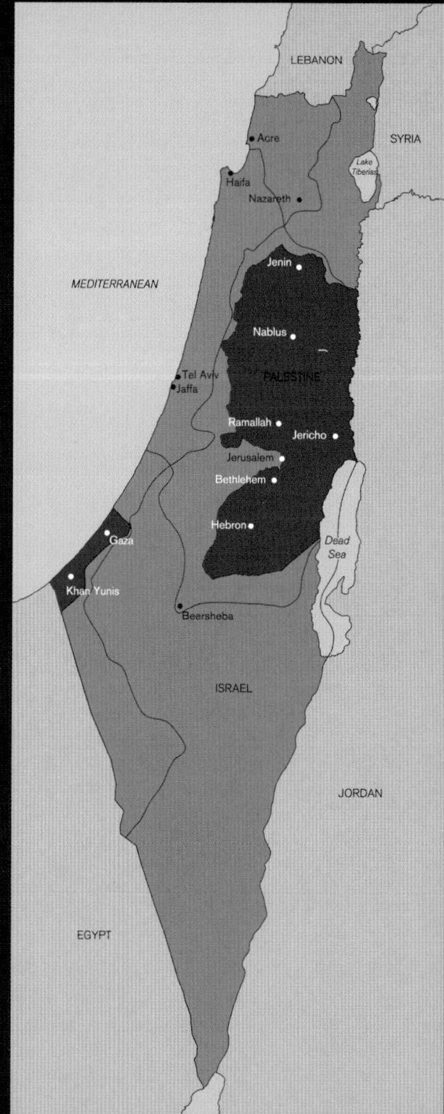

1949 Rhodes armistice line

1967-2008 Israeli incursions

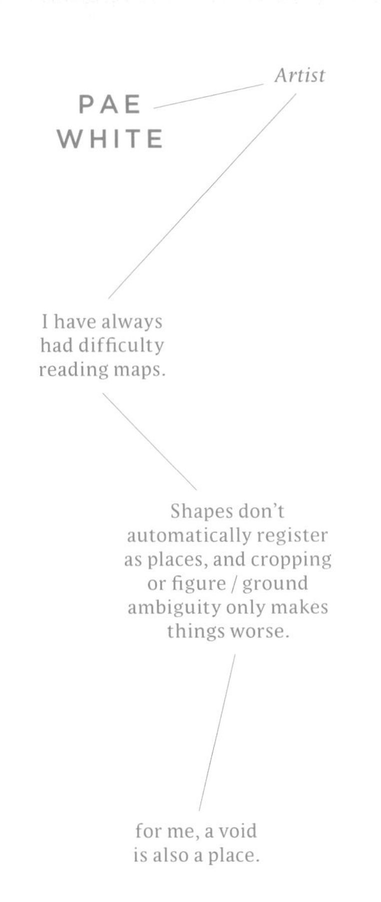
Artist
PAE WHITE
I have always had difficulty reading maps.
Shapes don't automatically register as places, and cropping or figure / ground ambiguity only makes things worse.
for me, a void is also a place.

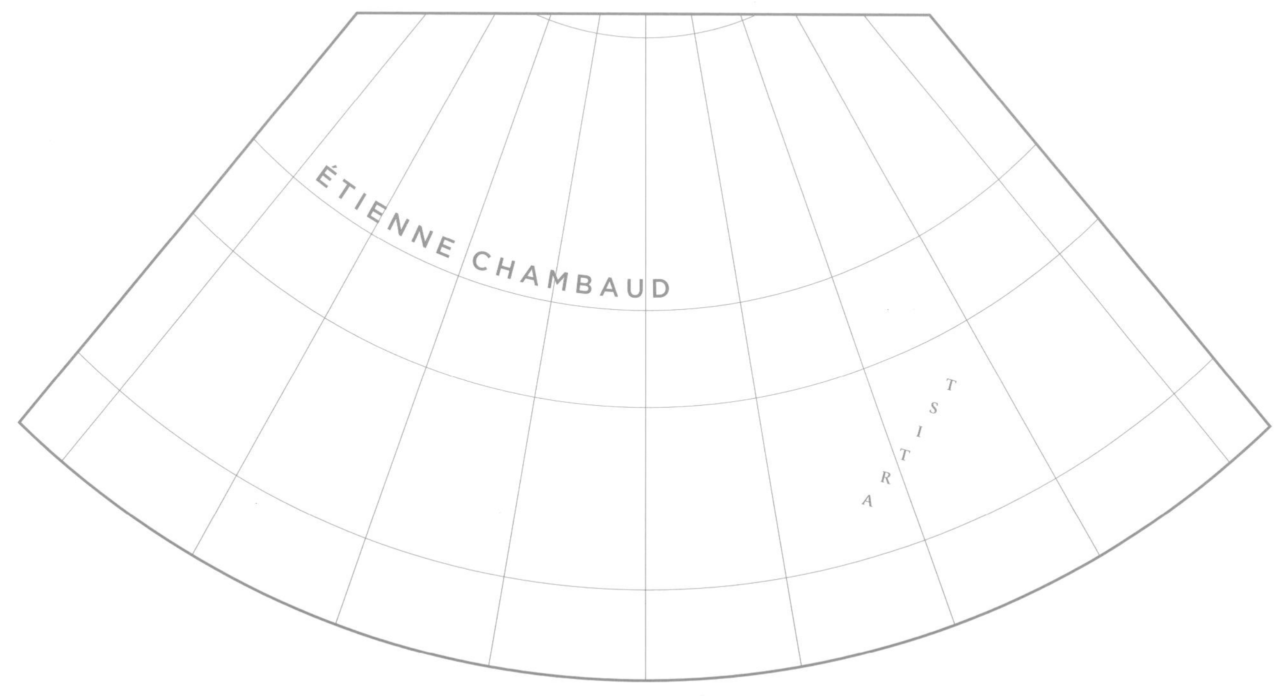
ÉTIENNE CHAMBAUD
ARTIST

ITALY
178

AUSTRIA, HUNGARY, CZECHOSLOVAKIA, and YUGOSLAVIA
AUSTRIA AFTER WORLD WAR II
1. UNITED STATES ADMINISTRATION
2. BRITISH ADMINISTRATION
3. FRENCH ADMINISTRATION
4. SOVIET ADMINISTRATION
VIENNA—INTER-ALLIED ADMINISTRATION
RUSSIAN SOVIET FED
179

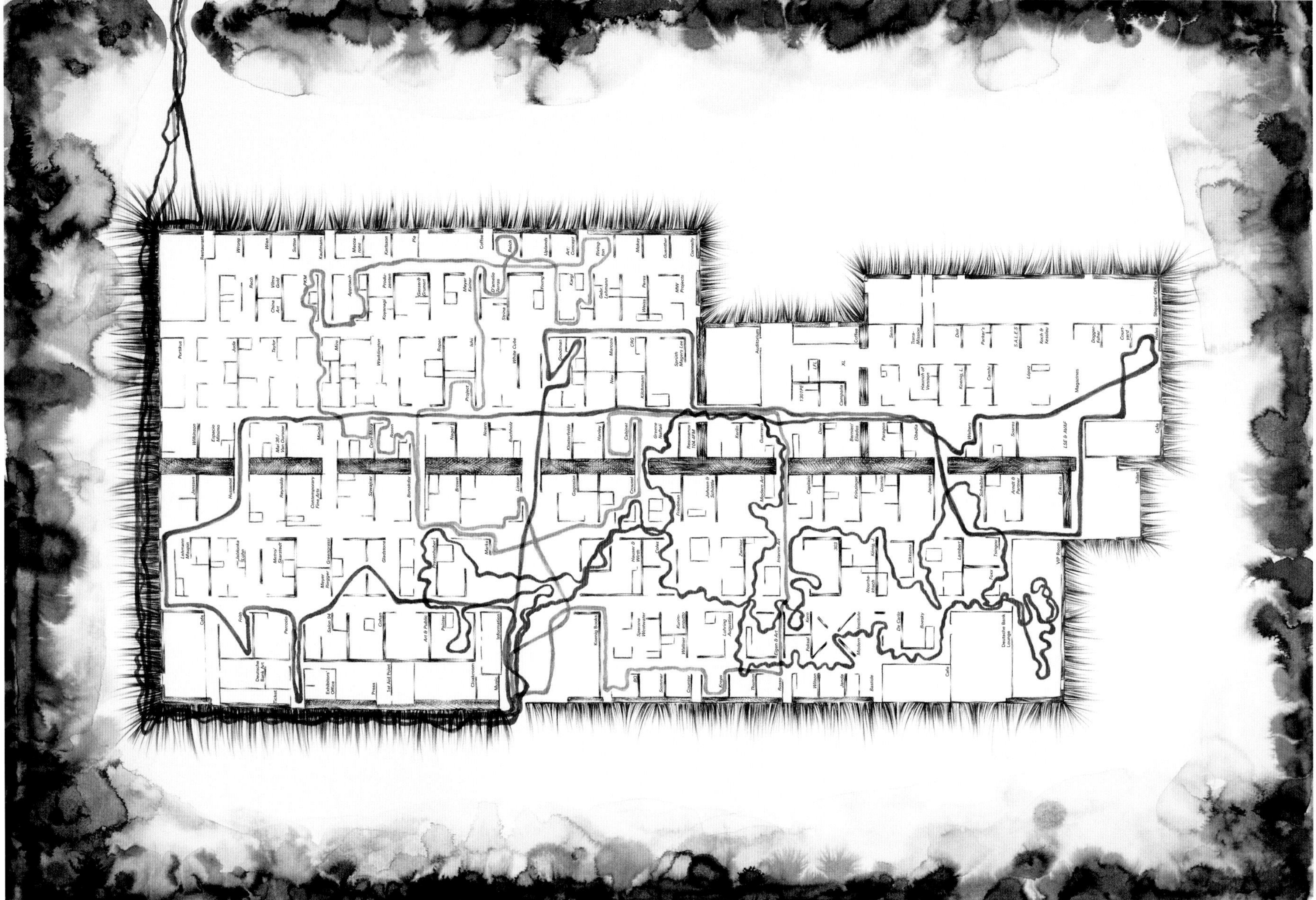

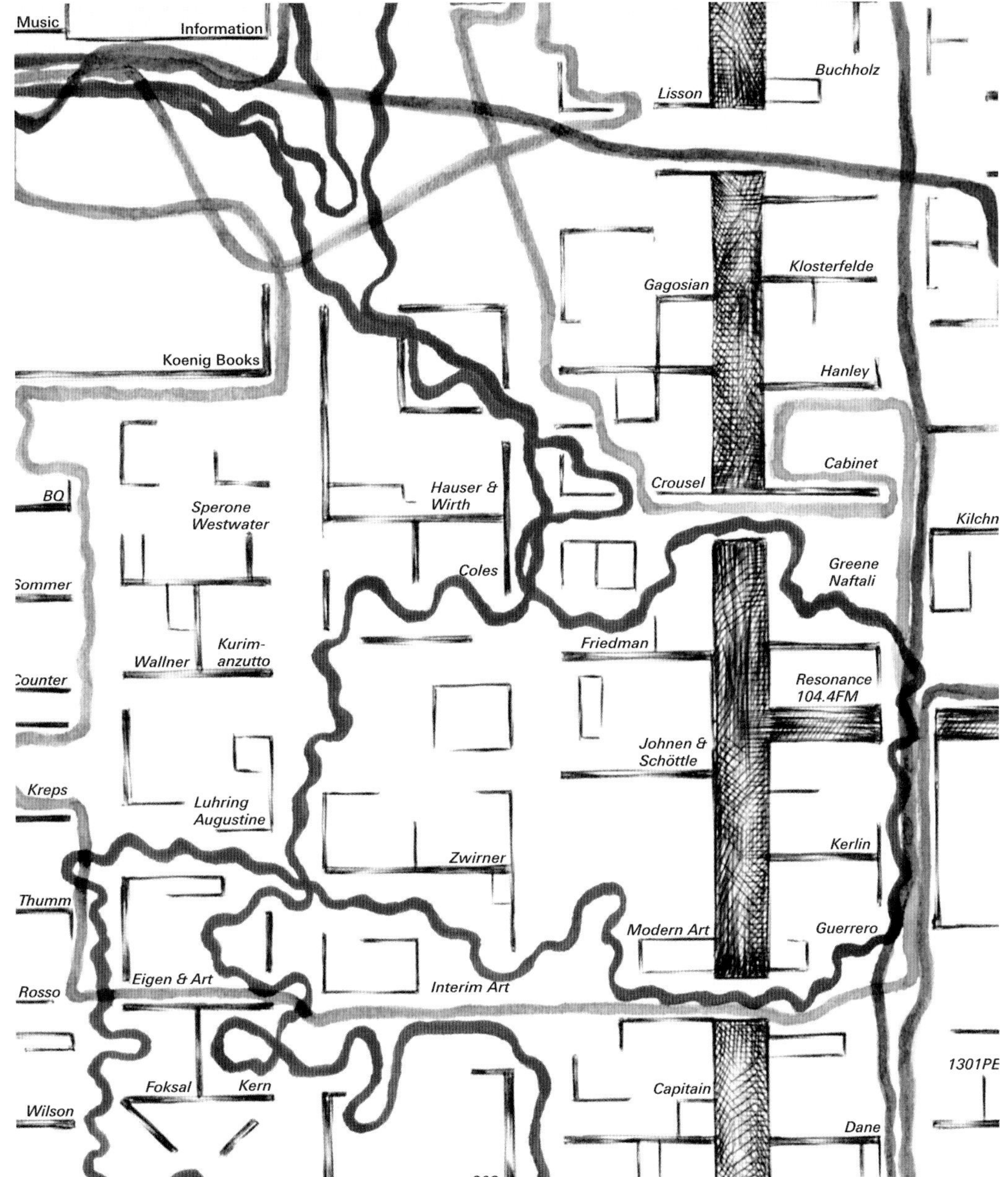

ADAM CHODZKO

ARTIST | *Night Shift* | 2004

The Wrong Map

I often use the wrong map. Sometimes by accident. Sometimes on purpose. Either way, the coordinates of where I could be going (or coming from) get projected from their two dimensions onto the specificity of me, here, now. An accident to be explored, to look for better – perhaps, momentarily, ideal – translations in this new set of alignments.

The official map of London's Frieze Art Fair is 'for the public', yet its paucity of detail suggests that it is aimed at a small group of collectors. Who else would need to identify the shortest route to Hauser and Wirth, say, or Hollybush Gardens (a route selected just as much for avoidance as it is for coincidence)? You look at the official map and see only a frame magnifying your lack of inside knowledge. ¶ *Night Shift* is an alternative map for the public visiting the 2004 fair – held in an enormous tent in a park so close to London Zoo. This map offers the navigation of an empathic pathway. A trail of a different kind of consciousness. Within its plan of the maze configured by numerous commercial galleries' plots are the traces of three journeys: the routes taken by a wolf, a skunk and a python on consecutive nights leading up to the opening of the fair. ¶ These nocturnal visitors entered the tent when the humans had left for the night, building a sporadic carnival parade through its labyrinths. On subsequent nights, paths were made by a red deer stag, a rat, a toad and a scorpion. Their routes are advice for the fair's daylight visitors. They give a purpose. Follow the wolf path and therefore become a wolf in order to see art.

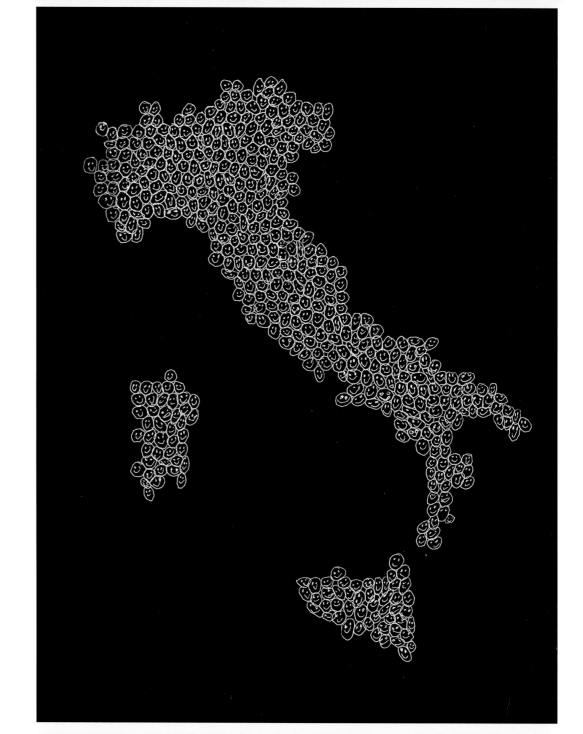

MAURIZIO CATTELAN

MICHAEL CRAIG-MARTIN

A — R — T — I — S — T

Globalisation, 2011

ASIAN COUNTRIES	EU COUNTRIES	ASIAN CITIES	US CITIES
Afghanistan	Bulgaria	Bangkok	Las Vegas
Bangladesh	Luxembourg	Beijing	Washington
Burma	Finland	Colombo	Omaha
Cambodia	Latvia	Dhaka	Minneapolis
China	Germany	Hanoi	Phoenix
India	France	Hong Kong	San Francisco
Indonesia	Sweden	Islamabad	Salt Lake City
Japan	United Kingdom	Jakarta	Honolulu
Kazakhstan	Poland	Kabul	Denver
Kyrgyzstan	Czech Republic	Kathmandu	Nashville
Laos	Estonia	Kuala Lumpur	San Diego
Malaysia	Denmark	Manila	New Orleans
Mongolia	Portugal	Mumbai	Los Angeles
Nepal	Austria	New Delhi	Philadelphia
North Korea	Belgium	Phnom Penh	St. Louis
Pakistan	Romania	Pyongyang	Detroit
Philippines	Greece	Rangoon	Boston
Russia	Spain	Seoul	Atlanta
South Korea	Netherlands	Shanghai	New York
Sri Lanka	Malta	Singapore	Miami
Taiwan	Ireland	Taipei	Dallas
Tajikistan	Slovakia	Tashkent	Milwaukee
Thailand	Italy	Tokyo	Chicago
Timor-Leste	Cyprus	Ulan Bator	Kansas City
Turkmenistan	Slovenia	Vladivostok	Baltimore
Uzbekistan	Hungary		
Vietnam	Lithuania		

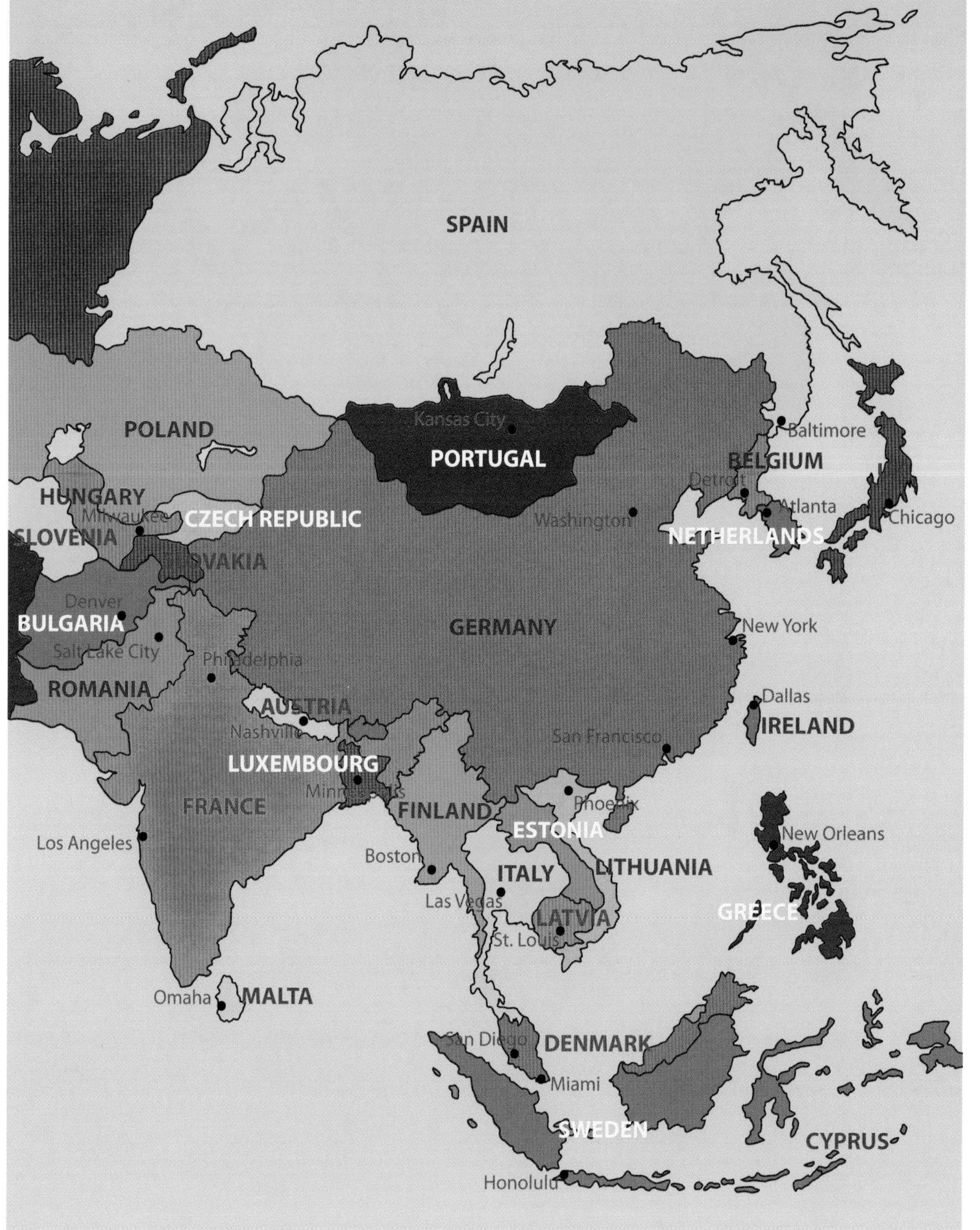

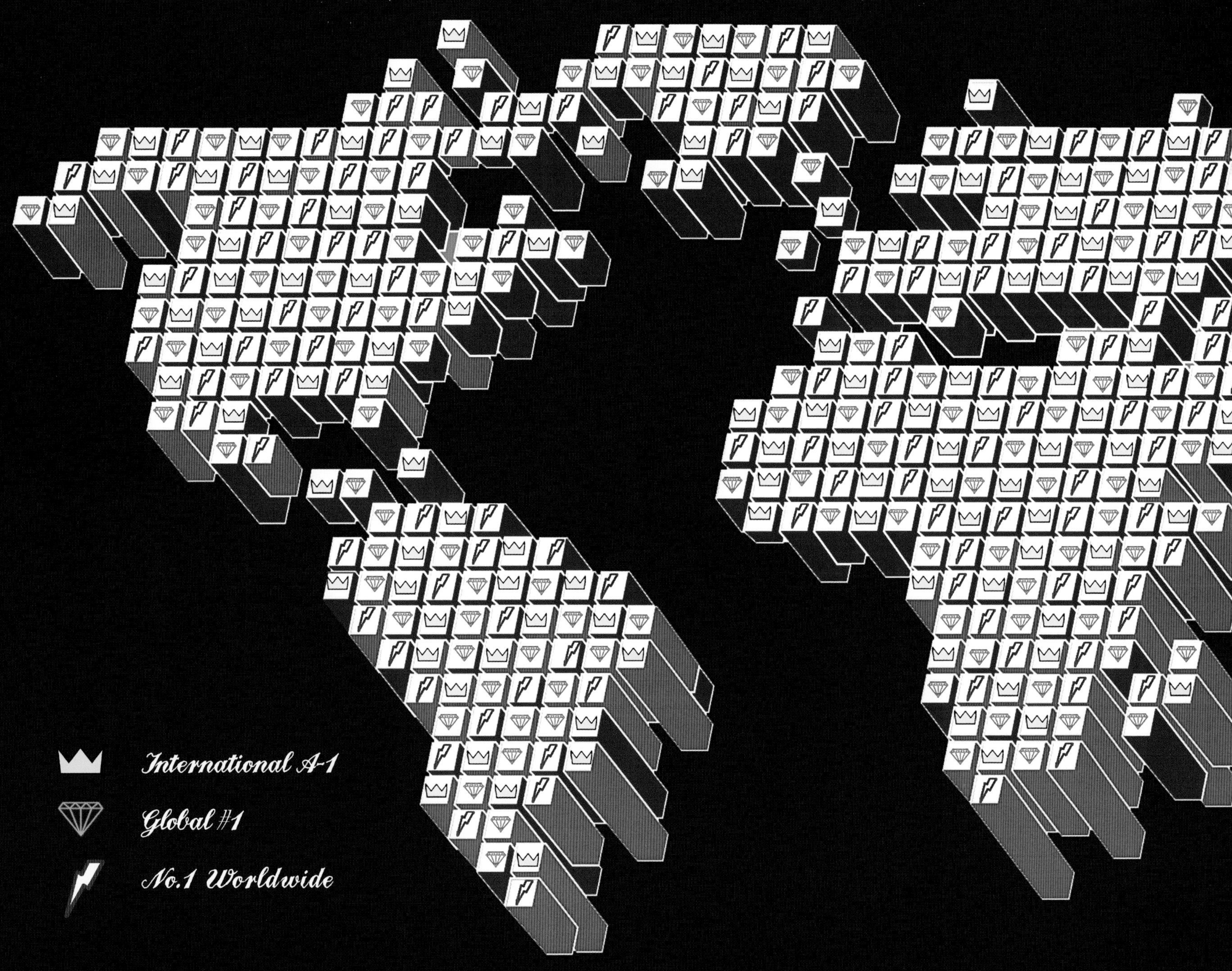

International A-1
Global #1
No.1 Worldwide

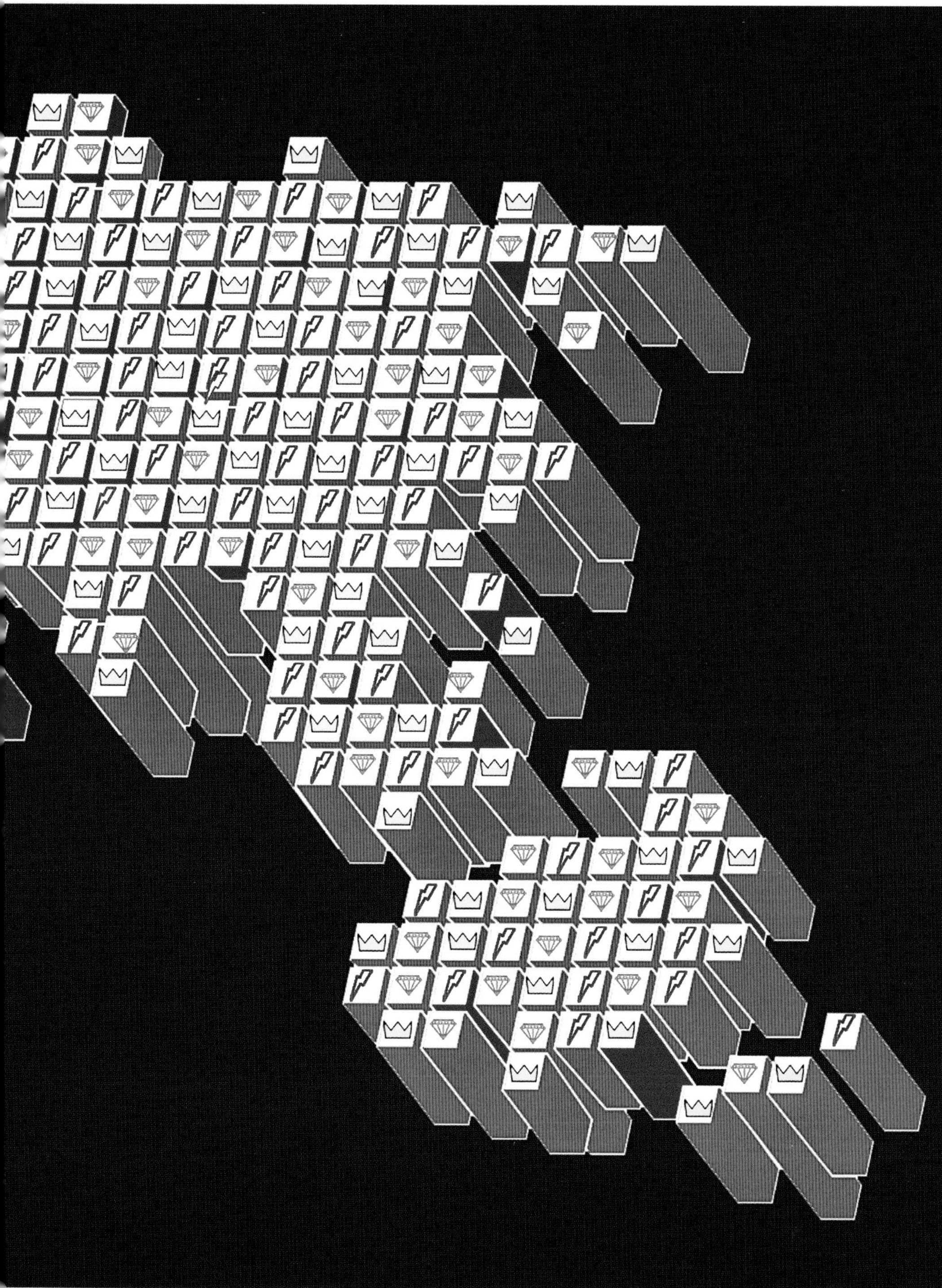

Super-Duper Helter-Skelter Lego-World

RAQS MEDIA COLLECTIVE

A R T I S T S

Super-Duper Helter-Skelter Lego-World is a map of the world in building blocks. Each block, repeated across the map, stands for some superlative claim or the other on the planet and its resources. Perhaps this is a completed puzzle waiting for an appropriately earth-shattering kick.

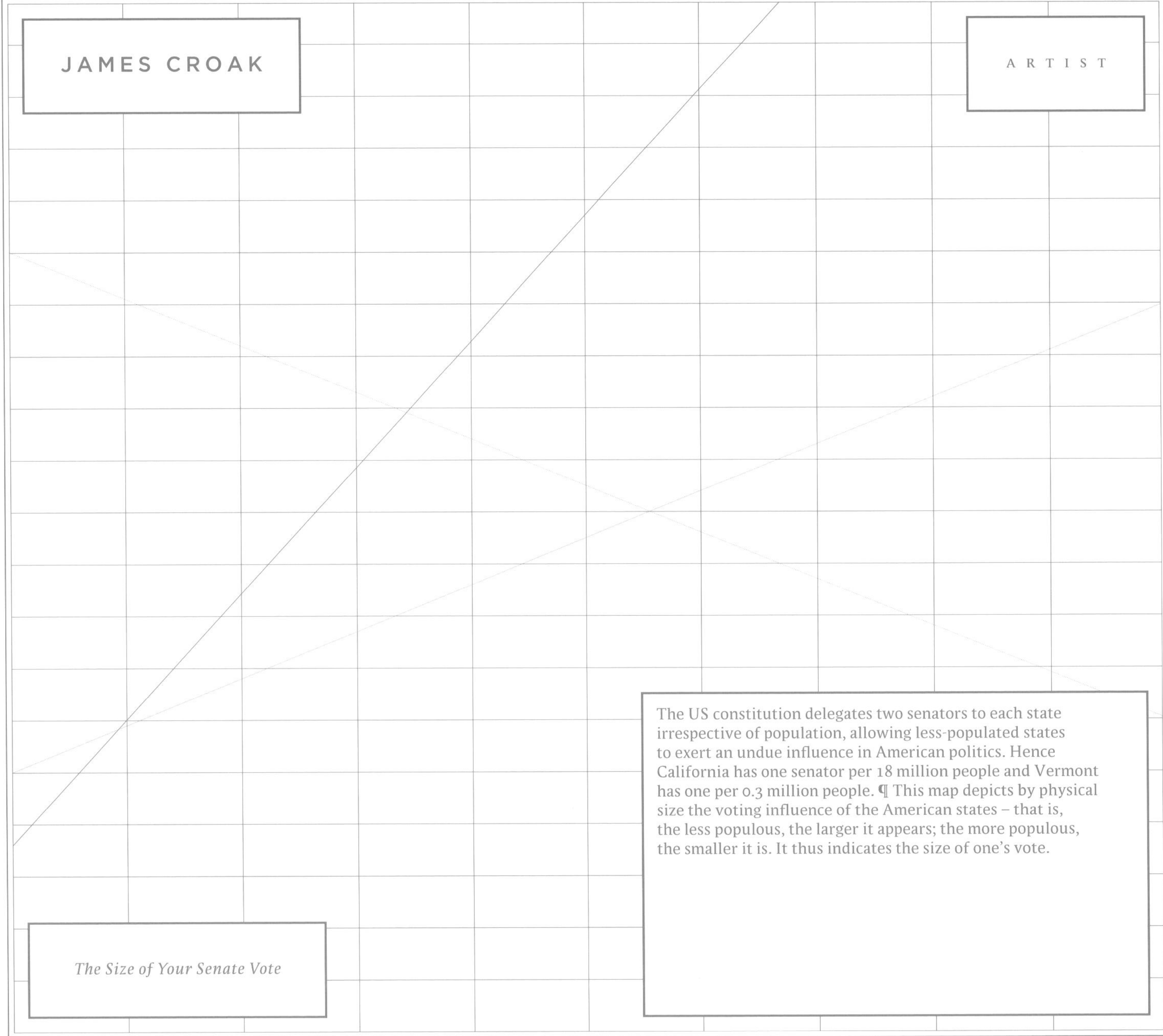

JAMES CROAK

ARTIST

The US constitution delegates two senators to each state irrespective of population, allowing less-populated states to exert an undue influence in American politics. Hence California has one senator per 18 million people and Vermont has one per 0.3 million people. ¶ This map depicts by physical size the voting influence of the American states – that is, the less populous, the larger it appears; the more populous, the smaller it is. It thus indicates the size of one's vote.

The Size of Your Senate Vote

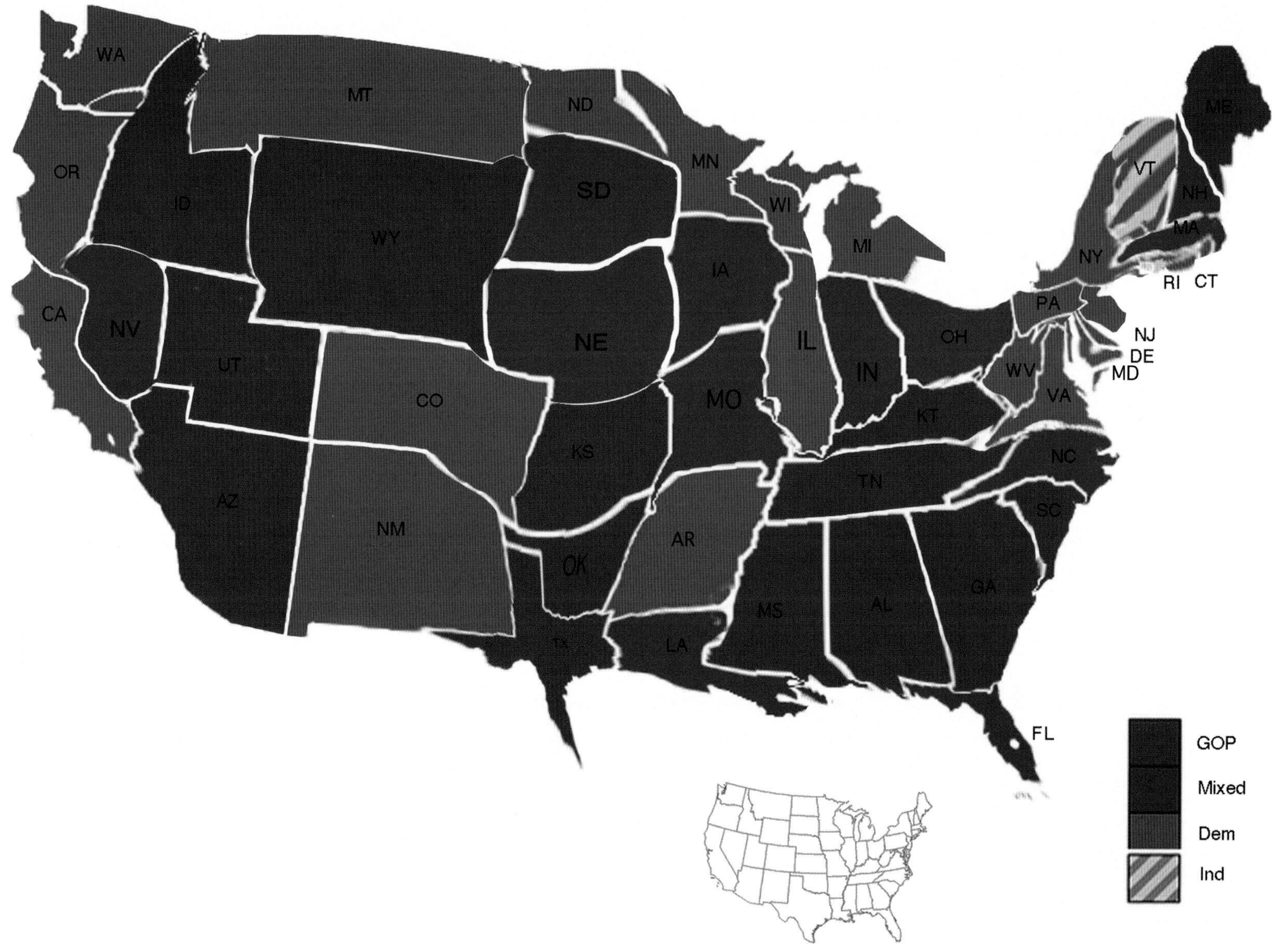

WA
OR
CA
ID
NV
MT
WY
UT
AZ
CO
NM
ND
SD
NE
KS
OK
TX
MN
IA
MO
AR
LA
WI
IL
MI
IN
OH
KT
TN
MS
AL
GA
SC
NC
FL
VA
WV
PA
NY
VT
NH
ME
MA
RI
CT
NJ
DE
MD
GOP
Mixed
Dem
Ind

18th CENTURY KÖNIGSBERG

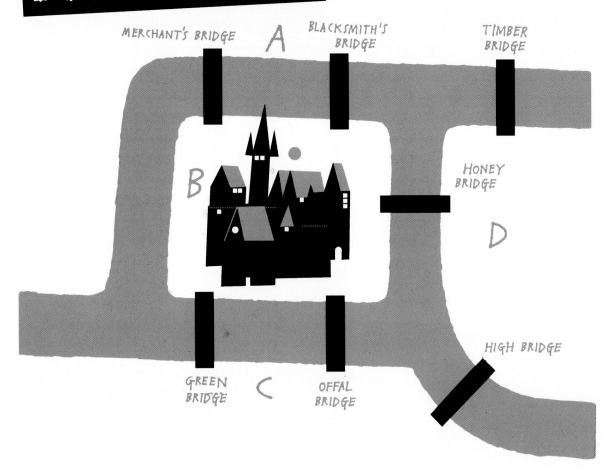

MERCHANT'S BRIDGE

A

BLACKSMITH'S BRIDGE

TIMBER BRIDGE

B

HONEY BRIDGE

D

HIGH BRIDGE

GREEN BRIDGE

C

OFFAL BRIDGE

MARCUS DU SAUTOY

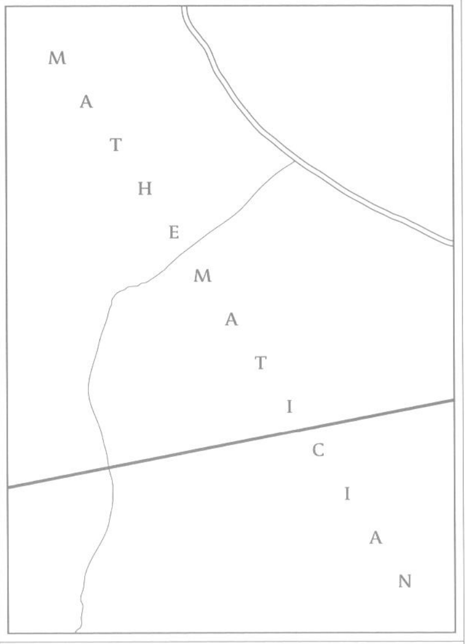

Can you cross all seven bridges once and once only? The eighteenth-century puzzle 'The Seven Bridges of Königsberg' introduced a new sort of map in mathematics. Rather than the physical geometry of the city, it was the way the city was connected together that was important. Topology was born. Topological maps are essential in navigating the plethora of networks that map the modern world: from the London Underground to the Internet, from neural networks to social networks. Although the eighteenth-century version proved an impossible puzzle to solve, it turns out that in modern-day Königsberg, or Kaliningrad as it is called today, you can cross the seven bridges that currently span the Pregel River once and once only.

21st CENTURY KALININGRAD

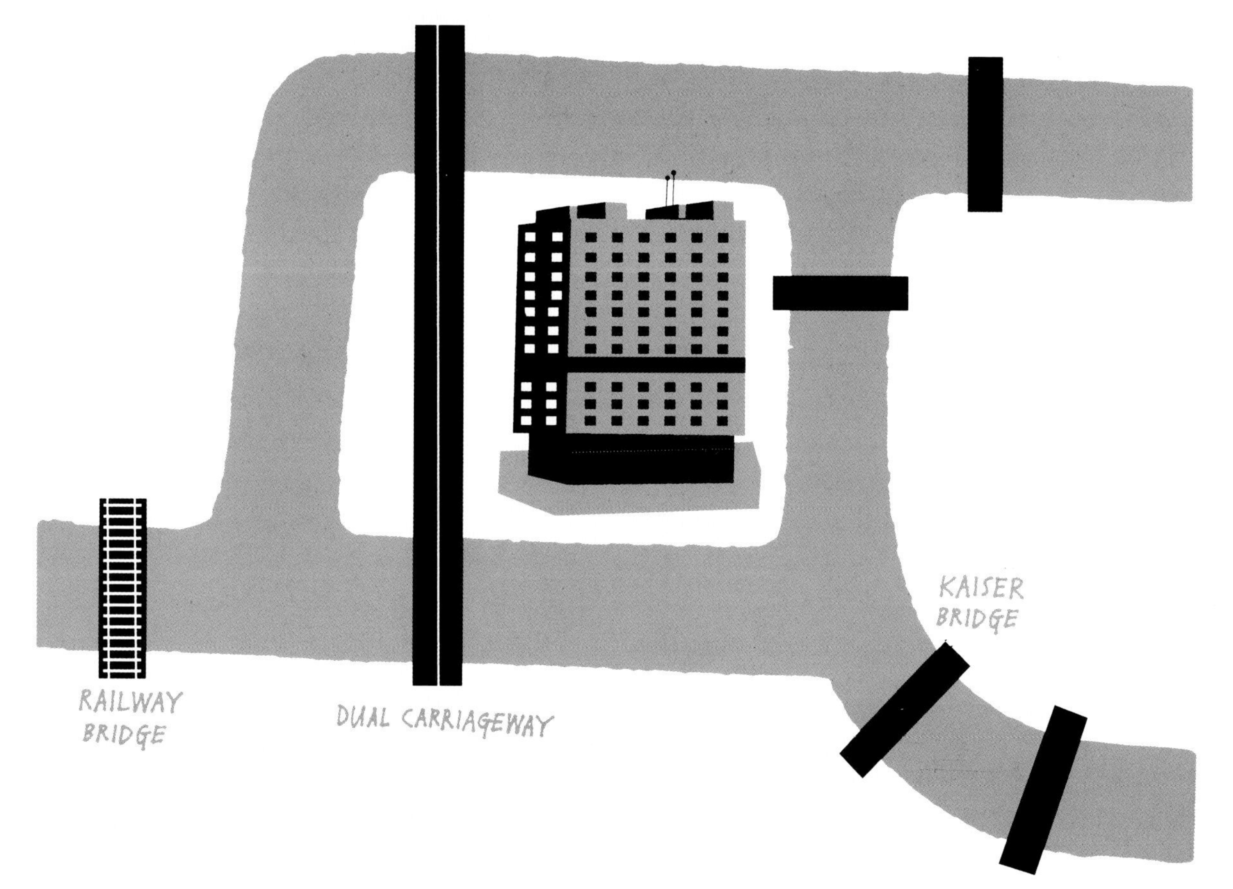

	A R T I S T	*Untitled*, 1990
CURTISLESLIE ANDERSON	And now the denouement was to be in scaled miniature? A thing of overlaid manuscript? The Doll composed himself. After everything that occurred? After Oe, Titania, E. T. Wawagawa and *The Good Fortune*, the smash!, slithering just in the nick of time through watershield to the already launching prowboat, the heavy g's of the launch, the freeze, the uncounted layers of varying silences before the slow melt, the drop! – flame-balling through the atmosphere (here the Doll had froze again in shock), finally plowing a seven-kilometre furrow into the leaf-beaten Atlantic infinity, into the wonders of the deep, the subsequent navigation, the acids, the shark plague, the sentient plank and, at an at-last laid upon a series of ever widening at-lasts, the discovery of the old Meuse delta in the frozen bed of now-flooded Netherlands, then at last again the winding, widening Rhine. And now here, this small mountain. After all of this, the Doll could not stifle Deary, the silvers and greens of her scales and flukes, the beating of her little multiple hearts. And so it was, at the selected coordinates, per her last request, beyond any possible series of endings, he produced the artificial intelligence.	

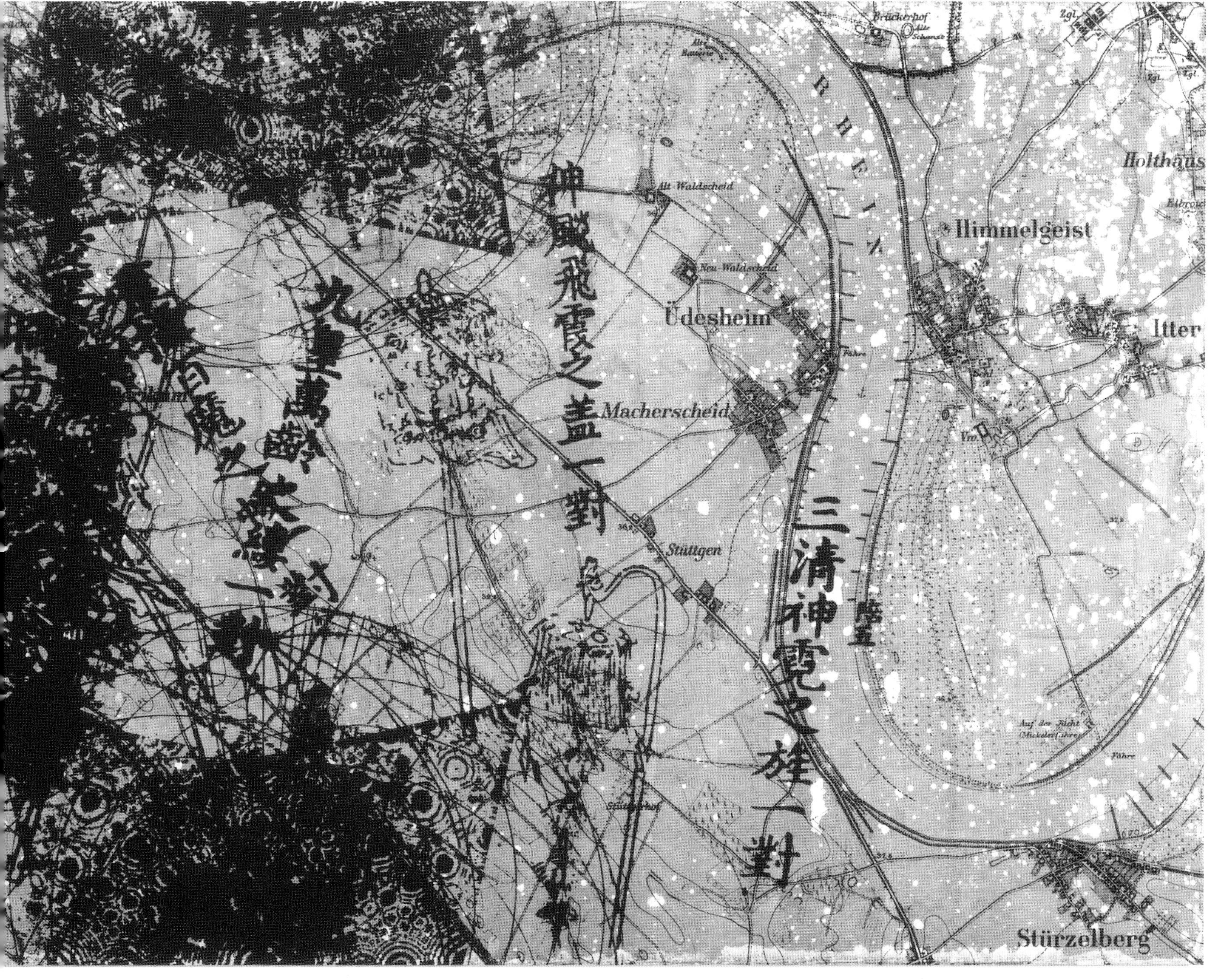

Brückerhof
Alt-Waldscheid
Neu-Waldscheid
Üdesheim
Macherscheid
Stüttgen
RHEIN
Himmelgeist
Itter
Fähre
Stürzelberg
神威飛霞之盖一對
三清神霓之旌一對

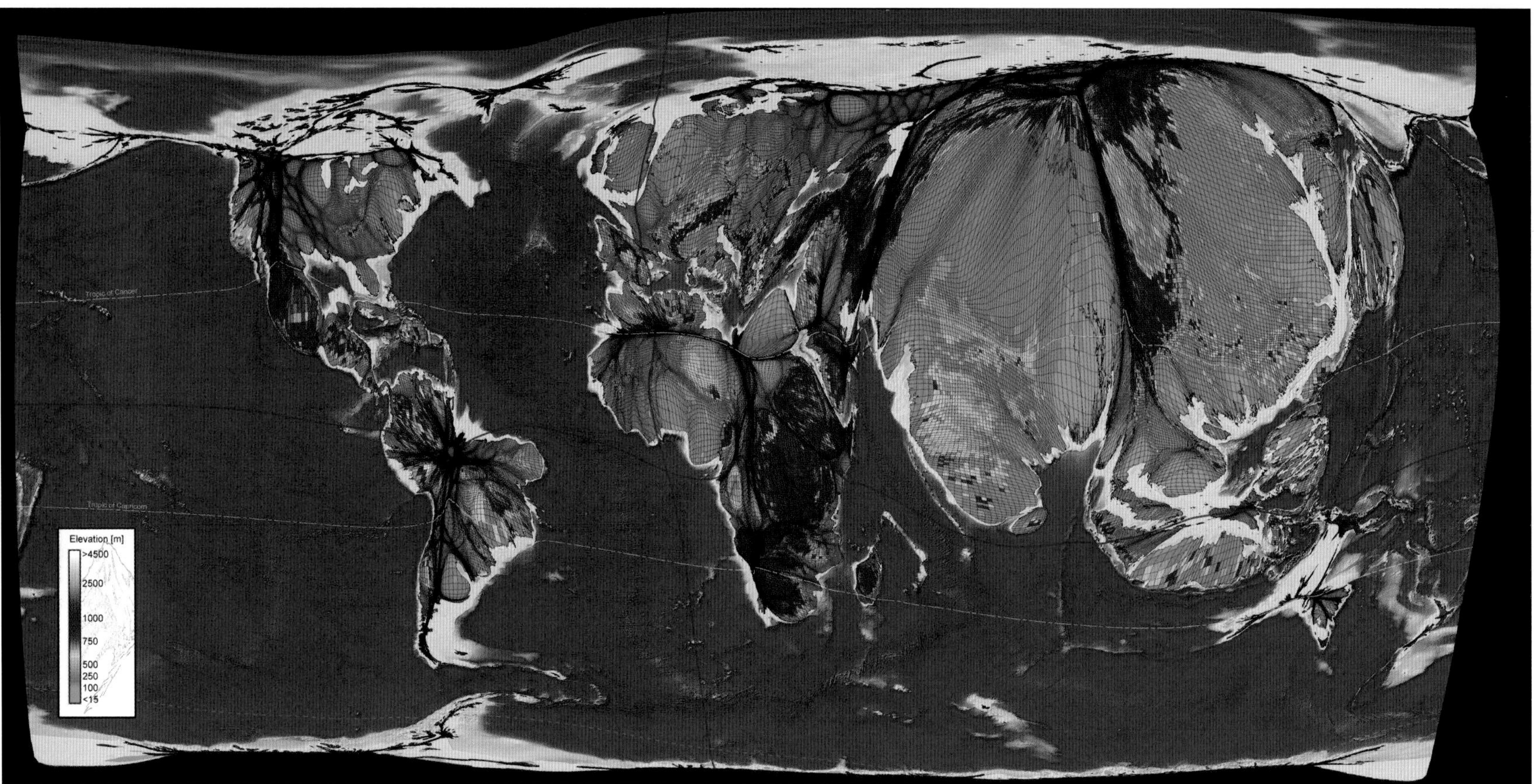
Tropic of Cancer
Tropic of Capricorn
Elevation [m]
>4500
2500
1000
750
500
250
100
<15

BENJAMIN D. HENNIG

A New World Population Cartogram with Topography, 2010

EARTH SCIENTIST

This new world map creates an unprecedented view of the world's population, which allows new perspectives for mapping the social dimension of our planet. The projection creates space in areas that matter most in the human world. Mapping the physical terrain onto this map reveals at which elevation most people live on Earth. Most people living at high elevations live in eastern and southern Africa, whereas in east Asia the densely populated coastal plains become apparent.

How to get to my house

LONDON

west

west

call first

EXIT

direction

roundabout right turn to

Turn left top of Hill (if you pass The wildlife and dinosaur park you're gone too far)

direction

my house

turn left before cattle grid

Two Big white stones

my driveway

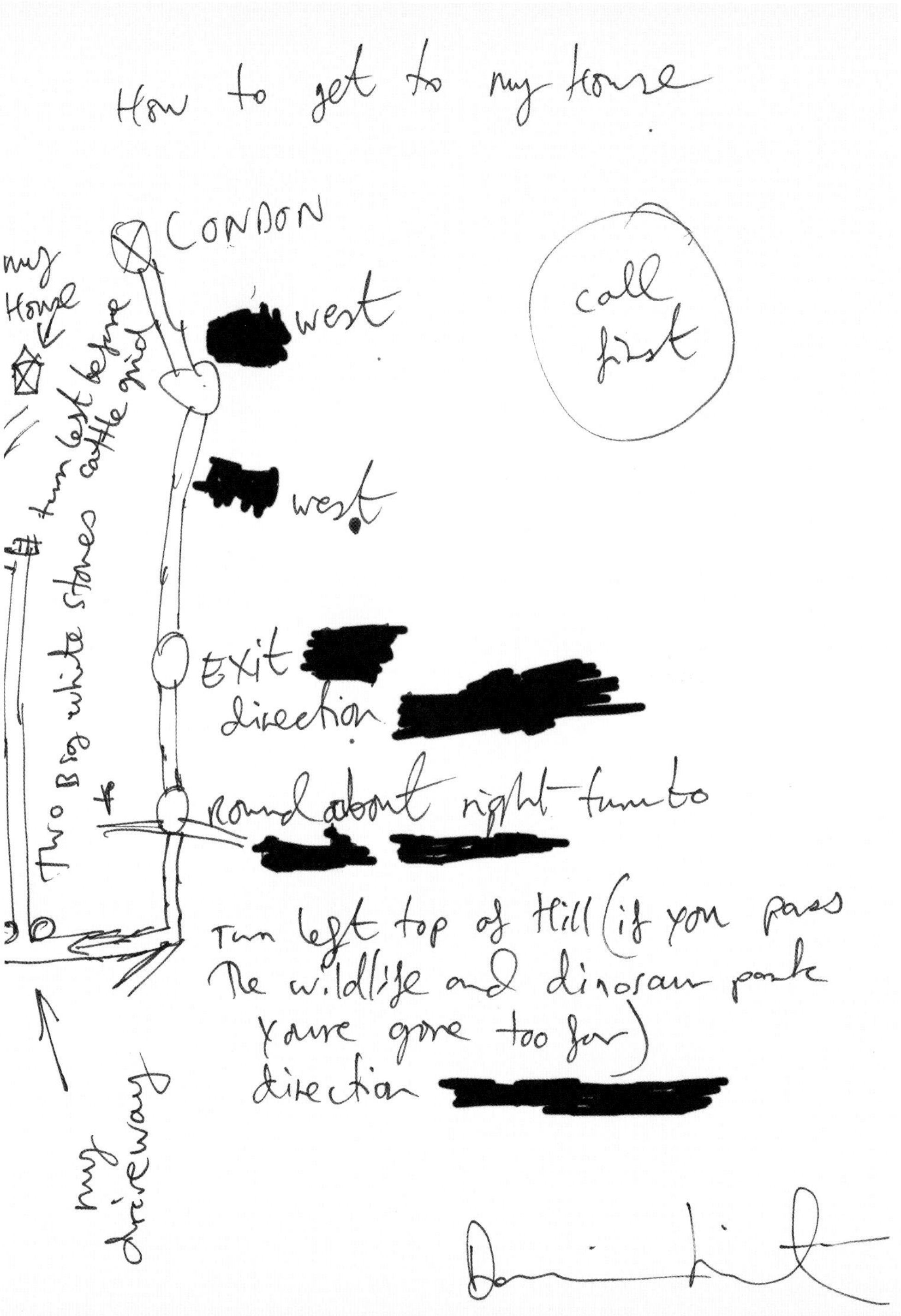

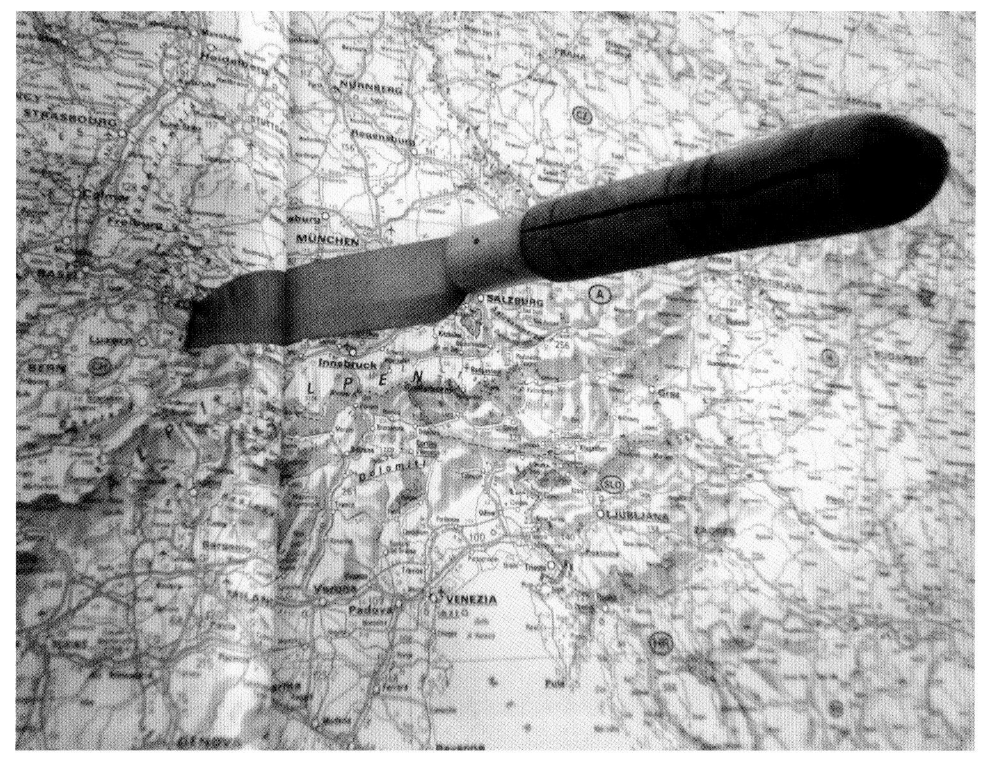

ARTUR BARRIO

a knife thrown from anywhere in portugal to nowhere in europe

1975

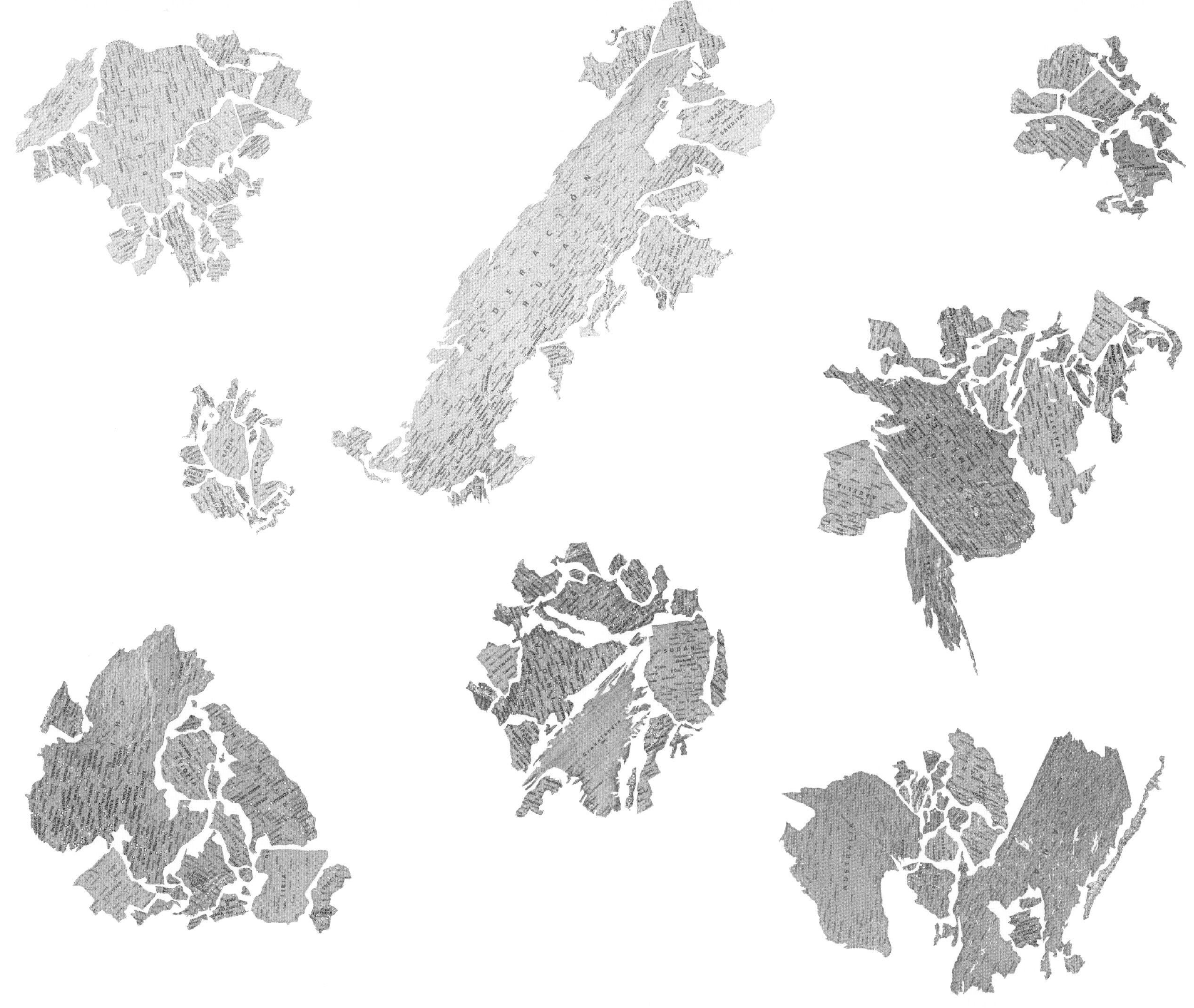

ARABIA SAUDITA
SUDAN
AUSTRALIA
LIBIA
BOLIVIA

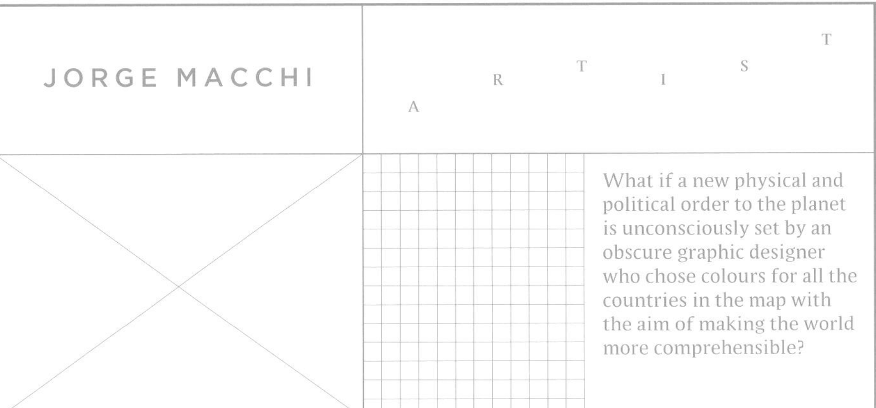

JORGE MACCHI

ARTIST

What if a new physical and political order to the planet is unconsciously set by an obscure graphic designer who chose colours for all the countries in the map with the aim of making the world more comprehensible?

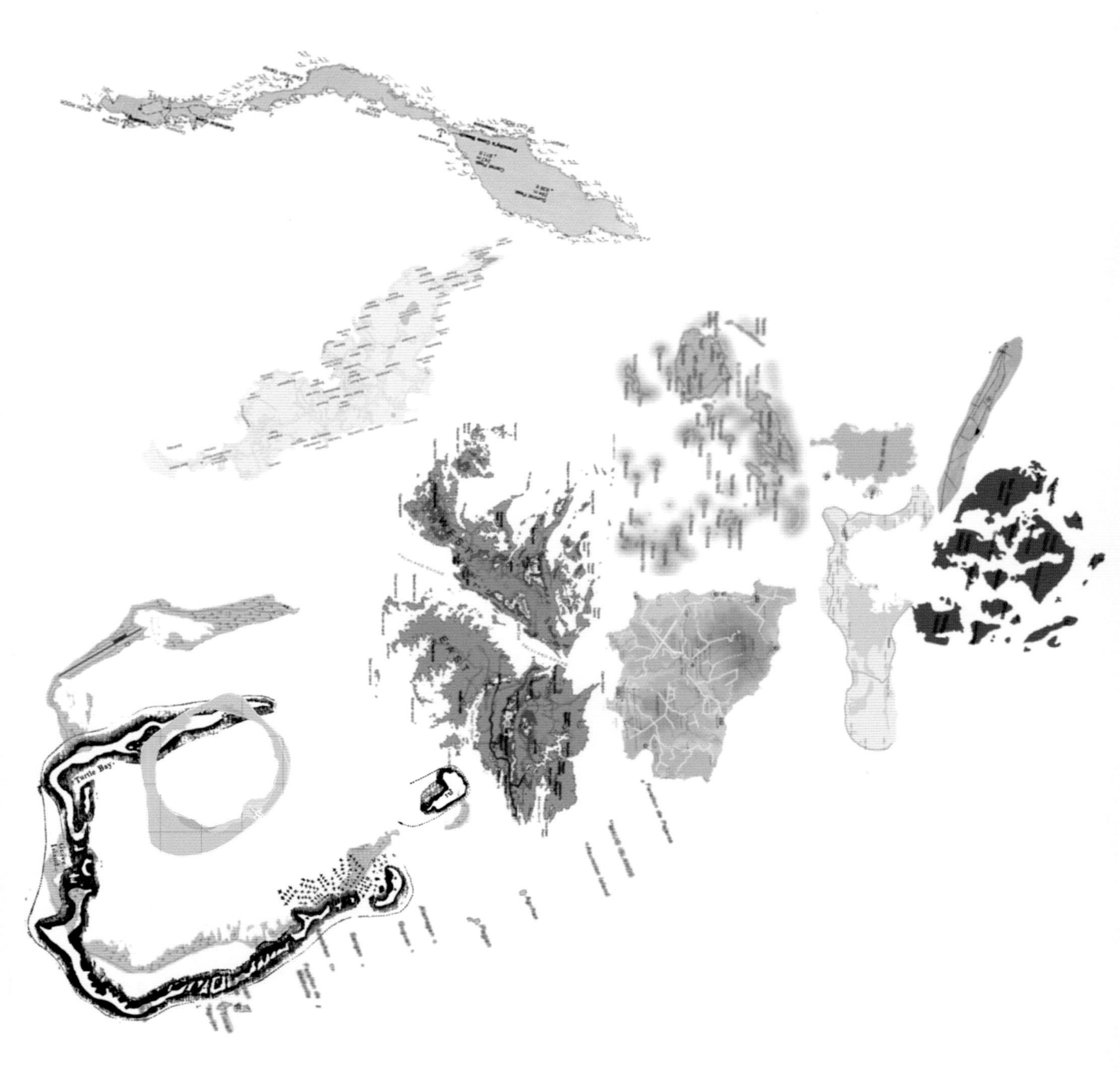
WEST
EAST
Turtle Bay

ANRI SALA

artist

THIS ARCHIPELAGO MAP REPRESENTS THE SILHOUETTE OF MR ARKADIN, THE ELUSIVE CHARACTER OF AN ORSON WELLES FILM OF THE SAME NAME WHO INITIATES AN INVESTIGATION INTO HIS OWN PAST WITH THE SOLE PURPOSE OF ERASING IT INSTEAD OF REVEALING IT.

A FRAGMENTED NARRATIVE OF AMNESIA, THE FILM SPANS VARIOUS PHYSICAL LOCATIONS AND PECULIAR CHARACTERS THAT HELP CONTOUR THE PERSONAGE FROM THE OUTSIDE, IN A SIMILAR WAY THAT EXPLORERS DID IN PAST AGES, WHEN IN ORDER TO MAP AND REVEAL A NEW LAND THEY WOULD SAIL AROUND IT TO DRAW ITS OUTLINES.

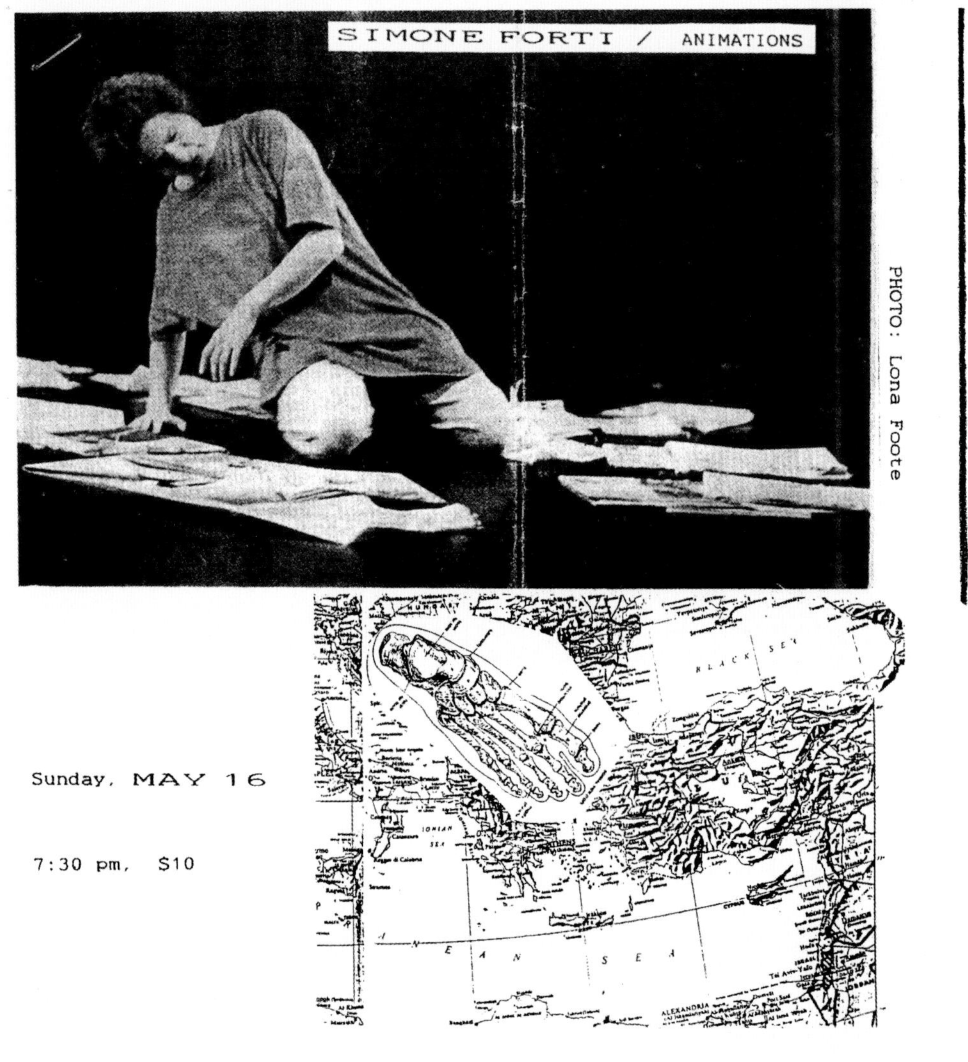

SIMONE FORTI / ANIMATIONS
PHOTO: Lona Foote
Sunday, MAY 16
7:30 pm, $10

HIGHWAYS PERFORMANCE SPACE
1651 18th St., Santa Monica, Ca. 90404

for reservations call TICKETS L.A. at 212 660-8587

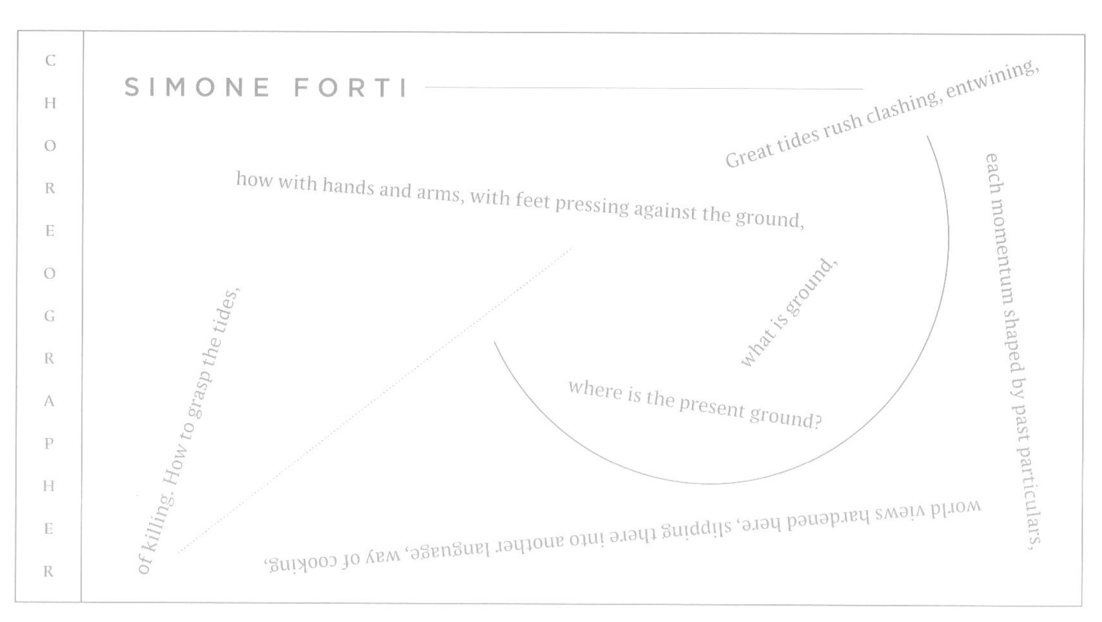

CHOREOGRAPHER
SIMONE FORTI
Great tides rush clashing, entwining,
each momentum shaped by past particulars,
world views hardened here, slipping there into another language, way of cooking,
of killing. How to grasp the tides,
how with hands and arms, with feet pressing against the ground,
what is ground,
where is the present ground?

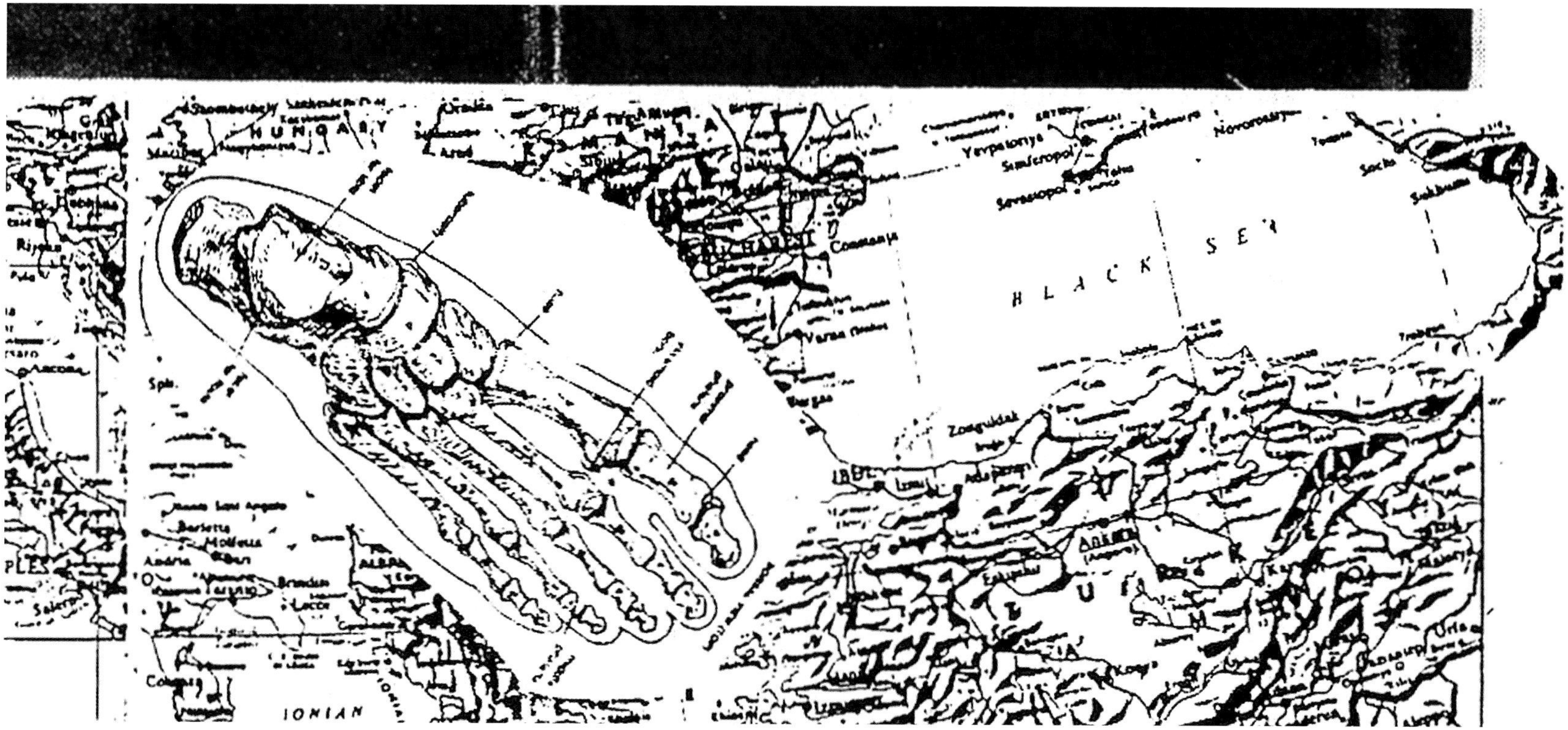

KAI KRAUSE

SOFTWARE PIONEER, PHILOSOPHER, AUTHOR

The True Size of Africa: A small contribution in the fight against rampant immappancy

A map about the complete inability of the general public to gauge relative sizes and distances, areas and population. Often people make extremely basic assumptions with distortions that would be hilarious if they weren't at the same time so deeply sad as well. I coined the term 'immappancy', analogous to illiteracy and innumeracy, meaning 'insufficient geographical knowledge'. A survey with random American school kids let them guess the population and land area of their country. Not entirely unexpected, but still rather unsettling, the majority of them chose '1–2 billion' and 'largest in the world', respectively. Even with Asian and European college students, geographical estimates were often off by factors of 2 to 3. This is partly due to the highly distorted nature of the predominantly used mapping projections (such as Mercator). A particularly extreme example is the worldwide misjudgment of the true size of Africa. This single image tries to embody the massive scale of the continent, which is larger than the USA, China, India, Japan and all of Europe – combined!

Country	Area (× 1000 km²)
USA	9,629
China	9,573
India	3,287
Mexico	1,964
Peru	1,285
France	633
Spain	506
Papua New Guinea	462
Sweden	441
Japan	378
Germany	357
Norway	324
Italy	301
New Zealand	270
United Kingdom	243
Nepal	147
Bangladesh	144
Greece	132
Total	30,102
Africa	30,221
The surface of the Moon (just for reference)	37,930

PLEASE NOTE | The graphical layout of this map is meant purely as a visualization to illustrate the fact: Africa is much larger than almost everyone assumes. Even totally blurred outlines could have been used to make that point, however the table above is very accurate. Note for instance that the figure for the area of the USA includes Alaska and Hawaii, even though they are not used in the map, as are a handful of other entries (such as Norway and Sweden). The reason for this is that the map purposely uses familiar shapes, as if you were moving pieces in Google Maps, because the mathematically exact depiction, using equal area scaling, would be even more drastic, but would appear highly distorted. I chose to retain the commonly known outlines and proportions to tell the story, even if this conservative size has left-over parts. The small maps on the far right are again the singular message: look at some of the countries in direct relation to Africa, a view that is quite unfamiliar and rarely seen. It is worth looking at Bucky Fuller's maps or the Peters equal area proposals, among many other beautiful attempts to display geographical information. Numerous other side-by-side comparisons have been made; this is by far not the first and hopefully not the last such map: someone should find the best fit of all puzzle pieces in a neutral projection. Until then, please do not take it all too literal ('where is Ibiza??') and simply take that one impression with you: Africa ... is immense.

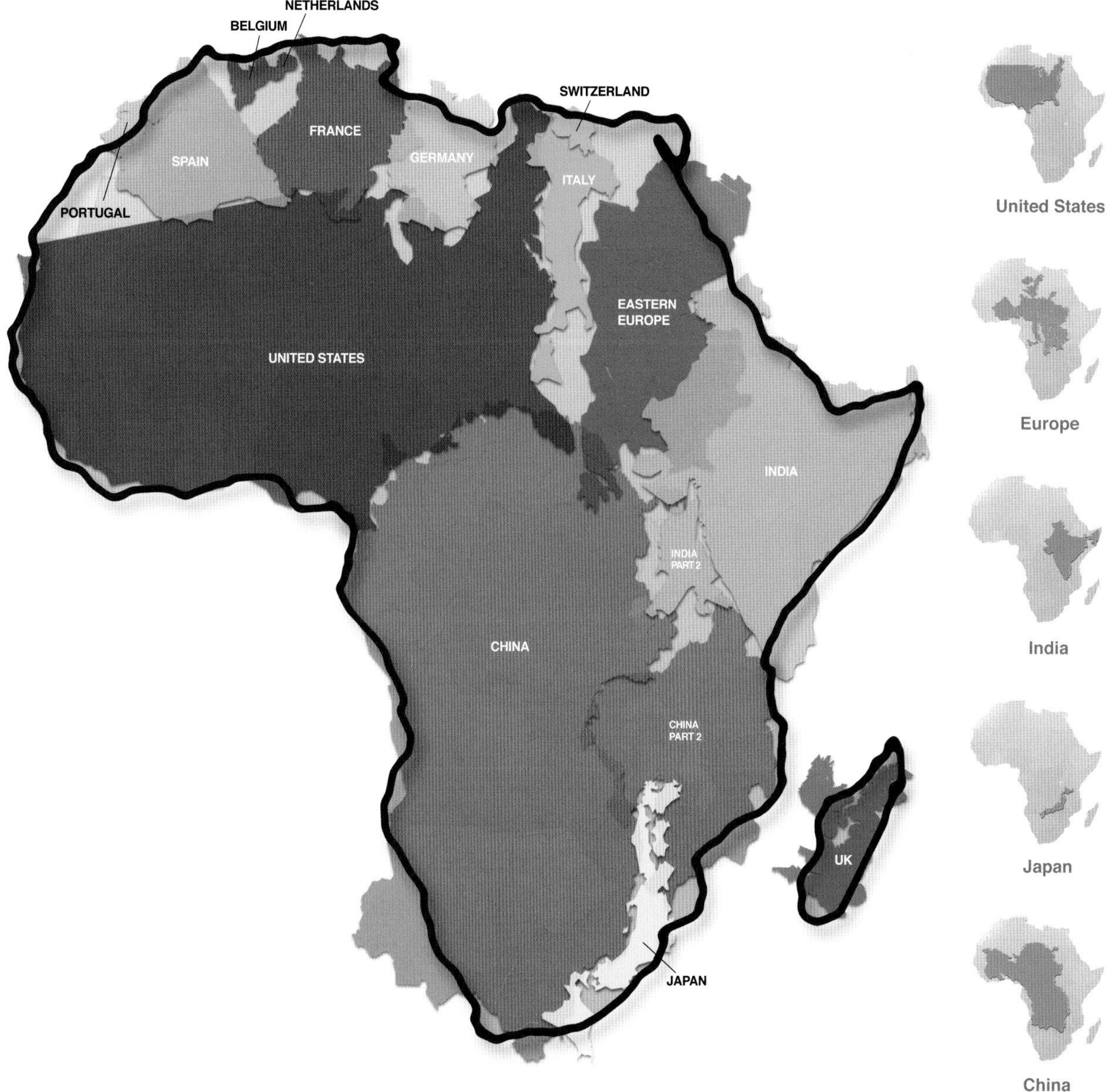
NETHERLANDS
BELGIUM
SWITZERLAND
FRANCE
SPAIN
GERMANY
ITALY
PORTUGAL
EASTERN EUROPE
UNITED STATES
INDIA
INDIA PART 2
CHINA
CHINA PART 2
UK
JAPAN
United States
Europe
India
Japan
China

DOUG AITKEN

ARTIST

Manhattan Metamorphosis

2007

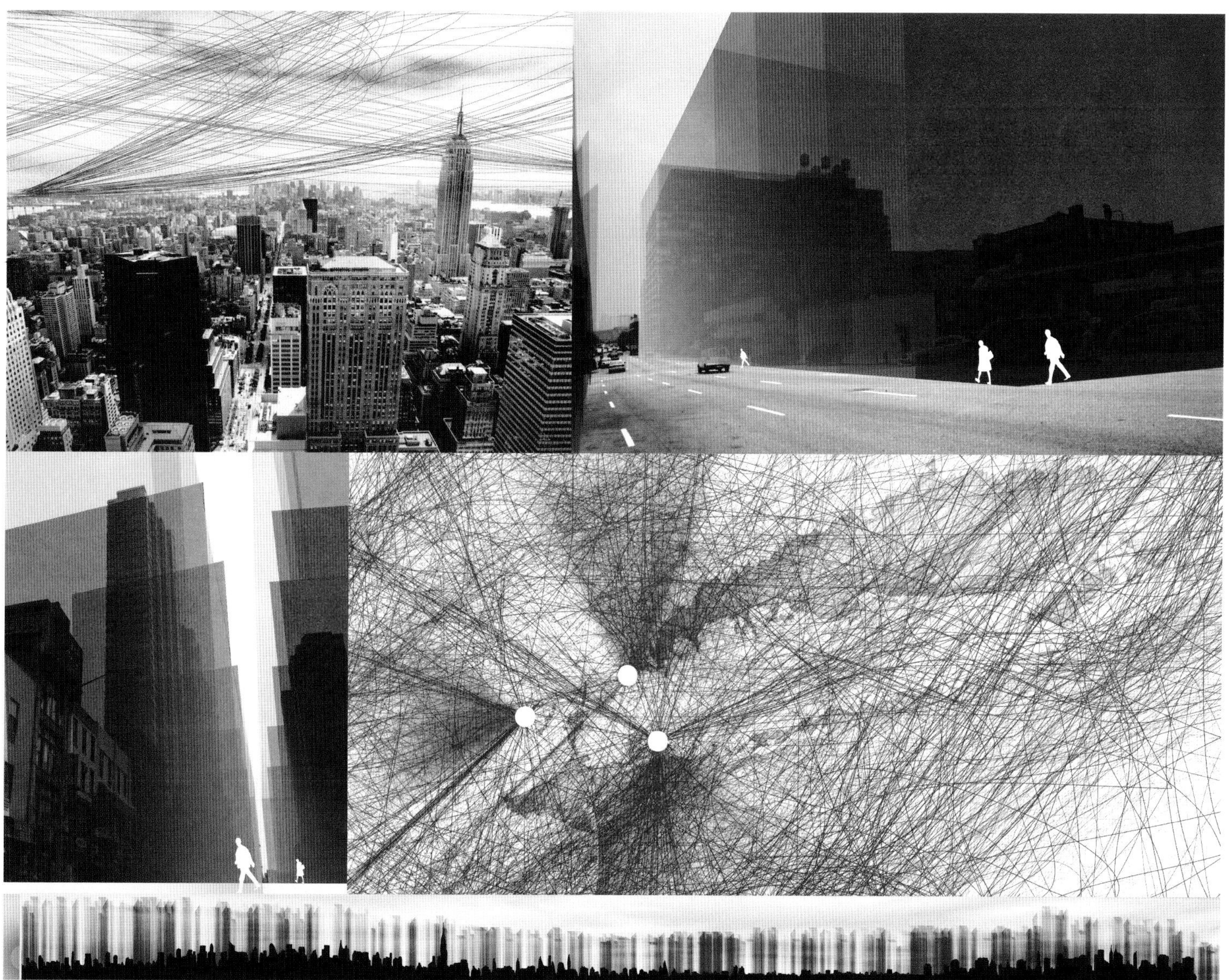

RIVANE NEUENSCHWANDER | ARTIST | *Diários de Pangaea / Pangaea's Diaries* | 2008

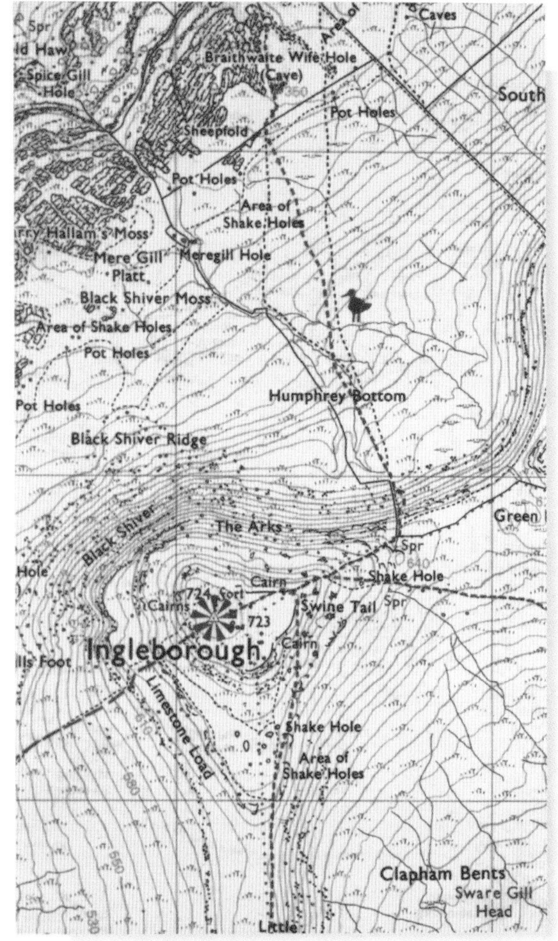

Caves
Braithwaite Wife Hole
(Cave)
South
Spice Gill
Hole
Pot Holes
Sheepfold
Pot Holes
Area of
Shake Holes
Mere Gill
Platt
Meregill Hole
Black Shiver Moss
Area of Shake Holes
Pot Holes
Humphrey Bottom
Pot Holes
Black Shiver Ridge
The Arks
Black Shiver
Spr
Cairn
Shake Hole
Cairns
724
723
Swine Tail
Ingleborough
Cairn
Limestone Road
Shake Hole
Area of
Shake Holes
Clapham Bents
Sware Gill
Head
Little

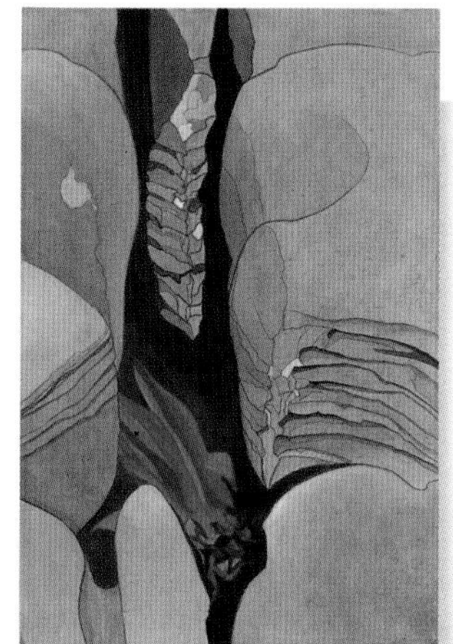

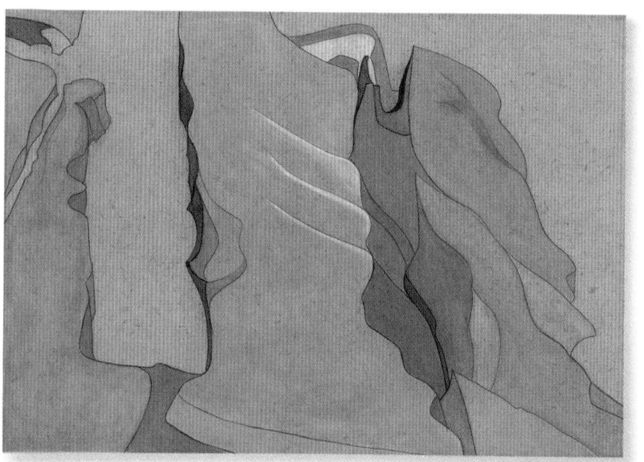

Ingleborough, 1998

PHILIP HUGHES

ARTIST

Ingleborough is one of the Three Peaks in Yorkshire, England (the others being Whernside and Pen-y-ghent). They are well known as a group for the challenge of climbing all three mountains in a circular walk in the shortest possible time. ¶ My interest in the peaks is not this fierce challenge, but rather the wonderful rock forms that emerge from the underlying geology. The various layers of rock type lead to the terracing of Ingleborough and to the striking flat summit caused by a cap of Millstone Grit. The valleys between the peaks are of Carboniferous limestone. This platform has eroded into a large area of crevices carved by water over time. ¶ My intent in combining the contoured map together with a series of small paintings is to link the large rock forms of the mountain directly to the detailed rock forms in the valley below.

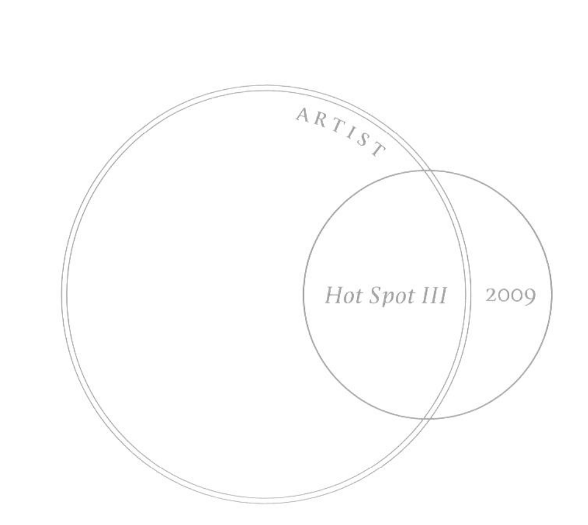

MONA HATOUM

Hot Spot is a cagelike steel globe, approximately the size of a person with arms stretched out, that tilts at the same angle as the Earth. Using delicate red neon to outline the contours of the continents on its surface, the work buzzes with an intense energy, bathing its surroundings in a luminescent red glow. It is both mesmerizing and seemingly dangerous. On the one hand it suggests that the whole world is a political hot spot caught up in conflict and unrest. It can also be seen as a reference to global warming, an impending concern.

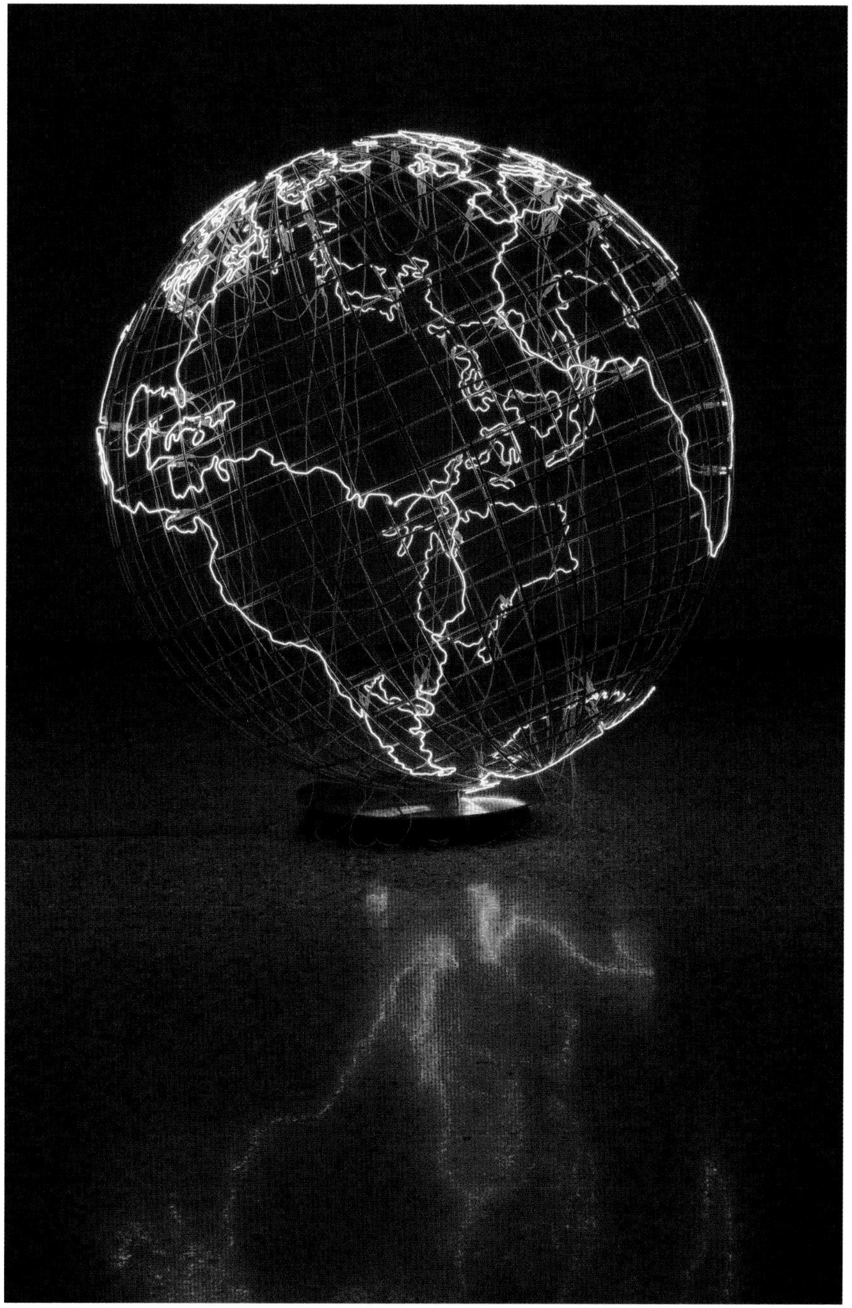

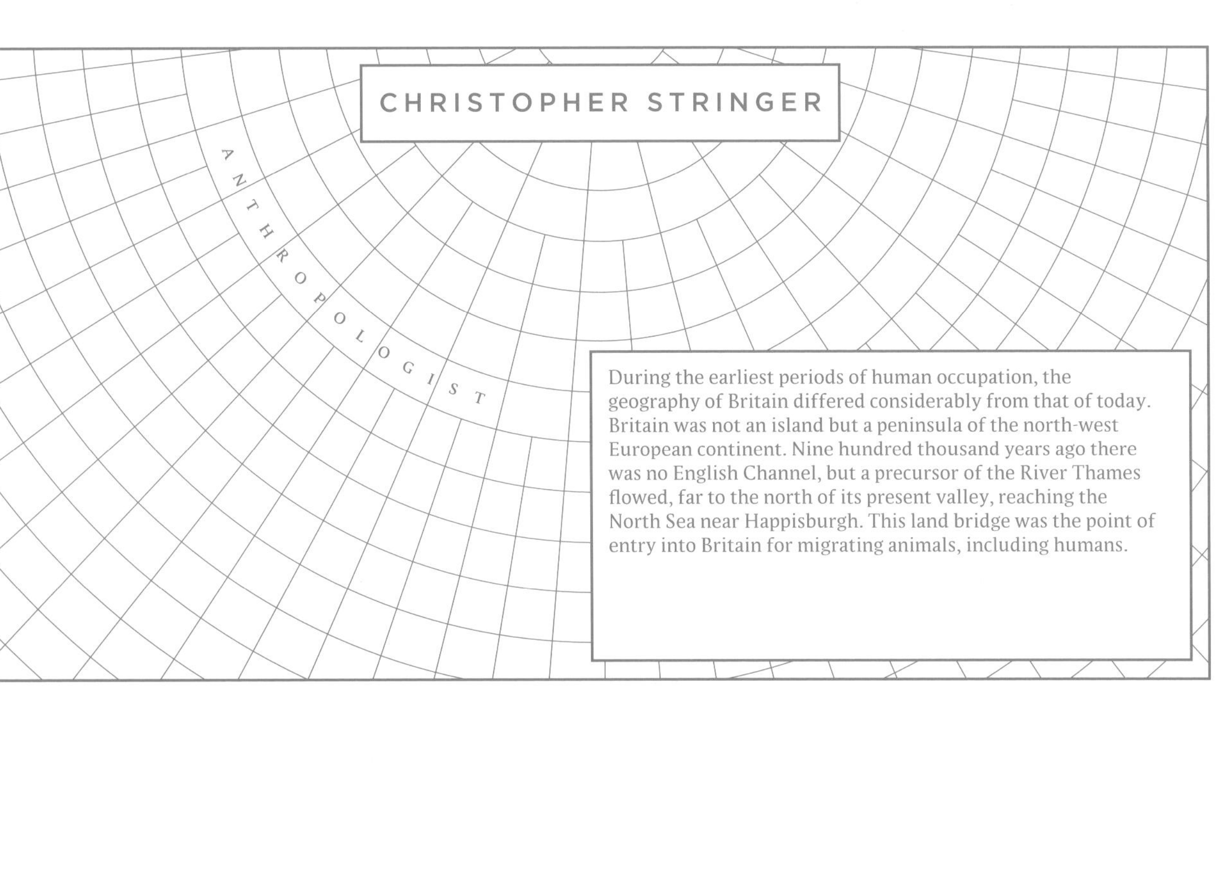

During the earliest periods of human occupation, the geography of Britain differed considerably from that of today. Britain was not an island but a peninsula of the north-west European continent. Nine hundred thousand years ago there was no English Channel, but a precursor of the River Thames flowed, far to the north of its present valley, reaching the North Sea near Happisburgh. This land bridge was the point of entry into Britain for migrating animals, including humans.

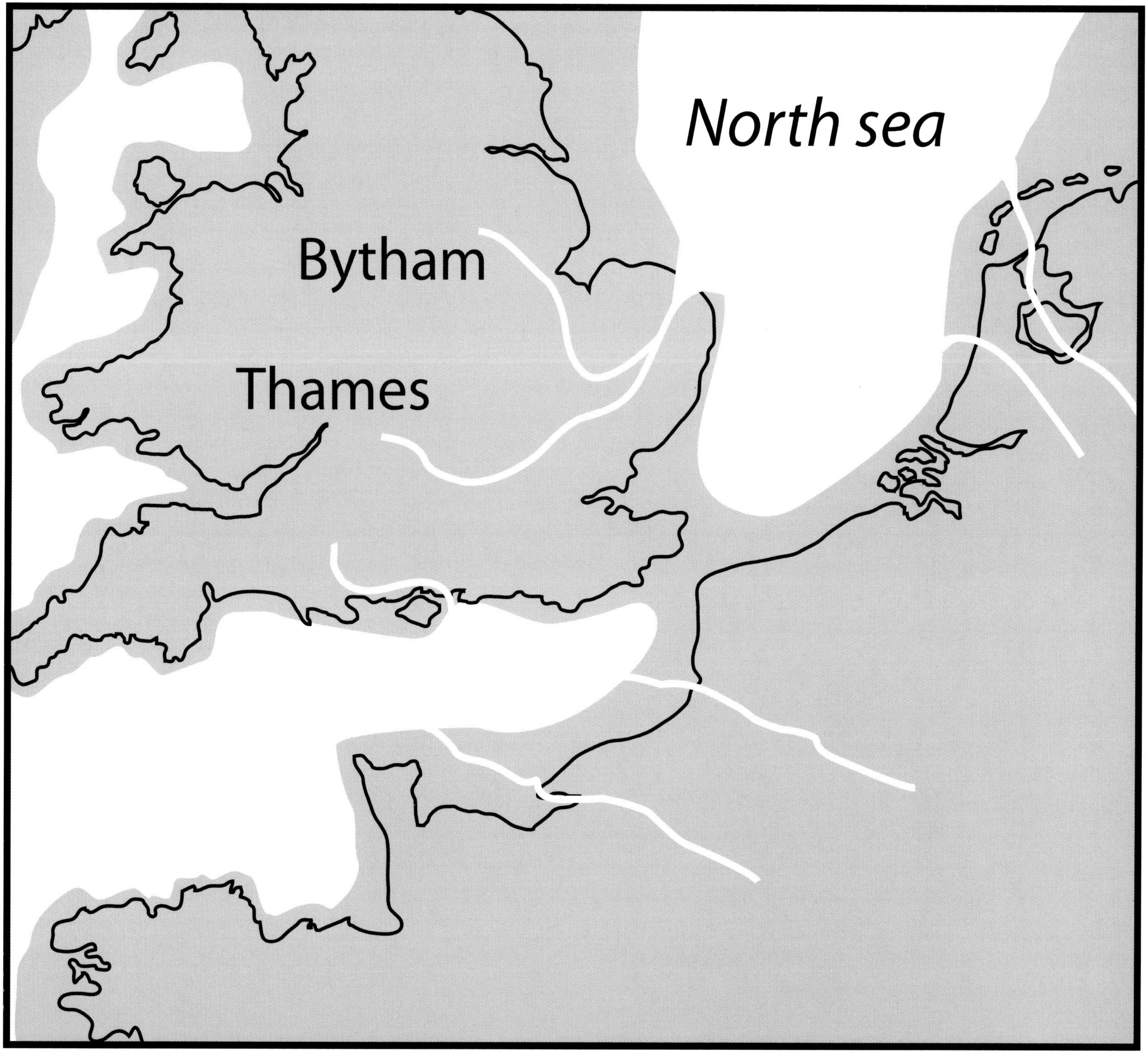

North sea

Bytham

Thames

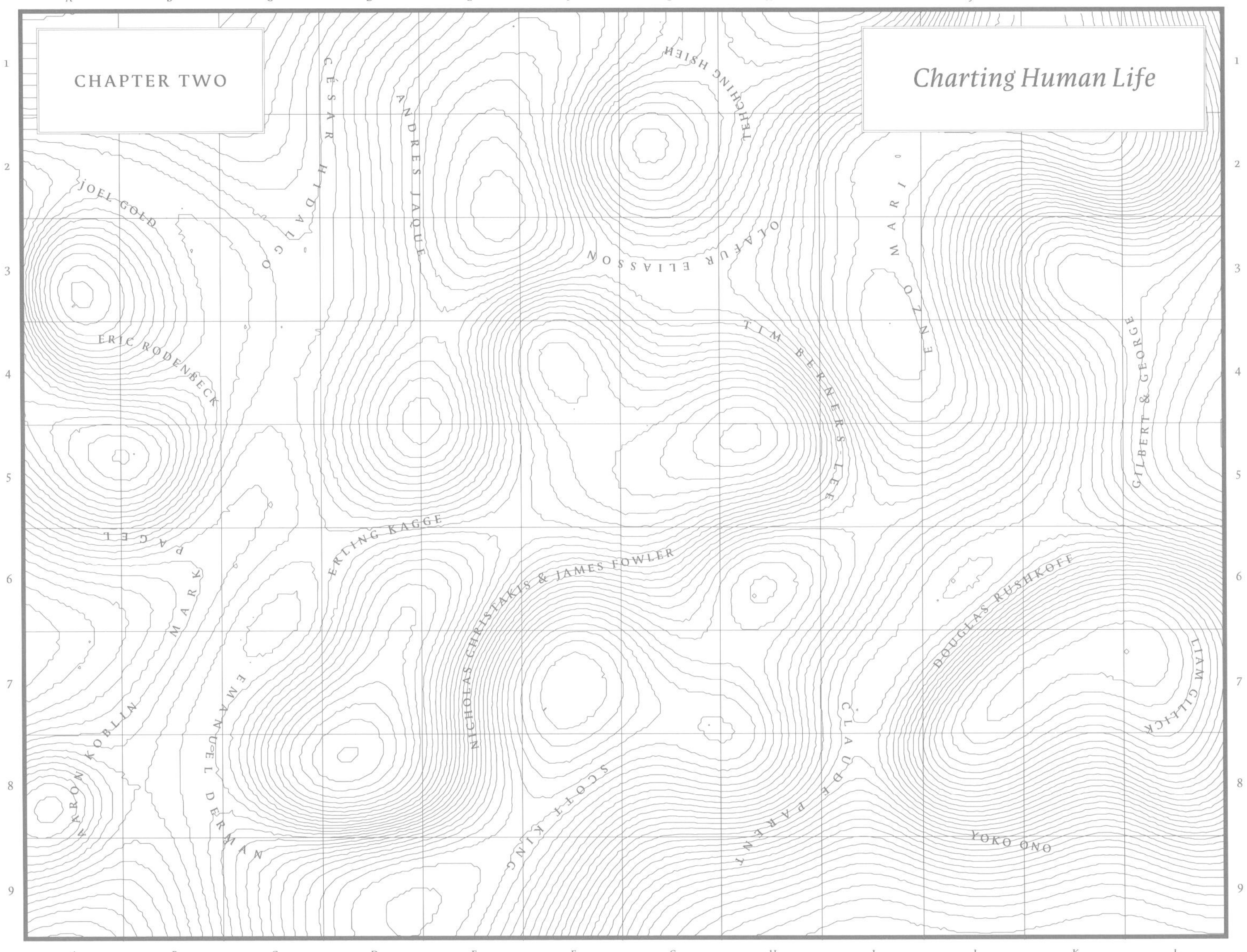
CHAPTER TWO
Charting Human Life
A B C D E F G H I J K L
1 2 3 4 5 6 7 8 9
JOEL GOLD
ERIC RODENBECK
MARK PAGEL
AARON KOBLIN
EMANUEL DERMAN
CÉSAR HIDALGO
ANDRES JAQUE
ERLING KAGGE
NICHOLAS CHRISTAKIS & JAMES FOWLER
SCOTT KING
OLAFUR ELIASSON
TEHCHING HSIEH
TIM BERNERS LEE
CLAUDE PARENT
DOUGLAS RUSHKOFF
YOKO ONO
GILBERT & GEORGE
LIAM GILLICK

All aspects of human existence can be plotted and followed, from a single person's habits or emotions to the shifting trends of a whole population or the historical course of an entire civilization. Changing patterns of personal behaviour and individual psychology; confrontations between competing ideologies; representations of psychogeography in action; or connections between elements of society both past and present – these maps chart the terrain of contemporary life and point towards a land of the future.

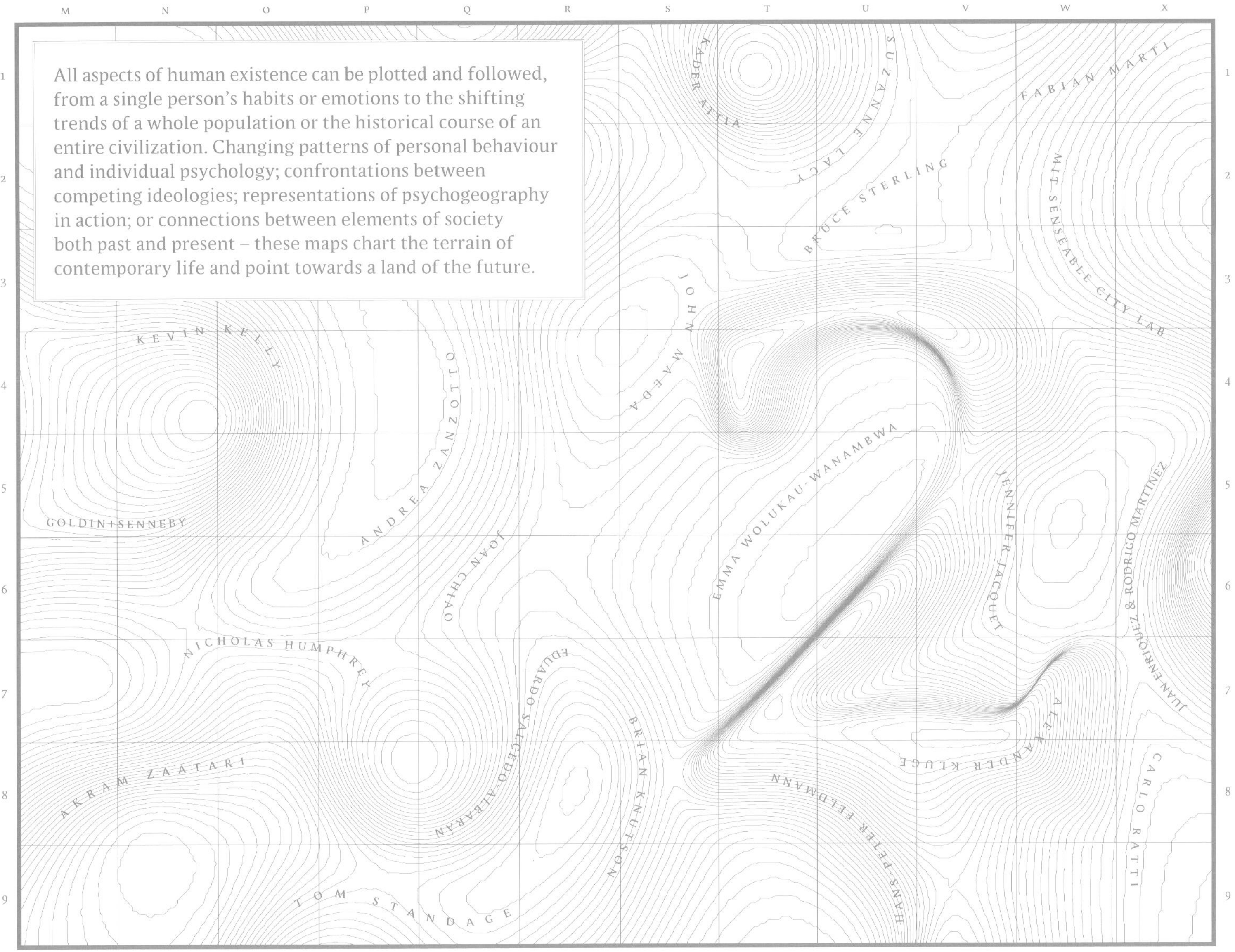

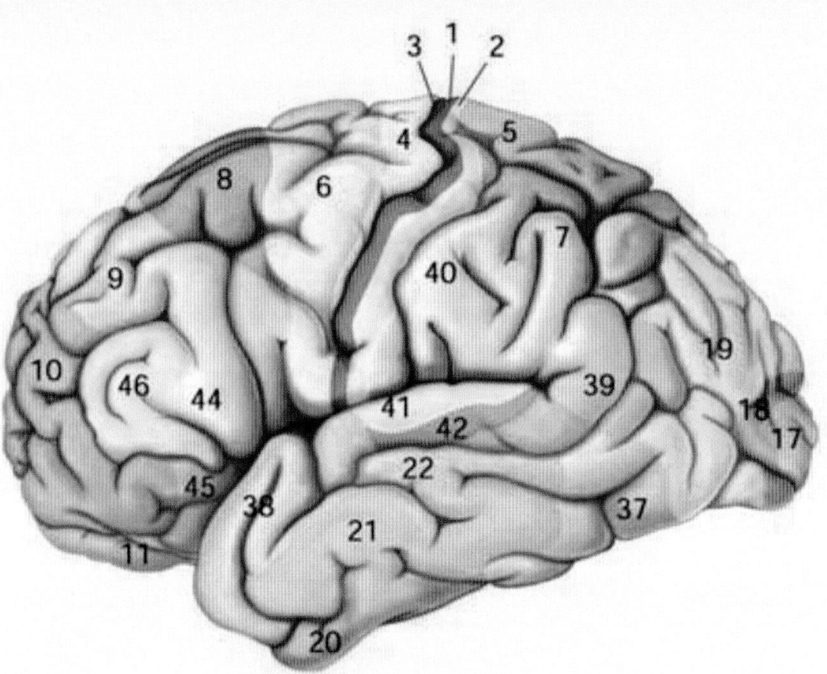

1 Loving Mother (Good Breast)
2 Hateful Mother (Bad Breast)
3 Father (Triadic World)
4 Elder Sister (Ambivalent Love)
5 Younger Brother (Protective/Competitive)
6 Grandmother Cells
7 Mrs Greenbaum (Third-Grade Teacher)
8 Douglas (Best Friend, Still)
9 Sophie Robbins (First Kiss)
10 Elena Roussel (First Sex)
11 Vanessa King (First Love)
17 Professor Ridge (Ego Ideal)
18 Martin (Bandmate)
19 Wife (Soulmate)
20 Ex-Wife (Soulless)
21 Daughter (Would Die For)
22 Son (Perfect/Inadequate)
37 Boss (Oedipal Victor)
38 Bastard Promoted Over Me
39 Caroline (Doubles Partner)
40 Caroline (Sexual Fantasy)
41 Robert (Drinks/Untrustworthy)
42 Psychotherapist (See All Above)
44 Alone (Peace/Reflection)
45 Alone (Lonely)
46 Books About The Brain

JOEL

GOLD

Object Relational Neuroanatomic Map of the Social Brain

PSYCHIATRIST

At university and in medical school, I examined the neuroanatomical structures governing functions such as cognition, language, movement and sensation. But in becoming a psychiatrist, particularly through the practice of psychotherapy and the study of psychoanalysis, I discovered that the brain is first and foremost a social brain. Relationships are the primary substance of life and are prominently symbolized in the mind. These mental representations of self and other are hardly homuncular, but are as vital as any island of grey matter.

Liam Gillick ARTIST

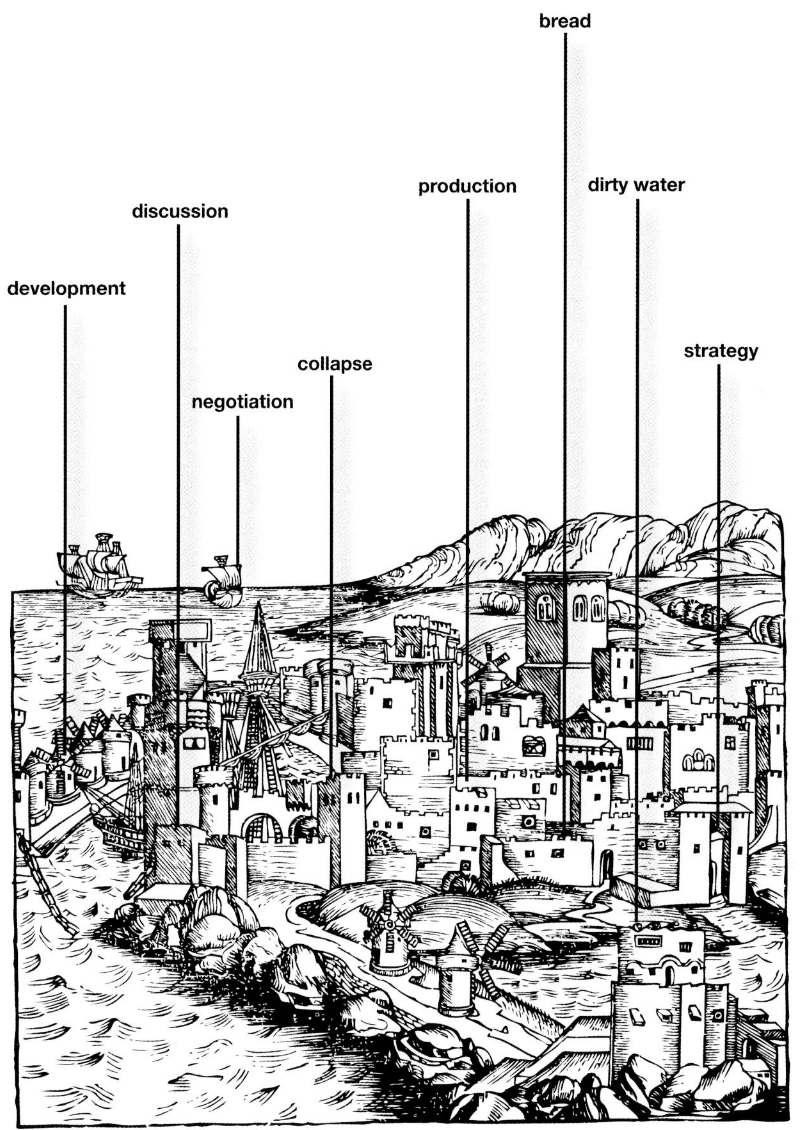
bread
production
dirty water
discussion
development
strategy
collapse
negotiation

EDUARDO SALCEDO ALBARÁN —

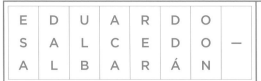

A social network mapping the arbitration of information (location of the node, higher in the nucleus) and amount of connections (size of the node) between narcotraffickers (NAR) and public servants (FUN) in the Mexican cartel La Familia Michoacana

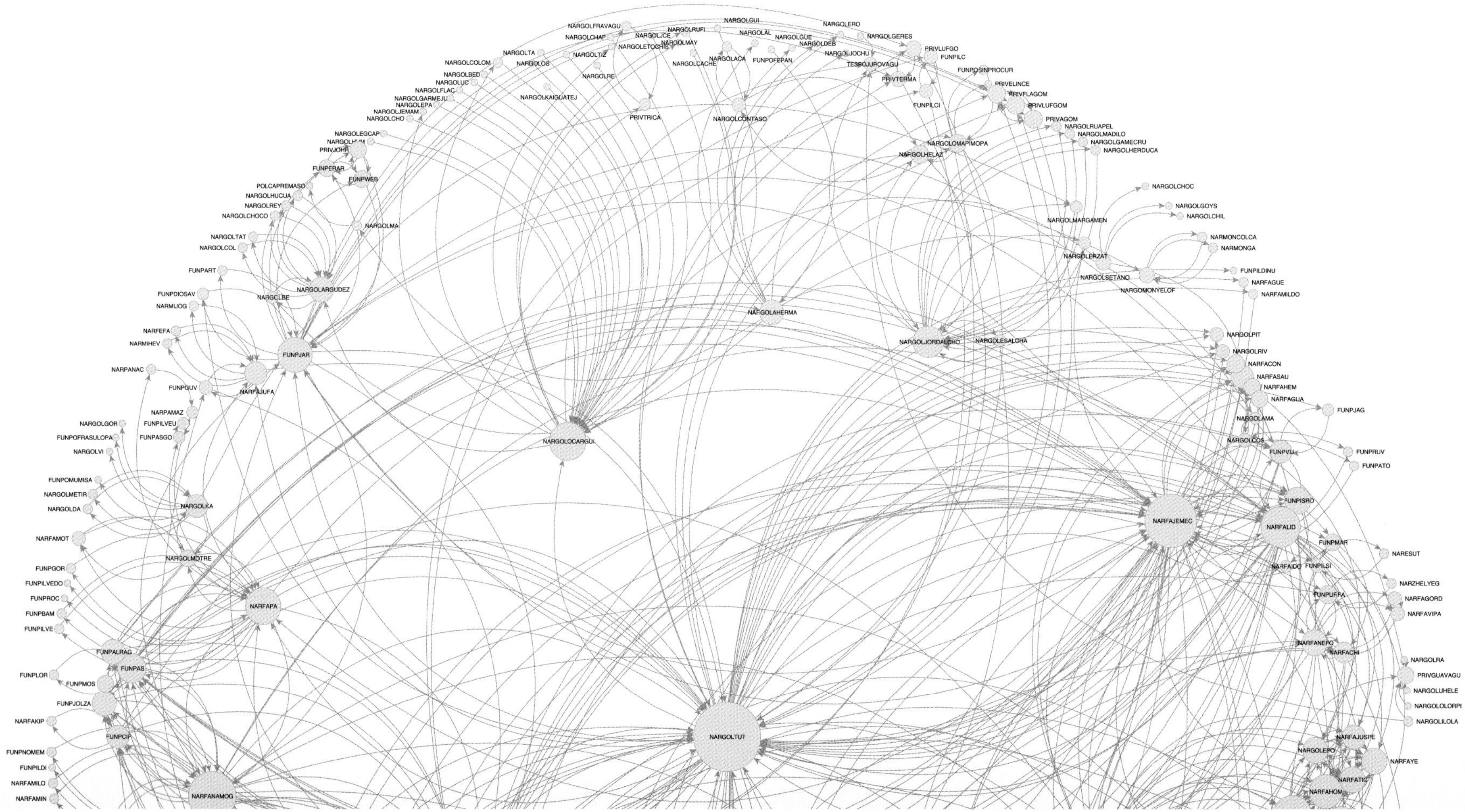

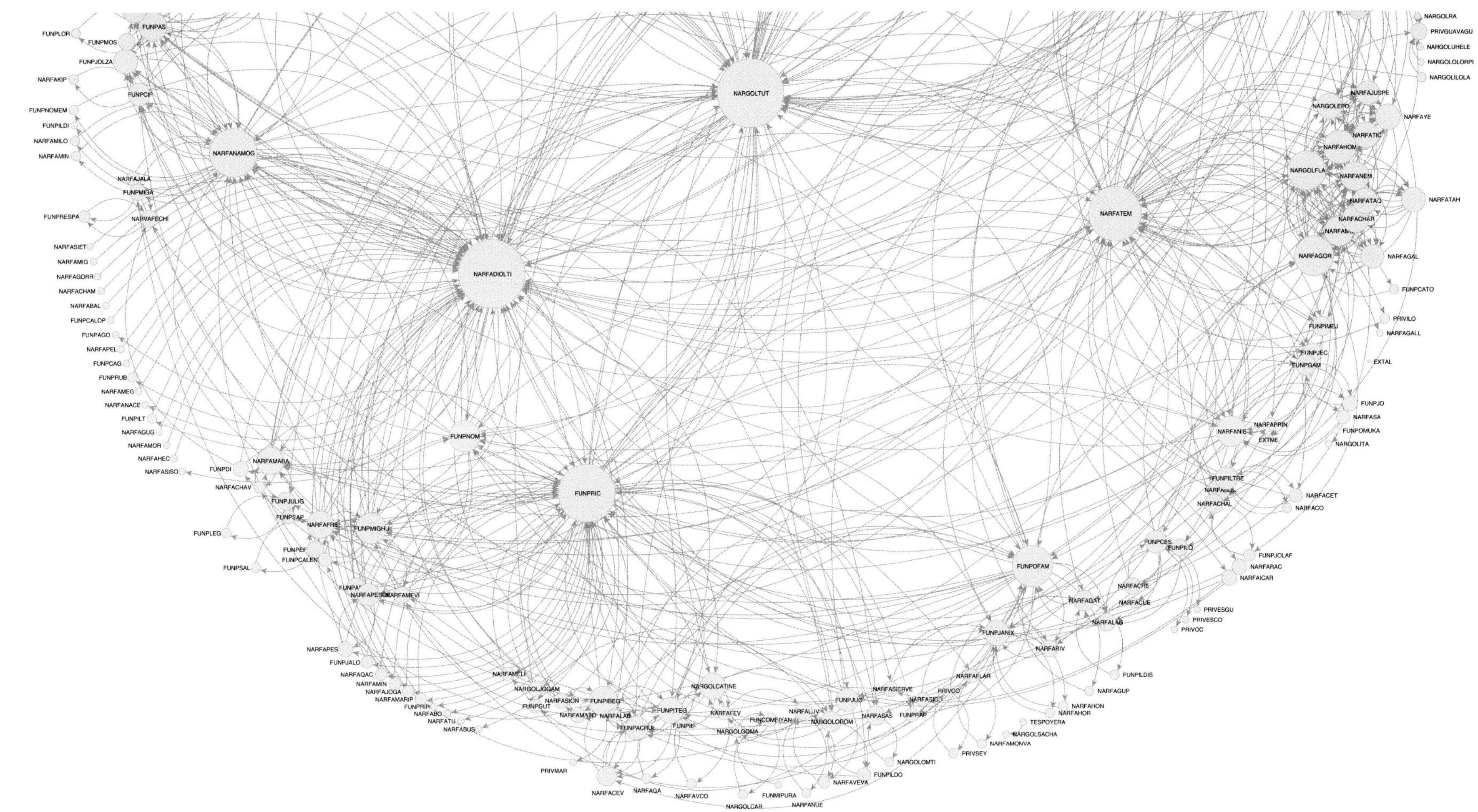

FUNPAS
FUNPLOR
FUNPMOS
FUNPJOLZA
NARFAKIP
FUNPCIP
FUNPNOMEM
FUNPILDI
NARFAMILO
NARFAMIN
NARFANAMOG
NARFAJALA
FUNPMIGA
FUNPRESPA
NARVAFECHI
NARFASIET
NARFAMIG
NARFAGORR
NARFACHAM
NARFABAL
FUNPCALOP
FUNPAGO
NARFAPEL
FUNPCAG
FUNPRUB
NARFAMEG
NARFANACE
FUNPILT
NARFAGUG
NARFAMOR
NARFAHEC
NARFASISO
NARGOLTUT
NARFADIOLTI
FUNPNOM
FUNPRIC
FUNPDI
NARFAMABA
NARFACHAV
FUNPJULIG
FUNPSAP
NARFAFRE
FUNPMIGHU
FUNPLEG
FUNPSAL
FUNPCALEN
NARFAPESOR
NARFAMEVI
NARFAPES
FUNPJALO
NARFAQAC
NARFAMIN
NARFAJOGA
NARFAMARIP
FUNPRIP
NARFABO
NARFATU
NARFASUS
NARFAMELI
NARGOLJOGAM
FUNPGUT
NARFASION
NARFAMATO
FUNPIBEG
NARFALAB
FUNPACRUL
FUNPITEG
FUNPIL
NARGOLCATINE
NARFAFEV
NARGOLGOMA
FUNCOMFIYAN
NARFALUV
NARGOLOROM
FUNPJUG
NARFASAS
FUNPRAP
NARFASIERVE
NARFASIG
PRIVCO
NARFAFLAR
FUNPJANIX
NARFARIV
NARFAGAT
NARFACUE
NARFACHE
NARFALAG
FUNPOFAM
FUNPCES
FUNPILO
PRIVESGU
PRIVESCO
PRIVOC
FUNPILDIS
NARFAGUP
NARFAHON
NARFAHOR
TESPOYERA
NARGOLSACHA
NARFAMONVA
PRIVSEY
NARGOLOMTI
FUNPILDO
NARFAVEVA
PRIVMAR
NARFACEV
NARFAGA
NARFAVCO
NARGOLCAR
FUNMIPURA
NARFANUE
NARFATEM
NARGOLRA
PRIVGUAVAGU
NARGOLUHELE
NARGOLOLORPI
NARGOLILOLA
NARGOLEPO
NARFAJUSPE
NARFAYE
NARFATIC
NARFAHOM
NARGOLFLA
NARFANEM
NARFATAC
NARFATAH
NARFACHAR
NARFAGOR
NARFAGAL
FUNPCATO
PRIVILO
NARFAGALL
FUNPIMEJ
FUNPJEC
FUNPGAM
EXTAL
FUNPJO
NARFASA
FUNPOMUKA
NARGOLITA
NARFANIB
NARFAPRIN
EXTME
FUNPILTRE
NARFACHAL
NARFACET
NARFACO
FUNPJOLAF
NARFARAC
NARFAICAR

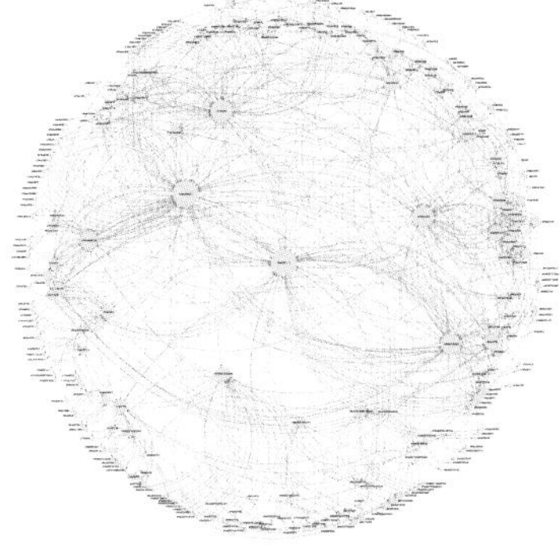

TIM BERNERS-LEE | Computer Scientist

2007

A mapping analogy for explaining to people the mingling and evolution of influences in the World Wide Web technology

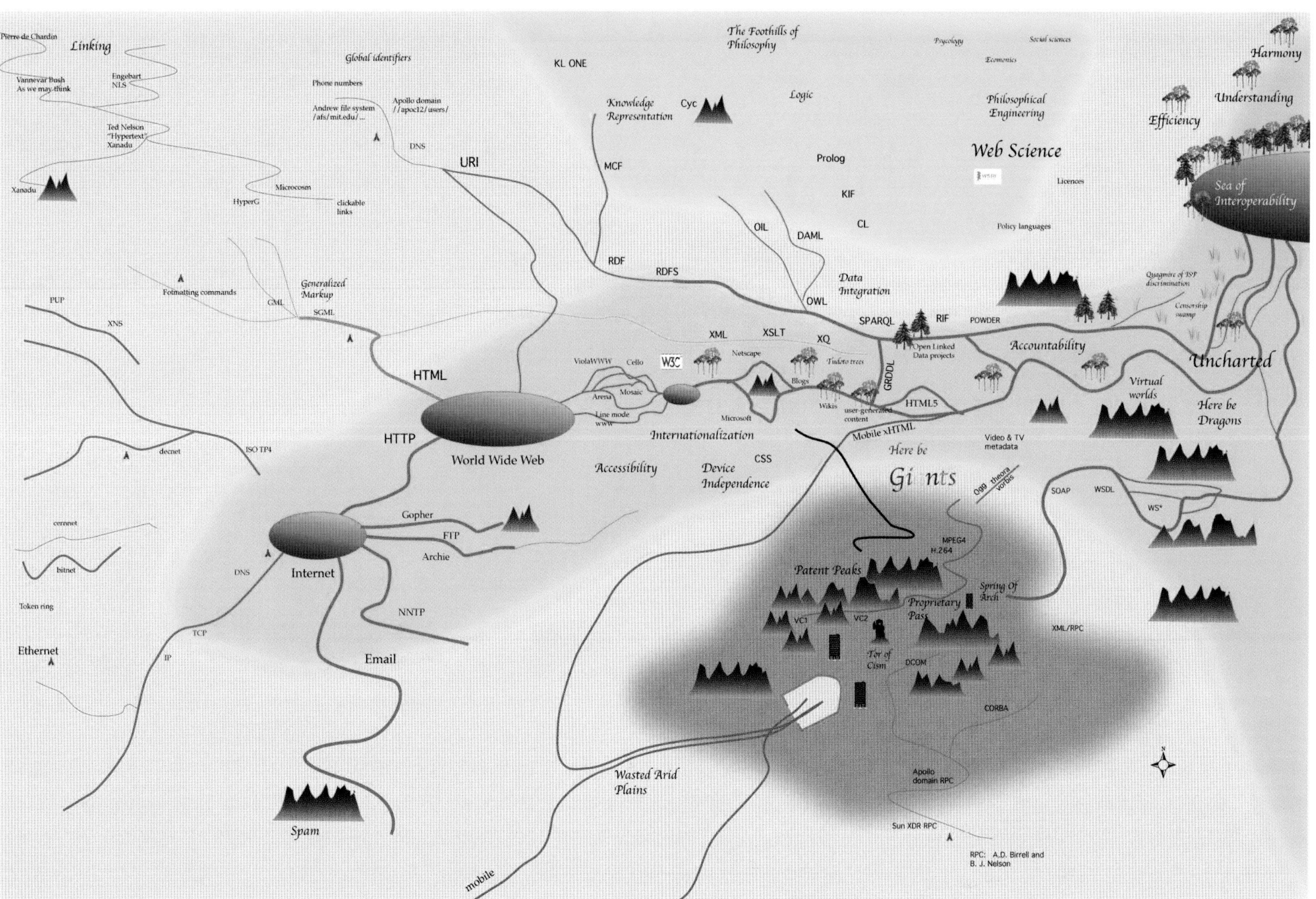

Pierre de Chardin
Linking
Vannevar Bush
As we may think
Engelbart
NLS
Ted Nelson
"Hypertext"
Xanadu
Xanadu
HyperG
Microcosm
clickable links
Global identifiers
Phone numbers
Andrew file system
/afs/mit.edu/...
Apollo domain
//apoc12/users/
DNS
URI
KL ONE
The Foothills of Philosophy
Knowledge Representation
Cyc
Logic
MCF
Prolog
KIF
CL
OIL
DAML
RDF
RDFS
Data Integration
OWL
Psycology
Social sciences
Economics
Philosophical Engineering
Web Science
Licences
Policy languages
Harmony
Understanding
Efficiency
Sea of Interoperability
Quagmire of ISP discrimination
Censorship swamp
Formatting commands
Generalized Markup
GML
SGML
PUP
XNS
HTML
XML
XSLT
XQ
SPARQL
RIF
POWDER
Accountability
Uncharted
ViolaWWW
Cello
W3C
Netscape
Tudoro trees
Open Linked Data projects
GRDDL
Arena
Mosaic
Line mode www
Blogs
Wikis
user-generated content
HTML5
Virtual worlds
Here be Dragons
Microsoft
Mobile xHTML
World Wide Web
HTTP
Internationalization
Accessibility
Device Independence
CSS
Here be Giants
Video & TV metadata
Ogg theora vorbis
decnet
ISO TP4
SOAP
WSDL
WS*
cernnet
bitnet
Token ring
Ethernet
Gopher
FTP
Archie
Internet
DNS
NNTP
MPEG4
H.264
Patent Peaks
Spring Of Arch
VC1
VC2
Proprietary Pass
XML/RPC
TCP
IP
Email
Tor of Cism
DCOM
CORBA
Spam
Wasted Arid Plains
Apollo domain RPC
Sun XDR RPC
RPC: A.D. Birrell and B. J. Nelson
mobile

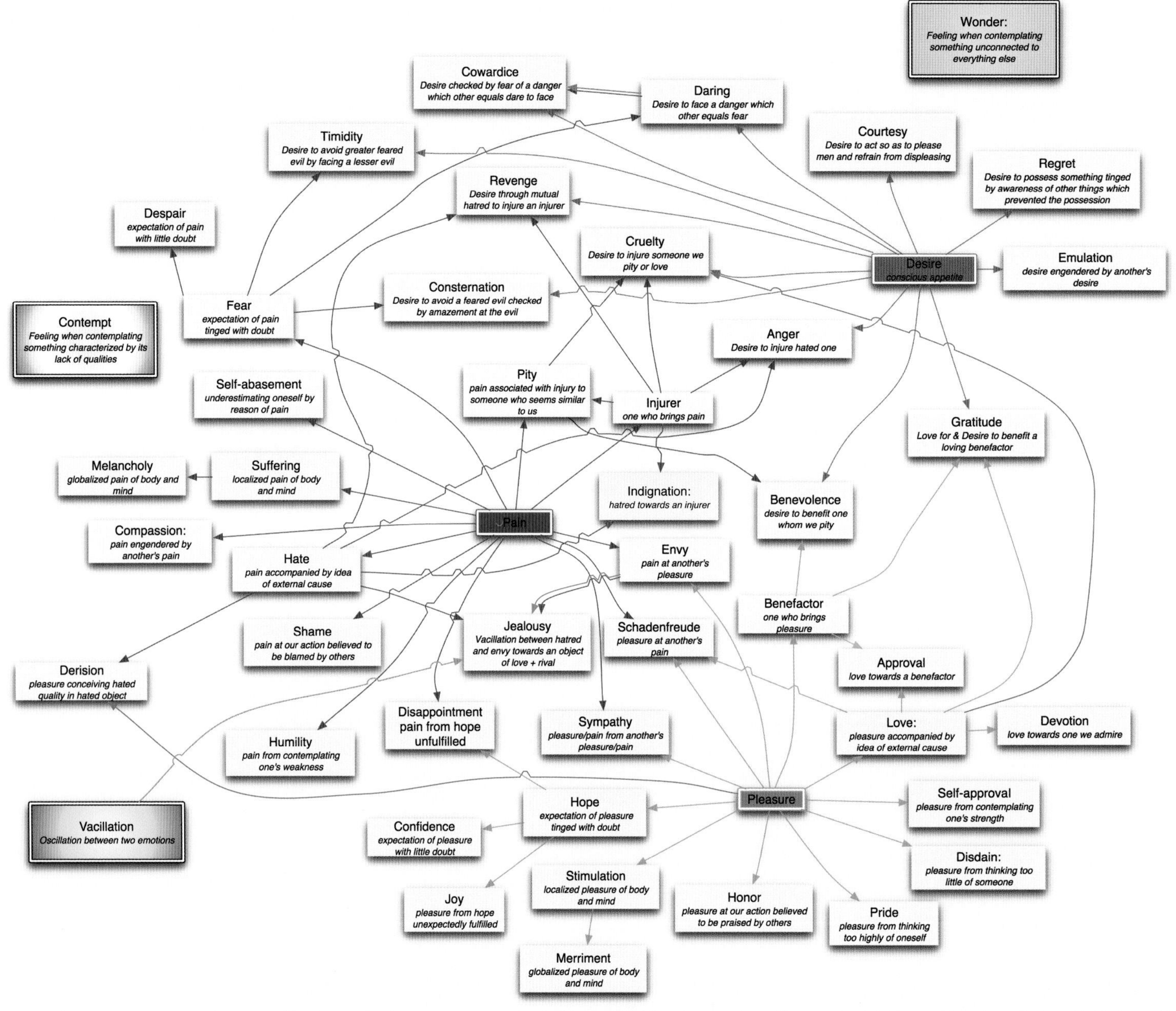

Wonder:
Feeling when contemplating something unconnected to everything else
Cowardice
Desire checked by fear of a danger which other equals dare to face
Daring
Desire to face a danger which other equals fear
Timidity
Desire to avoid greater feared evil by facing a lesser evil
Courtesy
Desire to act so as to please men and refrain from displeasing
Regret
Desire to possess something tinged by awareness of other things which prevented the possession
Revenge
Desire through mutual hatred to injure an injurer
Despair
expectation of pain with little doubt
Cruelty
Desire to injure someone we pity or love
Desire
conscious appetite
Emulation
desire engendered by another's desire
Contempt
Feeling when contemplating something characterized by its lack of qualities
Fear
expectation of pain tinged with doubt
Consternation
Desire to avoid a feared evil checked by amazement at the evil
Anger
Desire to injure hated one
Self-abasement
underestimating oneself by reason of pain
Pity
pain associated with injury to someone who seems similar to us
Injurer
one who brings pain
Gratitude
Love for & Desire to benefit a loving benefactor
Melancholy
globalized pain of body and mind
Suffering
localized pain of body and mind
Indignation:
hatred towards an injurer
Benevolence
desire to benefit one whom we pity
Compassion:
pain engendered by another's pain
Pain
Hate
pain accompanied by idea of external cause
Envy
pain at another's pleasure
Benefactor
one who brings pleasure
Shame
pain at our action believed to be blamed by others
Jealousy
Vacillation between hatred and envy towards an object of love + rival
Schadenfreude
pleasure at another's pain
Approval
love towards a benefactor
Derision
pleasure conceiving hated quality in hated object
Disappointment
pain from hope unfulfilled
Sympathy
pleasure/pain from another's pleasure/pain
Love:
pleasure accompanied by idea of external cause
Devotion
love towards one we admire
Humility
pain from contemplating one's weakness
Vacillation
Oscillation between two emotions
Hope
expectation of pleasure tinged with doubt
Pleasure
Self-approval
pleasure from contemplating one's strength
Confidence
expectation of pleasure with little doubt
Disdain:
pleasure from thinking too little of someone
Stimulation
localized pleasure of body and mind
Joy
pleasure from hope unexpectedly fulfilled
Honor
pleasure at our action believed to be praised by others
Pride
pleasure from thinking too highly of oneself
Merriment
globalized pleasure of body and mind

Pleasure Pain Desire:
*A Map of the Emotions**

EMANUEL

DERMAN

GOOD = EVERY KIND OF PLEASURE

EVIL = EVERY KIND OF PAIN

M	M	M	M	M	M
A	A	A	A	A	A
T	T	T	T	T	T
H	H	H	H	H	H
E	E	E	E	E	E
M	M	M	M	M	M
A	A	A	A	A	A
T	T	T	T	T	T
I	I	I	I	I	I
C	C	C	C	C	C
I	I	I	I	I	I
A	A	A	A	A	A
N	N	N	N	N	N

Spinoza's most fundamental affects are pain, pleasure and desire. They lie beneath all the other affects and can be thought of as closer to organic conditions than psychic ones. The more complex emotions bear an indirect link to the three just named.

*according to *Ethics*, BENEDICT DE SPINOZA

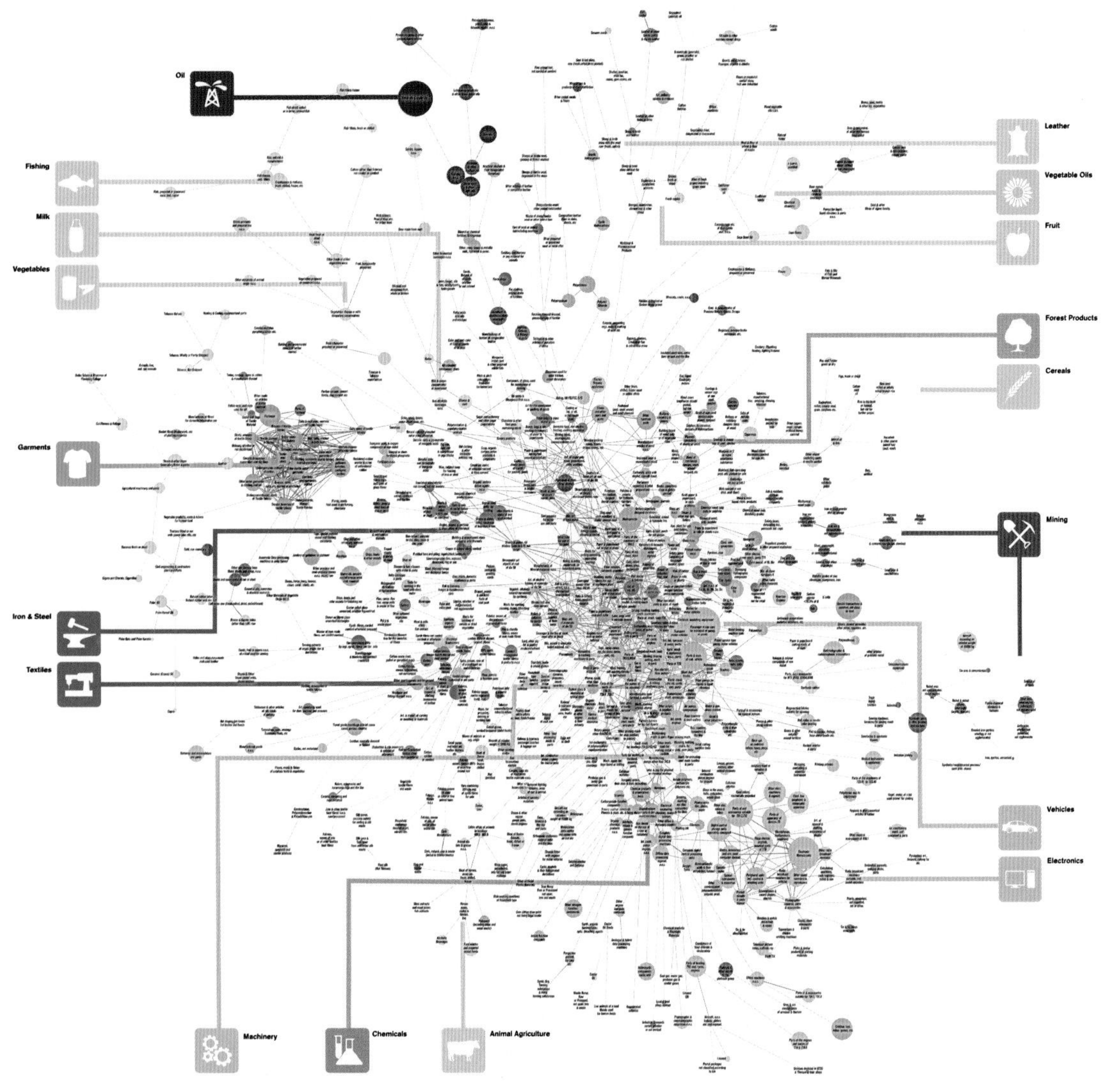

CÉSAR HIDALGO	SCIENTIST	*The Product Space*

In this visualization of the Product Space, each node (circle) represents a product. Links (lines) connect products that tend to be exported by the same countries. ¶ The size of a node is proportional to global trade in that good. Large nodes represent products with large world markets, such as oil and cars, whereas small nodes represent products in which global trade is relatively small. Node colours are based on 'Leamer' categories, which classify products in groups based on factor endowments. ¶ Link colours are proportional to the likelihood that two products will be exported in tandem. Red links connect products that are co-exported by at least 65% of all countries, whereas light blue links connect pairs of products that are co-exported by less than 40% of them. ¶ The structure of the Product Space is heterogeneous, with some densely connected regions or clusters, including the garments cluster (green), the electronics cluster (light blue), the textile cluster (blue), and the machinery cluster (light blue) and other parts where connections are sparse. In these peripheral parts of the Product Space, we find raw materials (red), mineral fuels (crimson) and agricultural products (yellow, light green and cream).

NODE COLOUR (Leamer classification)

- Petroleum
- Raw materials
- Forest products
- Tropical agriculture
- Animal agriculture
- Cereals
- Labour intensive
- Capital intensive
- Machinery
- Chemicals

LINK COLOUR (proximity)

- $\Phi > 0.65$
- $\Phi > 0.55$
- $\Phi < 0.4$
- $\Phi < 0.4$

Proximity measures the similarity between products based on the number of countries co-exporting them.

NODE SIZE (millions of dollars in 2000)

The scale of this diagram corresponds to the detail on the opposite page

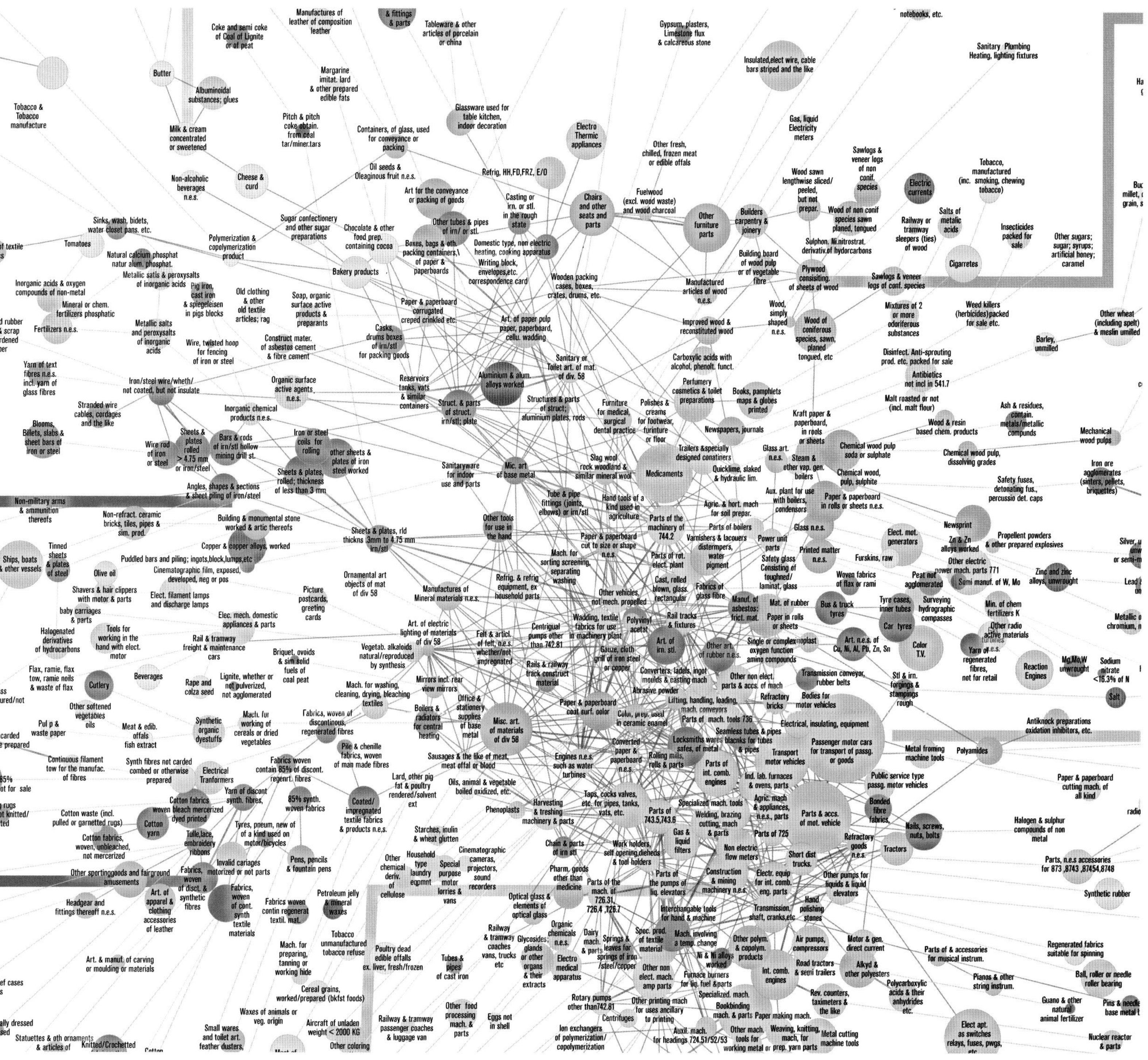

Manufactures of leather of composition leather
& fittings & parts
Tableware & other articles of porcelain or china
Coke and semi coke of Coal of Lignite or of peat
Gypsum, plasters, Limestone flux & calcareous stone
notebooks, etc.
Insulated,elect wire, cable bars striped and the like
Sanitary Plumbing Heating, lighting fixtures
Butter
Albuminoidal substances; glues
Margarine imitat. lard & other prepared edible fats
Tobacco & Tobacco manufacture
Milk & cream concentrated or sweetened
Pitch & pitch coke obtain. from coal tar/miner.tars
Glassware used for table kitchen, indoor decoration
Electro Thermic appliances
Containers, of glass, used for conveyance or packing
Gas, liquid Electricity meters
Other fresh, chilled, frozen meat or edible offals
Sawlogs & veneer logs of non conif. species
Tobacco, manufactured (inc. smoking, chewing tobacco)
Non-alcoholic beverages n.e.s.
Cheese & curd
Oil seeds & Oleaginous fruit n.e.s.
Refrig, HH,FD,FRZ, E/D
Wood sawn lengthwise sliced/ peeled, but not prepar.
Electric currents
Art for the conveyance or packing of goods
Casting or irn. or stl. in the rough state
Chairs and other seats and parts
Fuelwood (excl. wood waste) and wood charcoal
Other furniture parts
Builders carpentry & joinery
Wood of non conif species sawn planed, tongued
Salts of metallic acids
Sinks, wash, bidets, water closet pans. etc.
Sugar confectionery and other sugar preparations
Chocolate & other food prep. containing cocoa
Other tubes & pipes of irn/ or stl.
Domestic type, non electric heating, cooking apparatus
Railway or tramway sleepers (ties) of wood
Insecticides packed for sale
Other sugars; sugar; syrups; artificial honey; caramel
Tomatoes
Polymerization & copolymerization product
Boxes, bags & oth. packing containers,\ of paper & paperboards
Writing block, envelopes,etc. correspondence card
Sulphon. Ni.nitrostrat. derivativ.of hydrocarbons
Natural calcium phosphat natur alum. phosphat.
Bakery products
Building board of wood pulp or of vegetable fibre
Cigarettes
Metallic salts & peroxysalts of inorganic acids
Inorganic acids & oxygen compounds of non-metal
Pig iron, cast iron & spiegeleisen in pigs blocks
Old clothing & other old textile articles; rag
Soap, organic surface active products & preparants
Wooden packing cases, boxes, crates, drums, etc.
Manufactured articles of wood n.e.s.
Plywood consisting. of sheets of wood
Sawlogs & veneer logs of conf. species
Mineral or chem. fertilizers phosphatic
Paper & paperboard corrugated creped crinkled etc.
Art. of paper pulp paper, paperboard, cellu. wadding
Wood, simply shaped n.e.s.
Wood of coniferous species, sawn, planed tongued, etc
Mixtures of 2 or more odoriferous substances
Weed killers (herbicides) packed for sale etc.
Other wheat (including spelt) & meslin unmilled
Fertilizers n.e.s.
Metallic salts and peroxysalts of inorganic acids
Wire, twisted hoop for fencing of iron or steel
Construct mater. of asbestos cement & fibre cement
Casks, drums boxes of irn/stl for packing goods
Improved wood & reconstituted wood
Barley, unmilled
Carboxylic acids with alcohol, phenolt. funct.
Disinfect. Anti-sprouting prod. etc. packed for sale
Yarn of text fibres n.e.s. incl. yarn of glass fibres
Iron/steel wire/wheth/ not coated, but not insulate
Organic surface active agents n.e.s.
Reservoirs tanks, vats & similar containers
Aluminium & alum. alloys worked
Sanitary or Toilet art. of mat. of div. 58
Antibiotics not incl in 541.7
Perfumery cosmetics & toilet preparations
Books, pamphlets maps & globes printed
Malt roasted or not (incl. malt flour)
Stranded wire cables, cordages and the like
Inorganic chemical products n.e.s.
Struct. & parts of struct. irn/stl; plate
Structures & parts of struct; aluminium plates, rods
Furniture for medical, surgical dental practice
Polishes & creams for footwear, furniture or floor
Kraft paper & paperboard, in rools or sheets
Ash & residues, contain. metals/metallic compunds
Blooms, Billets, slabs & sheet bars of iron or steel
Wire rod of iron or steel
Sheets & plates rolled > 4.75 mm or iron/steel
Bars & rods of irn/stl hollow mining drill st.
Iron or steel coils for rolling
other sheets & plates of iron steel worked
Newspapers, journals
Wood & resin based chem. products
Mechanical wood pulps
Trailers &specially designed conatiners
Glass art. n.e.s.
Chemical wood pulp soda or sulphate
Chemical wood pulp, dissolving grades
Sheets & plates, rolled; thickness of less than 3 mm
Sanitaryware for indoor use and parts
Mic. art. of base metal
Slag wool rock woodland & similar mineral wool
Medicaments
Quicklime, slaked & hydraulic lim.
Steam & other vap. gen. boilers
Chemical wood, pulp, sulphite
Safety fuses, detonating fus., percussio det. caps
Iron ore agglomerates (sinters, pellets, briquettes)
Angles, shapes & sections & sheet piling of iron/steel
Non-military arms & ammunition thereofs
Tube & pipe fittings (joints, elbows) or irn/stl
Hand tools of a kind used in agriculture
Agric. & hort. mach for soil prepar.
Aux. plant for use with boilers, condensors
Paper & paperboard in rolls or sheets n.e.s.
Non-refract. ceramic bricks, tiles, pipes & sim. prod.
Building & monumental stone worked & artic thereofs
Other tools for use in the hand
Parts of the machinery of 744.2
Parts of boilers
Newsprint
Glass n.e.s.
Elect. mot. generators
Propellent powders & other prepared explosives
Sheets & plates, rld thickns 3mm to 4.75 mm irn/stl
Paper & paperboard cut to size or shape n.e.s.
Varnishers & lacours distempers, water pigment
Power unit parts
Zn & Zn alloys worked
Tinned sheets & plates of steel
Copper & copper alloys, worked
Mach. for sorting screening, separating washing
Parts of rot. elect. plant
Printed matter n.e.s.
Furskins, raw
Ships, boats & other vessels
Olive oil
Puddled bars and piling; ingots,block,lumps,etc
Safety glass Consisting of toughned/ laminat, glass
Other electric power mach. parts 771
Cinematographic film, exposed, developed, neg or pos
Ornamental art objects of mat of div 58
Cast, rolled blown, glass. rectangular
Woven fabrics of flax or rami
Peat not agglomerated
Semi manuf. of W, Mo
Zinc and zinc alloys, unwrought
Shavers & hair clippers with motor & parts
Elect. filament lamps and discharge lamps
Picture postcards, greeting cards
Manufactures of Mineral materials n.e.s.
Refrig. & refrig equipment, ex household parts
Other vehicles, not mech. propelled
Fabrics of glass fibre
Manuf. of asbestos: frict. mat.
Mat. of rubber
Bus & truck tyres
Tyre cases, inner tubes
Surveying hydrographic compasses
Min. of chem fertilizers K
baby carriages & parts
Elec. mech. domestic appliances & parts
Wadding, textile fabrics for use in machinery plant
Polyvinyl acetal
Rail tracks & fixtures
Paper in rolls or sheets
Car tyres
Other radio active materials
Halogenated derivatives of hydrocarbons
Tools for working in the hand with elect. motor
Rail & tramway freight & maintenance cars
Art. of electric lighting of materials of div 58
Felt & articl. of felt, n.e.s. whether/not impregnated
Centrigual pumps other than 742.81
Art. of irn. stl.
Other art. of rubber n.e.s.
Single or complex oxygen function amino compounds
Art. n.e.s. of Cu, Ni, Al, Pb, Zn, Sn
Color T.V.
Yarn of regenerated fibres, not for retail
Reaction Engines
Mg,Mo,W unwrought
Sodium nitrate <16.3% of N
Flax, ramie, flax tow, ramie noils & waste of flax
Cutlery
Beverages
Briquet, ovoids & sim solid fuels of coal peat
Vegetab. alkaloids natural/reproduced by synthesis
Gauze, cloth grill of iron steel or copper
Rails & railway track construct material
Rape and colza seed
Lignite, whether or not pulverized, not agglomerated
Mirrors incl. rear view mirrors
Converters, ladels, ingot moulds & casting mach
Other non elect. parts & accs. of mach
Transmission conveyor, rubber belts
Stl & irn. forgings & stampings rough
Other softened vegetables oils
Mach. for washing, cleaning, drying, bleaching textiles
Abrasive powder
Lifting, handling, loading, mach. conveyers
Refractory bricks
Bodies for motor vehicles
Salt
Boilers & radiators for central heating
Office & stationery supplies of base metal
Misc. art. of materials of div 58
Paper & paperboard coat surf. color
Color, prep. used in ceramic enamel
Parts of mach. tools 736
Electrical, insulating, equipment
Antiknock preparations oxidation inhibitors, etc.
Pul p & waste paper
Meat & edib. offals fish extract
Synthetic organic dyestuffs
Mach. for working of cereals or dried vegetables
Fabrics, woven of discontinous, regenerated fibres
Seamless tubes & pipes
Locksmiths wares blancks for tubes safes, of metal & pipes
Passenger motor cars for transport of passg. or goods
Metal froming machine tools
Polyamides
Pile & chenille fabrics, woven of man made fibres
Converted paper & paperboard n.e.s.
Rolling mills, rolls & parts
Transport motor vehicles
Continuous filament tow for the manufac. of fibres
Synth fibres not carded combed or otherwise prepared
Electrical Tranformers
Fabrics woven contain 85% of discont. regenrt. fibres
Sausages & the like of meat, meat offal or blood
Engines n.e.s. such as water turbines
Parts of int. comb. engines
Ind. lab. furnaces & ovens, parts
Public service type passg. motor vehicles
Paper & paperboard cutting mach. of all kind
Cotton fabrics woven bleach mercerized dyed printed
Yarn of discont synth. fibres,
85% synth. woven fabrics
Coated/ impregnated textile fabrics & products n.e.s
Lard, other pig fat & poultry rendered/solvent ext
Oils, animal & vegetable boiled oxidized, etc.
Taps, cocks valves, etc. for pipes, tanks, vats, etc.
Specialized mach. tools
Agric. mach & appliances, n.e.s., parts
Bonded fibre fabrics
Cotton waste (incl. pulled or garnetted rugs)
Cotton yarn
Tyres, pneum, new of a kind used on motor/bicycles
Phenoplasts
Harvesting & treshing machinery & parts
Parts of 743.5,743.6
Welding, brazing cutting, mach & parts
Parts & accs. of mot. vehicle
Halogen & sulphur compounds of non metal
Cotton fabrics, woven, unbleached, not mercerized
Tulle,lace, embroidery ribbons
Pens, pencils & fountain pens
Starches, inulin & wheat glutten
Gas & liquid filters
Parts of 725
Nails, screws, nuts, bolts
Refractory goods n.e.s.
Invalid cariages motorized or not parts
Cinematographic cameras, projectors, sound recorders
Chain & parts of irn stl
Work holders, self opening dieheds & tool holders
Non electric flow meters
Short dist trucks.
Tractors
Parts, n.e.s accessories for 873 ,8743 ,87454,8748
Other sportinggoods and fairground amusements
Fabrics, woven of disct. & synthetic fibres
Household type laundry eqpmnt
Special purpose motor lorries & vans
Other chemical deriv. of cellulose
Pharm. goods other than medicine
Parts of the mach. of 726.31, 726.4 ,726.7
Parts of the pumps of liq. elevators
Construction & mining machinery n.e.s.
Electr. equip for int. comb. eng. parts
Other pumps for liquids & liquid elevators
Synthetic rubber
Headgear and fittings thereoff n.e.s.
Art. of apparel & clothing accessories of leather
Fabrics woven of cont. synth textile materials
Fabrics woven contin regenerat textil. mat.
Petroleum jelly & mineral waxes
Optical glass & elements of optical glass
Interchangable tools for hand & machine
Transmission, shaft, cranks,etc
Hand polishing stones
Railway & tramway coaches vans, trucks etc
Glycosides; glands or other organs & their extracts
Organic chemicals n.e.s.
Electro medical apparatus
Dairy mach & parts
Springs & leaves for springs of iron /steel/copper
Spec. prod. of textile material
Mach. involving a temp. change
Other polym. & copolym. products
Air pumps, compressors
Motor & gen. direct current
Regenerated fabrics suitable for spinning
Art. & manuf. of carving or moulding or materials
Mach. for preparing, tanning or working hide
Tobacco unmanufactured tobacco refuse
Poultry dead edible offalls ex. liver, fresh/frozen
Tubes & pipes of cast iron
Other non elect. mach. amp parts
Ni & Ni alloys worked
Int. comb. engines
Road tractors & semi trailers
Alkyd & other polyesters
Parts of & accessories for musical instrum.
Pianos & other string instrum.
Ball, roller or needle roller bearing
Furnace burners for liq. fuel &parts
Specialized. mach.
Rev. counters, taximeters & the like
Polycarboxylic acids & their anhydrides etc.
Cereal grains, worked/prepared (bkfst foods)
Other food processing mach. & parts
Rotary pumps other than742.81
Other printing mach for uses ancillary to printing
Bookbinding mach. & parts
Paper making mach.
Guano & other natural animal fertilizer
Pins & needle base metal
Waxes of animals or veg. origin
Aircraft of unladen weight < 2000 KG
Railway & tramway passenger coaches & luggage van
Eggs not in shell
Centrifuges
Ion exchangers of polymerization/ copolymerization
Auxil. mach. for headings 724.51/52/53
Other mach. tools for working metal or
Weaving, knitting, mach. for prep. yarn parts
Metal cutting machine tools
Elect apt. as switches relays, fuses, pwgs,
Nuclear reactor & parts
Small wares and toilet art. feather dusters,
Statuettes & oth ornaments & articles of
Knitted/Crochetted
Other coloring

Motional City Map
2010
ARTIST
OLAFUR ELIASSON

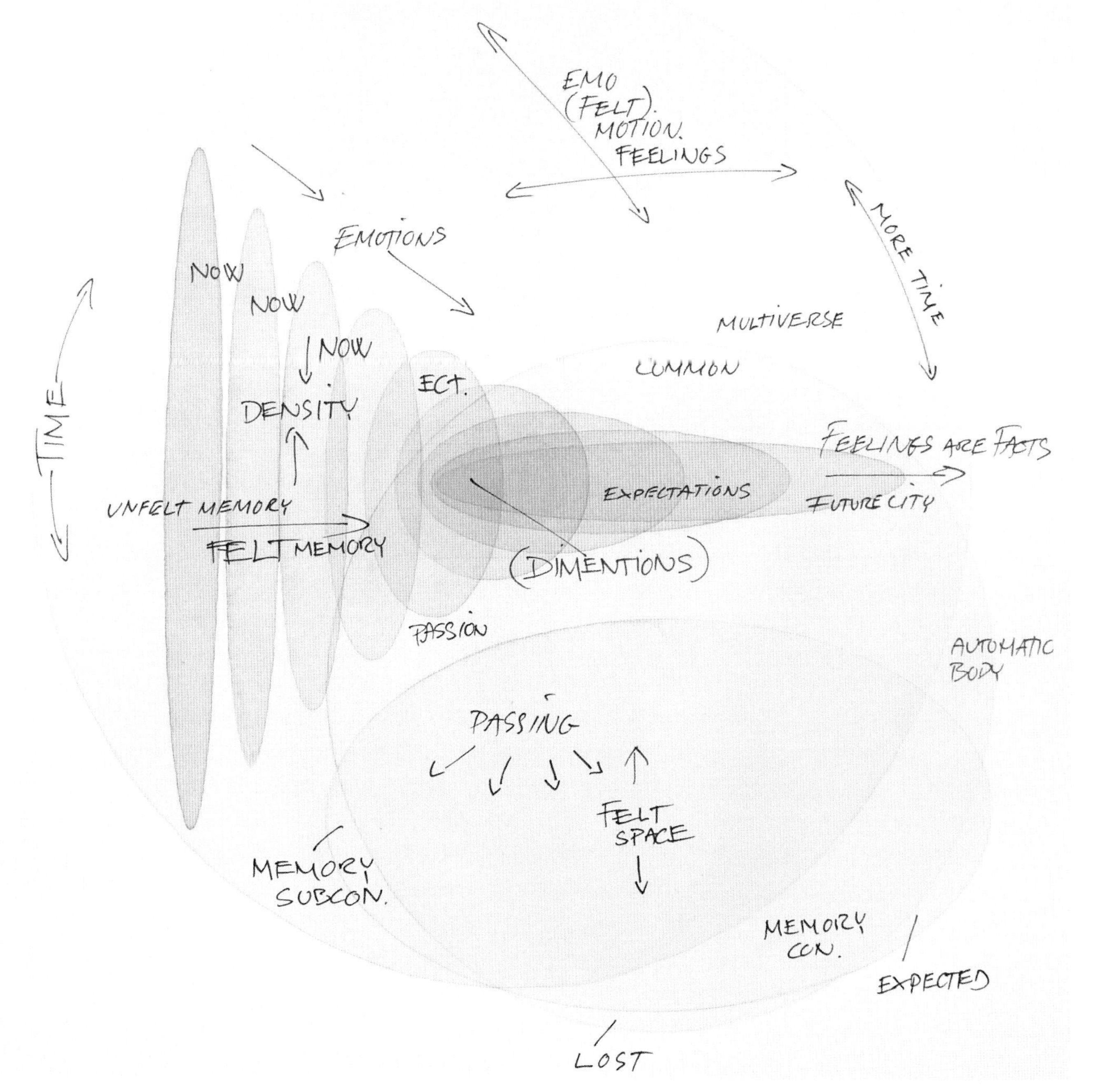
EMO
(FELT).
MOTION.
FEELINGS
MORE TIME
EMOTIONS
NOW
NOW
NOW
DENSITY
TIME
MULTIVERSE
COMMON
ECT.
FEELINGS ARE FACTS
EXPECTATIONS
FUTURE CITY
UNFELT MEMORY
FELT MEMORY
(DIMENTIONS)
PASSION
AUTOMATIC
BODY
PASSING
FELT
SPACE
MEMORY
SUBCON.
MEMORY
CON.
EXPECTED
LOST

ANDRES JAQUE

ARCHITECT	*Fray Foam Home*	2010

WHEN DECORATION BECOMES POLITICAL

Domestic interiors are arenas with the necessary conditions to make the political realm possible. FRAY FOAM HOME is the restoration of a network of spaces upon which a specific home – an apartment shared by four people, on Pez Street in Madrid – is truly built: the network of landscapes, resources and infrastructures that are necessary so that the forms of comfort, supplies and fictions that are activated in daily lives can be possible. The distribution of water, the exploitation of energy resources, the intellectual property rights or the ideology of audiovisual contents are compulsory transit points of the polemics that connect us as societies, and in which our collectivities take shape. And yet, are these political extensions of the domestic visible in the interior of houses? Is it possible to take the dispute to the point at which it originates? Architecture generates strategies to promote territorial distribution of uses, resources and consumptions that guarantee spheres of sweet peaceful localism. FRAY FOAM HOME stems from the acknowledgment of a discredited architectural periphery: the architecture of Christmas trees, of flower arrangements, of tablecloths, of birthday decorations and of photographs taped to mirrors. An architecture of the expression, exposure and dissemination of the personal realm, of the invitation to collective events, of the projection of dreamt futures. An architecture of the political that, far from creating new realities, could furnish the existing with parliamentary guarantees.

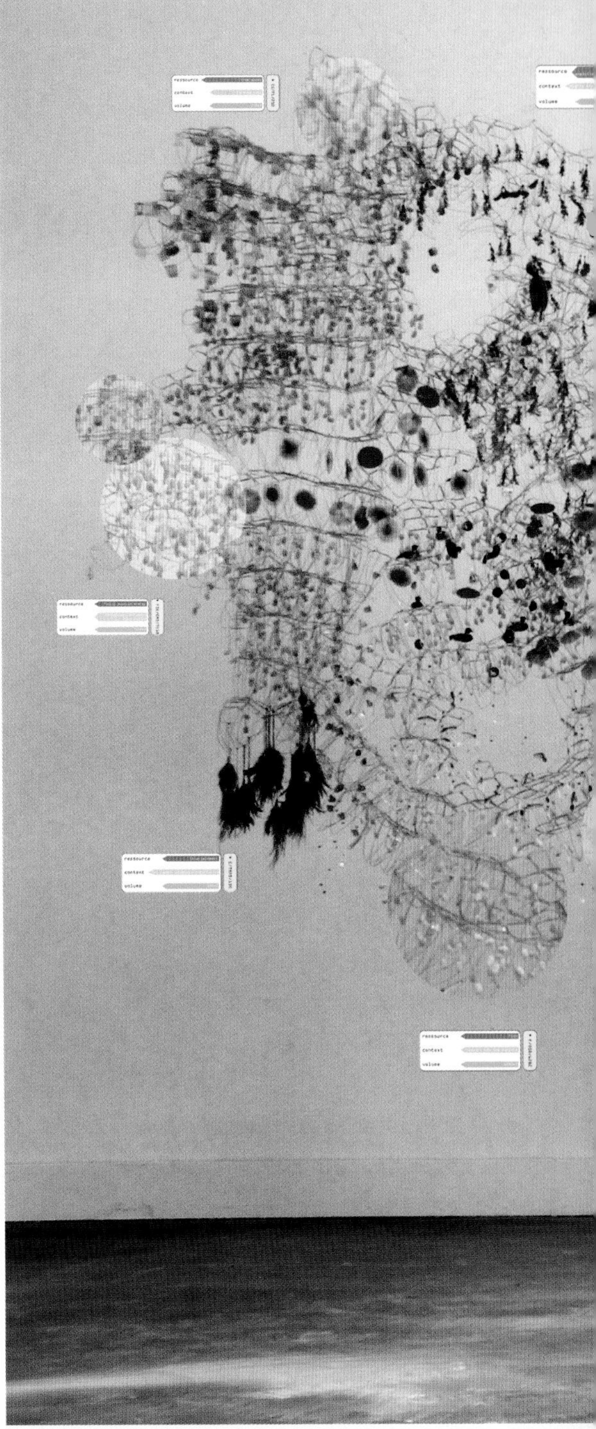

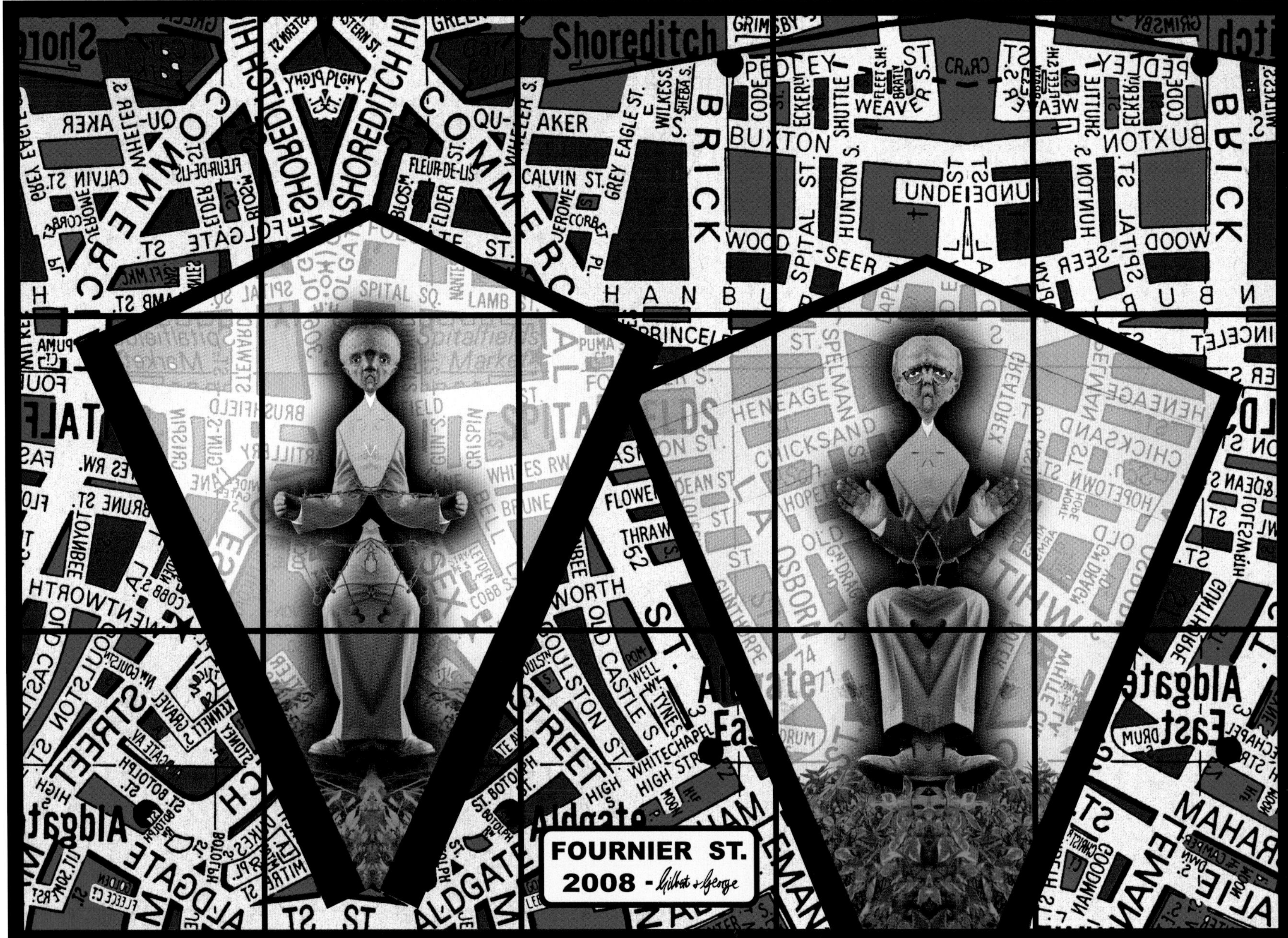

Fournier St, 2008, 226 × 317 cm

GILBERT & GEORGE

ARTISTS

My sister Lily is a whore down Piccadilly.

My mother is another down the Strand.

My father sells his arsehole down the Elephant & Castle.

We are the finest fucking family in the land.

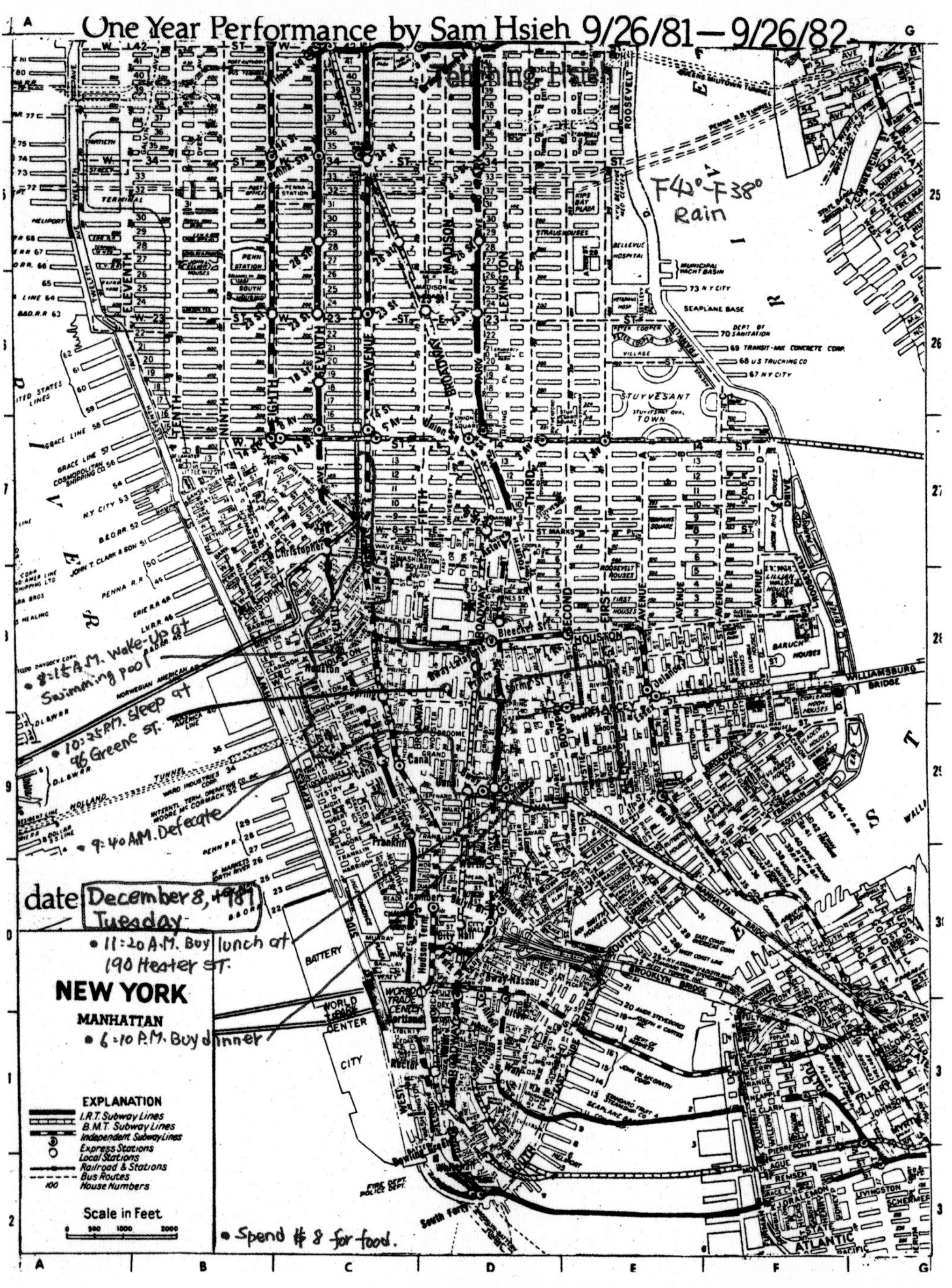

TEHCHING HSIEH

A
R T
I S T

One Year Performance 1981–2

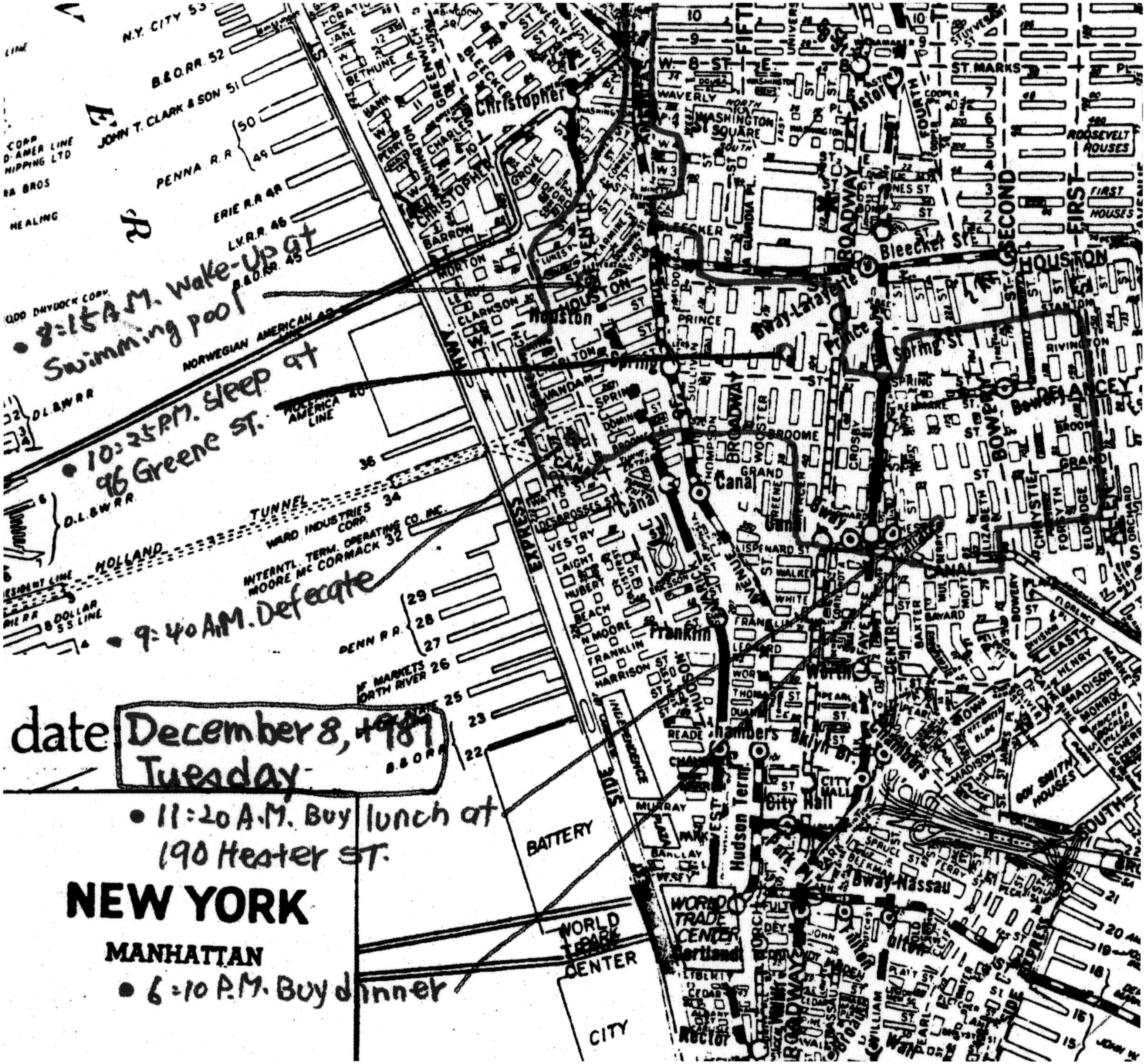

- 8:15 A.M. Wake-Up at Swimming pool
- 10:25 P.M. sleep at 96 Greene ST.
- 9:40 A.M. Defecate

date December 8, 1981 Tuesday

- 11:20 A.M. Buy lunch at 190 Hester ST.

NEW YORK

MANHATTAN

- 6:10 P.M. Buy dinner

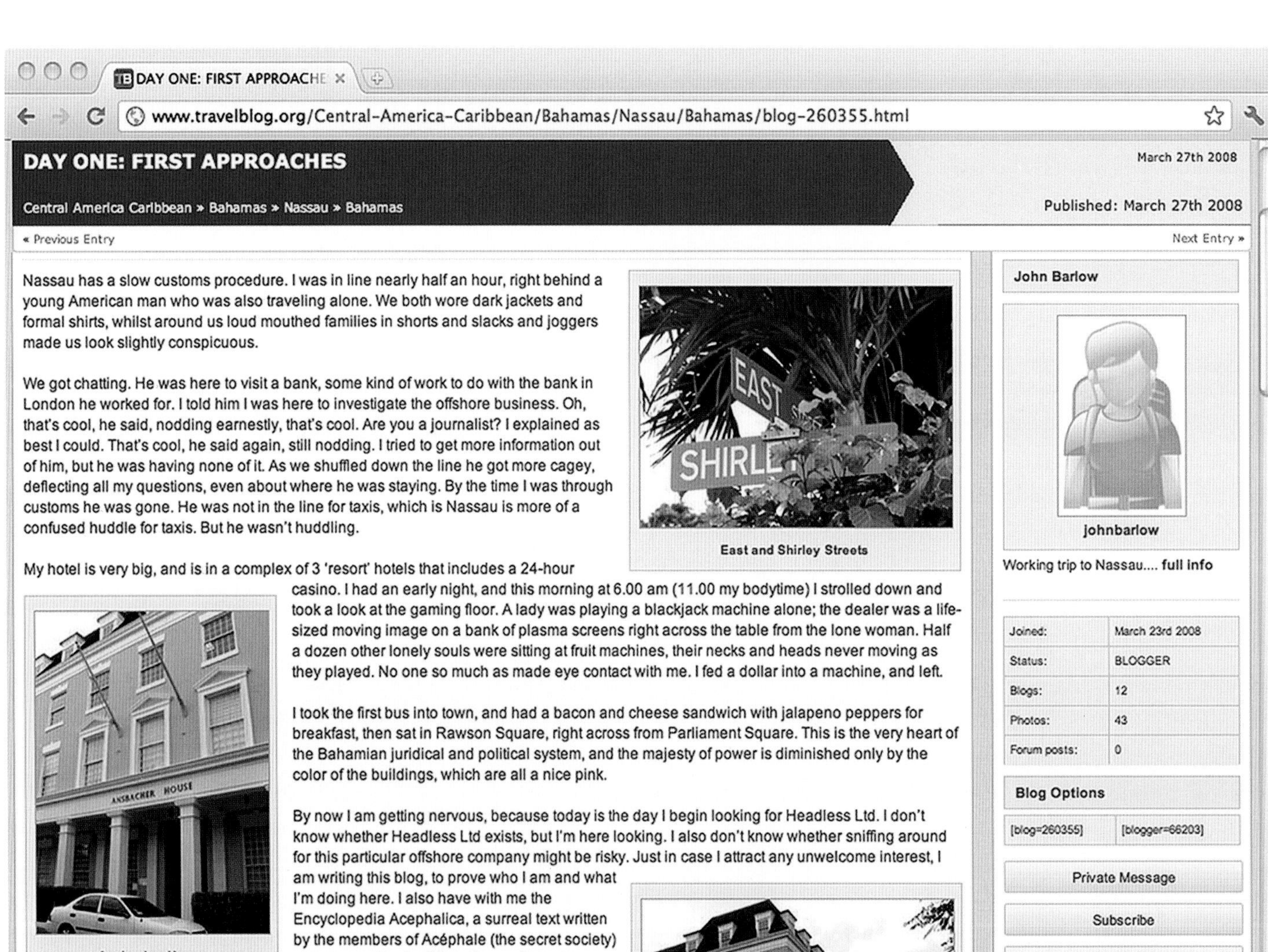

DAY ONE: FIRST APPROACHE ×

www.travelblog.org/Central-America-Caribbean/Bahamas/Nassau/Bahamas/blog-260355.html

DAY ONE: FIRST APPROACHES

March 27th 2008

Central America Caribbean » Bahamas » Nassau » Bahamas

Published: March 27th 2008

« Previous Entry

Next Entry »

Nassau has a slow customs procedure. I was in line nearly half an hour, right behind a young American man who was also traveling alone. We both wore dark jackets and formal shirts, whilst around us loud mouthed families in shorts and slacks and joggers made us look slightly conspicuous.

We got chatting. He was here to visit a bank, some kind of work to do with the bank in London he worked for. I told him I was here to investigate the offshore business. Oh, that's cool, he said, nodding earnestly, that's cool. Are you a journalist? I explained as best I could. That's cool, he said again, still nodding. I tried to get more information out of him, but he was having none of it. As we shuffled down the line he got more cagey, deflecting all my questions, even about where he was staying. By the time I was through customs he was gone. He was not in the line for taxis, which is Nassau is more of a confused huddle for taxis. But he wasn't huddling.

East and Shirley Streets

My hotel is very big, and is in a complex of 3 'resort' hotels that includes a 24-hour casino. I had an early night, and this morning at 6.00 am (11.00 my bodytime) I strolled down and took a look at the gaming floor. A lady was playing a blackjack machine alone; the dealer was a life-sized moving image on a bank of plasma screens right across the table from the lone woman. Half a dozen other lonely souls were sitting at fruit machines, their necks and heads never moving as they played. No one so much as made eye contact with me. I fed a dollar into a machine, and left.

Ansbacker House

I took the first bus into town, and had a bacon and cheese sandwich with jalapeno peppers for breakfast, then sat in Rawson Square, right across from Parliament Square. This is the very heart of the Bahamian juridical and political system, and the majesty of power is diminished only by the color of the buildings, which are all a nice pink.

By now I am getting nervous, because today is the day I begin looking for Headless Ltd. I don't know whether Headless Ltd exists, but I'm here looking. I also don't know whether sniffing around for this particular offshore company might be risky. Just in case I attract any unwelcome interest, I am writing this blog, to prove who I am and what I'm doing here. I also have with me the Encyclopedia Acephalica, a surreal text written by the members of Acéphale (the secret society) plus a paperback edition of one of my own books, which has a photo of me in it. I feel that together these books will serve as evidence if things get difficult. At least, I felt that when I packed. Now I feel like a fucking idiot.

John Barlow

johnbarlow

Working trip to Nassau.... **full info**

Joined:	March 23rd 2008
Status:	BLOGGER
Blogs:	12
Photos:	43
Forum posts:	0

Blog Options

[blog=260355] [blogger=66203]

Private Message

Subscribe

Blog Map

Guestbook

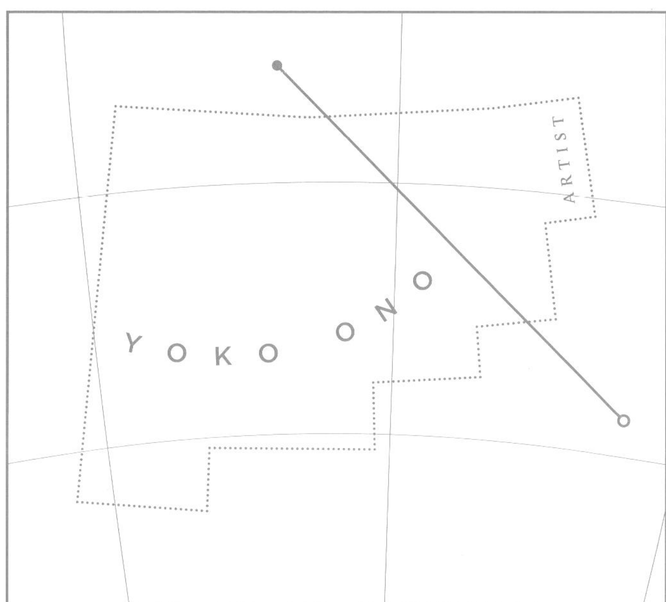

MAP PIECE

Draw an imaginary map.
Put a goal mark on the map where you want to go.
Go walking on an actual street according to your map.
If there is no street where it should be according to the map, make one by putting the obstacles aside.
When you reach the goal, ask the name of the city and give flowers to the first person you meet.
The map must be followed exactly, or the event has to be dropped all together.

Ask your friends to write maps.
Give your friends maps.

1962 summer

A

B

ERLING KAGGE

Expedition across Vatnajökull | late March 2010

(POLAR EXPLORER, PUBLISHER, PHILOSOPHER)

We are all born explorers. You, me and everybody else. Walking across Vatnajökull, Europe's biggest glacier, with the living polar legends Børge Ousland and Haraldur Örn Ólafsson, while the neighbouring volcano Eyjafjallajökull was erupting and making disruptions for air travel throughout Europe, I suddenly stopped and looked into the horizon, wondering what that was beyond it. To be an explorer is not something you become; it is something you are when you are born. Nobody starts to climb, or to wonder what's hidden deep in the oceans; it is a natural state of mind. But if you are not very careful in your daily life, you will quit early on. Years of school, parents' expectations and society's demands slowly grind your original spirit apart and you eventually start to behave in a civilized way.

It can feel both unpleasant and somewhat risky to explore the world. But perhaps it's even more risky to do nothing. What you will regret in times to come are the chances you didn't take, the initiative you didn't show, what you didn't do. If you say it's impossible and I say it's possible, we're probably both right.

JOHN

Designer

MAEDA

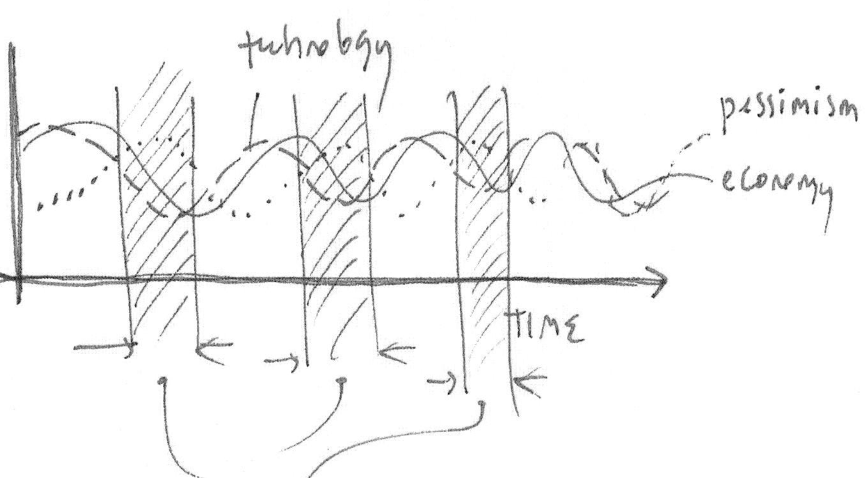

transformative
times → technology backlash
→ pessimism = lost-ness
→ money values deteriorate
∴ opportunity is v high

"map of the future" for TWO
WHAT WE CAN ALWAYS COUNT ON IS SIMPLY MORE OF THE SAME. Feb 3, 2010

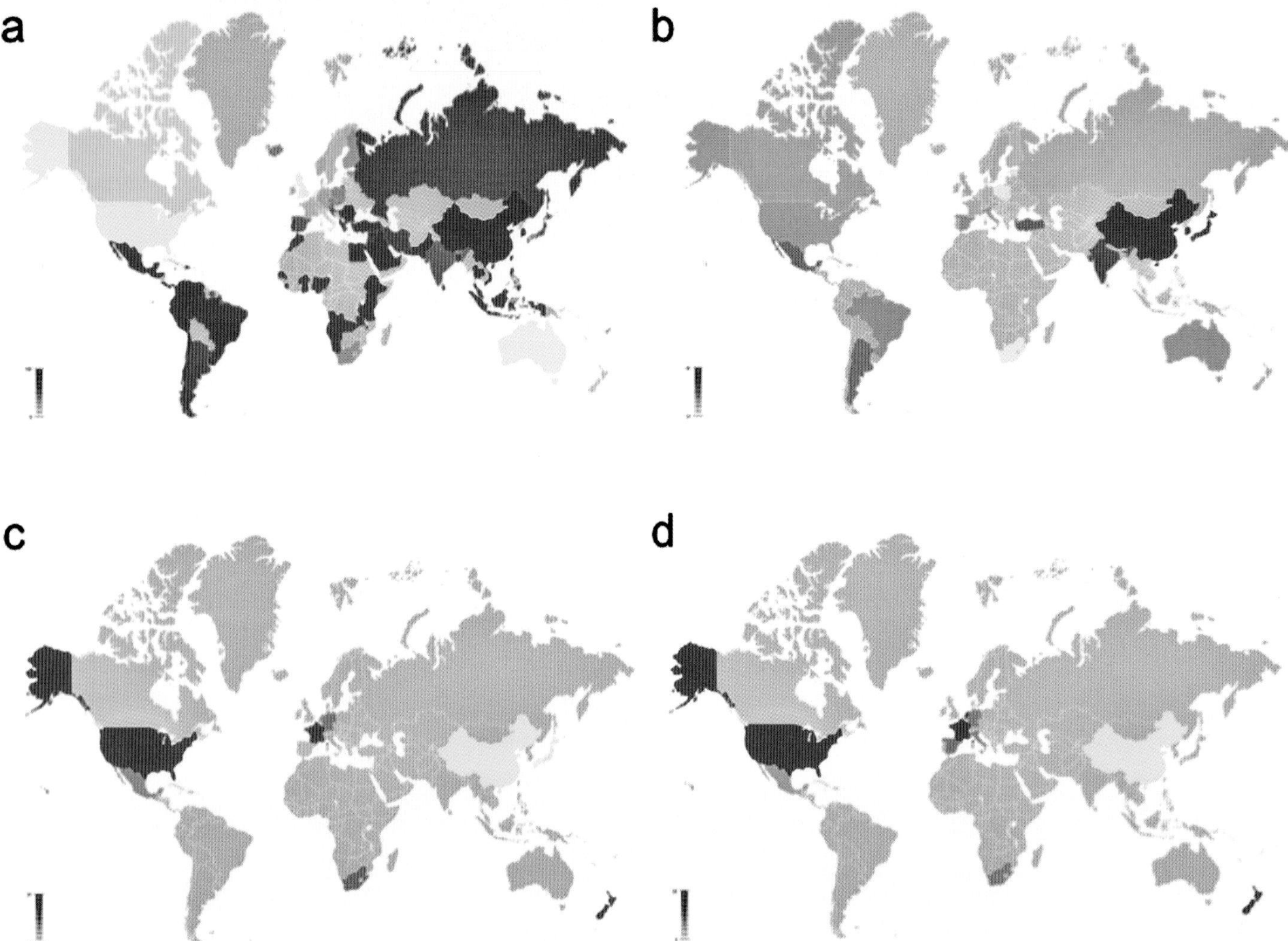
a
b
c
d

JOAN CHIAO

SCIENTIST

Maps examining the worldwide geographic coincidence between culture, genes and mood disorders from my paper with Kate Blizinsky published in 2010. The four charts show the geographical coincidence between serotonin transporter gene diversity and cultural traits of individualism–collectivism across countries, and include all available published data for each variable of interest. The yellow-to-red colour bar indicates low-to-high prevalence. Grey areas indicate geographical regions where no published data are available.

(a) Colour map of frequency distribution of IND-COL from Hofstede (2001)
(b) Colour map of frequency distribution of S alleles of 5-HTTLPR
(c) Colour map of frequency of global prevalence of anxiety
(d) Colour map of frequency of global prevalence of mood disorders

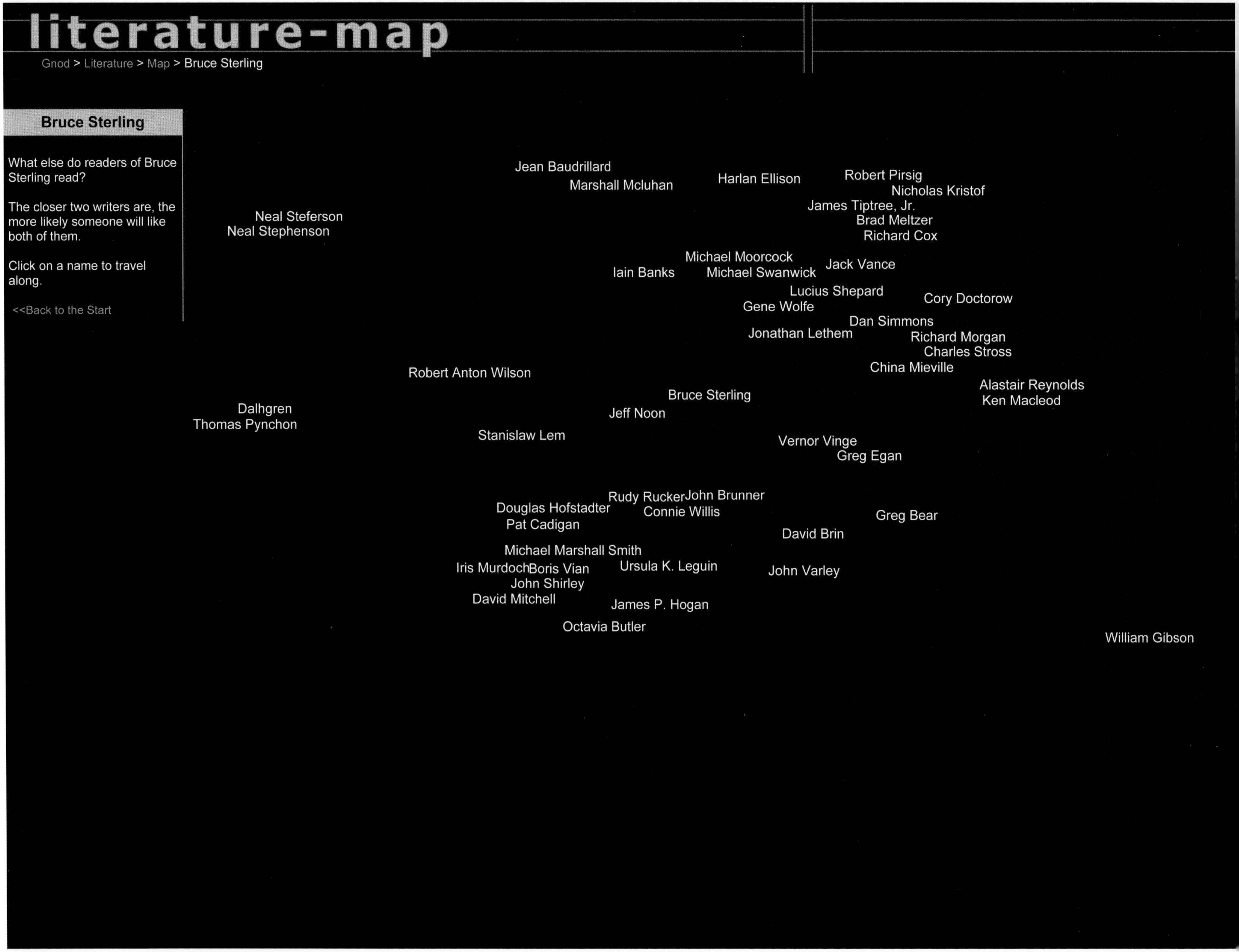
literature-map
Gnod > Literature > Map > Bruce Sterling
Bruce Sterling
What else do readers of Bruce Sterling read?
The closer two writers are, the more likely someone will like both of them.
Click on a name to travel along.
<<Back to the Start
Jean Baudrillard
Marshall Mcluhan
Harlan Ellison
Robert Pirsig
Nicholas Kristof
James Tiptree, Jr.
Brad Meltzer
Richard Cox
Neal Steferson
Neal Stephenson
Michael Moorcock
Iain Banks
Michael Swanwick
Jack Vance
Lucius Shepard
Gene Wolfe
Cory Doctorow
Dan Simmons
Jonathan Lethem
Richard Morgan
Charles Stross
China Mieville
Robert Anton Wilson
Alastair Reynolds
Ken Macleod
Bruce Sterling
Dalhgren
Thomas Pynchon
Jeff Noon
Stanislaw Lem
Vernor Vinge
Greg Egan
Rudy Rucker
John Brunner
Douglas Hofstadter
Connie Willis
Pat Cadigan
Greg Bear
David Brin
Michael Marshall Smith
Iris Murdoch
Boris Vian
Ursula K. Leguin
John Varley
John Shirley
David Mitchell
James P. Hogan
Octavia Butler
William Gibson

BRUCE STERLING

WRITER

Literature-Map: The Tourist Map of Literature

AKRAM ZAATARI

ARTIST

Hashem el Madani: Itinerary, 2008

Hashem el Madani: Itinerary explores the idea of 'returning' pictures, as opposed to the popular designation of the act of photography as 'taking' pictures, by placing framed photographs of shop owners in the locations where pictures had been taken fifty years ago in the old market in Saida, Lebanon. Forty-two photographs were placed in thirty-three locations indicated on a folded map of the old city.

هاشم المدني
جولة عمل

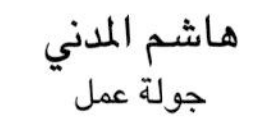

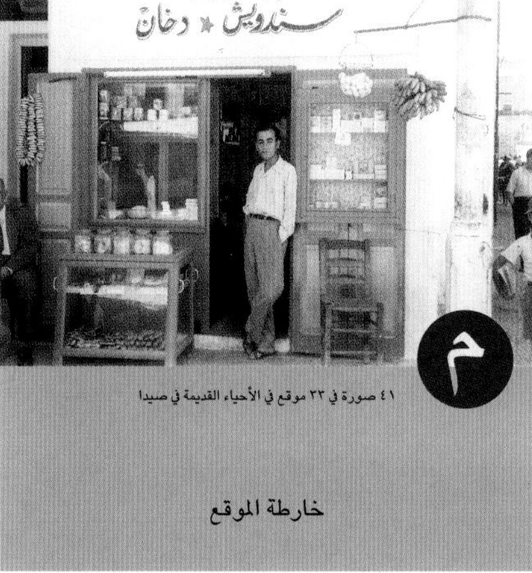

Hashem El Madani
Itinerary
An ongoing project by Akram Zaatari
The Arab Image Foundation

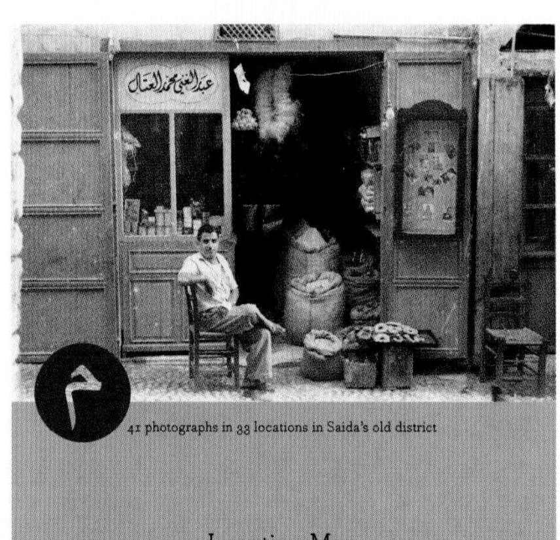

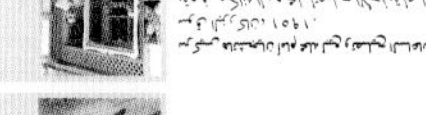

وفيق البابا أمام محله «نوفوتيه البابا» وإلى اليسار محله الثاني «ألعاب البابا».
شارع الحمام الجديد، باب السراي، أواخر الأربعينات.
يقع في مكانه اليوم «صالون الأنوار» لصاحبه محمد ناصر.

23
Wafiq el Baba at the door of his "Nouveauté el Baba". To the left is his second store, which sells toys.
Hammam el Jdid Street, Bab el Saray, late 1940s.
Now a barber shop "Salon el Anouar", owned by Mohamad Nasser.

محمد العطروني أمام محله «أزياء العطروني الحديثة». وفي يمين الصورة أحمد حفوضة.
شارع الحمام الجديد، باب السراي، بداية الخمسينات.
يقع في مكانه اليوم محل حلويات أبو عباس الغرمتي.

24
Mohamad el Aatrouni standing at the door of his shop "Rayon Bleu", with Ahmad Haffouda to the right.
Hammam el Jdid street, Bab el Saray, early 1950s.
Now Abu Aabbas el Gharamti's store for oriental pastries.

عفيف سوسان أمام محله للسندويشات.
ساحة باب السراي، ملاصق لقهوة باب السراي، بداية الخمسينات.
تمت إزالة هذا المحل في إطار مشروع إعادة تأهيل ساحة باب السراي.
صورة الغلاف.

25 A
Afif Soussan at the door of his sandwich and tobacco kiosk.
Bab el Saray square, next to Bab el Saray Café, early 1950s.
This kiosk was demolished as part of the Bab el Saray rehabilitation project. Cover Photograph.

من عائلتي أبو الغزالة وصقر. في الخلفية نوفوتيه زين والنادي المعني.
ساحة باب السراي، بداية الخمسينات.

26 A
From the families Abu Ghazaleh (left) and Sakr, behind them are Nouveauté Zein, and the Maani fitness club.
Bab el Saray Square, early 1950s.

نوفوتيه زين.
ساحة باب السراي، بداية الخمسينات.
تقع في مكانه اليوم «محمصة الفؤاد» لصاحبها فؤاد سرور.

27
Nouveauté Zein.
Bab el Saray Square, early 1950s.
Now "Mahmasat el Fouad" (el Fouad Roastery), owned by Fouad Srour.

ناصر الملاح (يمين) أمام محله لبيع و تصليح الأحذية. ومعه في أقصى اليسار أخوه محمود.
شارع الكيخيا، قرب مقهى الزجاج، بداية الخمسينات.
ما يزال المحل موجوداً اليوم.

28
Nasser el Mallah (right) standing at the door of his shoe shop, with his brother Mahmoud (far left).
Kikhia Street in front of the Glass Café, early 1950s.
Still open today.

أنيس الظريف جالساً أمام معمله للحلويات الشرقية.
شارع الكيخيا، مقابل مقهى الزجاج، بداية الخمسينات.
تقع في مكانه اليوم منشرة خضر درويش حداد.

29
Anis el Zarif sitting at the door of his oriental pastries store.
Kikhia Street, facing the Glass Café, early 1950s.
Now Khodr Darwish Haddad, the carpenter.

أحمد نعناعة (اليمين) أمام «صالون الأمير» للحلاقة.
شارع المحفل، قرب جامع الكيخيا، بداية الخمسينات.
يقع في مكانه اليوم محل سكاكر هيثم الاطرق.

30
Ahmad Naanaha (right) at the door of his barber shop "Salon el Empire".
El Mahfal Street next to Kikhia Mosque, early 1950s.
Now "Haytham el Otroq Grocery".

حسني الزين أمام محله للألبان و الأجبان.
شارع المحفل، المصلبية، مقابل جامع الكيخيا، ١٩٥٢.
يقع في مكانه اليوم محل ألبان و أجبان أبناء حسني الزين.

31
Husni el Zein standing at the door of his dairy shop.
El Mahfal street,1952.
Now "Husni el Zein sons Dairy".

محمد سمهون (أبو سعد) أمام محله للحلويات.
المصلبية، مقابل جامع الكيخيا، بداية الخمسينات.
يقع في مكانه اليوم محل بقالة، أجبان و ألبان إبراهيم الميسي.

32
Mohamad Samhoun (abu Saad) standing at the door of his oriental pastry store.
Msallabieh Crossing, facing Kikhia Mosque, early 1950s.
Now a grocery store, owned by Ibrahim el Meessi.

يوسف عجرم (الملقب بإدريس). أمام محله «المحمصة الوطنية».
شارع المصلبية، ملاصق لقهوة الغواصة، بداية الخمسينات.
هذا المحل مقفل اليوم.

33 C
Youssef Aajram (known as Idriss) standing at the door of his National Roastery.
Mssallabiyeh Street, next to the Ghawassa Café, early 1950s.
This shop is closed today.

صورة محل في هذا الموقع موضوعة هنا.
● Photograph placed in the location where it was initially taken.

صورة محل في هذا الموقع موضوعة في مكان آخر (مربع أحمر).
○ Photograph taken in this location but placed elsewhere (red squares).

صورة محل مأخوذة في موقع آخر وموضوعة هنا.
■ Photograph taken in a different location but placed here.

0 20 40 60 80 100 m

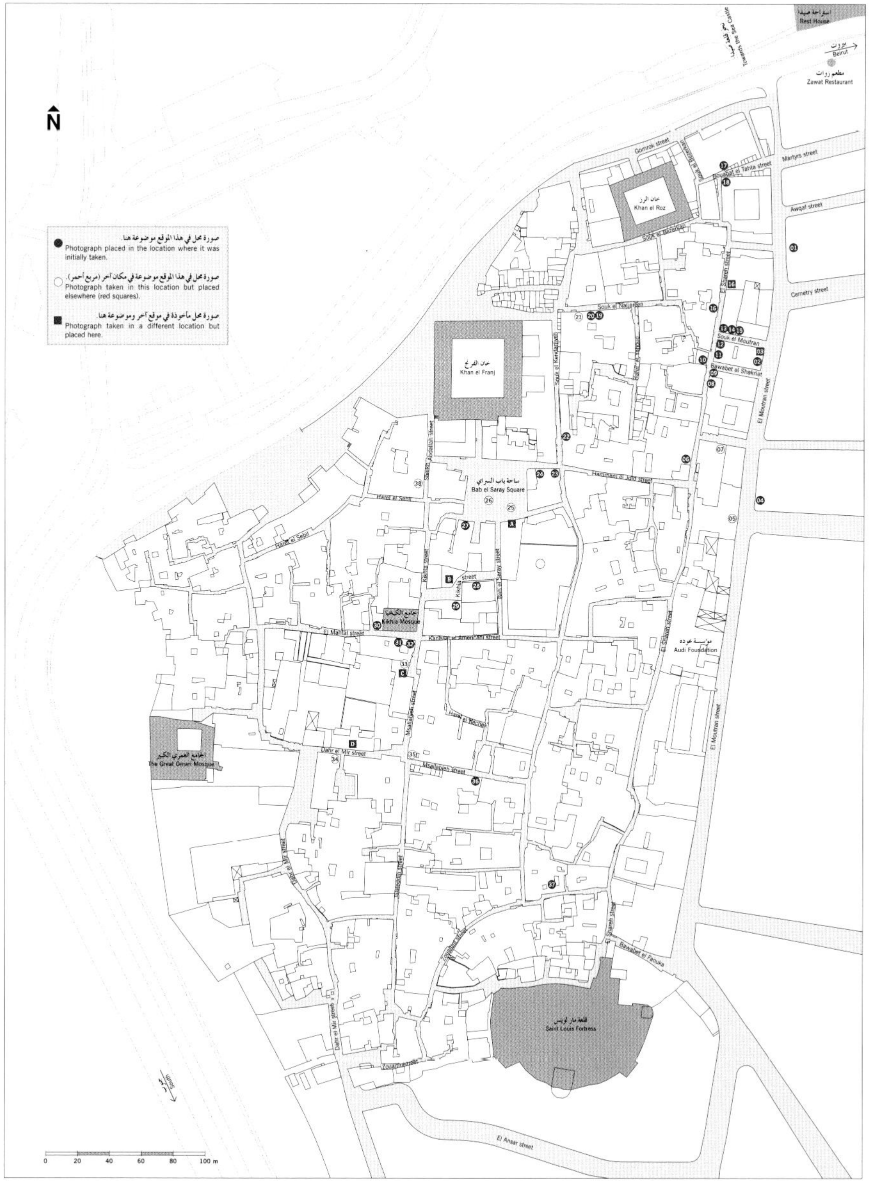

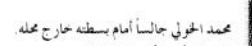

محمد الخولي جالساً أمام بسطته خارج محله.
شارع ظهر المير، ١٩٥١.
هذه البسطة غير موجودة اليوم.

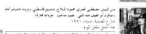

D 34
Mohamad el Khawli sitting next to his little vending table outside of his grocery store.
Dahr el Mir Street, 1951.
This vending table is not there today.

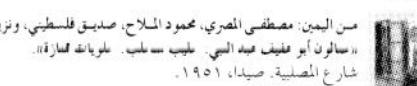

من اليمين: مصطفى المصري، محمود الملاح، صديق فلسطيني، ونزيه حشيشو أمام «صالون أبو عفيف عبد النبي. حليب سحلب. حلويات فاخرة».
شارع المصلبية. صيدا، ١٩٥١.
هذا المحل مقفل اليوم.

C 35
From right: Mustafa el Masri, Mahmud el Mallah, a Palestinian friend and Nazih Hashisho at the door of "Abu Aafif Abdelnabi lounge: milk, sahlab and best pastries".
Msallabieh street, 1951.
This shop is closed today.

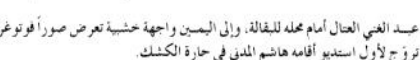

عبد الغني العتال أمام محله للبقالة. وإلى اليمين واجهة خشبية تعرض صوراً فوتوغرافية تروّج لأول استديو أقامه هاشم المدني في حارة الكشك.
شارع المصلبية، مدخل حارة الكشك، ١٩٤٩.
لا يزال المحل قائماً بإدارة الحاج محمد العتّال. صورة الغلاف.

36
Abdel Ghani el Aattal at the door of his grocery shop. To the right is a promotion of Madani's first studio nearby.
Al Moussallabiyya Street, at the entrance of Haret el Keshek, 1949.
The store is now managed by Mohamad el Aattal. Cover photograph.

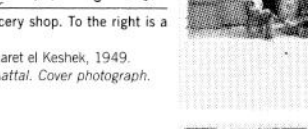

أحمد عمر الديماسي أمام محله للبقالة.
شارع الزويتيني، بداية الخمسينات.
يقع في مكانه اليوم محل «بقالة أبو مازن».

37
Ahmad Omar el Dimassi at the door of his grocery store.
Zouaitini Street, early 1950s.
Now "Abu Mazen's grocery".

حكمت الددا (اليمين) جالساً أمام محله للخياطة مع محمد النقوزي (واقفاً أمام ماكينة الخياطة)، وعبد الغني المارديني.
مقابل مبنى الجمرك القديم، ١٩٥٢.

C 38
Hikmat el Dada (right) at his tailor shop with Mohamad el Naquzi (by the sewing machine) and the tailor Abdel Ghani el Mardini.
Next to the old customs building, 1952.

سلامة أمام محله لبيع لوازم الكندرجية.
سوق النجارين، ١٩٥١.
موقع هذا المحل غير محدد بشكل دقيق.

B 39
Salameh at the door of his shop selling shoe repair accessories.
Souk el Najjareen, 1951.
The exact location of this shop has not been identified.

كوّا أمام مصبغته. (اليمين) من بيت أبو حلاوة.
مدخل حارة اليهود، بداية الخمسينات.
موقع هذا المحل غير محدد بشكل دقيق.

D 40
Owner of a laundry standing with friends at the door of his shop. (right) Abu Halawa.
Entrance to Haret el Yahood (Jewish neighborhood), early 1950s.
The exact location of this shop has not been identified.

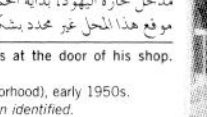

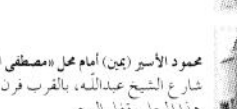

محمود الأسير (يمين) أمام محل «مصطفى الصباغ لبيع الصابون والخرضوات».
شارع الشيخ عبدالله، بالقرب فرن عيسى، بداية الخمسينات.
هذا المحل مقفل اليوم.

B 41
Mahmoud el Assir (right) at the door of Mustafa el Sabbagh store for soap and polishing products, next to present day Issa Bakery today.
Sheikh Abdallah Street, early 1950s.
This shop is closed today.

A Beb el Saray Café — مقهى باب السراي
Showing photographs — تعرض الصور
05 07 25 26

B Glass Café — مقهى الزجاج
Showing photographs — تعرض الصور
21 39 41

C Ghawassa Café — مقهى الغواصة
Showing photographs — تعرض الصور
33 35 38

D Zahra Café — مقهى زهرة
Showing photographs — تعرض الصور
31 10

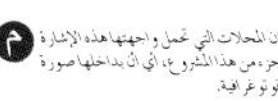

إن المحلات التي تحمل واجهتها هذه الإشارة جزء من هذا المشروع، أي أن بداخلها صورة فوتوغرافية.

Shops displaying this sign are part of the Itinerary Project and have photographs placed inside.

تفتح المحلات التجارية أبوابها يومياً من الساعة التاسعة صباحاً حتى الخامسة مساء، ما عدا يومي الجمعة والأحد حيث تفتح عادة قبل الظهر فقط.

Stores open daily from 9:00 am to 5:00 pm. Fridays and Sundays from 9:00 am to 1:00 pm.

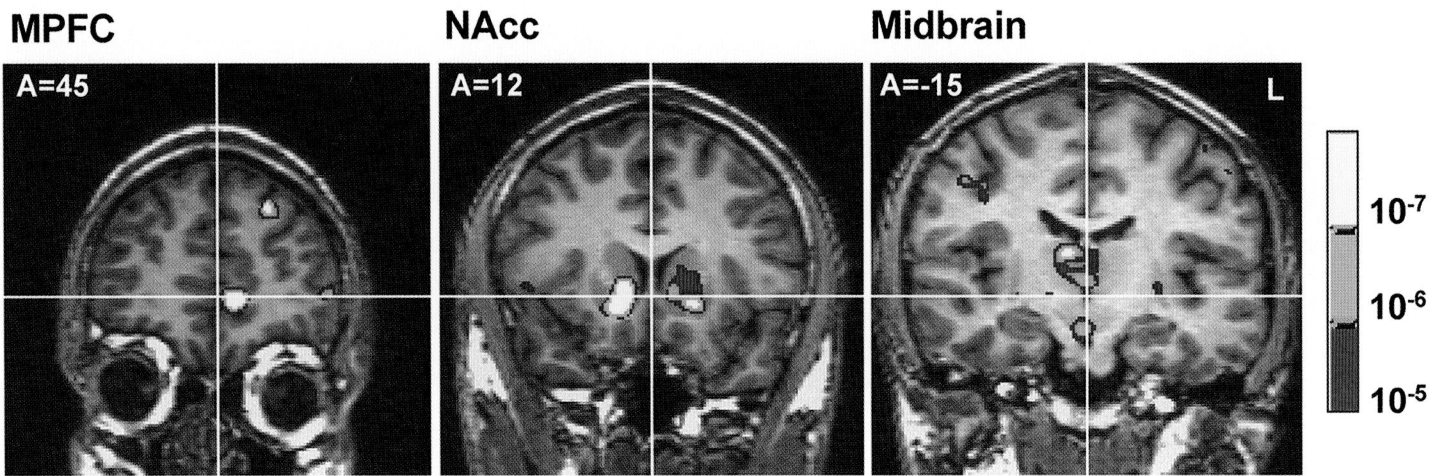

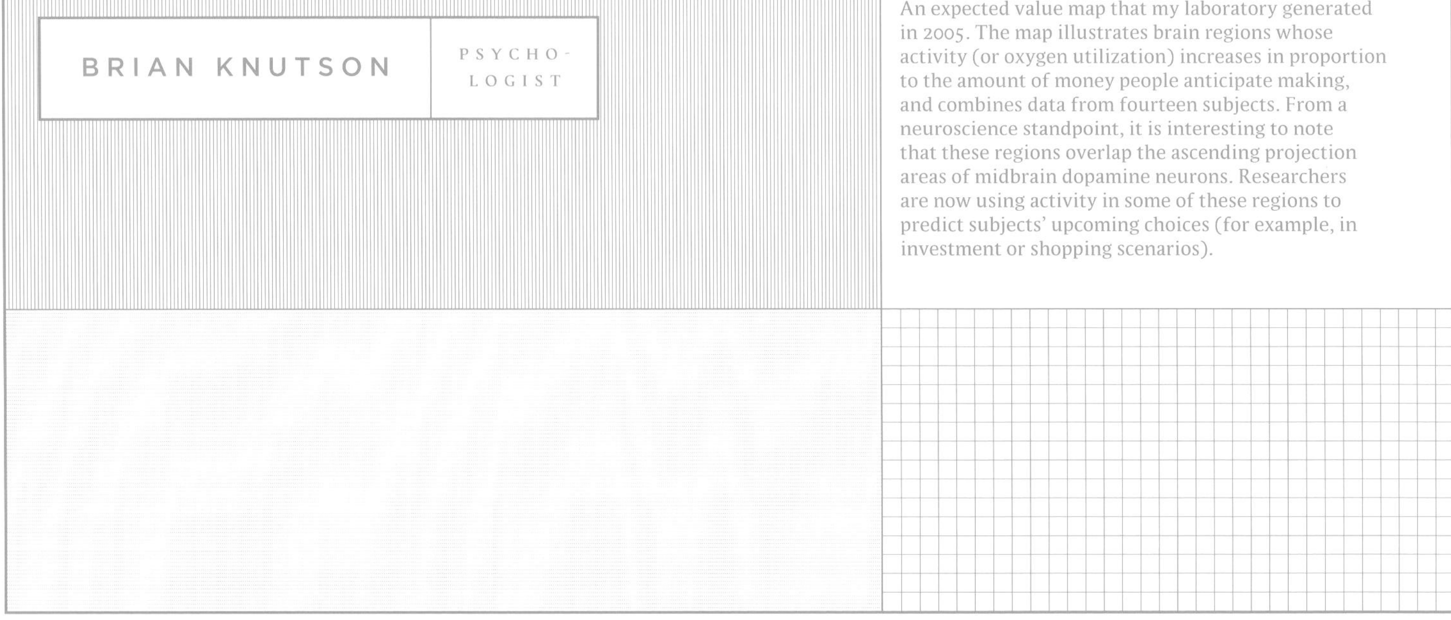

An expected value map that my laboratory generated in 2005. The map illustrates brain regions whose activity (or oxygen utilization) increases in proportion to the amount of money people anticipate making, and combines data from fourteen subjects. From a neuroscience standpoint, it is interesting to note that these regions overlap the ascending projection areas of midbrain dopamine neurons. Researchers are now using activity in some of these regions to predict subjects' upcoming choices (for example, in investment or shopping scenarios).

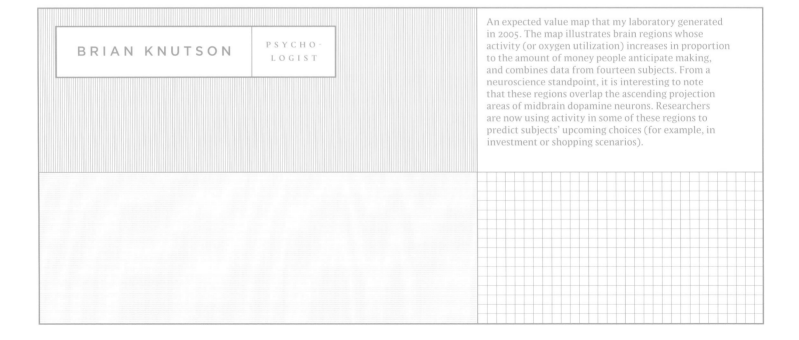

MARK PAGEL

SCIENTIST

A Speaker's Map of the Mind (the words we share)

The oldest words in our lexicon (largest font in image) change through history slowly enough that they might have been recognized by people living 15,000 years ago or more; younger words (small font) would not.

Our ancient shared speech is dominated in all languages by social relations – you, me (I), what we do, to whom – and has been throughout our history.

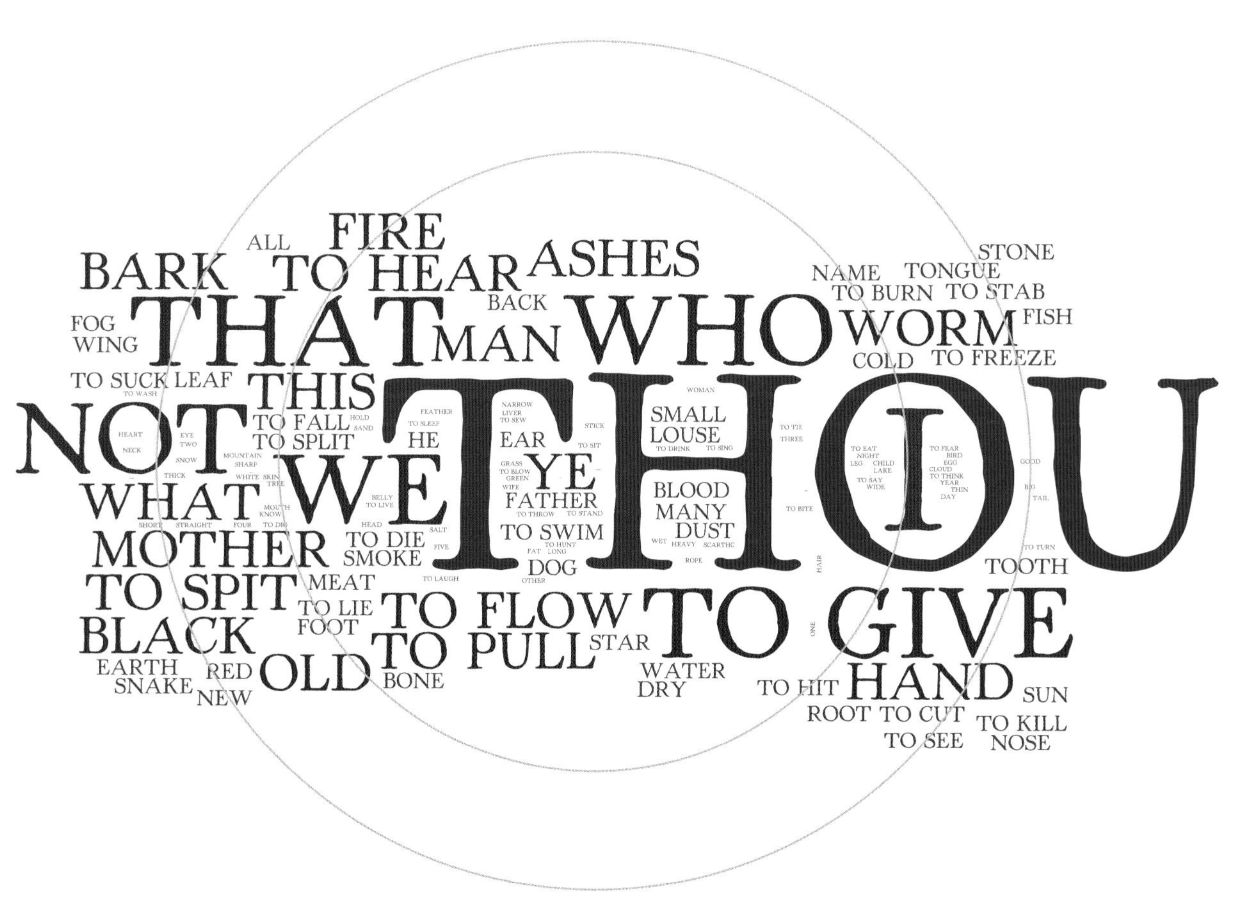

TOM STANDAGE

Writer

This is a map of the Internet in 1901. Surely there was no Internet in 1901? But each technology is built on top of the previous technology, and the Internet is no exception. It was built on top of the telephone network, which was built, in turn, on top of the telegraph network, which already girdled the world by the end of the Victorian era, in 1901. So here it is. The Internet in 1901.

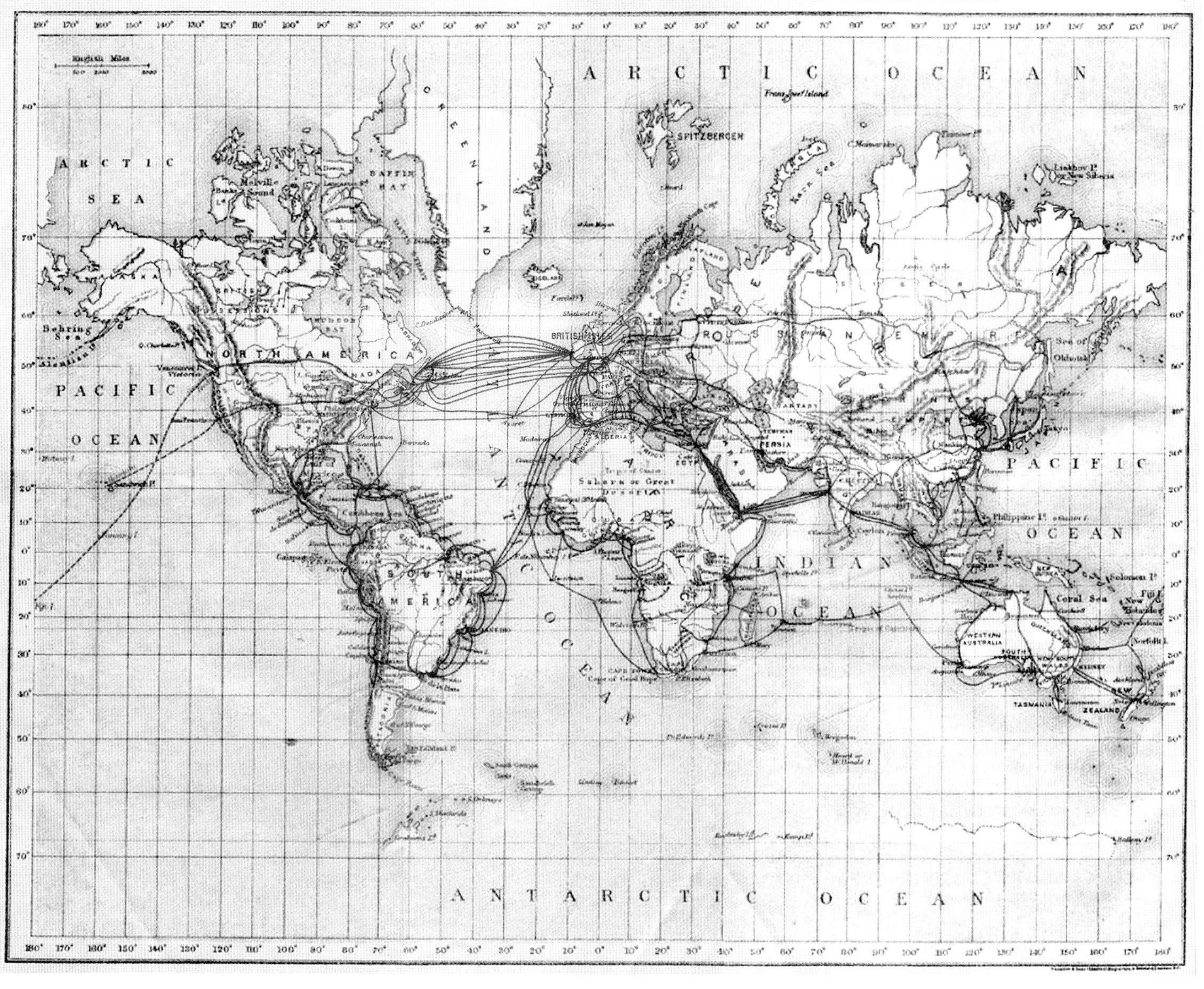
EASTERN TELEGRAPH C^O'S SYSTEM AND ITS GENERAL CONNECTIONS.
ARCTIC OCEAN
ARCTIC SEA
SPITZBERGEN
BAFFIN BAY
GREENLAND
NORTH AMERICA
PACIFIC OCEAN
BRITISH ISLES
PERSIA
EGYPT
INDIAN OCEAN
SOUTH AMERICA
PACIFIC OCEAN
Coral Sea
WESTERN AUSTRALIA
TASMANIA
ZEALAND
CAPE TOWN
ANTARCTIC OCEAN

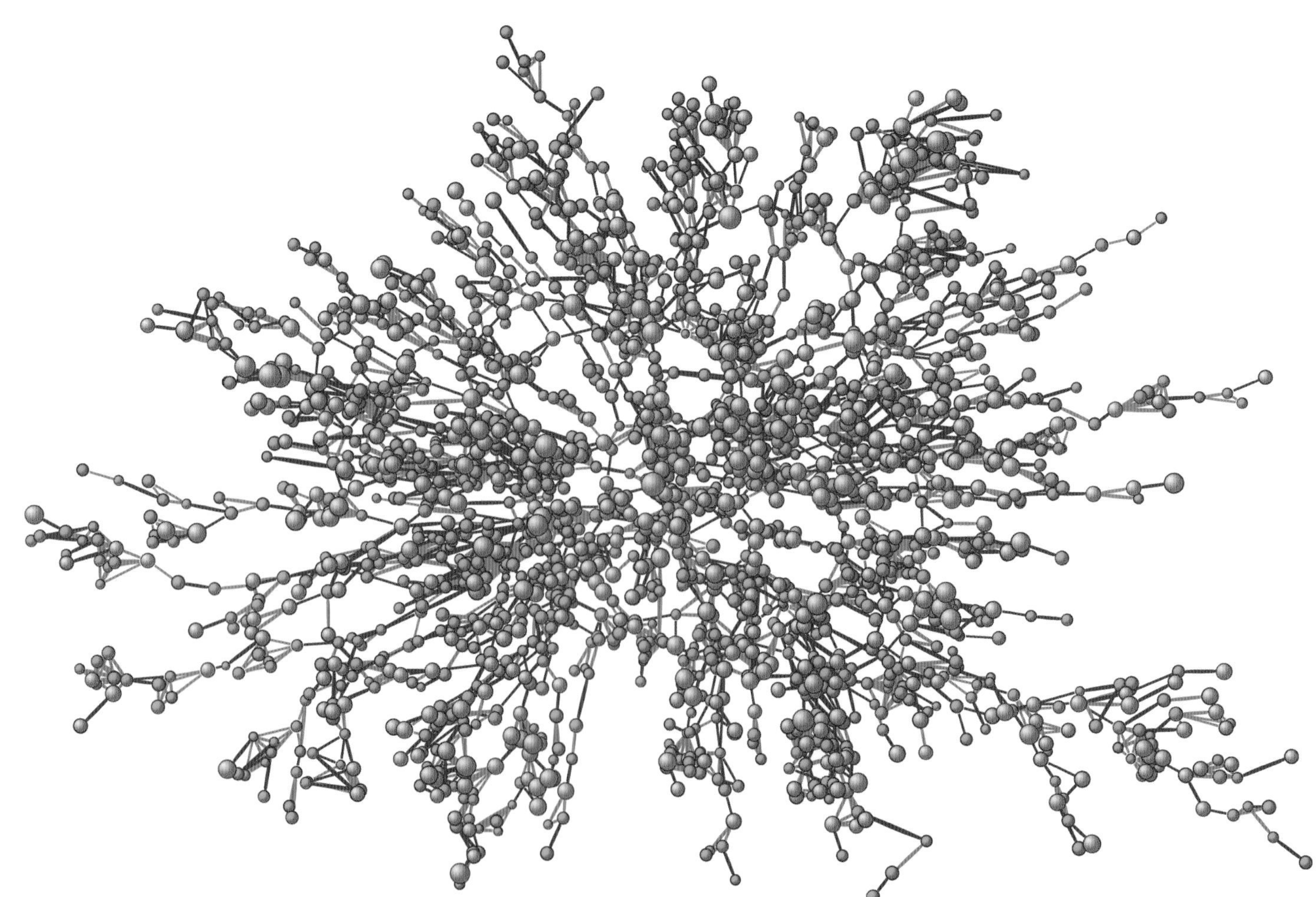

NICHOLAS CHRISTAKIS & JAMES FOWLER

A map of obesity within the kind of social network we all inhabit. There are 2,200 people (nodes) and many thousands of ties (lines) between them. Nodes with blue borders are men and red borders are women. Bigger nodes are bigger people, and the interior colour of the nodes indicates whether the person is obese: yellow are obese and green are non-obese people. The colours of the ties between the nodes indicate the kind of relationship (e.g., friend, spouse, sibling). Clusters of obese and non-obese individuals are visible, and these arise not only because individuals of similar body size preferentially form ties, but also because one person's body size affects that of another to whom they are connected. This map sent us on a new direction in our research, orienting us to new possibilities that network science had for understanding the human condition, and for improving it.

social scientists

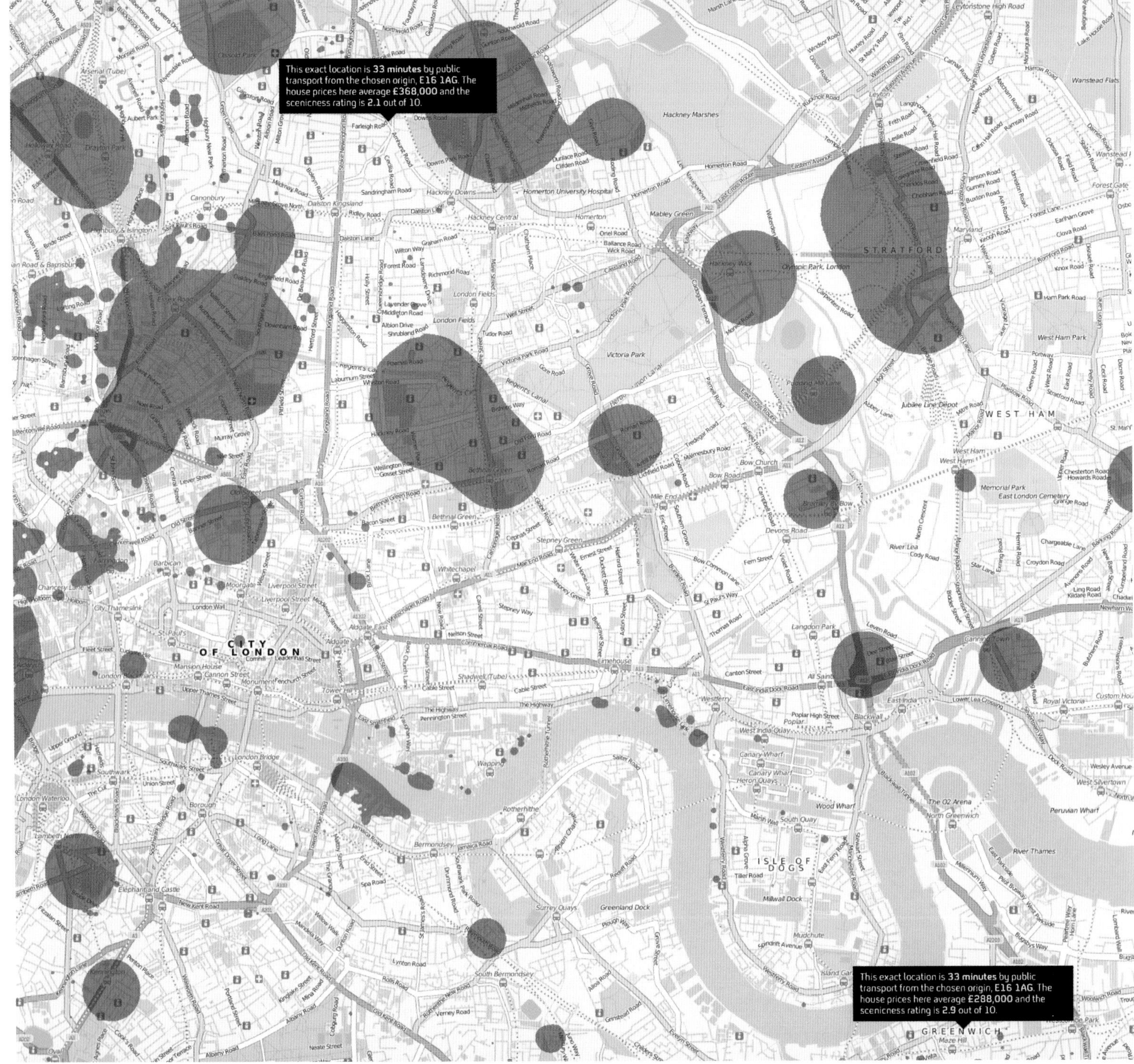
This exact location is **33 minutes** by public transport from the chosen origin, **E16 1AG**. The house prices here average **£368,000** and the scenicness rating is **2.1** out of 10.
This exact location is **33 minutes** by public transport from the chosen origin, **E16 1AG**. The house prices here average **£288,000** and the scenicness rating is **2.9** out of 10.
CITY OF LONDON
STRATFORD
WEST HAM
ISLE OF DOGS
GREENWICH

ERIC RODENBECK

DESIGNER

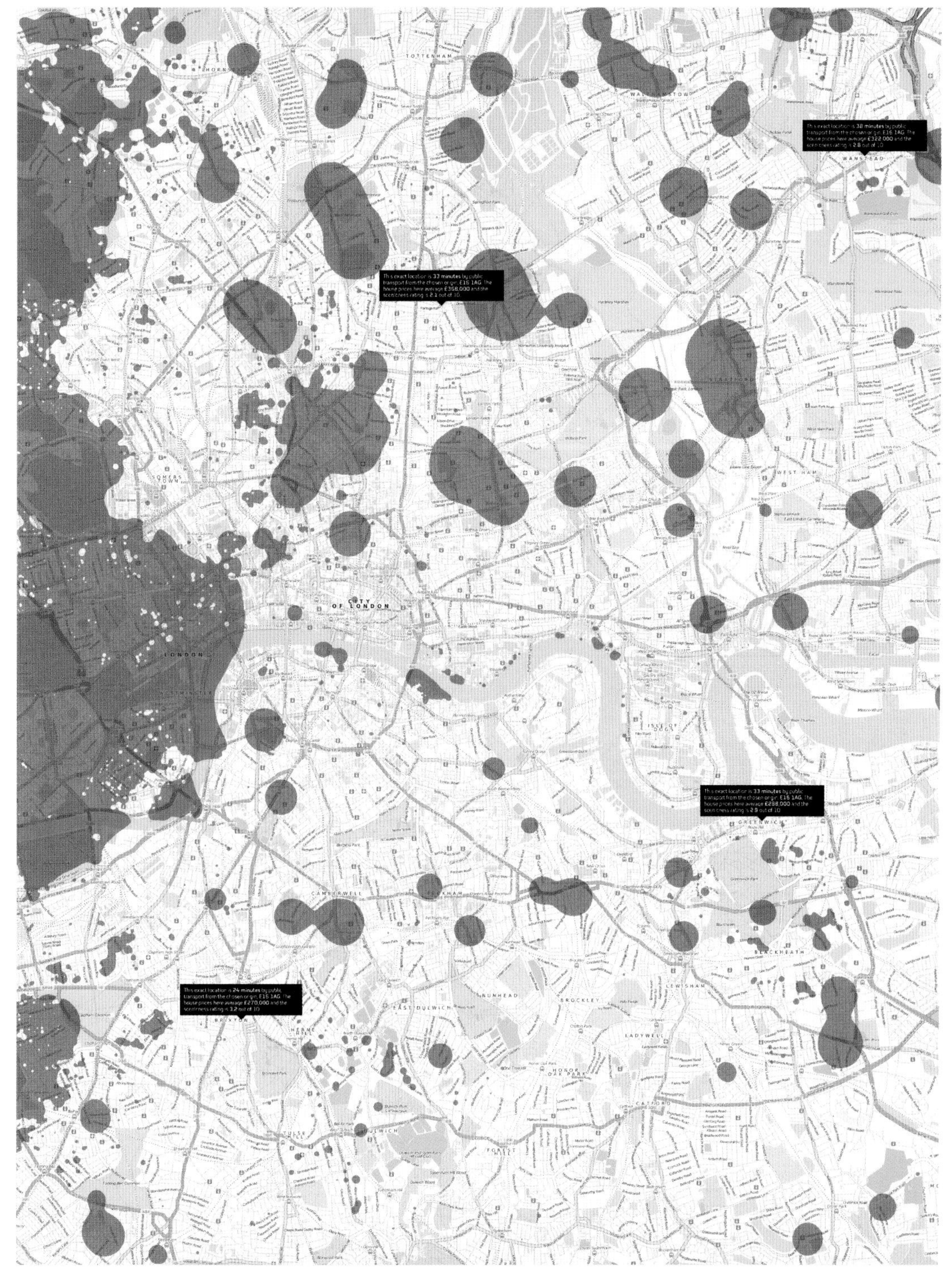

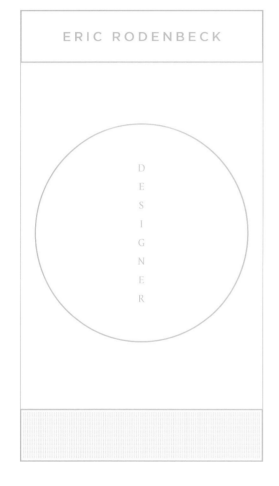

EDITOR

I asked people to draw a map of the Internet as they pictured it in their mind. What was the image they used as they ventured into it? To illustrate what I meant, I drew my own version. This was what I thought of as the conceptual topography and geography of the Internet in 2009.

IRC chat rooms
CHINESE CHAT ROOMS
PIRATE BAY
BIT TORRENT
Pop up WINDOWS
Google Books
usenet forums
SKYPE
Games
MY HOME
Back up
FLICKR
WEB 3.0
WEB 2.0
MOZI
SOUNDPEDIA
last.fm
Kottke
TWITTER
FACEBOOK
YOUTUBE
POPURLS
Google Reader
KK
BLOGS
WEB
J-walk
AOL
YAHOO
swiss miss
seth godin
boing-boing
MINT.COM
ebay
TWINE
NYTIMES
etrade
evernote
delicious
Fandango
weather
NETFLIX
Google
AMAZON
THE CLOUD
GMAIL
G CALENDAR
G VOICE
G DOCS
GMAPS
GEARTH

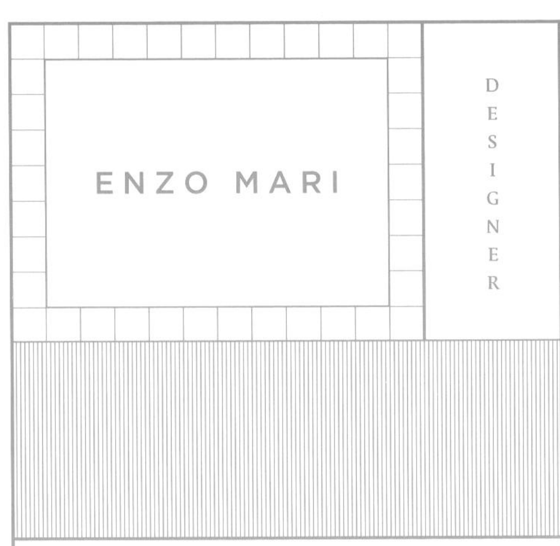

Cultural Map of the Cultural Intervention

This map refers to the level of class struggle, the fundamental social struggle, as it functions in the field of culture. Excluded here is the idea of a proletarian culture (working or popular) in opposition to the existing bourgeois culture, since that is utopian or somewhat contradictory; this is the conception of a new, alternative culture in formation. ¶ It recognizes instead the specific social motivation, contrary to bourgeois rule, of all authentic cultural research, which is always continuously conditioned by bourgeois ideology (in both the research and the dissemination of knowledge). Culture, while having modes of particular struggle or tension, is not defined as autonomous or capable of opposition. Of these modes, the unifying pole is Marxism, which remains critical of separate fields of knowledge within the existing division of labour. Its intervention seeks to replace any philosophical-ideological generalization that may be performed on the results of research and experimentation with a strict connection between intellectual labour and social use and the needs of the general base of society. ¶ The representation of the set of controls, brakes, misinformation and justifications with which the social power administers this secondary field (which is as important as that of production) is well developed here. In addition, the map is twofold and problematic because it aims to show the ineffectiveness of the same outlet of power if the final purpose directing its development comes from forces that lead, reduce and summarize it in another ideology or system of ideas, and thus results in another form of bureaucratic or somewhat functionary authority.

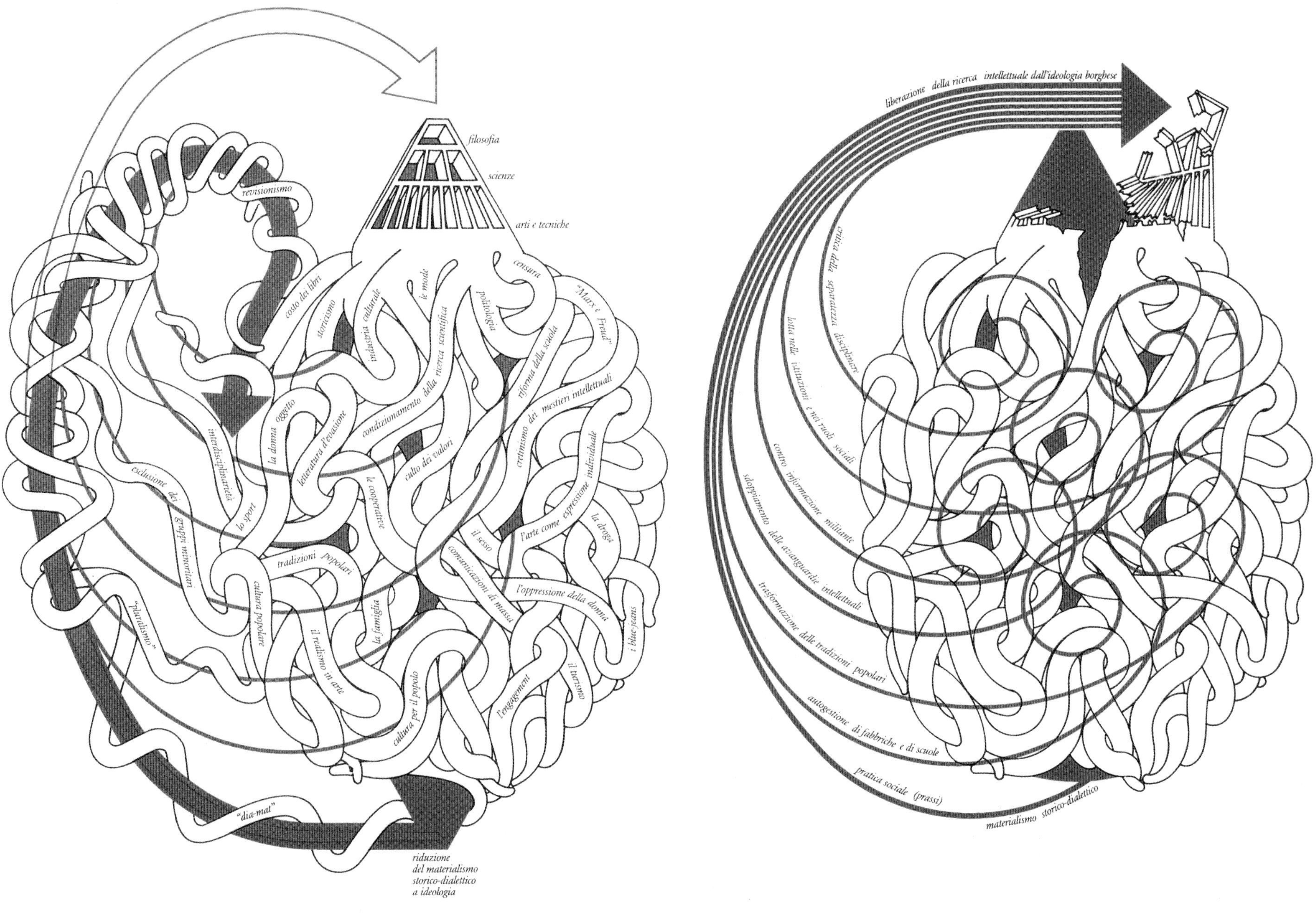

atlante secondo Lenin CARTA CULTURALE (1976 - E. Mari, F. Leonetti)

Enzo Mari 14/150

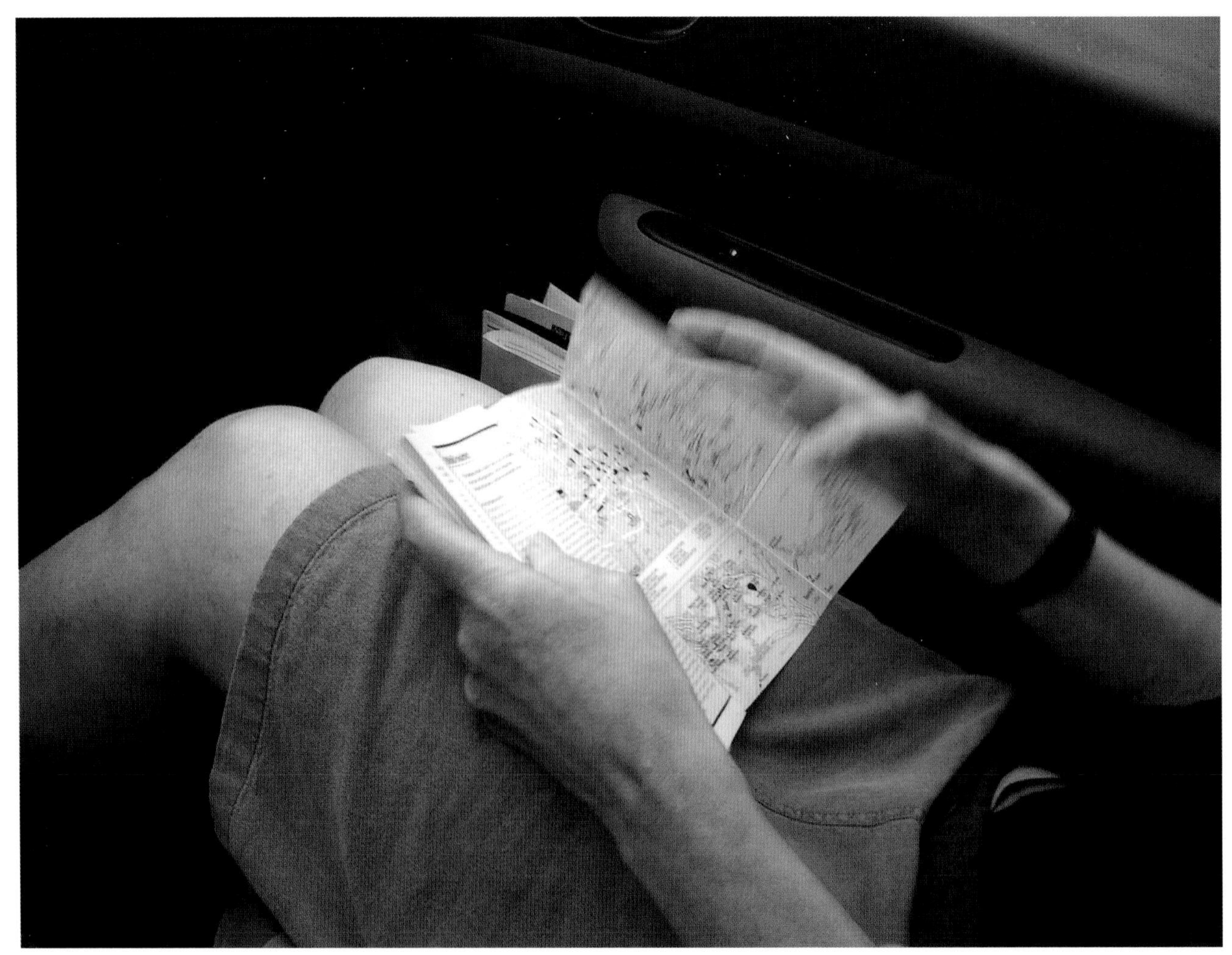

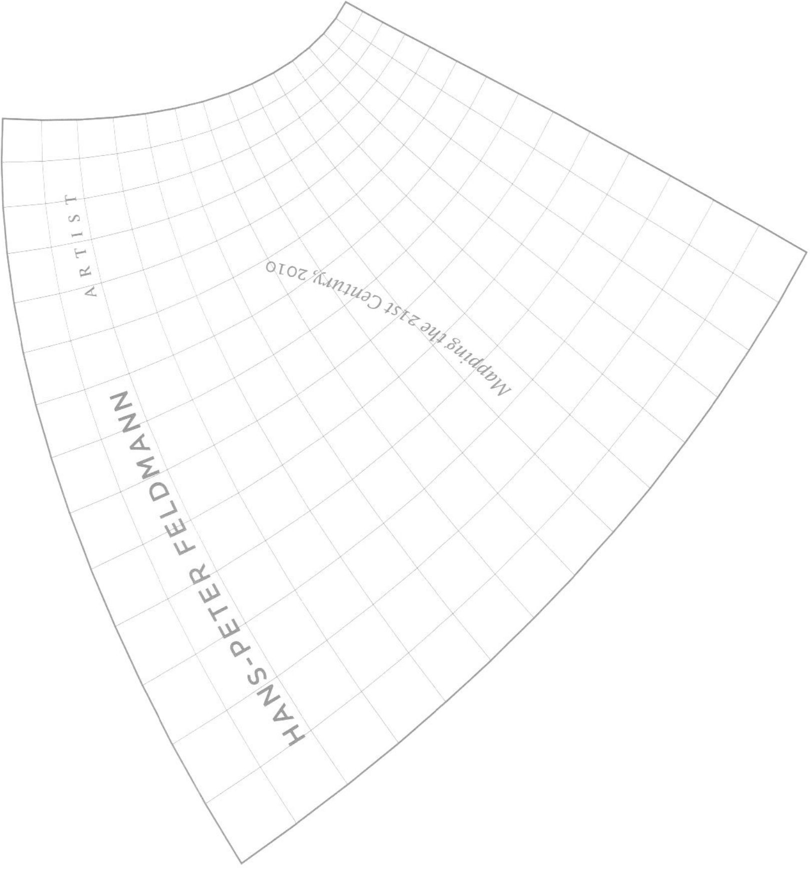
HANS-PETER FELDMANN
ARTIST
Mapping the 21st Century, 2010

KADER ATTIA

ARTIST

Nowadays, it looks like borders between political ideologies are more and more porous, where they have not faded altogether. Nevertheless, nothing has really changed over the years: ideologies still exist. Whether those who claim there are no ideologies any more agree or not, I believe they are still very present, but totally mixed with both old and new ones. Whereas twenty years ago, you were clearly right or left wing, nowadays borders are blurred. To come to power, a political ideology does not need to be strictly opposite. Economically also, what was still unbelievable twenty years ago, happens today. China – a socialist country – is about to become the first economical power of the world. Even more unbelievable, it is the creditor of the most capitalist country of the West: the United States of America. Today feminists fight for Sudanese women's right to wear a bra, the same item they had fought against in the 1970s, as a symbol of their oppression. Does that make sense? I don't know. What is sure is that we get lost in anachronistic representations; from one extreme to the other, as neither the Right nor the Left exists any more. From politics to art, all these visual and discursive expressions sound obsolete. When the notion of extremes is pushed away by a wider and wider centre that keeps absorbing them, what possible novelty is there left, in what we believe is a democratic scene?

SUFFRAGISMO E M I I N CONFUCIANIS
MONARCHIS N I I A S S ELITISM E T L S
CHIISM T E I S S Y M M ISLAMISMO I E
I M I X S M M LEFTISM M I P S R
A O V I M O E B N I M A
L N I SPLAGIARISM I A STALINISM B
HINDUISMMLUTHERISM S P P E SM R I
S I M E S M T R S M E L
B M ATAVISM D M CALVINISM B A T G I
R SALAFISM O O S A I I N E I S
U I SUNNISM M M P N A I R O M
THEISM PROSAISM M E I O N E R N C
A M P S SUFISM S R I R O PAUPE
L ANACHRONISM N B M I S I R L C
I N I O T M S I I T
MS IDEALISM ECOLOGISM

ALEXANDER KLUGE

AUTHOR AND FILM DIRECTOR

Garden of Information

2010

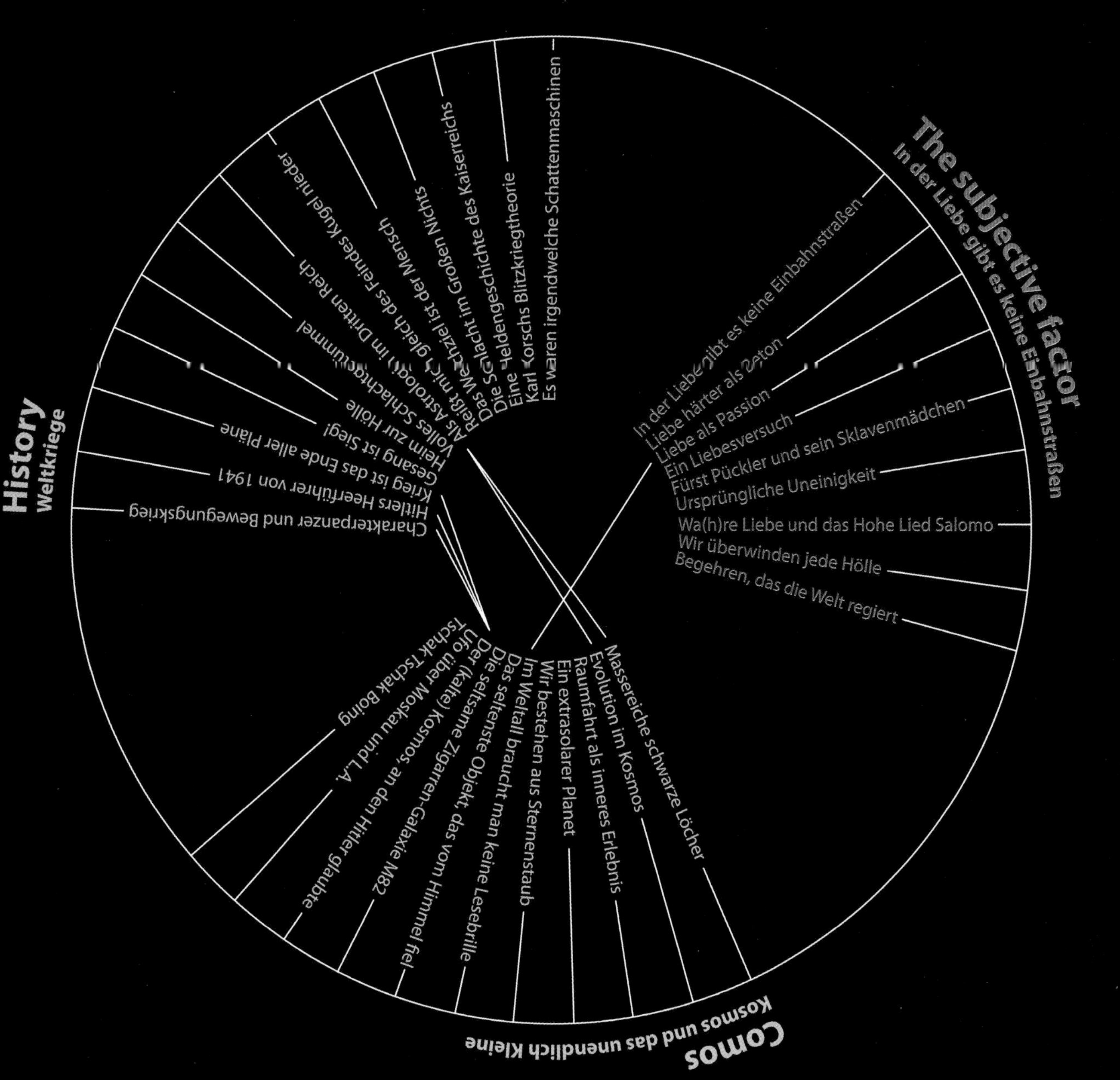

History
Weltkriege
Charakterpanzer und Bewegungskrieg
Hitlers Heerführer von 1941
Krieg ist das Ende aller Pläne
Gesang ist Sieg!
Heim zur Hölle
Volles Schlachtgetümmel
Als Astrologe im Dritten Reich
Reißt mich gleich des Feindes Kugel nieder
Das Weltziel ist der Mensch
Die Schlacht im Großen Nichts
Eine Heldengeschichte des Kaiserreichs
Karl Korschs Blitzkriegtheorie
Es waren irgendwelche Schattenmaschinen
The subjective factor
In der Liebe gibt es keine Einbahnstraßen
In der Liebe gibt es keine Einbahnstraßen
Liebe härter als Beton
Liebe als Passion
Ein Liebesversuch
Fürst Pückler und sein Sklavenmädchen
Ursprüngliche Uneinigkeit
Wa(h)re Liebe und das Hohe Lied Salomo
Wir überwinden jede Hölle
Begehren, das die Welt regiert
Comos
Kosmos und das unendlich Kleine
Massereiche schwarze Löcher
Evolution im Kosmos
Raumfahrt als inneres Erlebnis
Ein extrasolarer Planet
Wir bestehen aus Sternenstaub
Im Weltall braucht man keine Lesebrille
Das seltenste Objekt, das vom Himmel fiel
Die seltsame Zigarren-Galaxie M82
Der (kalte) Kosmos, an den Hitler glaubte
Ufo über Moskau und L.A.
Tschak Tschak Boing

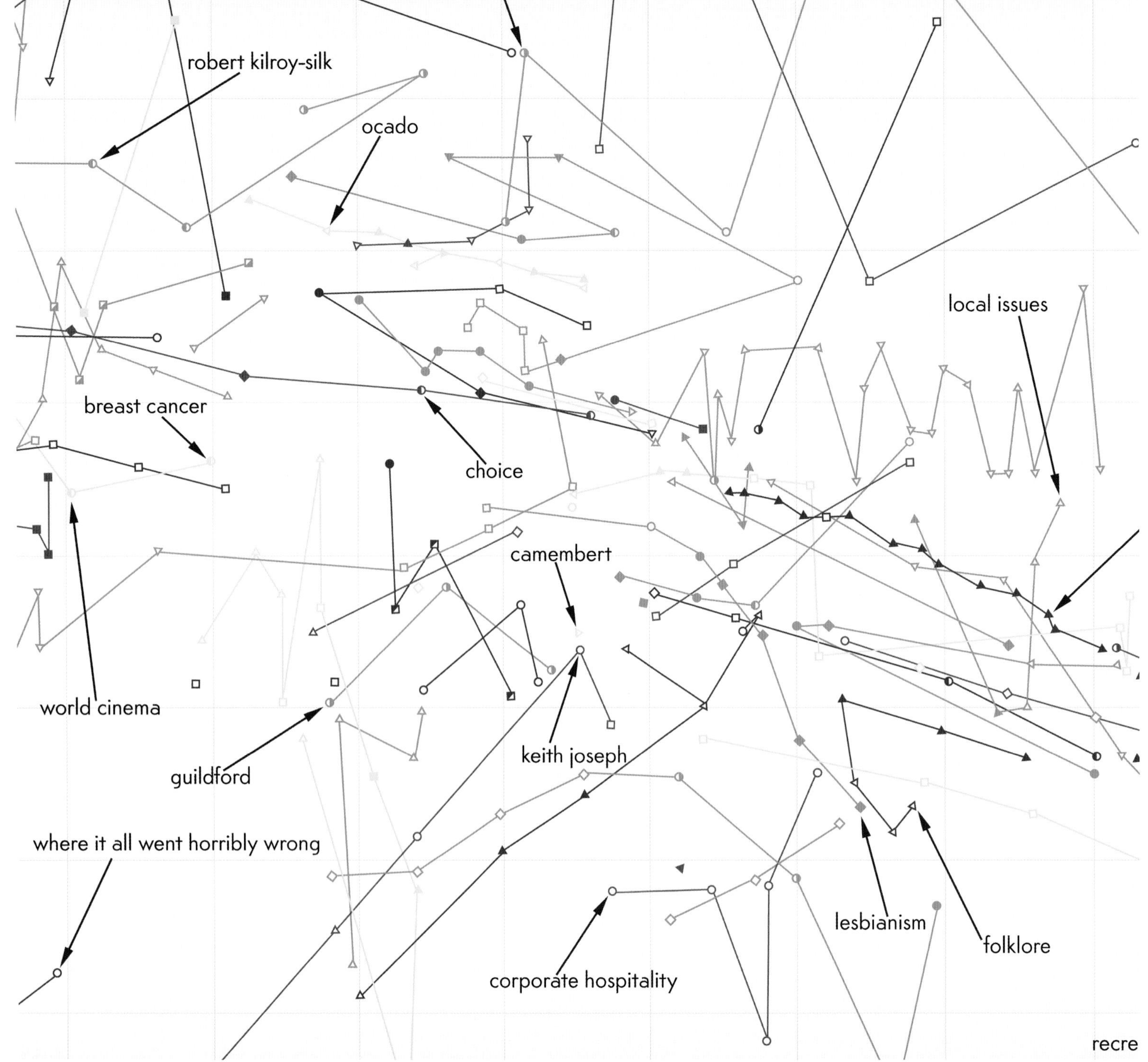
robert kilroy-silk
ocado
local issues
breast cancer
choice
world cinema
camembert
guildford
keith joseph
where it all went horribly wrong
lesbianism
folklore
corporate hospitality
recre

EMMA WOLUKAU-WANAMBWA

A Continuing Survey of Syntactic Parsing, 2010 (detail)

In England, as in many other countries, the production and organization of social class is not only physically but also psychically spatialized. This is most clearly evidenced by the language: if the class system in England were not internalized as a sort of 3D conceptual landscape it would be impossible to speak, as one can in British English, of 'social mobility' and latterly of 'social exclusion'; one could not describe or even think of certain people as 'being from the wrong part of town', 'getting above themselves' or 'not knowing their place'. ¶ By the late twentieth century, the middle classes had become the central reference point of English culture, and the class whose range of practices, beliefs and values were represented as universally 'normal', 'good' and 'appropriate'. Taken in conjunction with their historical resistance to the idea of collective consciousness, this colonization of the social meant that, even as they policed and produced their space by emphatically and pathologically marking that and those who do not live up to its values as 'Other', the English middle classes became increasingly invisible to themselves. Within English political discourse, to be middle class became merely to be normal. ¶ My aim in making *A Continuing Survey of Syntactic Parsing* was to see if it was possible to visualize and materialize (however contingently) the extensive yet largely unacknowledged terrain of England's middle classes – to map it through the objects, words, people, phenomena and events that constitute its topography and mark its limits. ¶ This psychic landscape is arguably much more culturally visible now than it was at the time I made the work – essentially because the English middle class feel they are (to stick with the spatial metaphors) 'losing ground'. The recession has forced 'the squeezed middle' out into the open, as have the policies of a right-wing government that clearly does not have their best interests at heart. ¶ The English middle classes continue to insist on the normality of their values and practices, but as they feel increasingly under threat, as their borders are redrawn, the debates about precisely who and what qualifies as normal are becoming ever more intense and acrimonious.

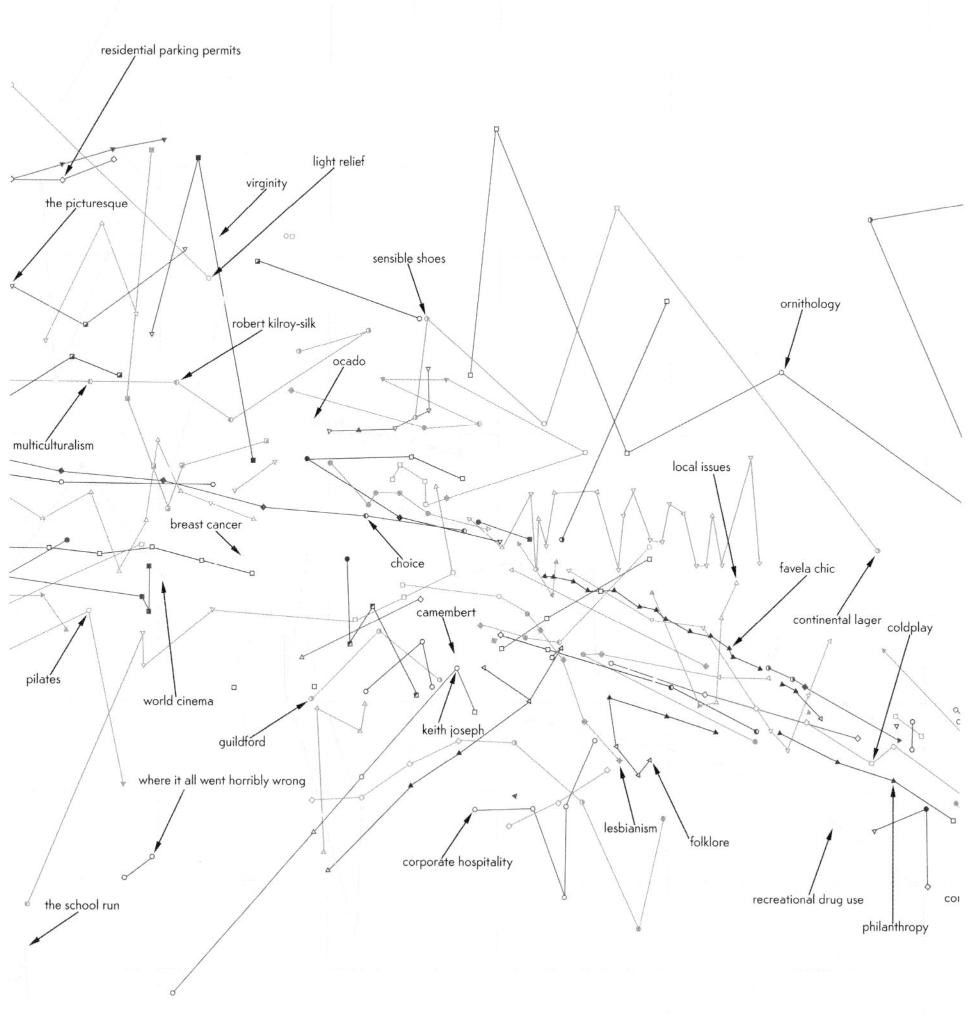

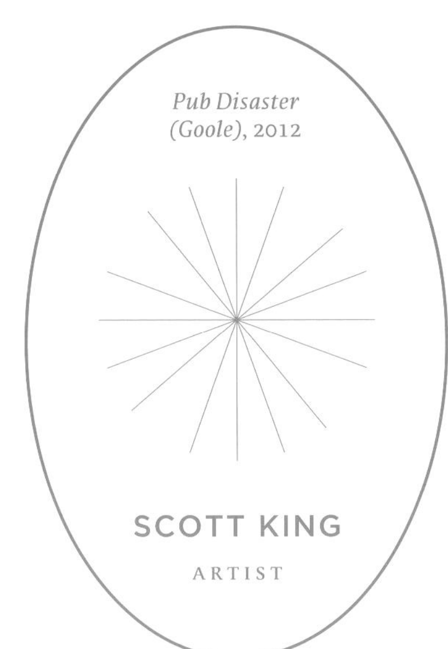

I SHALL

NEVER

FORGET

THAT

DAY

THOUGH

I WANT TO

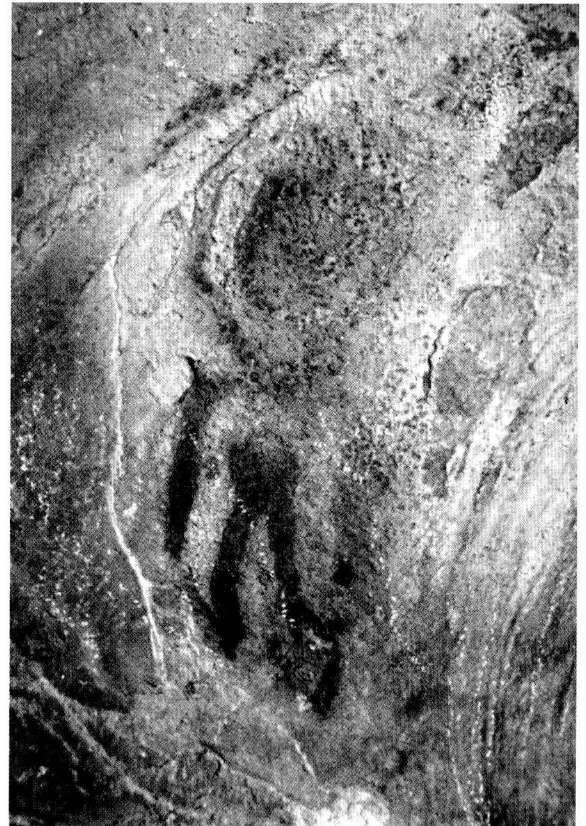

NICHOLAS HUMPHREY

PSYCHOLOGIST

Rock painting at Vilafamés, Valencia, Spain, *c.* 15,000 BC, listed (but not illustrated) as UNESCO World Heritage Site 874-359 (1998), http://whc.unesco.org/en/list/874; height 25cm. The image here is taken from my photograph, which was then subjected to 'contour tracing' by the CorelDraw software program.

The Speciation of Religion

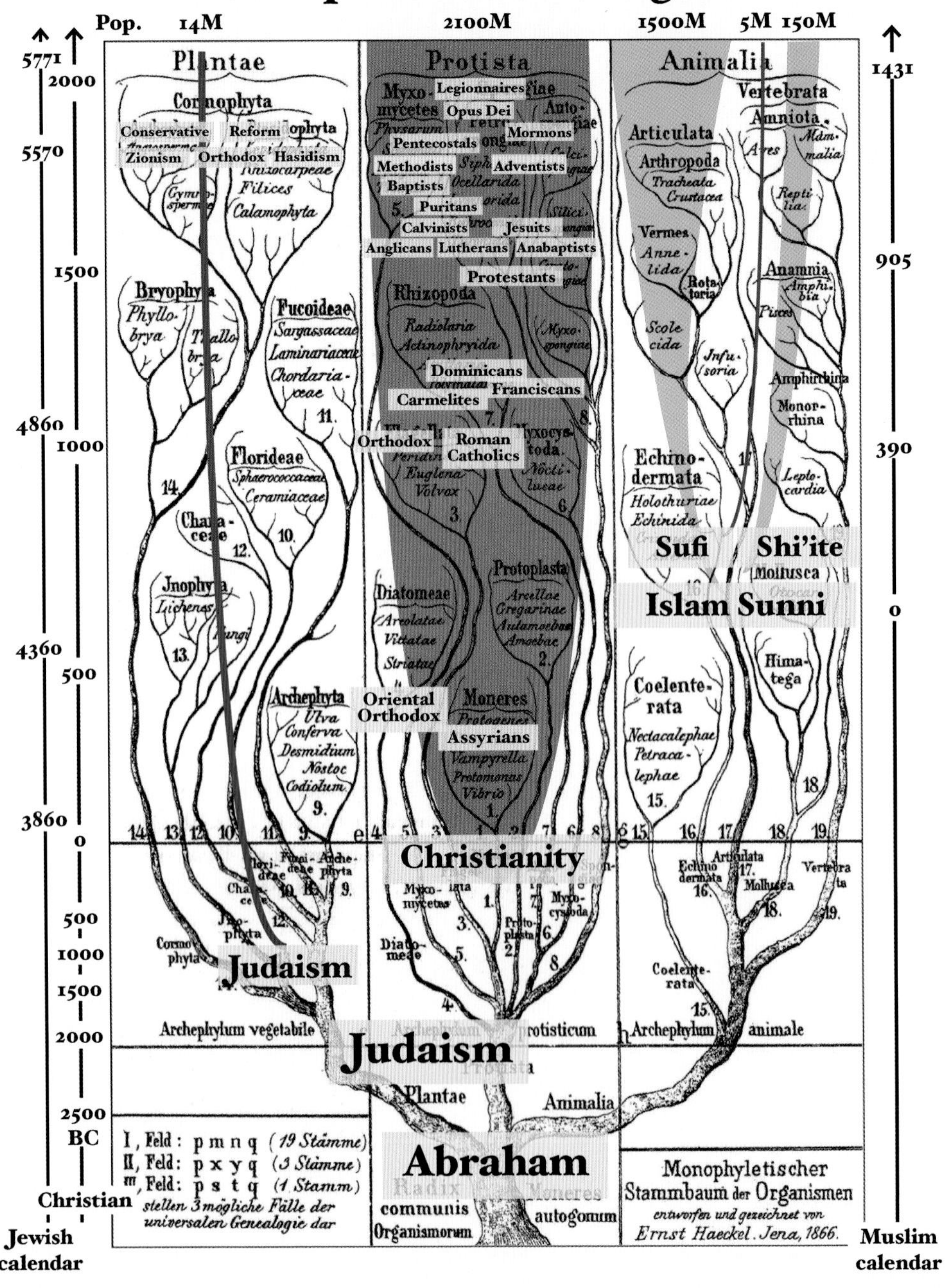

JUAN ENRIQUEZ & RODRIGO MARTINEZ

(S) (&)
(C) (D)
(I) (E)
(E) (S)
(N) (I)
(T) (G)
(I) (N)
(S) (E)
(T) (R)

Religions, like animals, plants and bacteria, speciate. If beliefs and institutions don't adapt and adopt as the environment changes, they too go extinct. This map illustrates some of the speciation that occurred with three of the world's great religions after originating from a common Abrahamic belief. (PS Most don't adapt, which is why more than ninety per cent of the world's religions and gods are now extinct.)

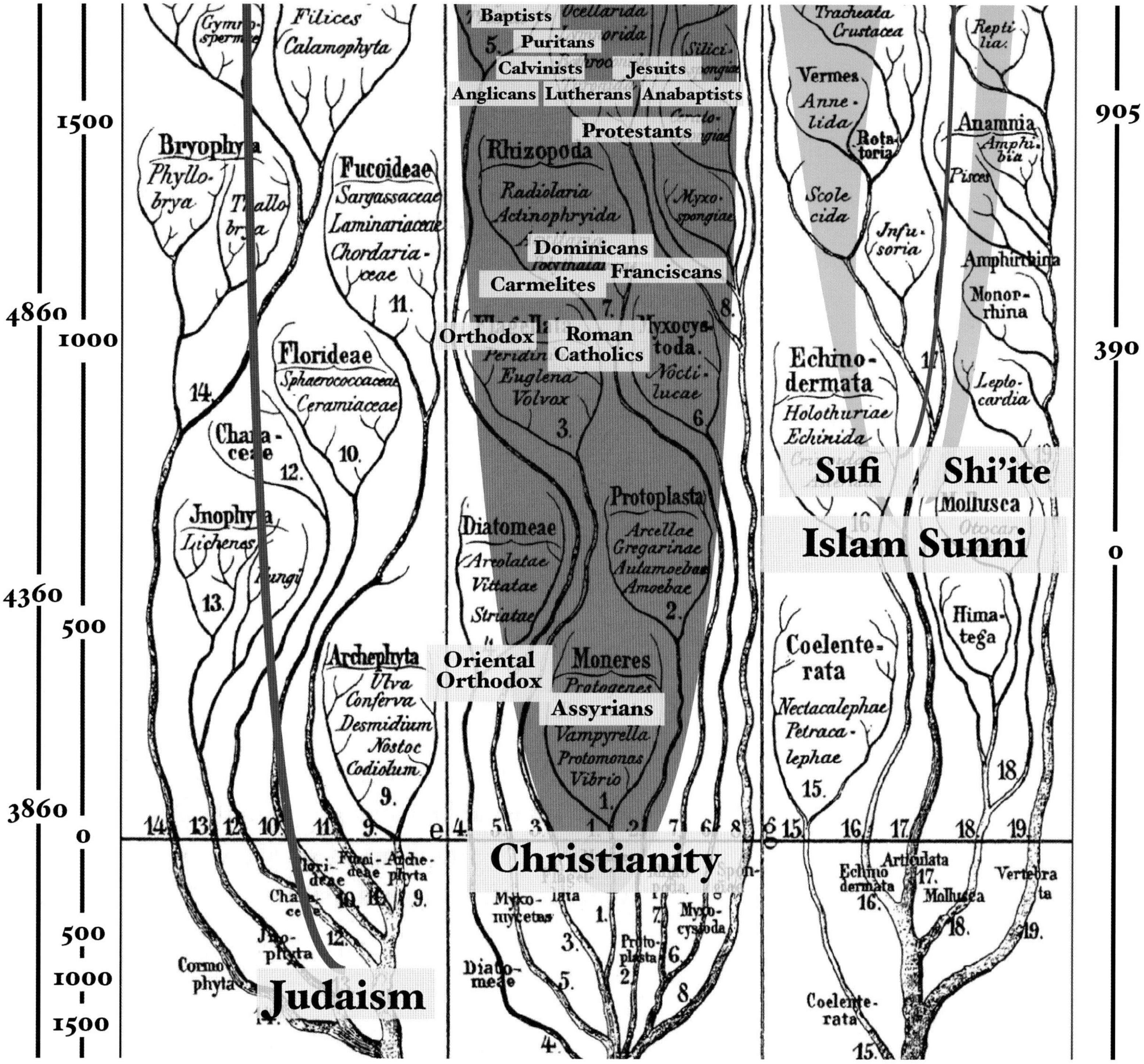

1500
4860
1000
4360
500
3860
0
500
1000
1500

Baptists
Puritans
Calvinists
Jesuits
Anglicans
Lutherans
Anabaptists
Protestants
Dominicans
Franciscans
Carmelites
Orthodox
Roman Catholics
Oriental Orthodox
Assyrians
Christianity

Judaism

Sufi
Shi'ite
Islam Sunni

905
390
0

Gymnospermae
Filices
Calamophyta
Bryophyta
Phyllobrya
Thallobrya
Fucoideae
Sargassaceae
Laminariaceae
Chordariaceae
11.
14.
Florideae
Sphaerococcaceae
Ceramiaceae
Characeae
12.
10.
Jnophyta
Lichenes
Fungi
13.
Archephyta
Ulva
Conferva
Desmidium
Nostoc
Codiolum
9.
14 13 12 10 11 9 e
Florideae
Fungi-deae
Archephyta
Characeae
10. 11. 9.
12.
Jnophyta
Cormophyta
14.

5.
Rhizopoda
Radiolaria
Actinophryida
Myxospongiae
Silicispongiae
7.
8.
Myxocystoda
Peridinium
Euglena
Volvox
Noctilucae
3.
6.
Protoplasta
Arcellae
Gregarinae
Autamoebae
Amoebae
Diatomeae
Areolatae
Vittatae
Striatae
2.
Moneres
Protogenes
Vampyrella
Protomonas
Vibrio
1.
4. 5. 3. 1. 2. 7. 6. 8.
Myxomycetes
1.
7.
Myxocystoda
3.
Protoplasta
6.
Diatomeae
5.
2.
8.
4.

Tracheata
Crustacea
Vermes
Annelida
Rotatoria
Scolecida
Infusoria
Reptilia
Anamnia
Amphibia
Pisces
Amphirhina
Monorrhina
Leptocardia
17.
Echinodermata
Holothuriae
Echinida
19.
Mollusca
16
Himatega
Coelenterata
Nectacalephae
Petracalephae
15.
18.
g 15. 16. 17. 18. 19.
Articulata
Echinodermata
16.
17.
Mollusca
18.
Vertebrata
19.
Coelenterata
15.

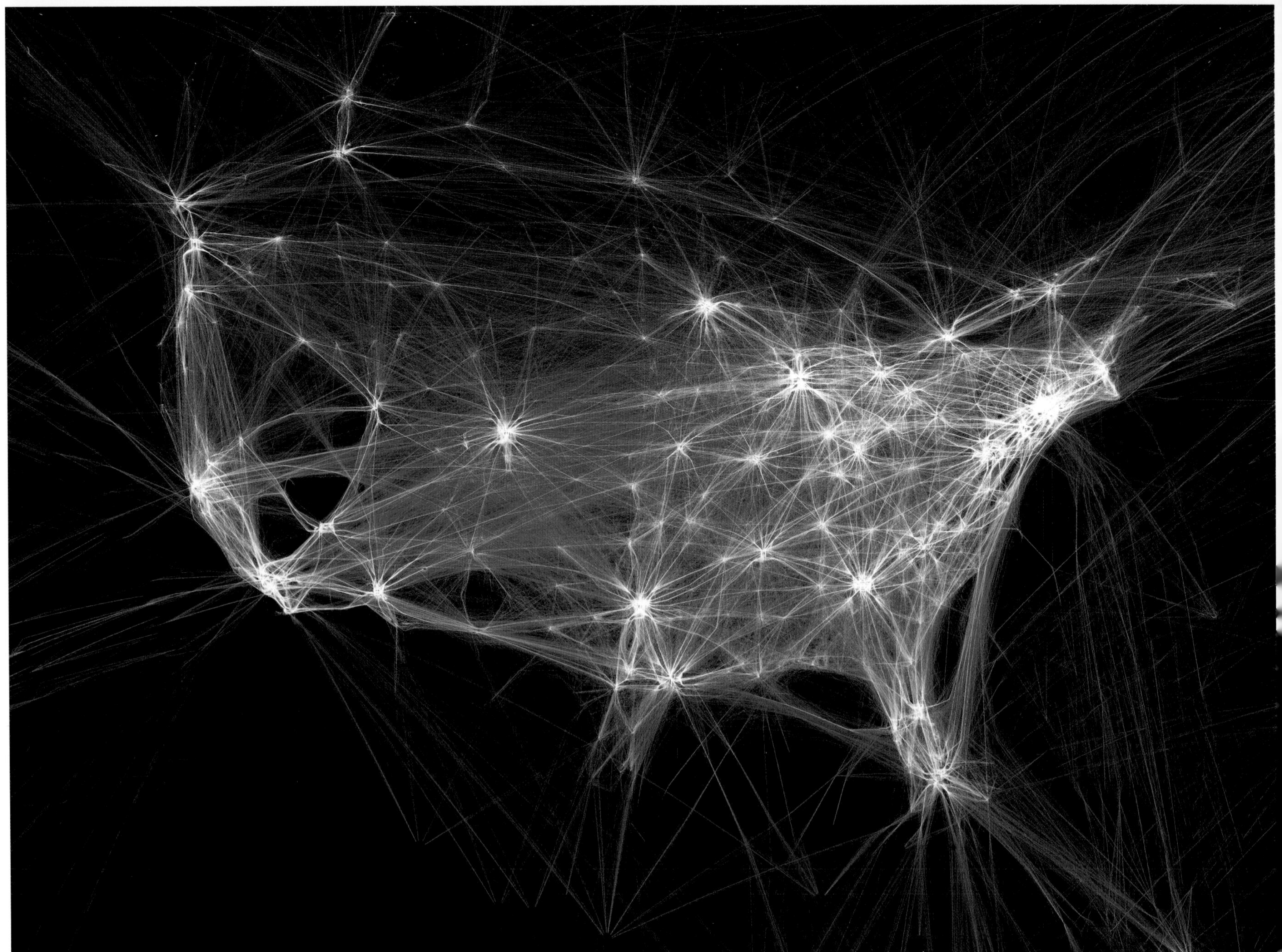

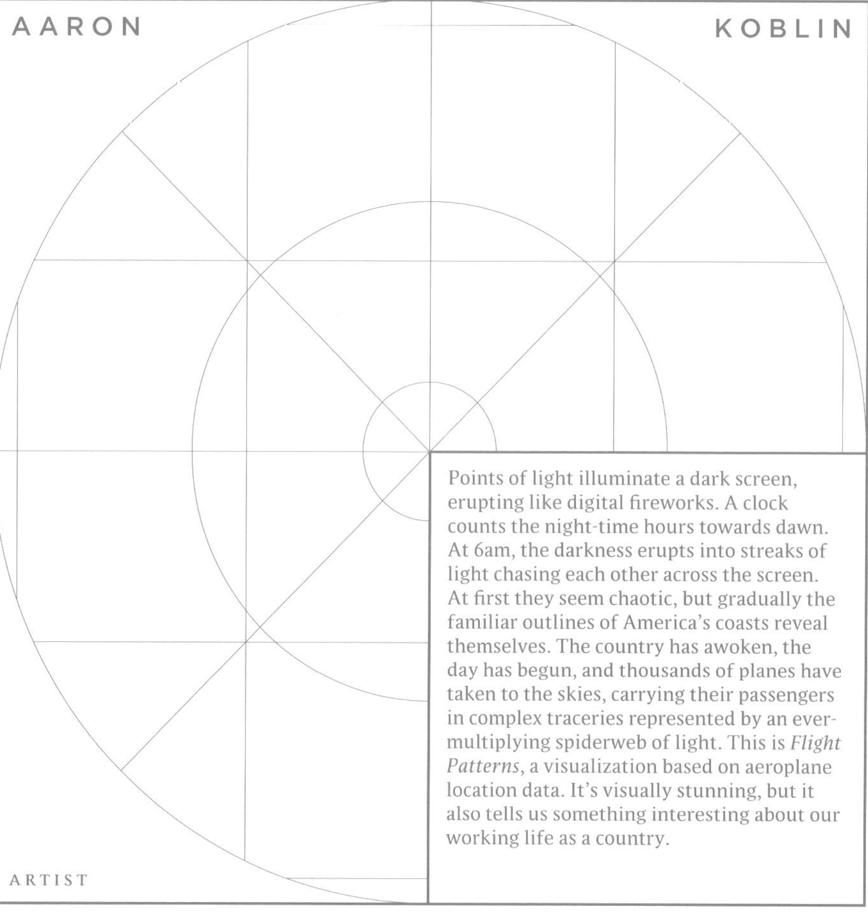

AARON KOBLIN

ARTIST

Points of light illuminate a dark screen, erupting like digital fireworks. A clock counts the night-time hours towards dawn. At 6am, the darkness erupts into streaks of light chasing each other across the screen. At first they seem chaotic, but gradually the familiar outlines of America's coasts reveal themselves. The country has awoken, the day has begun, and thousands of planes have taken to the skies, carrying their passengers in complex traceries represented by an ever-multiplying spiderweb of light. This is *Flight Patterns*, a visualization based on aeroplane location data. It's visually stunning, but it also tells us something interesting about our working life as a country.

FABIAN MARTI

ARTIST

VRNTYNHZLN CLGKNNMNLYN WKOHZ
MARTI KERAMIK 0041765653946, 2011

My intention is to build a memorial to future generations, reminding them to come to its inauguration by means of a time machine. In the event that nobody from the future shows up at the inauguration, it shall prove to me that I will fail as an artist. I then shall stop doing art for ever.

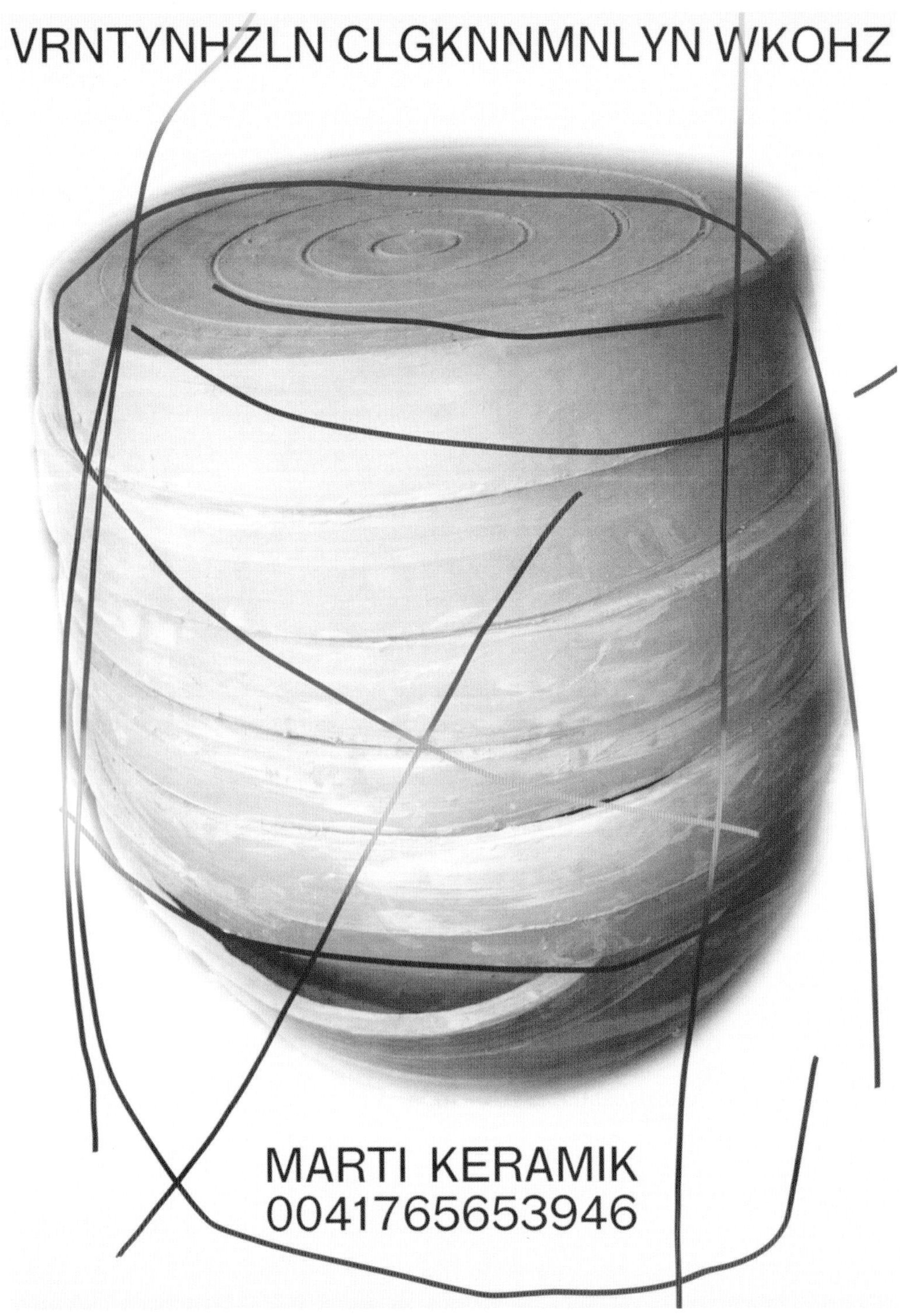

MIT SENSEABLE CITY LAB

ARCHITECTS AND URBAN PLANNERS

Globe Encounters 2010

In the Information Age, the flow of Internet traffic between locations is nearly ubiquitous. *Globe Encounters* visualizes the volumes of Internet data flowing between New York and cities around the world over the past 24 hours. The size of the glow on a particular city location corresponds to the amount of traffic flowing between the the place and New York City. A larger glow implies a greater IP flow.

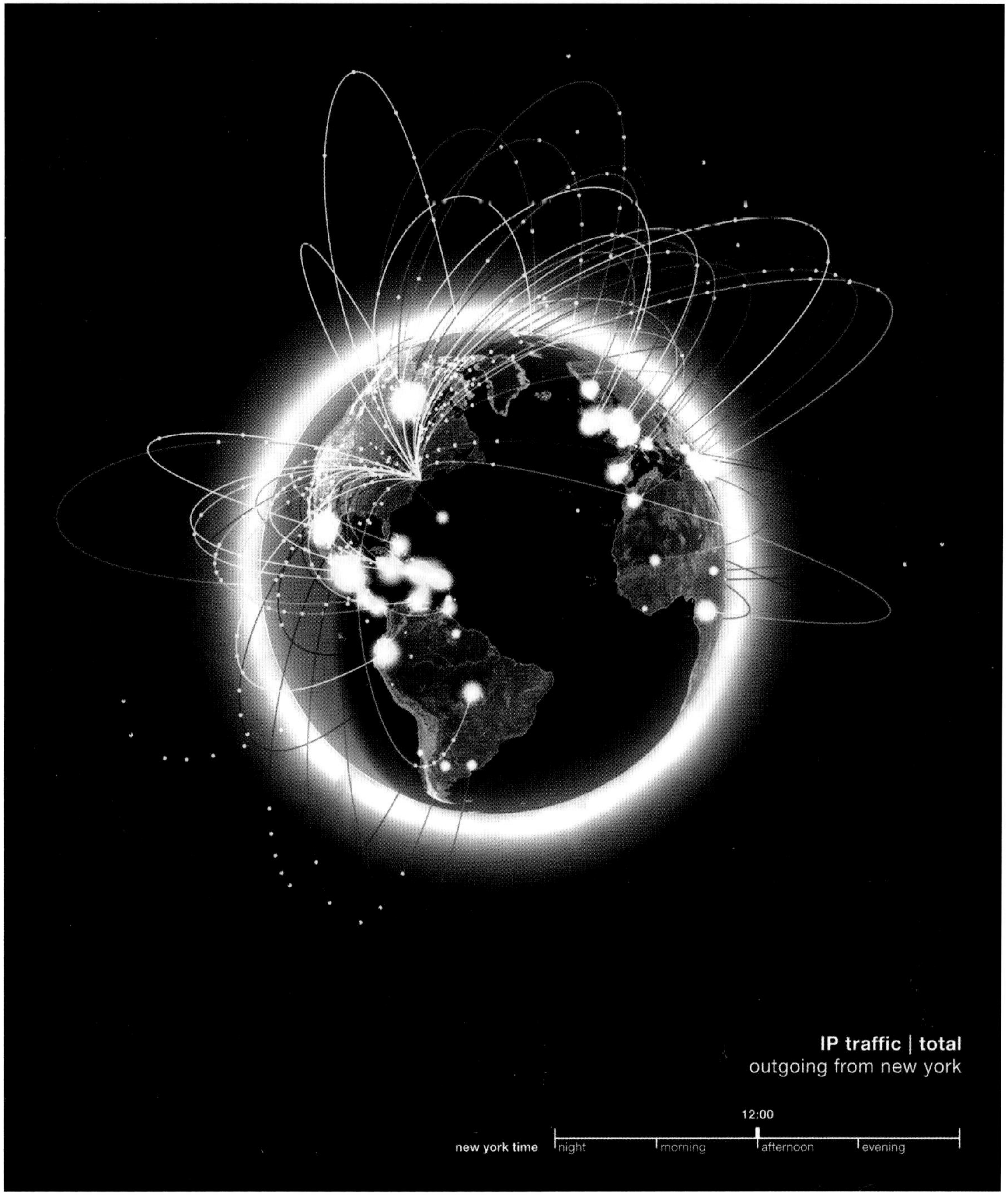

IP traffic | total
outgoing from new york

12:00
new york time night morning afternoon evening

JULY 20 A NIGHT OUT WITH THE BOYS

Brian and I dress up at my house. Brian is a friend who used to be a male prostitute ... who fucked men... we're going out to see the spots. We take off, me with lots of make-up and looking rather hard and ho-like. We drive to Selma ave and there Brian stands alone on a street corner. I lean against a church on the other side of the street watching. Brian certainly does out-class the other hookers on the street tonight. A guy parked in a car honks and motions me over... I ignore him and he comes over. I am aware of men driving by who think I am trick-ing. This guy Dino asks if I'm tricking and says he can fix me up at the Beverly Hilton, where he works. I say I'm not but he doesn't quite believe me. I invite him to join Brian and me for coffee. We go to Gold Cup and he tells us he is a high-class hooker, only works calls, makes one or two Bills per eve. He also says he is straight. It is obvious he is bullshitting and trying to think of a way to hit on me. Dino leaves, leaving us with Bill. The G.C. is filled with gay men, T.V.'s and an occasional woman hooker. They know and are protective of one another, although I don't sense hostility.

Brian points out the old men who cluster around the corner, hoping to blow a young boy who is down on his money and who needs a cup of coffee or a hamburger. He says you can often spot a hooker by her shoulder bag. Two men dressed very convincingly like women come in. One of the male hookers is feeling her (his) breast. We go to the outside and stand looking at nude magazines. B. says this is a good pick-up spot. We go to Spotlight bar. B. says this is sleezy or low life hustling, and will take me to the class joints when we're dressed better. I walk behind him on the Boulevard and watch the older men turn and stare at him. At the newstand I bought a Playgirl and an Advocate and a free press.

HOLLYWOOD BLVD

SELMA

LEXINGTON

LA BREA

HIGHLAND

McCADDEN

LAS PALMAS

HUDSON

CAHUENGA

Drag queens used to cruise here.

Diamond Jims

where high class pimps & ho's hang out.

Gold Cup

LONG JOHNS

Pioneer Chicken

News stand

GALLEON ROOM

male hookers hitching

SPOTLIGHT

Super M

YMCA

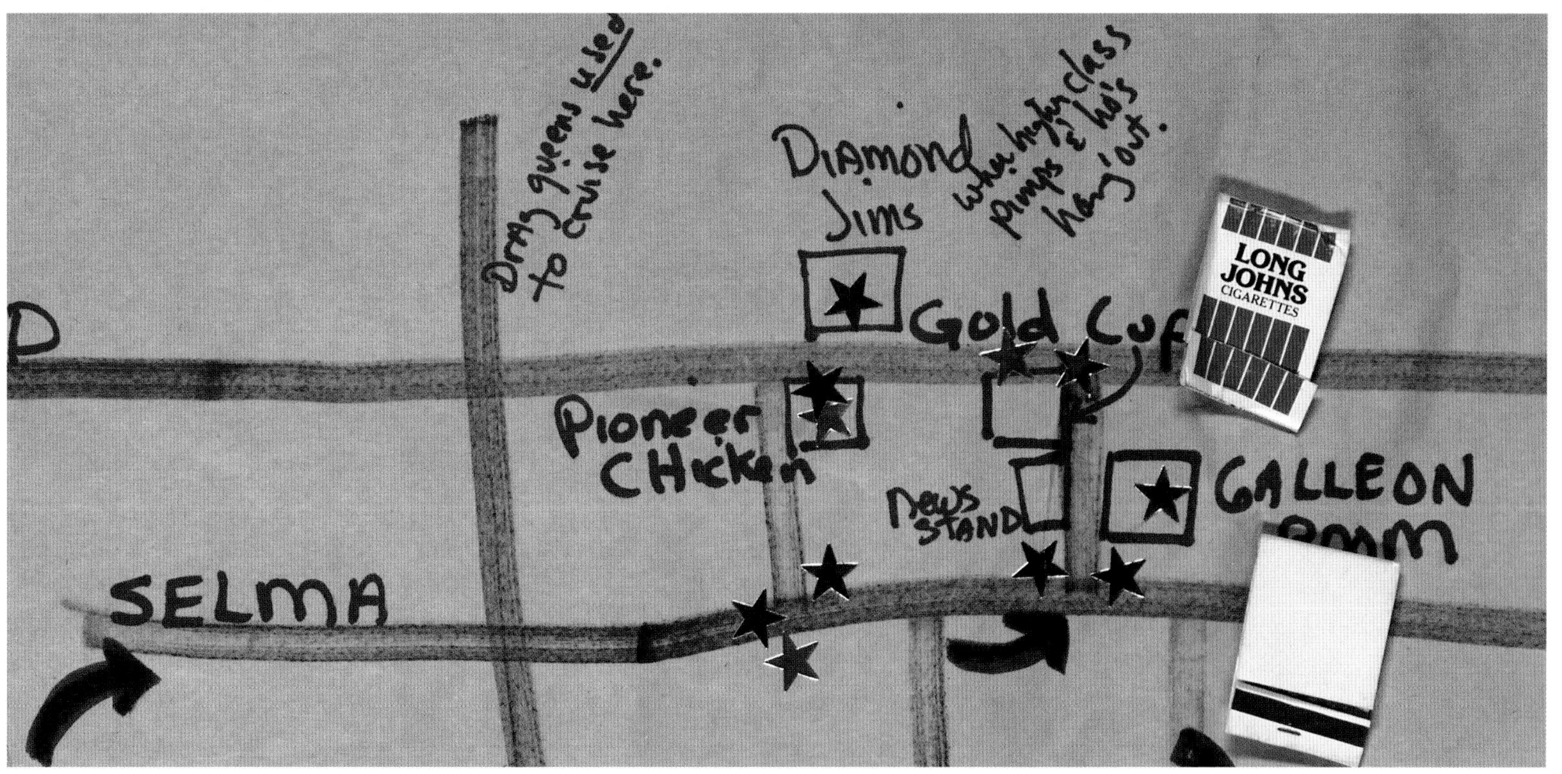

SUZANNE LACY

PROSTITUTION NOTES, 1974

In 1974, I decided to do a project on prostitution. I wondered who they were, these women whose lives were such powerful icons for my gender. How did I carry their condition inside my own experience? I didn't want to put myself inside their shoes, walk the streets as an art performance or dress up like a prostitute in order to flirt with their reality or to relate their individual stories, except as their stories appeared along my journey. Rather, I thought to locate the work in my own experience, to record the process of my entry into an understanding of 'The Life' as I looked for the echo of their situation inside my own. ¶ *Prostitution Notes* represents an early example of performative research, a series of 'notes' recorded on brown paper. I set myself the task of understanding the (at that time) little-known specifics of the lives of prostitutes. I began by drawing circles within circles on large pieces of brown craft paper, representing my friendships, acquaintances and contacts. I explored the mythologies and realities of prostitution through my meetings with people in and around 'The Life'. I contacted people, met with them and their contacts in their social spaces such as bars or coffee shops, itemized what they ate during their conversations, and also collected items from those locations to affix to the maps, such as restaurant matchbook covers. The documentation included photographs and annotations of my 'tracking' prostitutes around Los Angeles. The journey took me across LA in three dimensions: the sociology and fabric of relationships, the geography and specific places where prostitution occurs, and my own psychological terrain.

LA FOULE EN DELIRE MEURTRIER
1. le TSUNAMI HUMAIN
détruit tout sur son passage

CLAUDE PARENT

SKETCH ONE Where is the world heading if not towards its ruin, towards its autodestruction because we have released each individual's 'opinion' from any obligation of profound thought, from any responsible commitment, and, dare we say, from any morality?

A	R	C	H	I	T	E	C	T
A	R	C	H	I	T	E	C	T
A	R	C	H	I	T	E	C	T
A	R	C	H	I	T	E	C	T
A	R	C	H	I	T	E	C	T

'L'ARC' protecteur de la future architecture
LA VIE
EN SOUS-SOL LA VIE
" l'incision urbaine "
2. Le TSUNAMI HUMAIN est passé.
L'ONDULATION de l'ARCHITECTURE (L'ARC) a RÉSISTÉ.
Les hommes troglodytes ont survécu dans "l'incision": RENAÎTRE!

SKETCH TWO How to remedy this gesture of death, this will to disappear by destroying the architectural envelope of the world? ¶ How, if not through a total transformation of human habitation by denying that to build confers a right of ownership of the surface of the Earth? ¶ The crime is to confuse habitation and circulation. The crime is to make inhabiting the equivalent of locking up by transforming the planet into so many protected prisons. ¶ To respond to this tragedy that leads a desperate crowd to find its rightful place, to destroy the established status quo, it is essential first and foremost to build a protective carapace that will itself serve as a means of 'universal' communication. ¶ Habitation thus conceived as seamless and continuous will allow social relations to be entirely unhindered, free from obstacles preventing us from encountering everyone. ¶ The model that seems most suitable for this future could be that of a UNIVERSAL MIGRATION, even if that means it must invent its own manners, habits and ultimately its own culture. ¶ The permanent MIGRATION of men across immense and continuously habitable practicabilities would avoid for ever the fatal risk that our current ways of enclosing cities increasingly engenders every day; it would give man a second chance to LIVE his EARTH without harming anyone. ¶ Only then will life rediscover all of its meaning and energy. The world will become once again HABITABLE.

Global War on Terror OVERSEAS CONTINGENCY OPERATION Stefani Germanotta LADY GAGA Love Canal BLACK CREEK VILLAGE Federation of Atomic Scientists FEDERATION OF AMERICAN SCIENTISTS AIG AIU HOLDINGS, LTD. Stumpknocker SPOTTED SUNFISH South-Central SOUTH LOS ANGELES Department of Health, Education, and Welfare DEPARTMENT OF HEALTH AND HUMAN SERVICES Philip Morris ALTRIA Jenny Hamm XENI JARDIN Napalm MARK 77 Kentucky Fried Chicken KITCHEN FRESH CHICKEN School of the Americas WESTERN HEMISPHERE INSTITUTE FOR SECURITY High Fructose Corn Syrup CORN SUGAR Patagonian Toothfish CHILEAN SEABASS Federal Homeloan Bank Board OFFICE OF THRIFT SUPERVISION Christ the Good Shepherd Worldwide Church WORD OF FAITH CHURCH Jamaat-ud Dawa TEHREEK-E-TAHAFUZ QIBLA AWAL Aspartame AMINOSWEET Jon Stewart JONATHAN LEIBOWITZ ValuJet AIRTRAN Guest Choice Network CENTER FOR CONSUMER FREEDOM Lehman Brothers Merchant Banking TRIATLANTIC CAPITAL PARTNERS Halfway, Oregon HALF.COM, OREGON Slimehead ORANGE ROUGHY WorldCom MCI AIG Financial Advisors SAGEPOINT FINANCIAL, INC. Radio Shack THE SHACK Blackwater XE Stimulus RECOVERY ACT Torture ENHANCED INTERROGATION TECHNIQUE

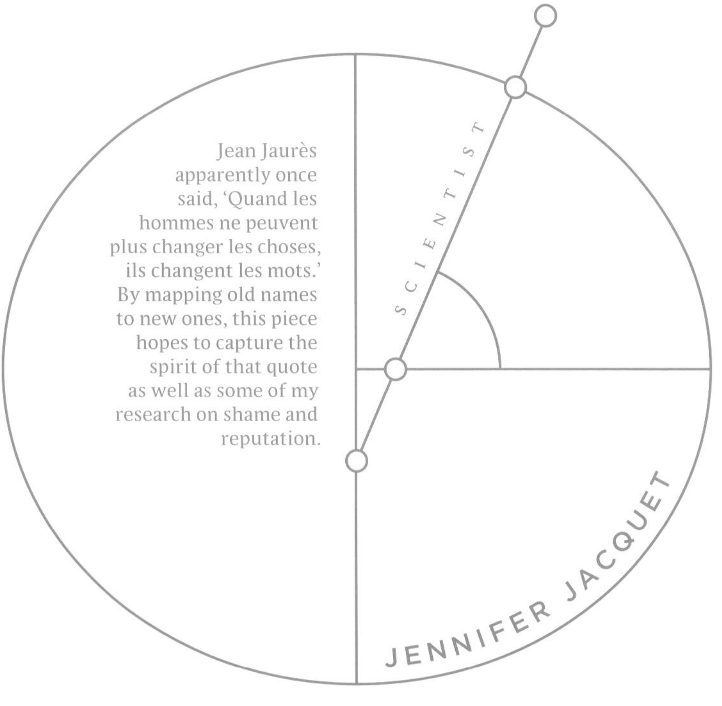

Jean Jaurès apparently once said, 'Quand les hommes ne peuvent plus changer les choses, ils changent les mots.' By mapping old names to new ones, this piece hopes to capture the spirit of that quote as well as some of my research on shame and reputation.

EPARTMENT OF HEALTH AND HUMAN S

Philip Morris ALTRIA Jenny Hamm XENI

Napalm MARK 77 Kentucky Fried Chicken

RESH CHICKEN School of the A

WESTERN HEMISPHERE INSTITUTE FOR S

High Fructose Corn Syrup CORN

Patagonian Toothfish CHILEAN SEABASS

Homeloan Bank Board OFFICE OF

SUPERVISION Christ the Good S

Worldwide Church WORD OF FAITH

Jamaat-ud Dawa TEHREEK-E-TAHAFUZ

AWAL Aspartame AMINOSWEET Jon

JONATHAN LEIBOWITZ ValuJet AIRTRA

Choice Network CENTER FOR CO

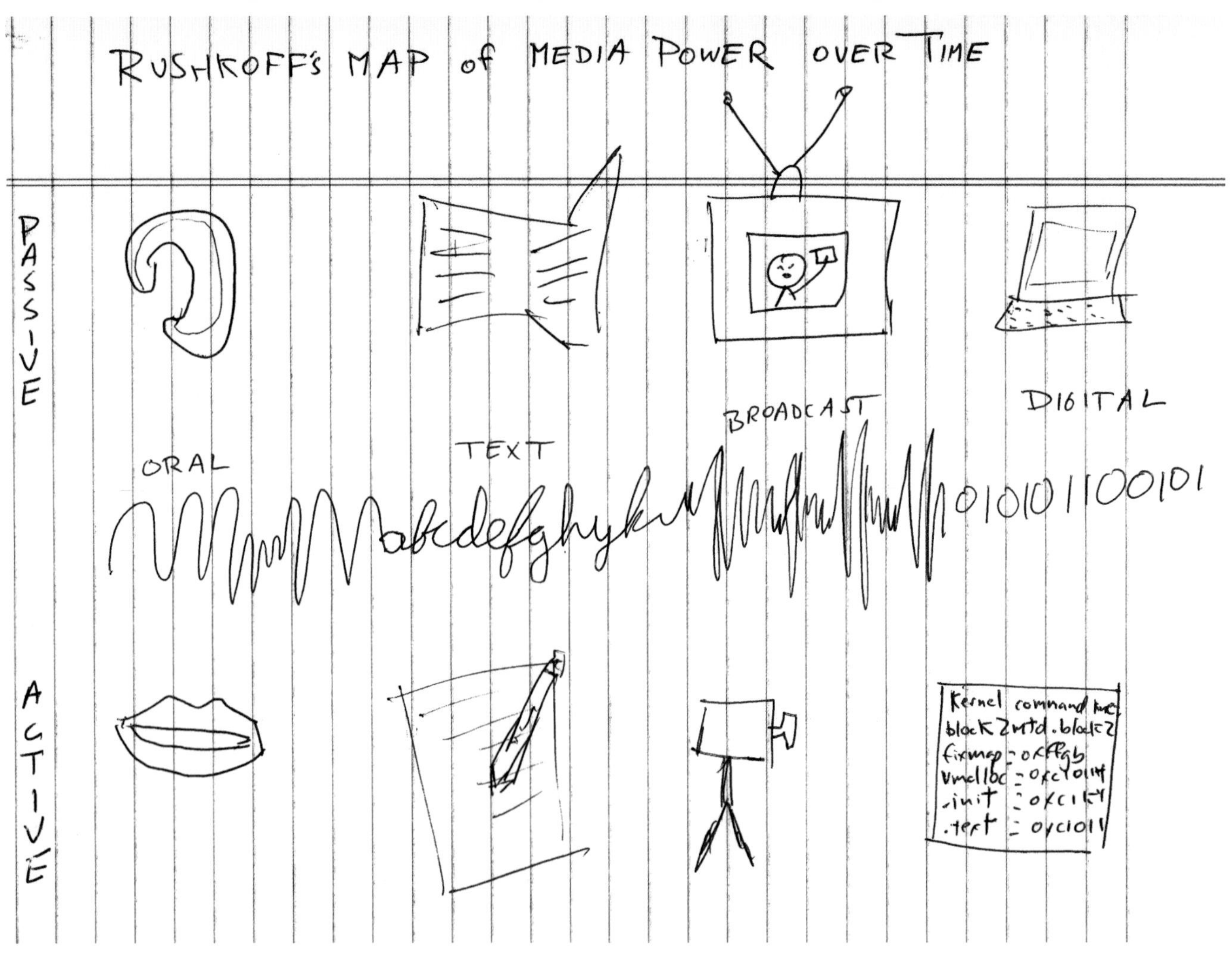

DOUGLAS RUSHKOFF

MEDIA THEORIST

Redrawing the map of Great Britain from a network of human interactions

ARCHITECT

CARLO RATTI

Do regional boundaries defined by governments respect the more natural ways that people interact across space? This map proposes a novel, fine-grained approach to regional delineation, based on analysing networks of billions of individual human transactions. Given a geographical area and some measure of the strength of links between its inhabitants, we show how to partition the area into smaller, non-overlapping regions while minimizing the disruption to each person's links. We tested our method on the largest non-Internet human network, inferred from a large telecommunications database in Britain. Our partitioning algorithm yields geographically cohesive regions that correspond remarkably well with administrative regions, while unveiling unexpected spatial structures that had previously only been hypothesized in the literature. We also quantify the effects of partitioning, showing for instance that the effects of a possible secession of Wales from Britain would be twice as disruptive for the human network than that of Scotland.

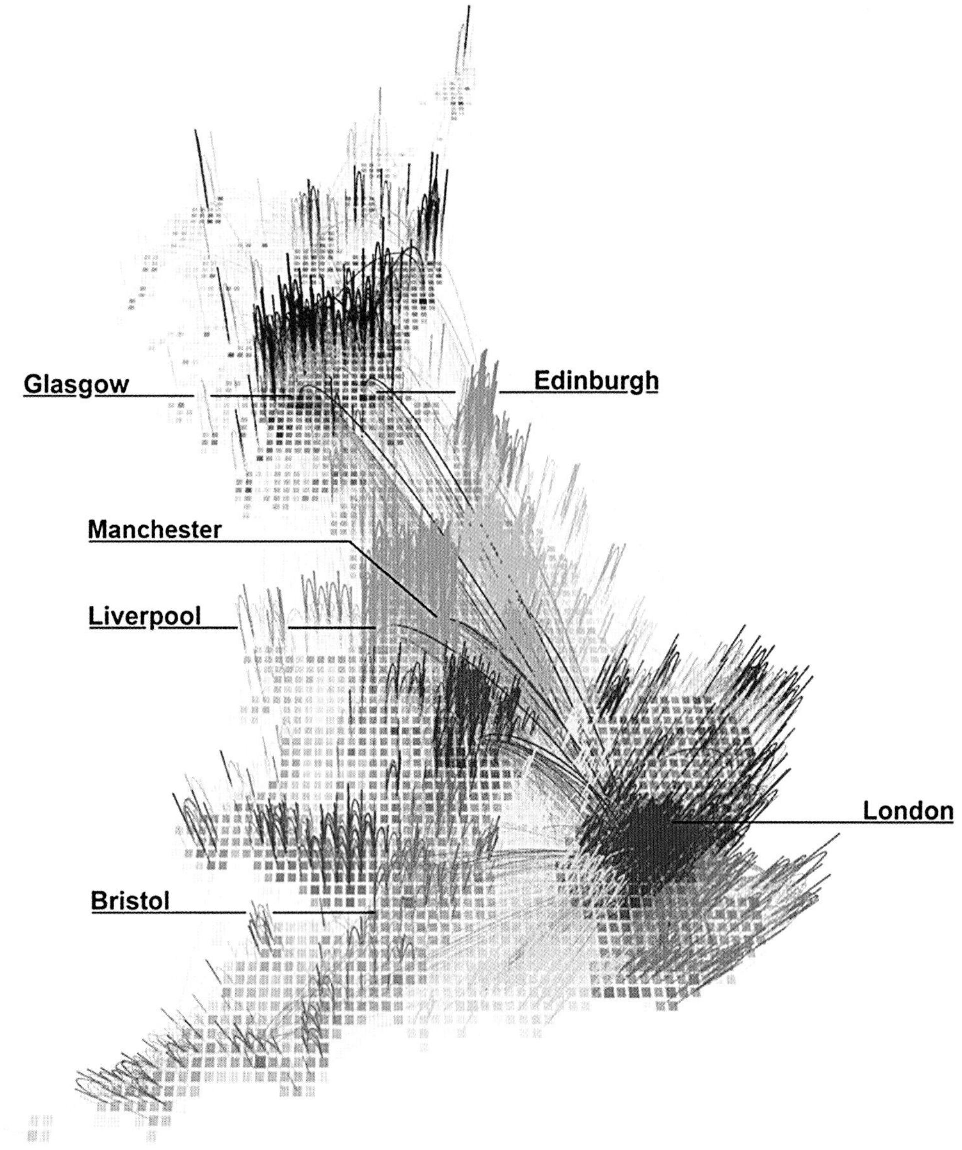

Glasgow
Edinburgh
Manchester
Liverpool
London
Bristol

In Networks of Neurons and Astral Synapses

ANDREA ZANZOTTO

POET

with ELISABETTA DI MAGGIO

... in endless councils of snow and ice ...
in networks of neurons and astral synapses [1]

... like a red-hot ganglion hardening
in the uranic / vacuous soma ... [2]

... the most attenuated non-divisions and intergamies ...
which practised intergamies along each synapse ... [3]

Tell me what I have lost / tell me in
what I am lost ... in this beloved city [4]

---

1 — Andrea Zanzotto, *Pasque: Lanternina cieca*, in Andrea Zanzotto, *Le poesie e prose scelta*, Milan, Mondadori, 1998, p.418
2 — Andrea Zanzotto, *IX Ecloghe: Un libro di Ecloghe*, in ibid., p.201
3 — Andrea Zanzotto, *Fosfeni: Silicio, Carbonio, Castellieri*, in ibid., p.659
4 — Andrea Zanzotto, *Fosfeni: Collassare e pomerio*, in ibid., p.661

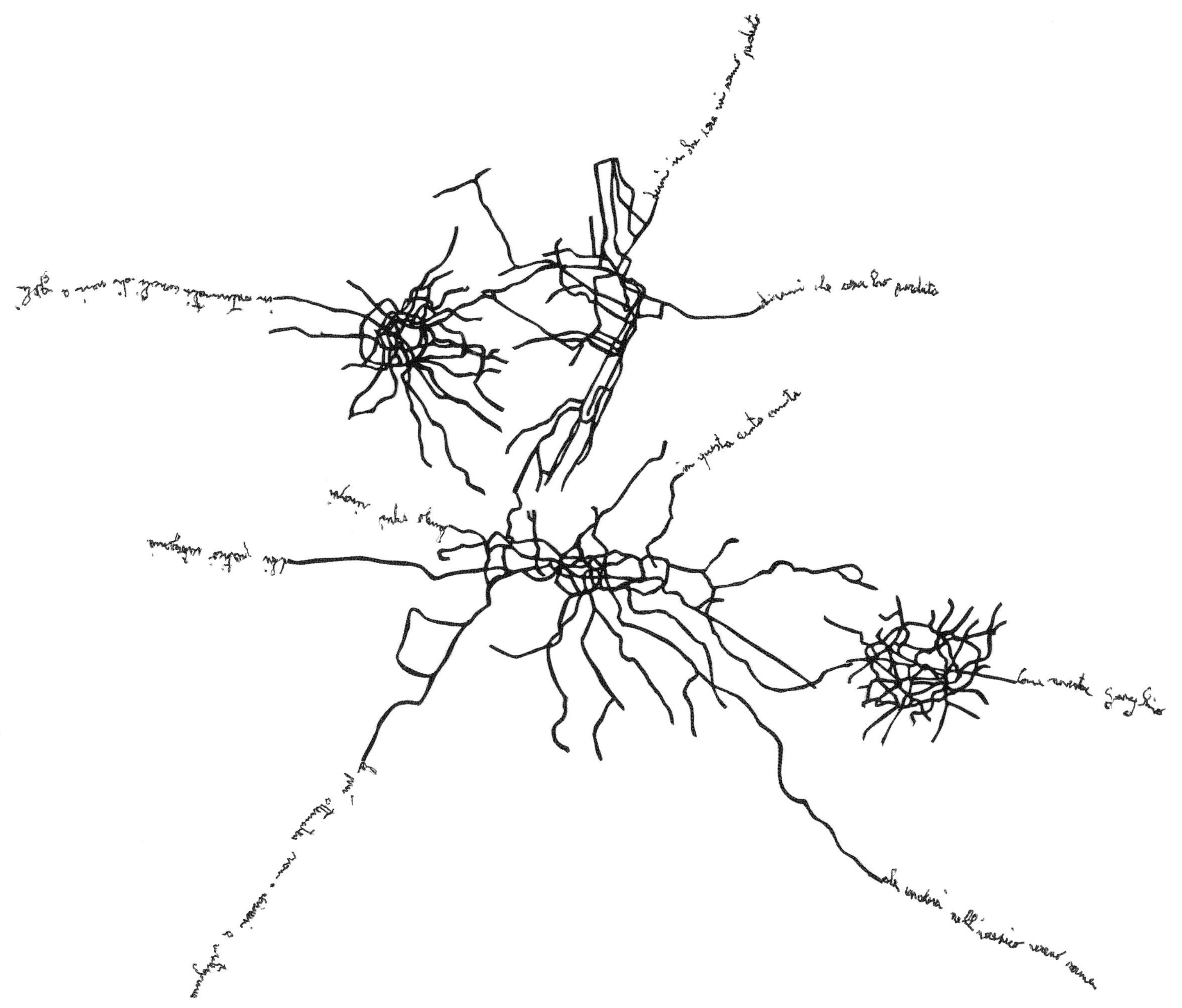

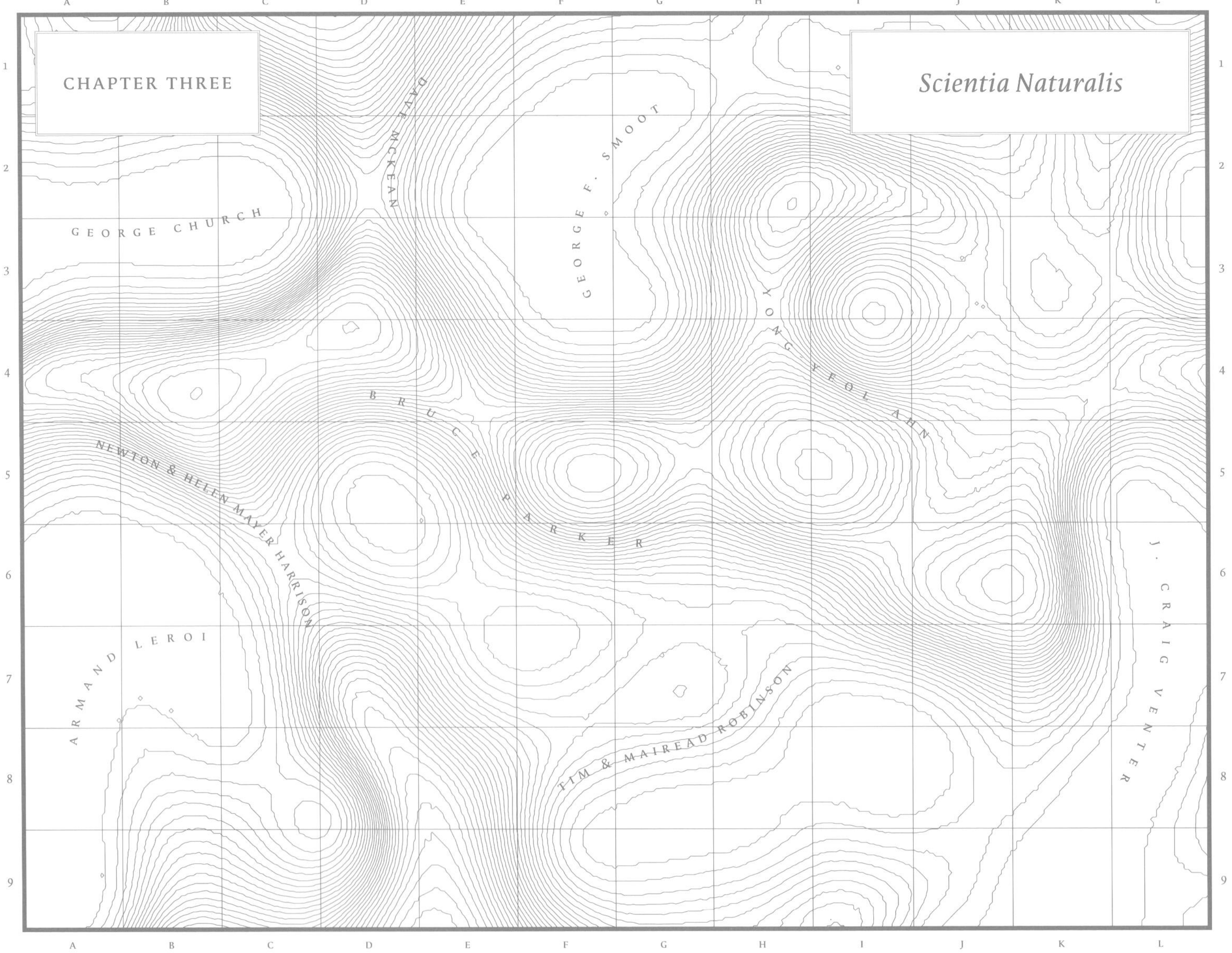
CHAPTER THREE
Scientia Naturalis
DAVE MCKEAN
GEORGE F. SMOOT
GEORGE CHURCH
YONG YEOL AHN
BRUCE PARKER
NEWTON & HELEN MAYER HARRISON
J. CRAIG VENTER
ARMAND LEROI
TIM & MAIREAD ROBINSON

The first maps were created to enable humans to measure and make sense of the world around them. These early charts either defined a particular physical, political or social space, recorded a route through a difficult terrain that might otherwise be forgotten, or else revealed to others a path across unfamiliar lands. Today those working in scientific fields use mapping techniques for much the same reasons: to help them to identify and delineate an area of study; to document and understand the results of their research; and to communicate their findings to non-specialists. Whether scientist or artist, the contributors to this chapter all use maps to reach some truth of the natural world.

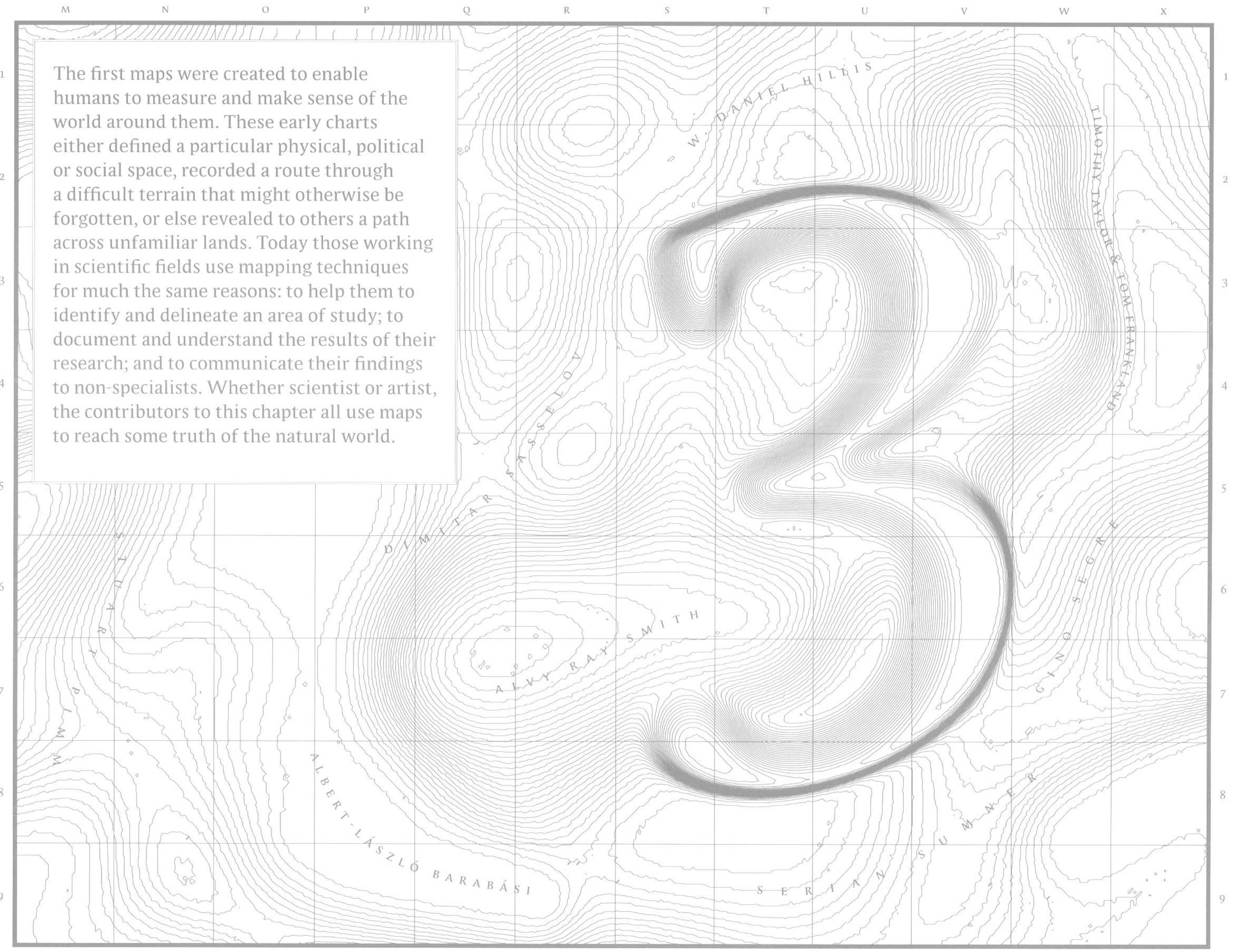

A map of a human proteome. The molecules from a drop of human blood are mapped by weight (left to right), and by slipperiness (top to bottom). The reason that multiple stripes appear in series is that the atoms in proteins come in different isotopes creating variations that differ in weight by a single neutron.

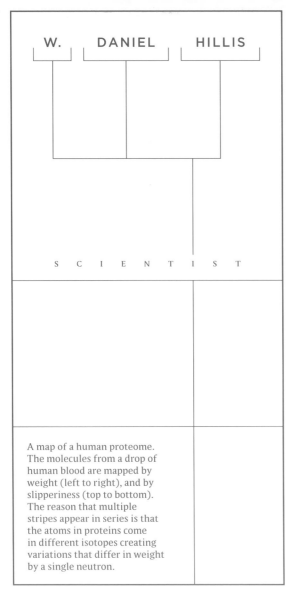

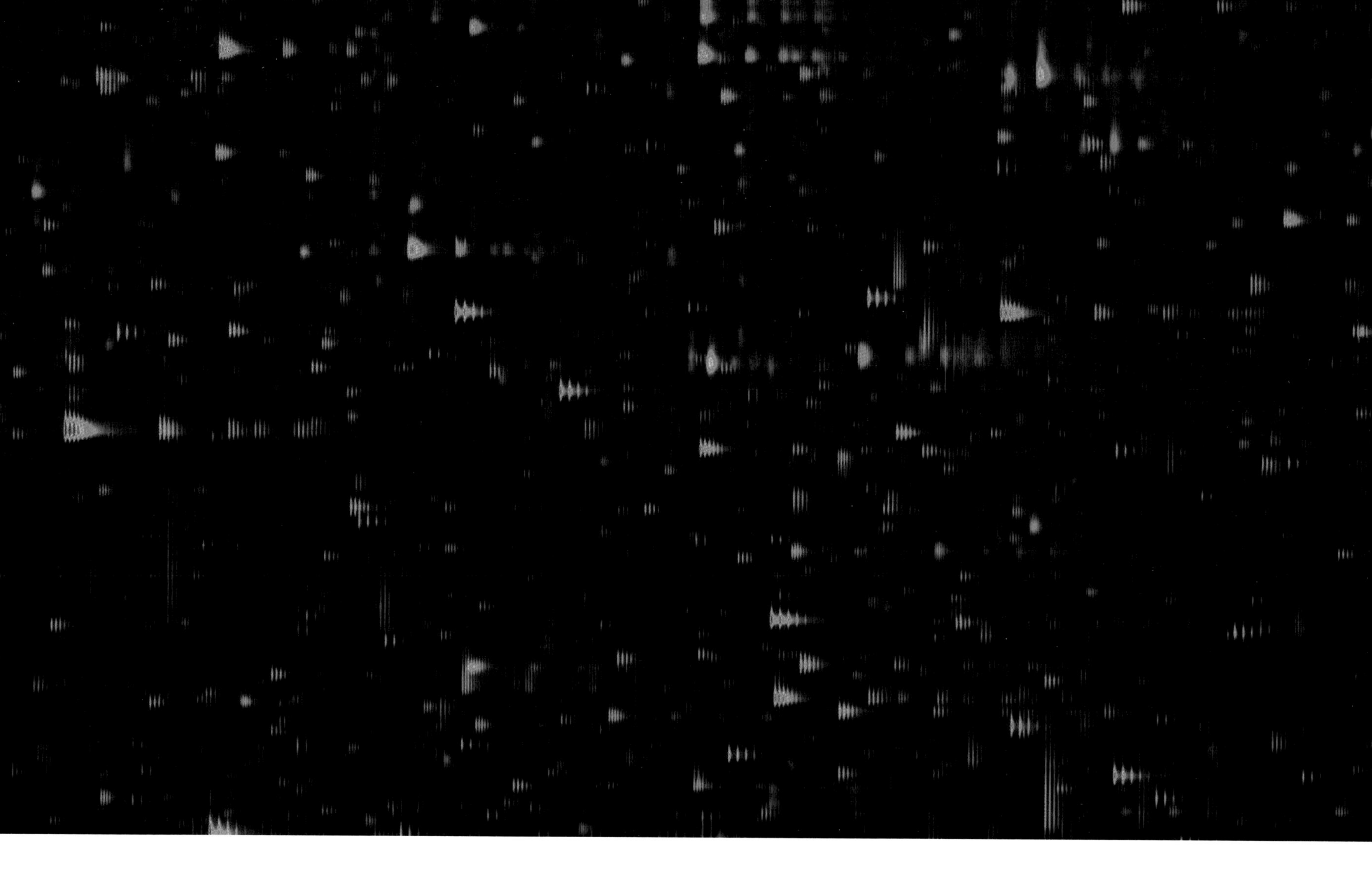

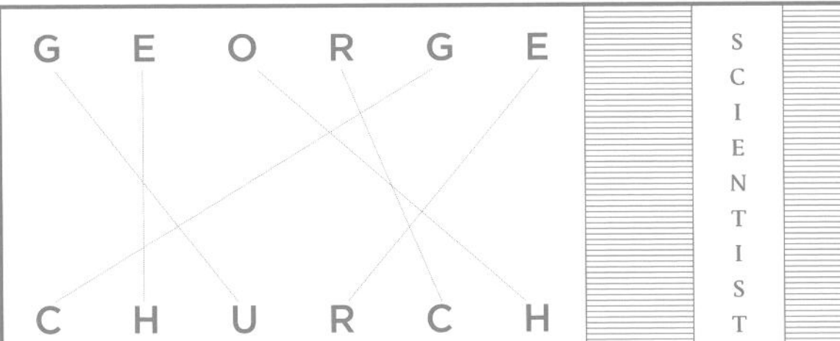

SCIENTIST

A roadmap for eliminating viruses from industrial microbes (and possibly agriculture and humans). It shows the genetic code used in every living thing on our planet: all sixty-four possible triplet 'codon' combinations of four bases: A, C, G, U. The numbers represent how many times each of these occurs in the star of genome engineering, E.coli. The three-letter names in black are the twenty amino acids encoded by the triplets. The three-colour uppercase symbols represent the 'anti-codons' in the tRNA molecules responsible for the decoding. We are using this map to design and construct new genomes with new codes.

1st base	2nd base: U	2nd base: C	2nd base: A	2nd base: G	3rd base
U	Phe 21841 GAAms^{2}i^{6}A 29334	Ser 11332 GGAA 10992	Tyr 16088 GUAms^{2}i^{6}A 21069	Cys 8486 GCAms^{2}i^{6}A 6707	C U
U	Leu 18097 cmnm^{5}UAAms^{2}i^{6}A 18006	9159 Ser VGA ms^{2}i^{6}A 11759	2682 RF2 RF1 288	1178 Trp 20071 CCAms^{2}i^{6}A	A G
C	Leu 14709 GAGm^{1}G 14410	Pro 7142 GGG ms^{2}i^{6}A 9130	His 12830 GUGA 16952	29308 27864 Arg ICGA 4529	C U A
C	Leu 5079 UAGG 70443	11063 Pro VGGm^{1}G 30994	Gln 20216 cmnm^{5}s^{2}UUGA 38169	6991 Arg CCGm^{1}G	G
A	Ile 33359 GAUt^{6}A 40223	Thr 31001 GGUt^{6}A 11581	Asn 28329 GUUt^{6}A 22786	Ser 21132 GCUt^{6}A 11323	C U
A	5356 Ile k2CAUt^{6}A Met CAUt^{6}A 36724	8979 Thr VGUt^{6}A 18989	Lys 44272 SUUt^{6}A 13398	Arg 2495 mnm^{5}UCUt^{6}A 1366	A G
G	Val 20240 GACA 24056	Ala 33911 GGCA 20010	Asp 25234 GUCA 42161	Gly 39395 GCCA 32678	C U
G	14337 Val VACA 34817	26551 Ala VGCA 44924	Glu 52362 SUCA 23474	Gly 10226 U*CCA 14472	A G

G ---- C

A ---- U

Arg His Lys Asp Glu

Ser Thr Asn Gln Cys Sec Gly Pro

Ala Val Ile Leu Met Phe Tyr Trp

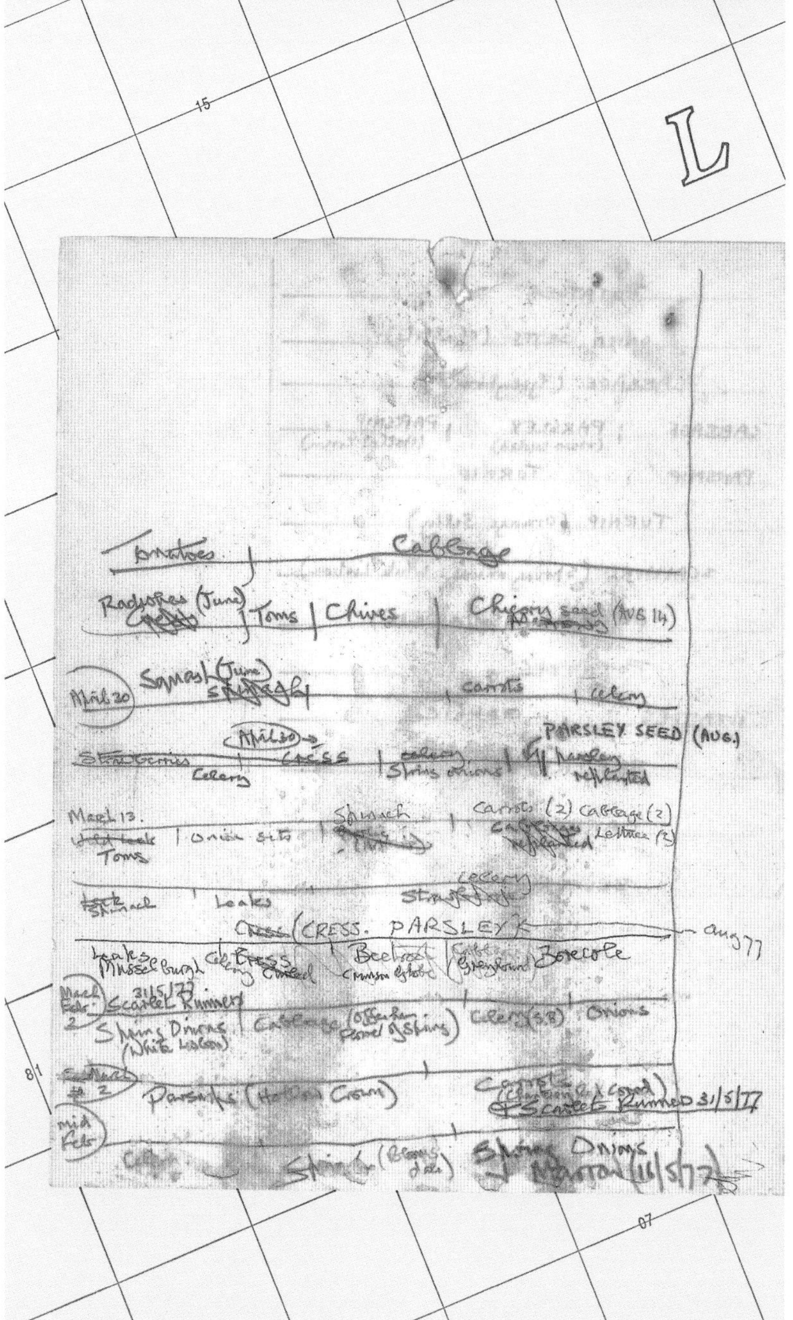

TIM & MAIREAD ROBINSON

A — R — T — I — S — T — S

The Vegetable Plot at L8511

In 1977 in the Aran Islands, Mairead and I tried our hands at growing vegetables for the first time, in a plot ridged like the traditional west of Ireland potato field, beside our garden path. I kept the weather-beaten bit of paper recording our muddled efforts as a memento, and on looking at it again I am reminded of how, when we were at work there, paths and ridges defined our private sense of direction, throwing the north, south, east, and west of the National Grid out of kilter. Nevertheless, the unchanging abstractions of official cartography insensibly penetrated the time-bound little domain, and I was always conscious of the angle, the argument, between so-called True North and our Garden North.

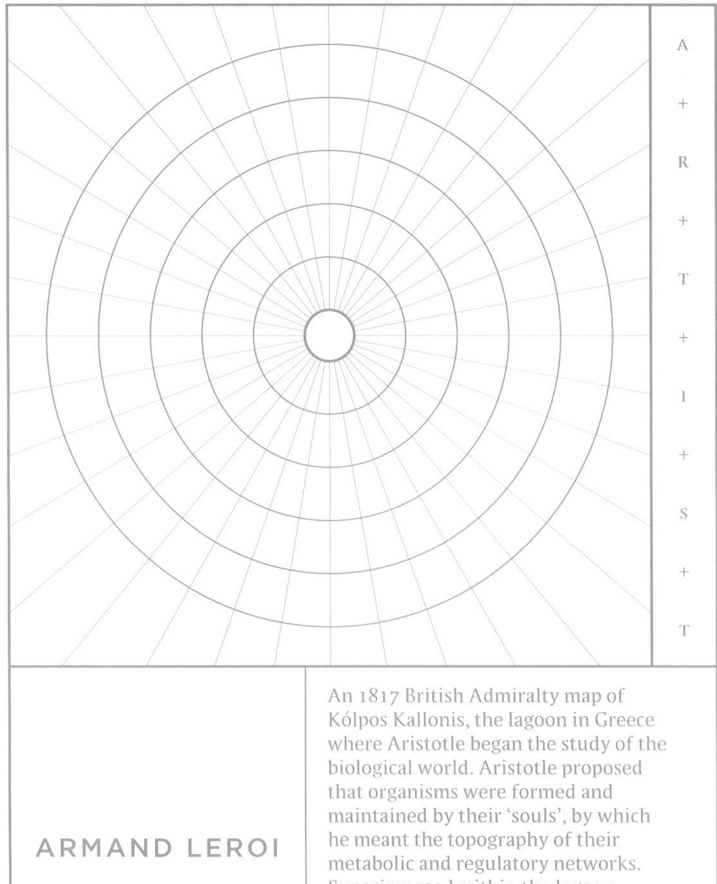

ARMAND LEROI

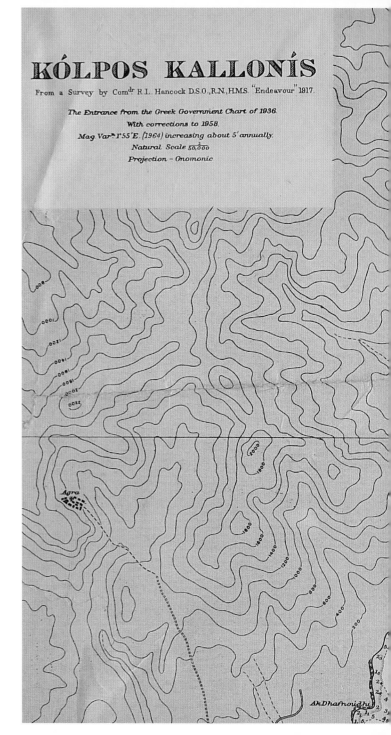

An 1817 British Admiralty map of Kólpos Kallonis, the lagoon in Greece where Aristotle began the study of the biological world. Aristotle proposed that organisms were formed and maintained by their 'souls', by which he meant the topography of their metabolic and regulatory networks. Superimposed within the lagoon, therefore, is a map of the metabolic network of a worm: Aristotle's vision realized in the twenty-first century.

KÓLPOS KALLONÍS

From a Survey by Com[dr] R.L. Hancock D.S.O., R.N., H.M.S. "Endeavour" 1917.

The Entrance from the Greek Government Chart of 1936.
With corrections to 1958.
Mag. Var.n 1°55'E. (1964) increasing about 5' annually.
Natural Scale $\frac{1}{50,000}$
Projection – Gnomonic

Agra

Ak Dhafnoúdhi

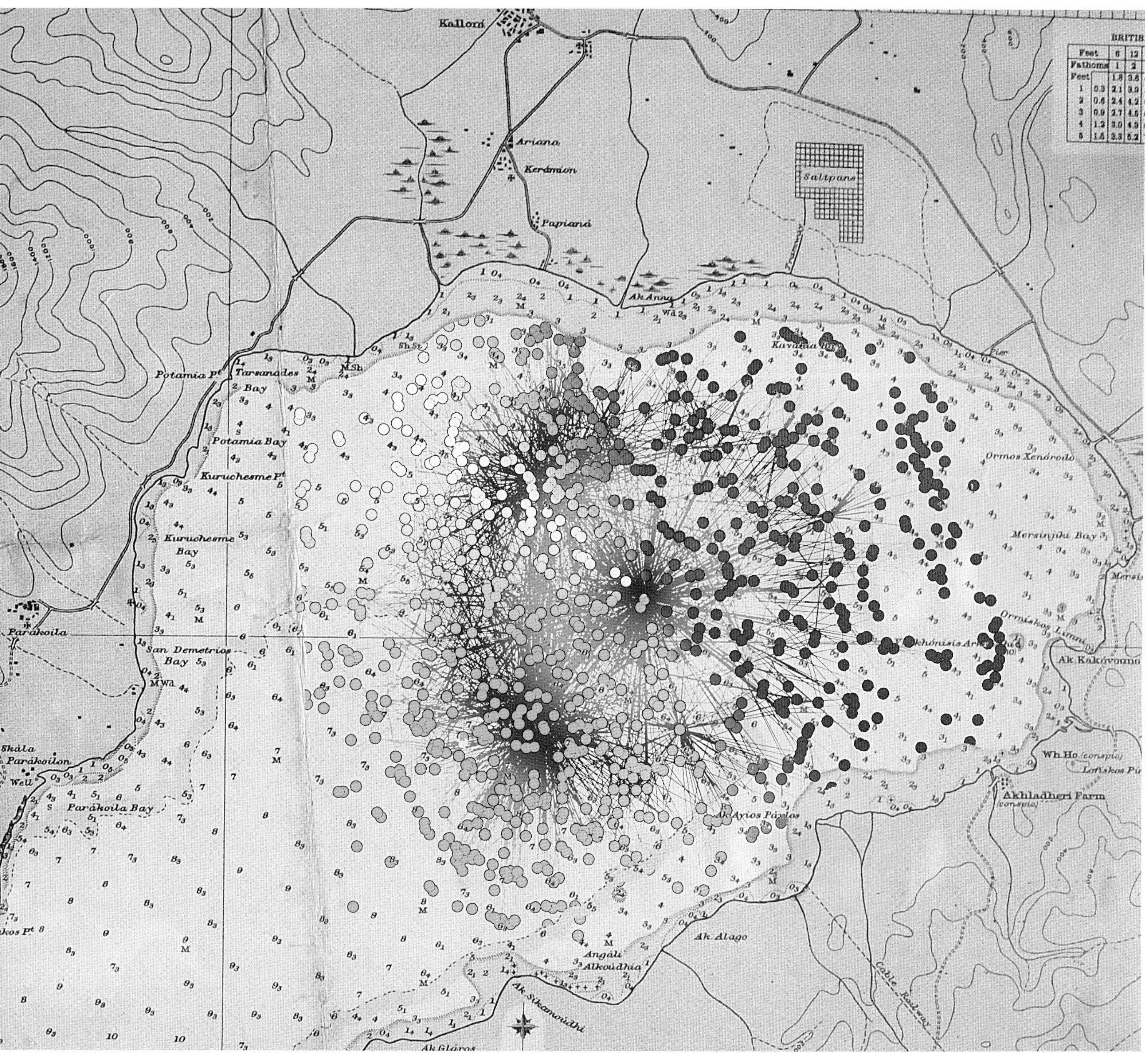

Kalloní
Ariana
Kerámion
Papianá
Saltpans
Ak.Anna
Kavalaia Bay
Potamia Pt
Tarsanades Bay
Potamia Bay
Kuruchesme Pt
Kuruchesme Bay
Parákoila
San Demetrios Bay
Skála Parákoilon
Well
Parákoila Bay
Ormos Xenórodo
Mersinjiki Bay
Ak.Kakóvouno
Wh.Ho (conspic)
Akhladheri Farm (conspic)
Ak.Ayios Pávlos
Ak.Alago
Angáli Alkoúdhia
Ak.Sikamoúdhi
Ak.Gláros
Cable Railway
Pier

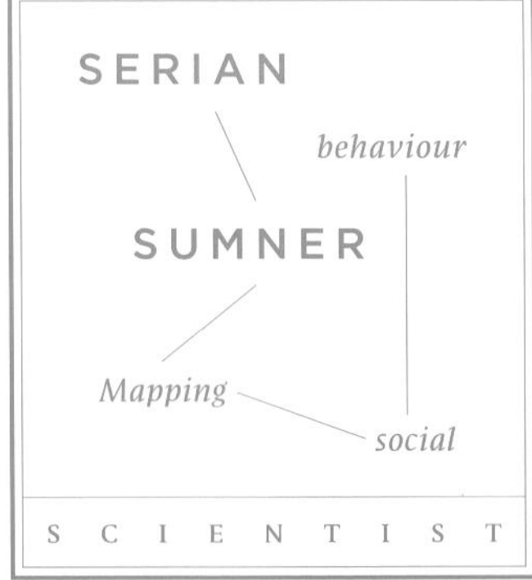

Social insects should be faithful to their nests because they gain genetic fitness benefits
from raising kin . However , monitoring the movements of individually
radio-tagged wasps reveals that fifty per cent of paper wasp workers ‘ drift
’ between different nests : workers appear to help raise related broods on the
nests they visit. These social networks , mapped from the movements of 455
radio-tagged wasps from 32 nests (represented as nodes in the map
) , show the relative drifting rates (represented as the ‘ edges
’ or lines in the map) of tagged workers between nests within four
nest aggregations . Without radio-tagging technology , these maps could not
have been generated , and hence a potentially important aspect of
social behaviour would have gone unnoticed .

N221
N124
N224
N222
N125
N223
N126
N120
N123
N121
N503
N502
N501
N507
N506
N504
N505
N101
N102
N103
N104
N105
N107
N196
N204
N199
N197
N205

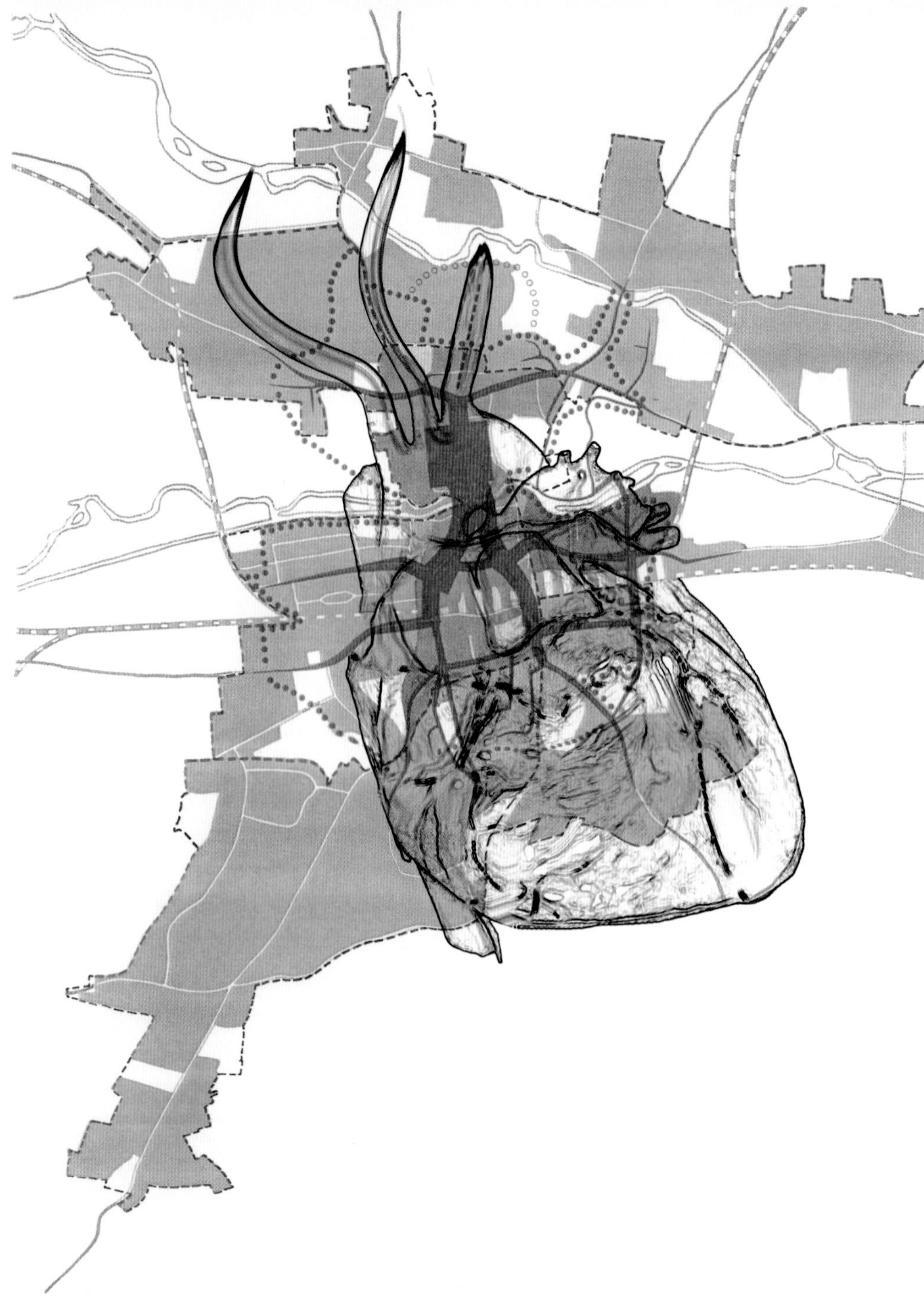

A map of the human heart

This image began with my contributions to psychogeographer and national treasure Iain Sinclair's love letter to the M25 motorway, *London Orbital*, and blossomed, or bled, from there.

ARTIST

DAVE McKEAN

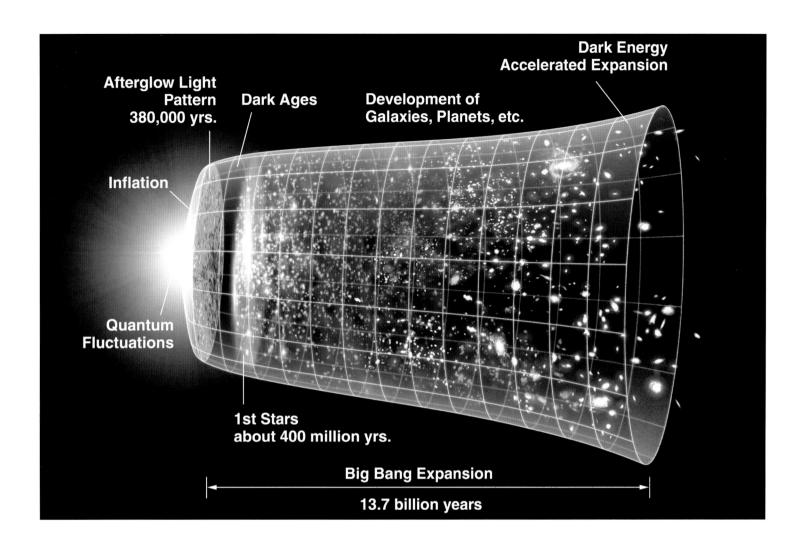

GEORGE F. SMOOT

ASTRONOMER

This is a map of the space–time for our observable universe. It shows two of three spatial dimensions and the time. It shows the beginning of time to the present epoch. You have to imagine the third spatial dimension as the continuation of the sphere of space around us for which the two dimensions show a circular cross-section.

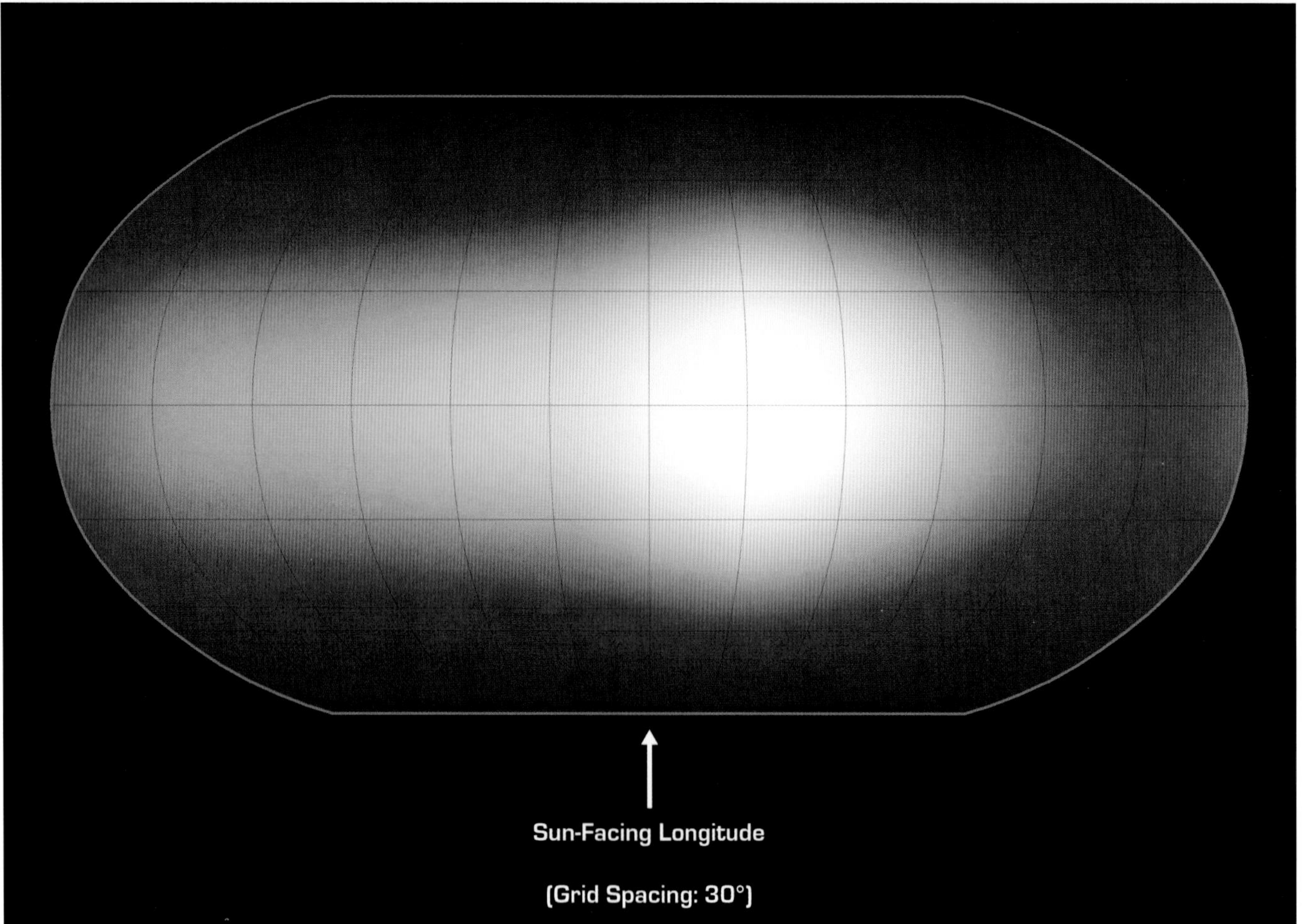
Sun-Facing Longitude
(Grid Spacing: 30°)

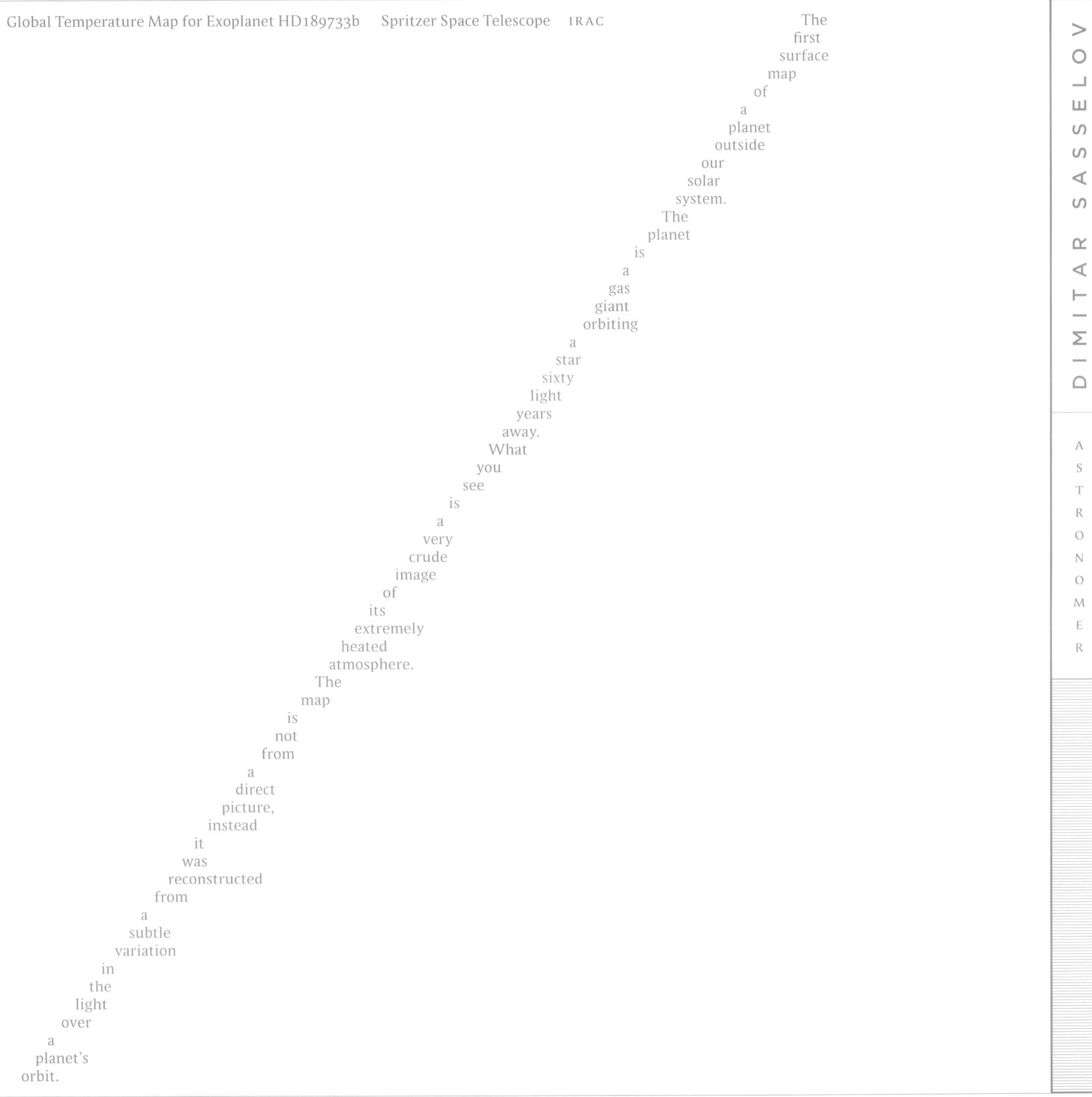

Global Temperature Map for Exoplanet HD189733b
Spritzer Space Telescope
IRAC
The first surface map of a planet outside our solar system. The planet is a gas giant orbiting a star sixty light years away. What you see is a very crude image of its extremely heated atmosphere. The map is not from a direct picture, instead it was reconstructed from a subtle variation in the light over a planet's orbit.

DIMITAR SASSELOV

ASTRONOMER

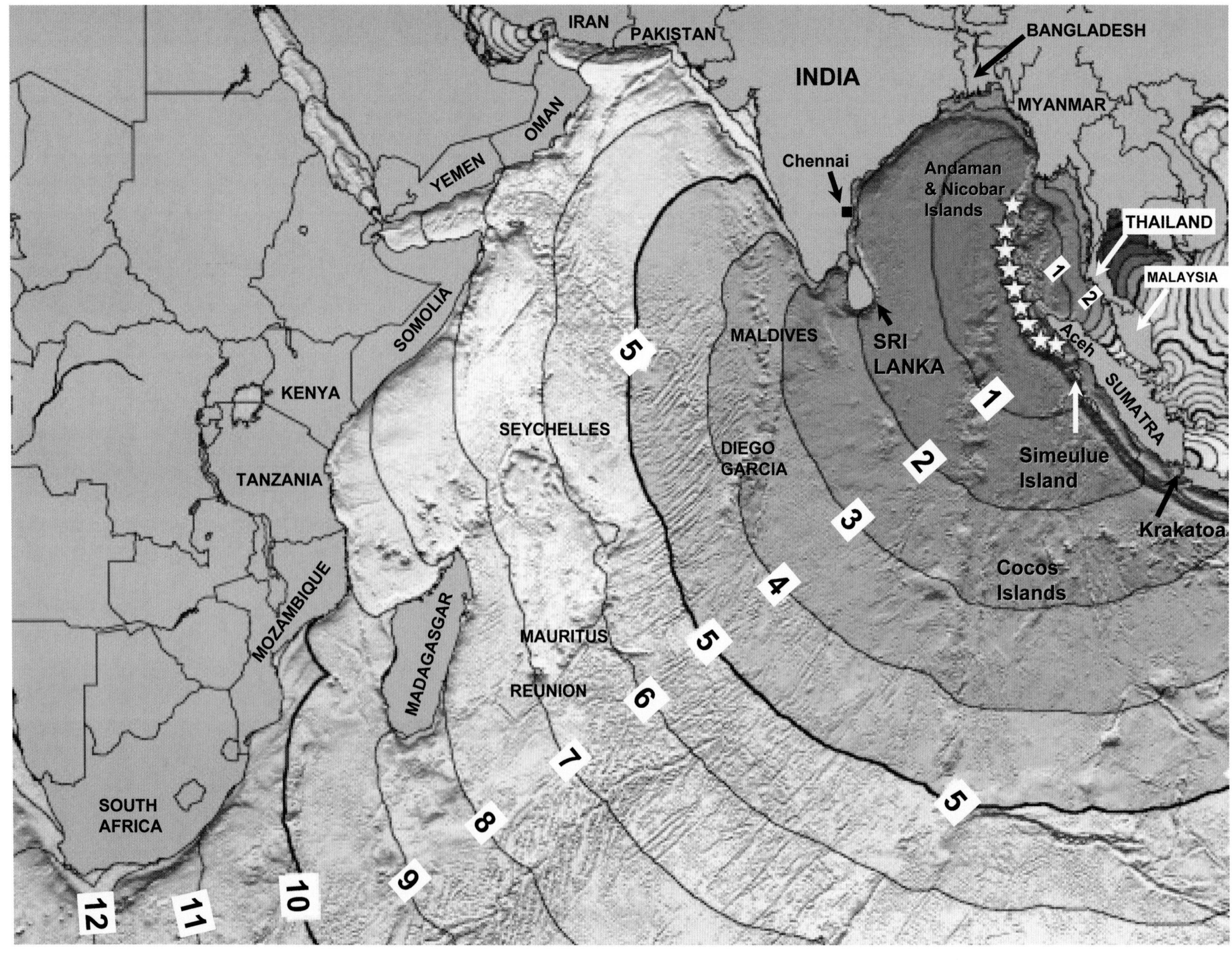
IRAN
PAKISTAN
BANGLADESH
INDIA
MYANMAR
OMAN
YEMEN
Chennai
Andaman & Nicobar Islands
THAILAND
MALAYSIA
SOMOLIA
MALDIVES
SRI LANKA
Aceh
SUMATRA
KENYA
SEYCHELLES
DIEGO GARCIA
Simeulue Island
TANZANIA
Krakatoa
Cocos Islands
MOZAMBIQUE
MADAGASGAR
MAURITUS
REUNION
SOUTH AFRICA
1
2
3
4
5
6
7
8
9
10
11
12

BRUCE PARKER

The first twelve hours of the 2004 Indian Ocean tsunami were caused by a 900-mile long submarine earthquake (indicated by the stars). But it was the first two hours that were most devastating. Only 17 minutes after the earthquake, a 100-foot tsunami bulldozed towns out of existence along the Aceh coast of northern Sumatra, Indonesia. In less than an hour, 240,000 were dead. In less than two hours, smaller but still powerful tsunami waves had killed 7,500 in Thailand, 31,000 in Sri Lanka, and 16,000 in India. Submarine ridges focused the tsunami wave energy like a lens focuses light, eventually guiding them out of the Indian Ocean and up the Atlantic, though now greatly reduced in size. It was that same bathymetric effect that sometimes determined who would live and who would die. More than 8,500 Sri Lankans died in Kalmunai at the shoreward end of a submarine ridge, while eight miles south only 2 died in Oluvil at the shoreward end of a submarine canyon. This is a modified version of a model-produced map from NOAA's National Geophysical Data Center.

EARTH SCIENTIST

NEWTON & HELEN MAYER HARRISON	*The Great Draughtsman*, 2009	Where it can be seen that the world's ocean is a great draughtsman, redrawing the island of Britain by rising its waters, first fifteen metres, then twenty-five, then fifty, then seventy-five, then one hundred metres.
A | R | T | I | S | T | S		

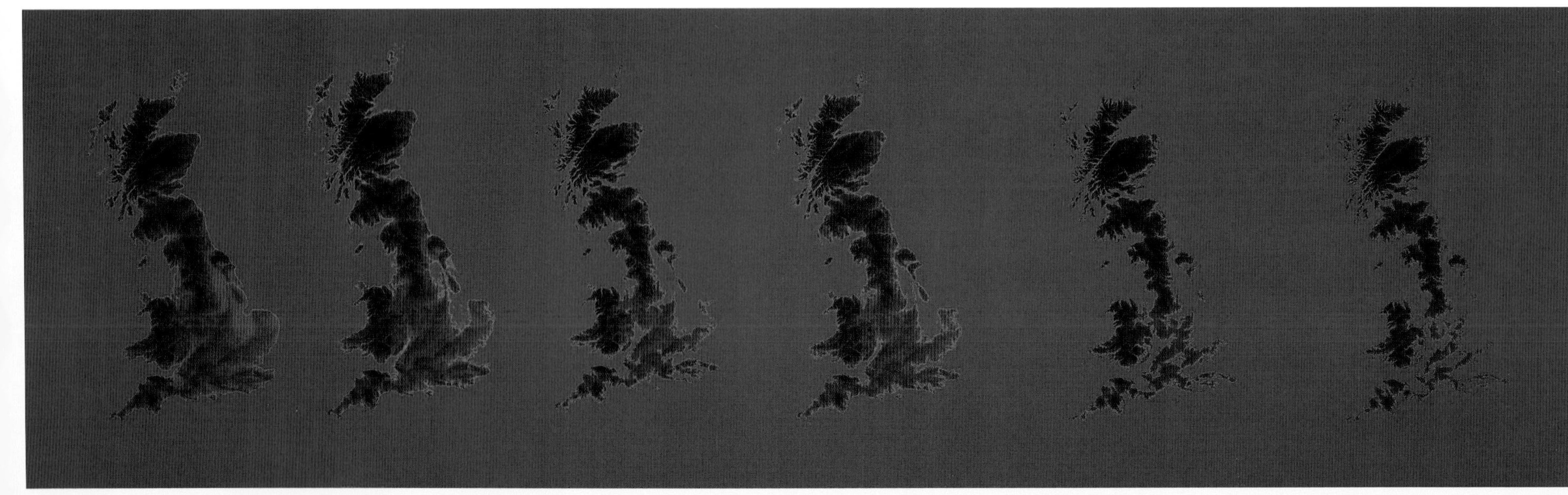

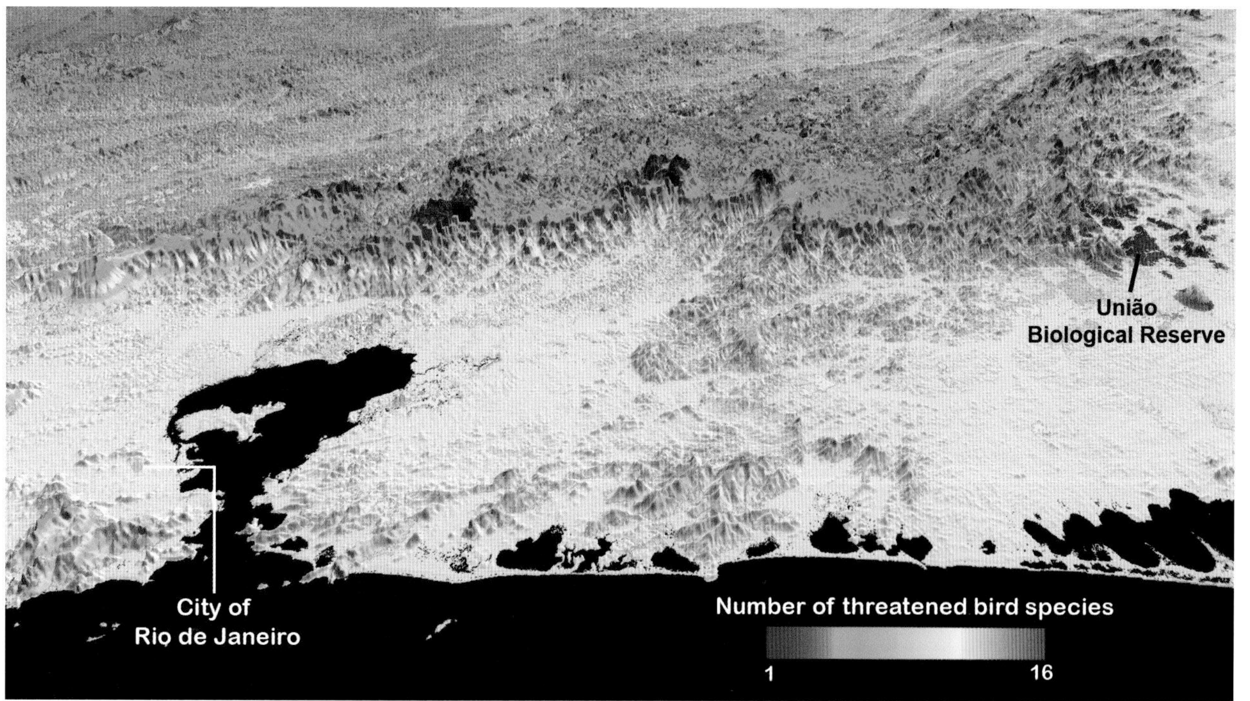

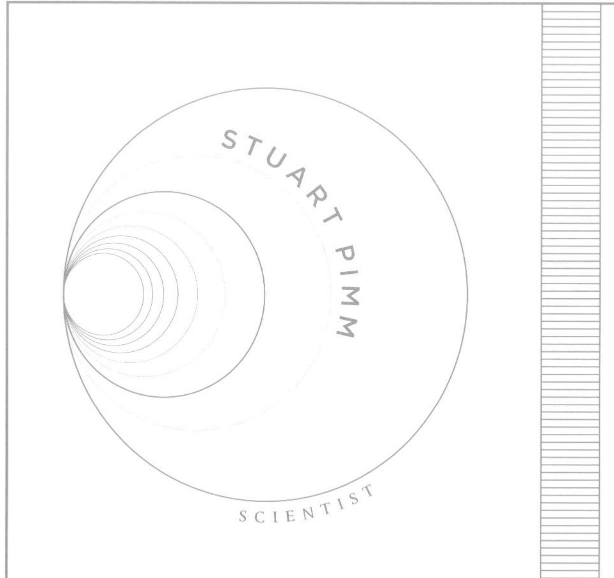

A joint effort with my colleague Dr Clinton Jenkins, this is a map of a portion of south-east Brazil, with the city of Rio de Janeiro at the bottom left. Only areas with substantial remaining 'rainforest' – technically tropical moist forest – are coloured, showing the numbers of threatened species of birds, and are draped over a 3D rendering of elevation. This is a map that immediately conveys where (and what) conservation actions are most needed to save biodiversity. And, indeed, with Brazilian colleagues we have now connected the red 'island' to the rest of the areas with forest restoration.

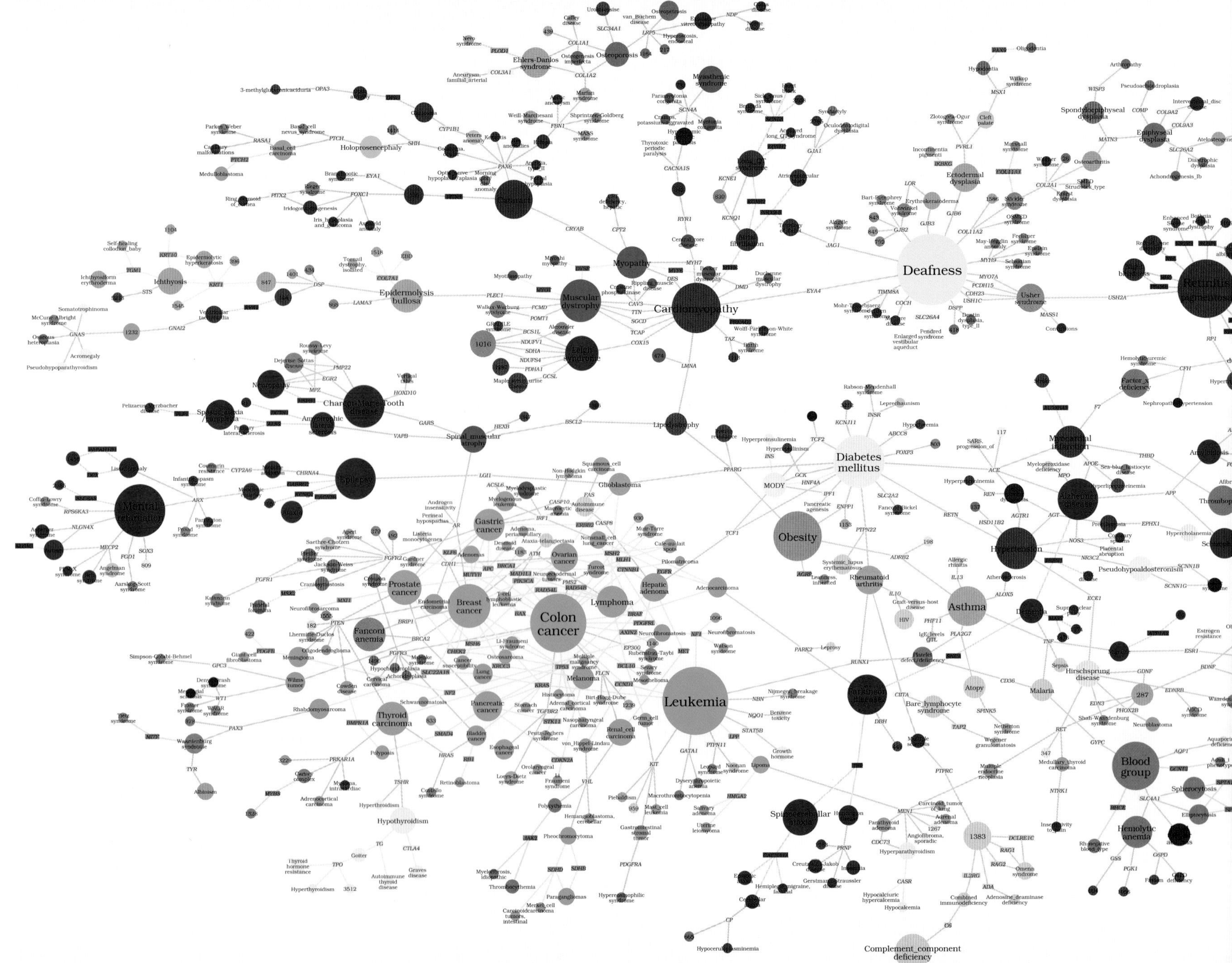

Deafness
Cardiomyopathy
Colon cancer
Leukemia
Diabetes mellitus
Obesity
Breast cancer
Prostate cancer
Gastric cancer
Ovarian cancer
Lymphoma
Thyroid carcinoma
Pancreatic cancer
Fanconi anemia
Asthma
Rheumatoid arthritis
Hypertension
Myocardial infarction
Alzheimer disease
Blood group
Hemolytic anemia
Spherocytosis
Ectodermal dysplasia
Usher syndrome
Retinitis pigmentosa
Epidermolysis bullosa
Ichthyosis
Muscular dystrophy
Myopathy
Leigh syndrome
Charcot-Marie-Tooth disease
Spinal muscular atrophy
Epilepsy
Mental retardation
Lipodystrophy
Osteoporosis
Ehlers-Danlos syndrome
Holoprosencephaly
Cataract
Myasthenic syndrome
Glioblastoma
Melanoma
Lung cancer
Renal cell carcinoma
Hepatic adenoma
Meningioma
Wilms tumor
Hypothyroidism
Pheochromocytoma
Spinocerebellar ataxia
Parkinson disease
Atopy
Malaria
Hirschsprung disease
Complement component deficiency
MODY
Epiphyseal dysplasia
Spondyloepiphyseal dysplasia
Pseudohypoaldosteronism
Factor x deficiency

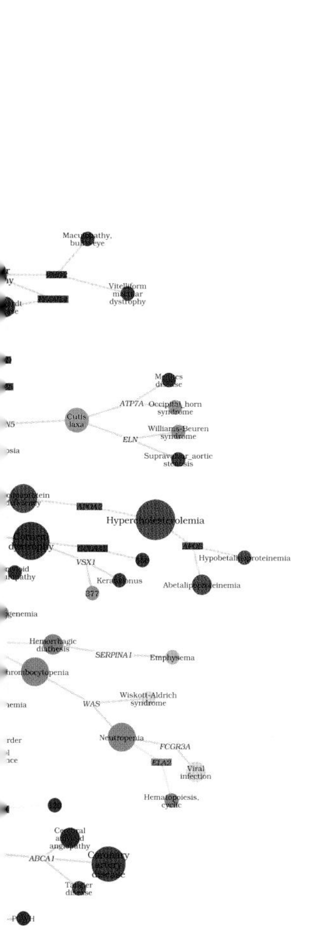
Vitelliform macular dystrophy
Cutis laxa
ATP7A
ELN
Williams-Beuren syndrome
VSX1
Abetalipoproteinemia
SERPINA1
Emphysema
Wiskott-Aldrich syndrome
WAS
Neutropenia
FCGR3A
Viral infection
ABCA1

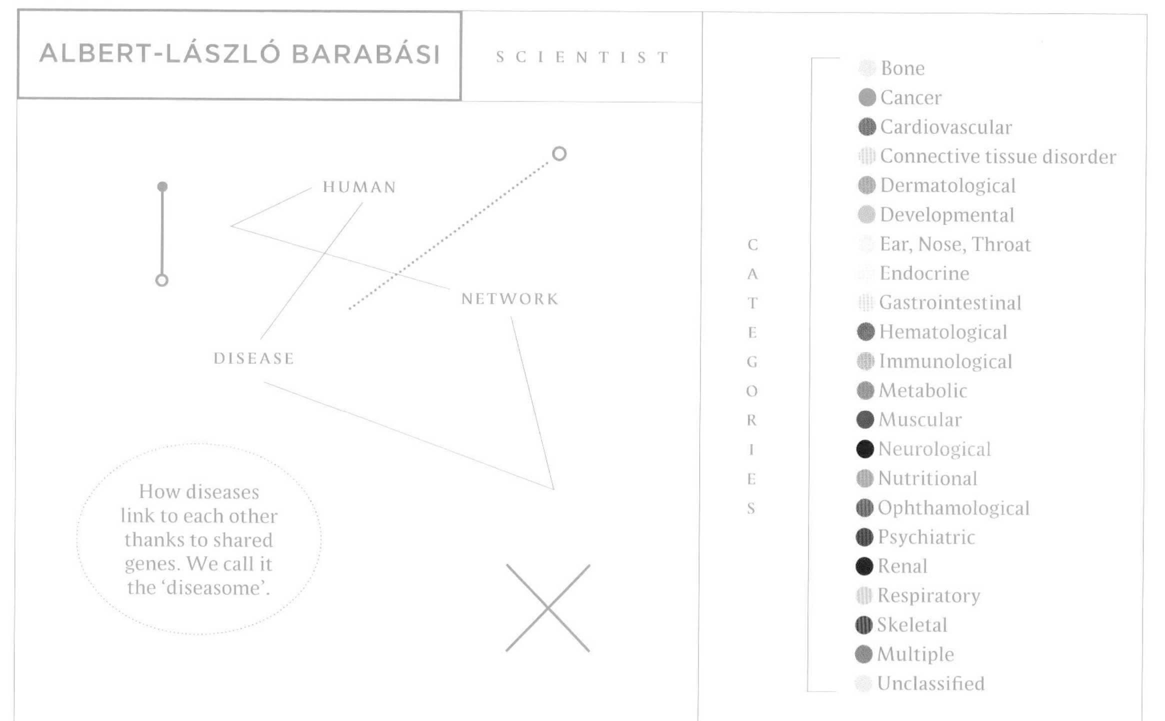
ALBERT-LÁSZLÓ BARABÁSI
SCIENTIST
HUMAN
NETWORK
DISEASE
How diseases link to each other thanks to shared genes. We call it the 'diseasome'.
CATEGORIES
Bone
Cancer
Cardiovascular
Connective tissue disorder
Dermatological
Developmental
Ear, Nose, Throat
Endocrine
Gastrointestinal
Hematological
Immunological
Metabolic
Muscular
Neurological
Nutritional
Ophthamological
Psychiatric
Renal
Respiratory
Skeletal
Multiple
Unclassified

A SCHEMATIC GRAPHIC OF THE BASICS OF HUMAN EVOLUTION (TO BE READ CLOCKWISE)

A reconstruction of *Sabelanthropus tchadensis* is shown at 2 o'clock; it may not actually be the common ancestor species of both chimpanzees (1 o'clock) and modern humans (11 o'clock), but it is currently one of the closest candidates. From this bifurcation point, gracile australipithecines arise (3 o'clock) and from them robust australipithecines (also known as paranthropines, 4 o'clock).

These go extinct, but early genus *Homo* also evolves from the australopiths (5 o'clock: the reconstruction can be read as *H. habilis* or *H. rudolfensis*). Whether *Homo ergaster* (7 o'clock) arises from the habilines or from some as yet unknown line of descent from gracile austropiths is not known for certain. From *H. ergaster* comes *H. erectus* (8 o'clock), which eventually goes extinct, as well as the line that leads to *Homo heidelbergensis* (9 o'clock), which many see as the last common ancestor of Neanderthals (10 o'clock) and moderns.

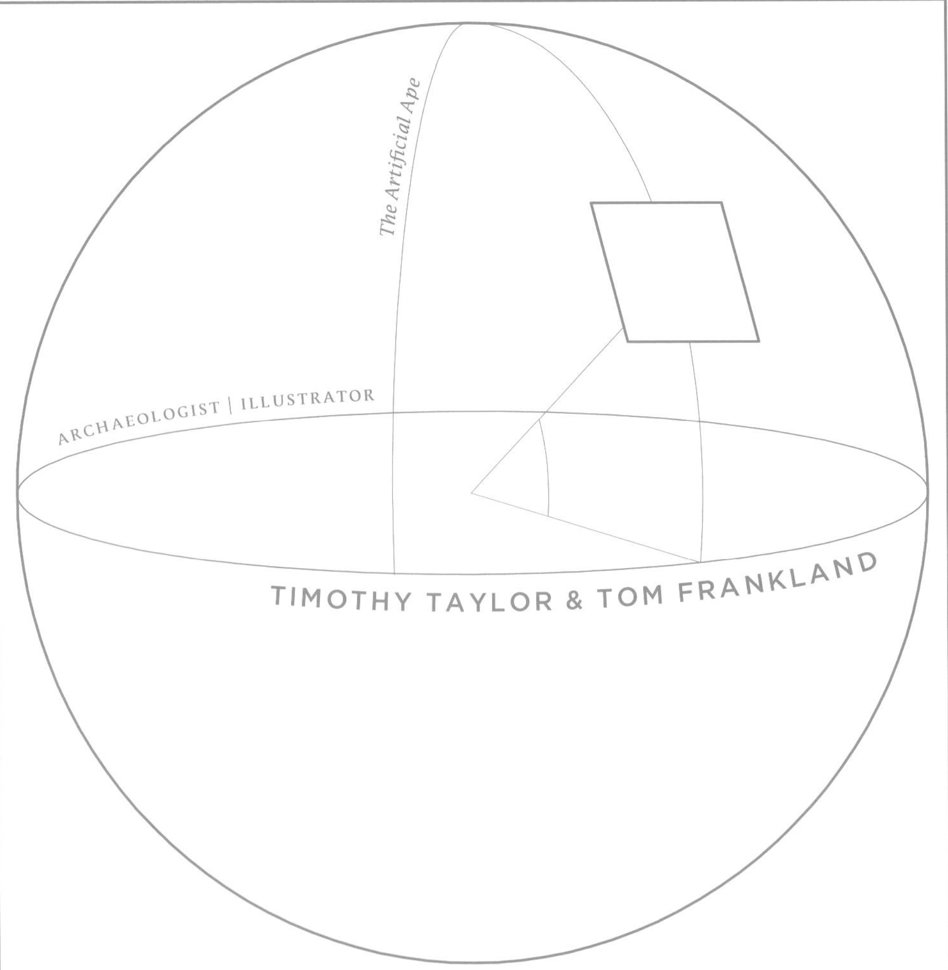

The Artificial Ape
ARCHAEOLOGIST | ILLUSTRATOR
TIMOTHY TAYLOR & TOM FRANKLAND

J. CRAIG VENTER | *Scientist*

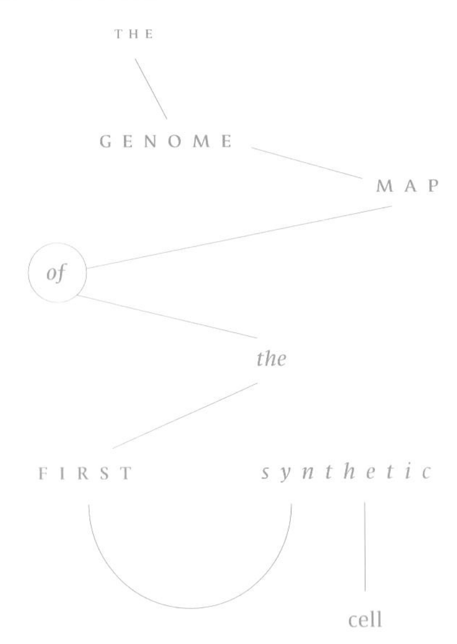

Every component in the cell comes from the synthetic genome. This cell, its lineage is a computer.... It is the first self-replicating species we've had on the planet whose parent is a computer. ¶ We can digitize life, and we generate life from the digital world. Just as the ribosome can convert the analogue message in mRNA into a protein robot, it's becoming standard now in the world of science to convert digital code into protein viruses and cells. Scientists send digital code to each other instead of sending genes or proteins. There are several companies around the world that make their living by synthesizing genes for scientific labs. It's faster and cheaper to synthesize a gene than it is to clone it, or even to get it by Federal Express.

Mycoplasma mycoides JCVI-syn1.0

Gibson, D. G., J. I. Glass, C. Lartigue, V. N. Noskov, R.-Y. Chuang, M. A. Algire, G. A. Benders, M. G. Montague, L. Ma, M. M. Moodie, C. Merryman, S. Vashee, R. Krishnakumar, N. Assad-Garcia, C. Andrews-Pfannkoch, E. A. Denisova, L. Young, Z.-Q. Qi, T. H. Segall-Shapiro, C. H. Calvey, P. P. Parmar, C. A. Hutchison III, H. O. Smith, and J. C. Venter. 2010. Creation of a bacterial cell controlled by a chemically synthesized genome. Science, Published online May 20 2010.

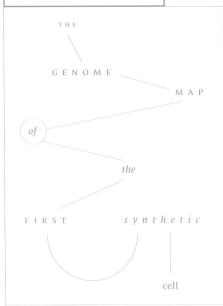

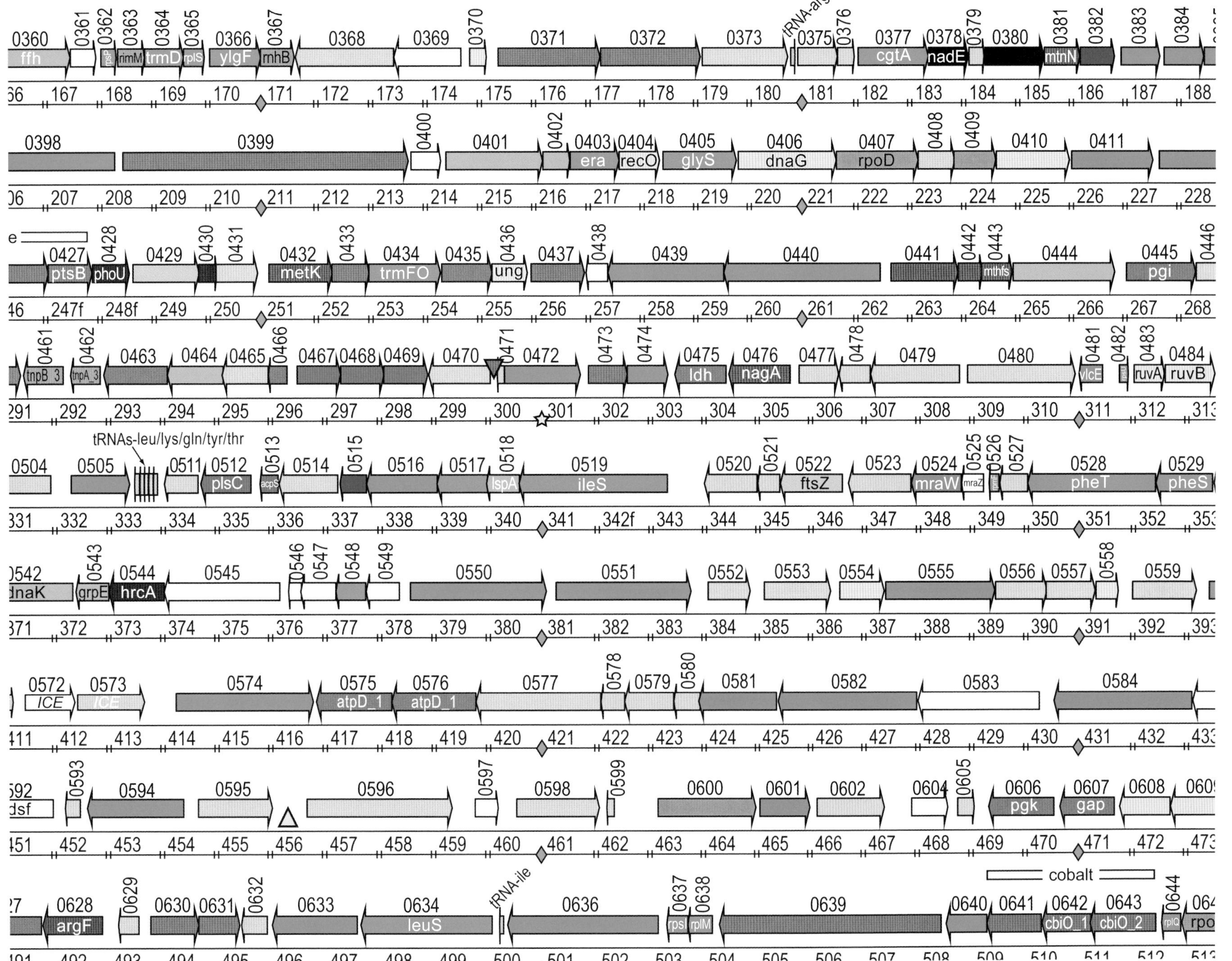

0360 0361 0362 0363 0364 0365 0366 0367 0368 0369 0370 0371 0372 0373 tRNA-arg 0375 0376 0377 0378 0379 0380 0381 0382 0383 0384
ffh rpsP rimM trmD rplS ylgF rnhB cgtA nadE mtnN
167 168 169 170 171 172 173 174 175 176 177 178 179 180 181 182 183 184 185 186 187 188
0398 0399 0400 0401 0402 0403 0404 0405 0406 0407 0408 0409 0410 0411
era recO glyS dnaG rpoD
207 208 209 210 211 212 213 214 215 216 217 218 219 220 221 222 223 224 225 226 227 228
0427 0428 0429 0430 0431 0432 0433 0434 0435 0436 0437 0438 0439 0440 0441 0442 0443 0444 0445 0446
ptsB phoU metK trmFO ung mthfs pgi
247f 248f 249 250 251 252 253 254 255 256 257 258 259 260 261 262 263 264 265 266 267 268
0461 0462 0463 0464 0465 0466 0467 0468 0469 0470 0471 0472 0473 0474 0475 0476 0477 0478 0479 0480 0481 0482 0483 0484
tnpB_3 tnpA_3 ldh nagA ylcE ruvA ruvB
291 292 293 294 295 296 297 298 299 300 301 302 303 304 305 306 307 308 309 310 311 312
tRNAs-leu/lys/gln/tyr/thr
0504 0505 0511 0512 0513 0514 0515 0516 0517 0518 0519 0520 0521 0522 0523 0524 0525 0526 0527 0528 0529
plsC acpS lspA ileS ftsZ mraW mraZ pheT pheS
331 332 333 334 335 336 337 338 339 340 341 342f 343 344 345 346 347 348 349 350 351 352
0542 0543 0544 0545 0546 0547 0548 0549 0550 0551 0552 0553 0554 0555 0556 0557 0558 0559
dnaK grpE hrcA
371 372 373 374 375 376 377 378 379 380 381 382 383 384 385 386 387 388 389 390 391 392
0572 0573 0574 0575 0576 0577 0578 0579 0580 0581 0582 0583 0584
ICE ICE atpD_1 atpD_1
411 412 413 414 415 416 417 418 419 420 421 422 423 424 425 426 427 428 429 430 431 432
0593 0594 0595 0596 0597 0598 0599 0600 0601 0602 0604 0605 0606 0607 0608
dsf pgk gap
451 452 453 454 455 456 457 458 459 460 461 462 463 464 465 466 467 468 469 470 471 472
cobalt
0628 0629 0630 0631 0632 0633 0634 tRNA-ile 0636 0637 0638 0639 0640 0641 0642 0643 0644
argF leuS rpsI rplM cbiO_1 cbiO_2 rplQ

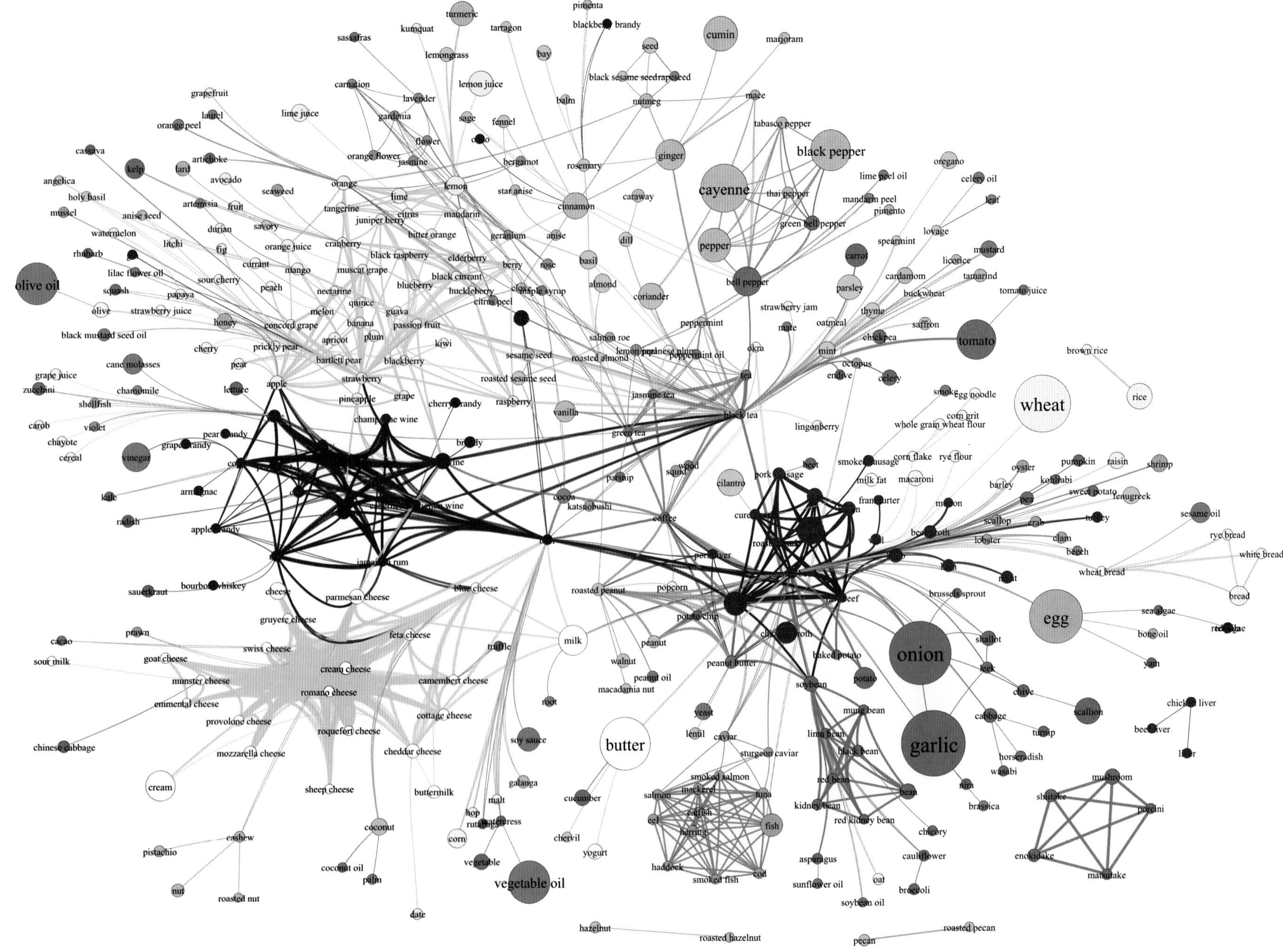
pimenta
blackberry brandy
turmeric
kumquat
tarragon
sassafras
cumin
marjoram
seed
lemongrass
bay
black sesame seed
rapeseed
lemon juice
carnation
grapefruit
lavender
balm
nutmeg
mace
laurel
lime juice
gardenia
sage
fennel
tabasco pepper
orange peel
flower
black pepper
cassava
artichoke
orange flower
jasmine
bergamot
rosemary
ginger
oregano
kelp
lard
avocado
orange
lime peel oil
celery oil
angelica
lemon
cayenne
holy basil
seaweed
star anise
caraway
thai pepper
artemisia
fruit
lime
mandarin peel
leaf
mussel
anise seed
tangerine
citrus
mandarin
cinnamon
pimento
juniper berry
durian
savory
green bell pepper
lovage
watermelon
bitter orange
geranium
anise
dill
litchi
orange juice
cranberry
pepper
spearmint
mustard
rhubarb
fig
black raspberry
elderberry
carrot
lilac flower oil
currant
mango
muscat grape
berry
rose
basil
licorice
black currant
cardamom
tamarind
sour cherry
olive oil
squash
papaya
peach
nectarine
blueberry
huckleberry
maple syrup
almond
bell pepper
coriander
parsley
buckwheat
tomato juice
quince
citrus peel
olive
strawberry juice
melon
guava
strawberry jam
thyme
honey
concord grape
banana
passion fruit
mate
peppermint
oatmeal
saffron
black mustard seed oil
apricot
plum
salmon roe
chickpea
tomato
kiwi
cherry
prickly pear
mint
brown rice
lemon peel
japanese plum
peppermint oil
okra
sesame seed
roasted almond
pear
bartlett pear
blackberry
octopus
grape juice
endive
tea
celery
roasted sesame seed
apple
strawberry
lettuce
zucchini
chamomile
pineapple
jasmine tea
wheat
rice
smoke
egg noodle
shellfish
grape
cherry brandy
raspberry
vanilla
corn grit
black tea
carob
violet
champagne wine
whole grain wheat flour
green tea
lingonberry
chayote
pear brandy
grape brandy
brandy
cereal
vinegar
corn flake
rye flour
smoked sausage
beet
wood
pumpkin
raisin
shrimp
oyster
squid
milk fat
macaroni
kohlrabi
parsnip
pork sausage
barley
cilantro
sweet potato
fenugreek
kale
armagnac
cocoa
katsuobushi
frankfurter
pea
melon
sesame oil
coffee
scallop
turkey
cured pork
rye bread
apple brandy
crab
lobster
clam
white bread
beef broth
radish
pork liver
beech
jamaican rum
wheat bread
bourbon whiskey
roasted peanut
popcorn
sauerkraut
cheese
blue cheese
brussels sprout
beef
parmesan cheese
bread
gruyere cheese
potato chip
sea algae
egg
prawn
feta cheese
cacao
bone oil
swiss cheese
milk
peanut
shallot
truffle
onion
goat cheese
walnut
sour milk
cream cheese
peanut butter
baked potato
yam
leek
munster cheese
peanut oil
camembert cheese
chive
macadamia nut
potato
soybean
romano cheese
chicken liver
emmental cheese
root
scallion
yeast
mung bean
beef liver
provolone cheese
cottage cheese
cabbage
lentil
roquefort cheese
caviar
lima bean
turnip
chinese cabbage
soy sauce
butter
black bean
sturgeon caviar
garlic
liver
mozzarella cheese
cheddar cheese
horseradish
wasabi
galanga
smoked salmon
red bean
mushroom
cream
sheep cheese
salmon
mackerel
tuna
nira
buttermilk
malt
bean
brassica
cucumber
kidney bean
shiitake
porcini
catfish
hop
rutabaga
watercress
coconut
eel
fish
red kidney bean
chicory
herring
cashew
chervil
corn
pistachio
yogurt
asparagus
cauliflower
enokidake
vegetable
haddock
coconut oil
vegetable oil
cod
matsutake
oat
smoked fish
sunflower oil
palm
nut
broccoli
roasted nut
soybean oil
date
hazelnut
roasted pecan
roasted hazelnut
pecan

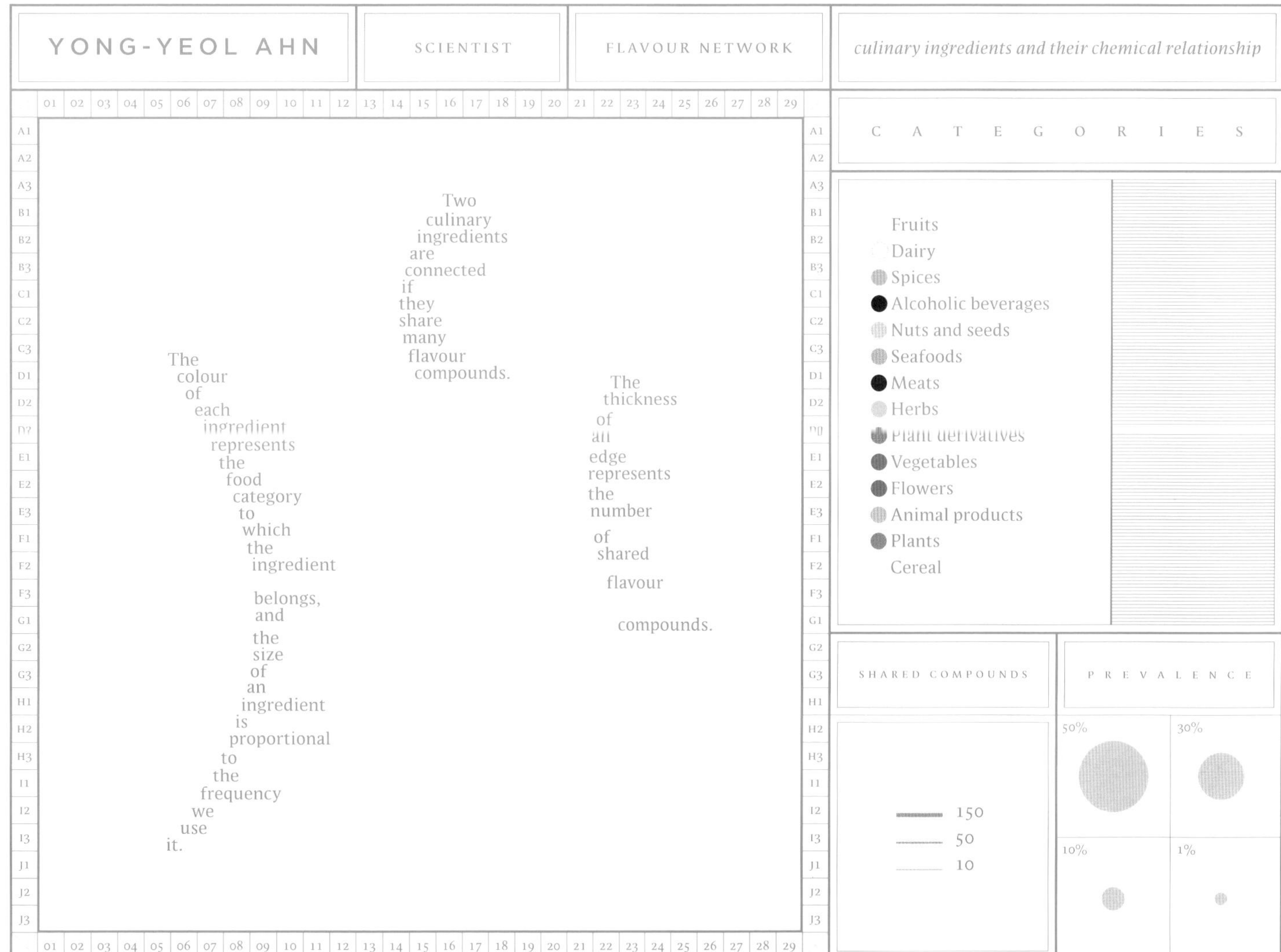
YONG-YEOL AHN
SCIENTIST
FLAVOUR NETWORK
culinary ingredients and their chemical relationship
Two culinary ingredients are connected if they share many flavour compounds.
The colour of each ingredient represents the food category to which the ingredient belongs, and the size of an ingredient is proportional to the frequency we use it.
The thickness of an edge represents the number of shared flavour compounds.
CATEGORIES
Fruits
Dairy
Spices
Alcoholic beverages
Nuts and seeds
Seafoods
Meats
Herbs
Plant derivatives
Vegetables
Flowers
Animal products
Plants
Cereal
SHARED COMPOUNDS
150
50
10
PREVALENCE
50%
30%
10%
1%

Cinna
Gaius Julius Caesar
Aurelia
Cornelia
Julius Caesar
Cleopatra
Julia
Marcus Atius Balbus
Pompey
Julia
Caesarion
Gaius Octavius
Atia
Lucius Marcus Philippus
Augustus
Scribonia
Livia
Tiberius Claudius Nero
Mark Antony
Octavia
Gaius Claudius Marcellus
Marcia
Cato
Agrippa
Julia
Tiberius
Nero Claudius Drusus
Antonia
Marcus Claudius Marcellus
Agrippina
Germanicus
Claudius
Gnaeus Domitius Ahenobarbus
Agrippina
Caligula
Octavia
Nero

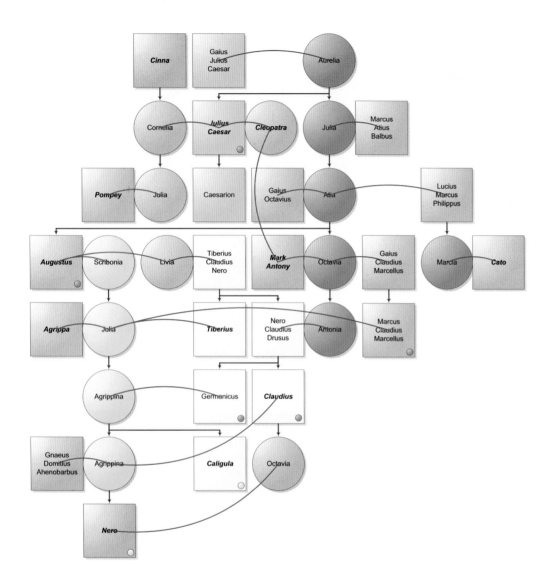

ALVY RAY SMITH

COMPUTER SCIENTIST

DNA of the Early Roman Emperors and Famous Associates

Squares are males. Disks are females. Blue arrows show direction of descent. Horizontal blue bars bind siblings. Red curves join 'spouses' – that is, procreative couples. In cases of multiple spouses, the child goes with the most tightly bound spouse. Yellow squares represent one strain of Y-chromosome DNA (YDNA) passed down via males only; orange, another. Magenta disks represent one strain of mitochondrial DNA (mtDNA) passed down via females only; green, another. Small disks within squares are males carrying the designated mtDNA, who could not, being male, pass it on. The surprise is the predominance of the mtDNA lines over the YDNA – that is, of the feminine connections over the masculine.

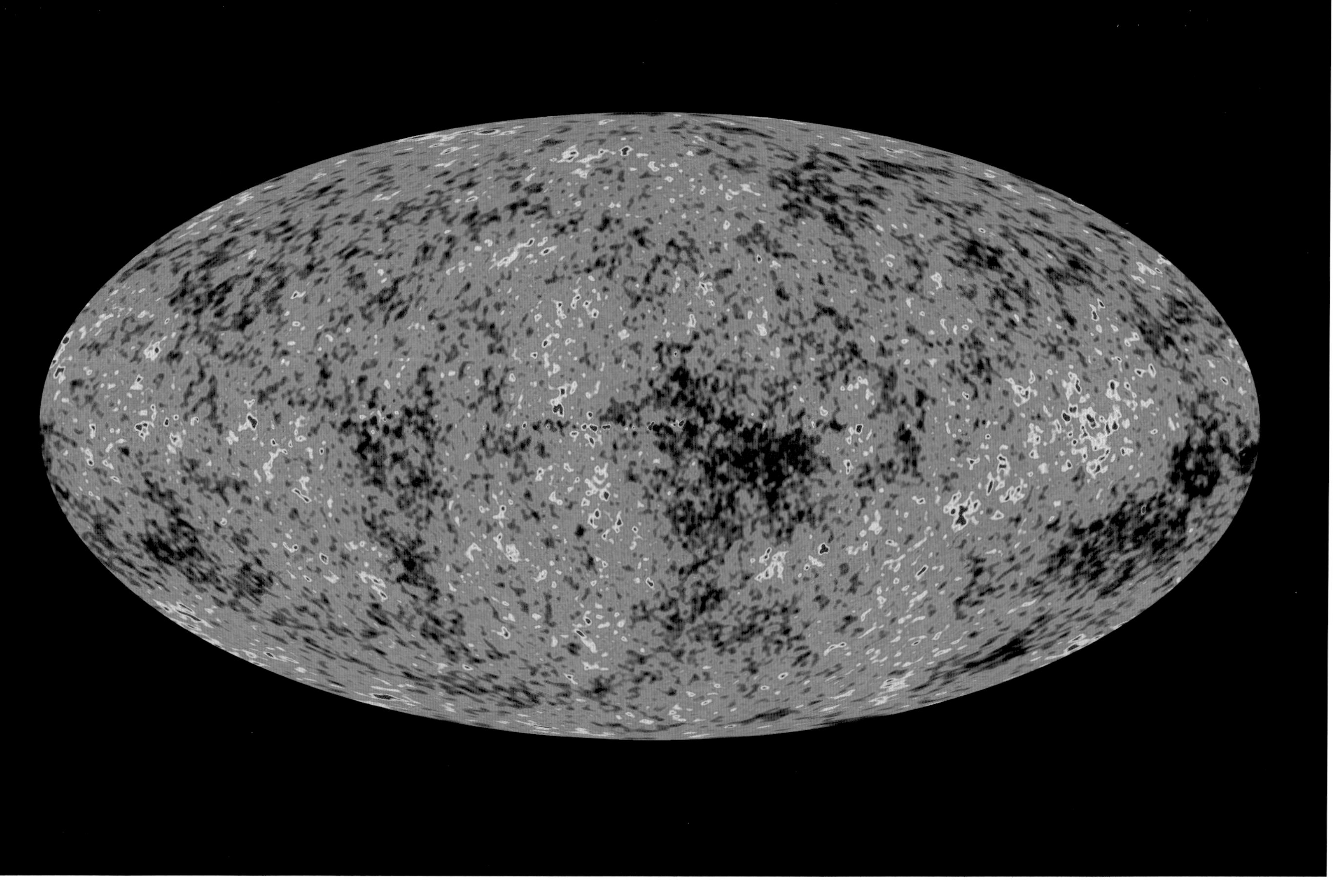

GINO SEGRE

scientist

A temperature map of the Universe 400,000 years after the Big Bang. This was the end of thermal equilibrium and the beginning of all we see now.

CHAPTER FOUR
Invented Worlds
DAVID ADJAYE
JOHN BALDESSARI
MARGARITA GLUZBERG
ETEL ADNAN
SEAN CARROLL
YONA FRIEDMAN
MATTHEW BARNEY
MARIANA CASTILLO DEBALL & AMALIA PICA
QIU ZHIJIE
JOOST GROOTENS
ROSA BARBA
SUSAN HILLER
INTERNATIONAL NECRONAUTICAL SOCIETY
SANAA

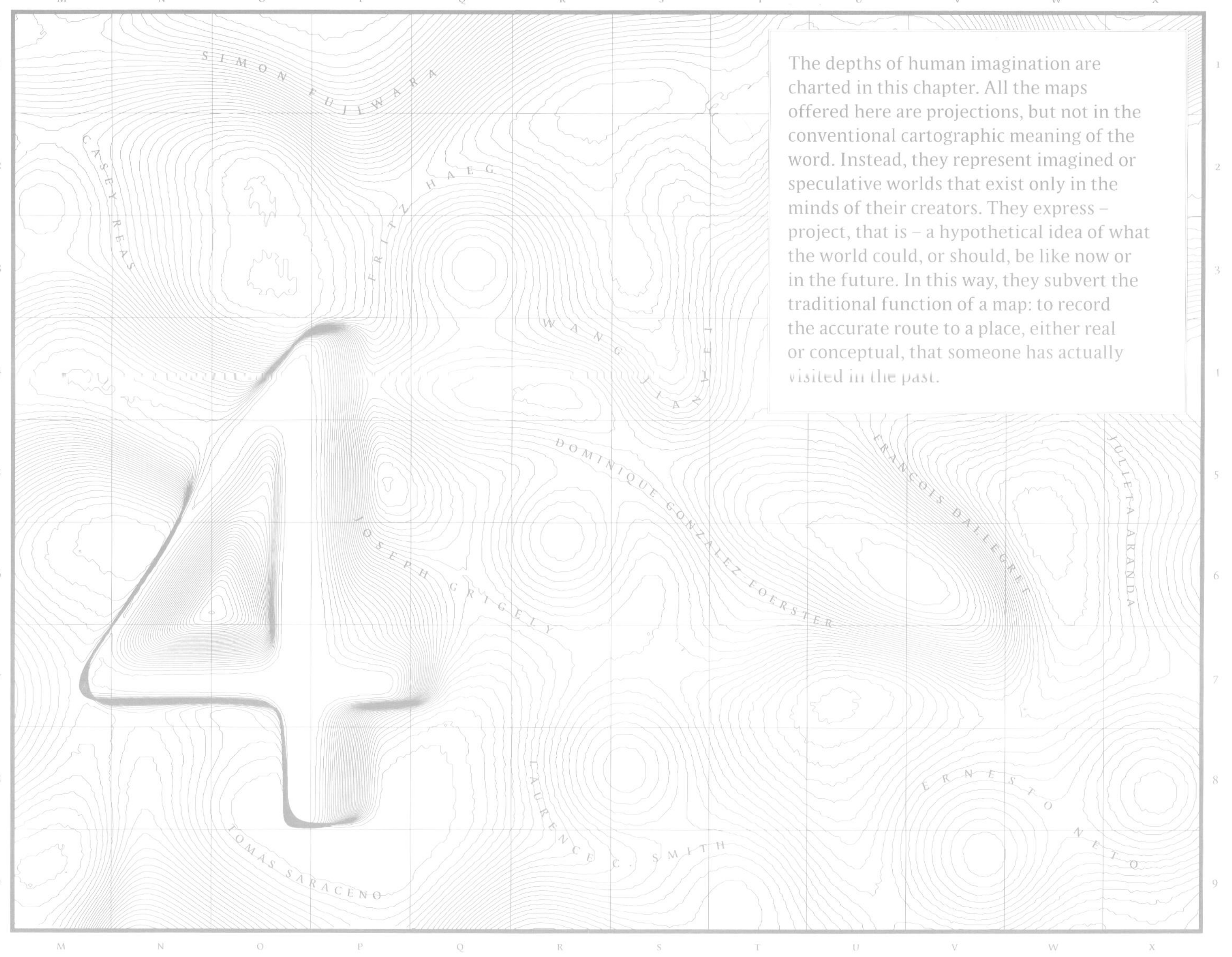

The depths of human imagination are charted in this chapter. All the maps offered here are projections, but not in the conventional cartographic meaning of the word. Instead, they represent imagined or speculative worlds that exist only in the minds of their creators. They express – project, that is – a hypothetical idea of what the world could, or should, be like now or in the future. In this way, they subvert the traditional function of a map: to record the accurate route to a place, either real or conceptual, that someone has actually visited in the past.

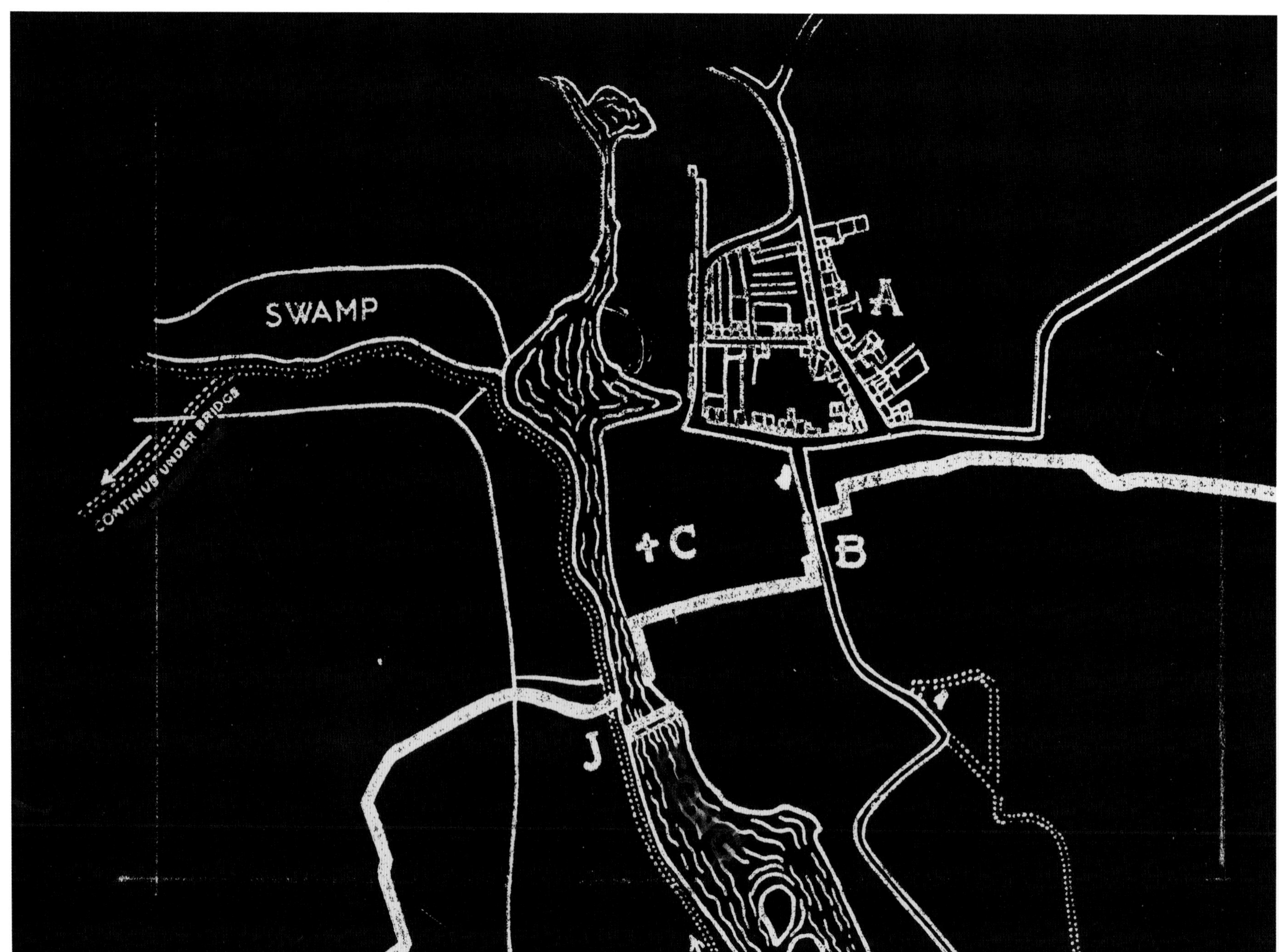

SWAMP
A
CONTINUE UNDER BRIDGE
C
B
J

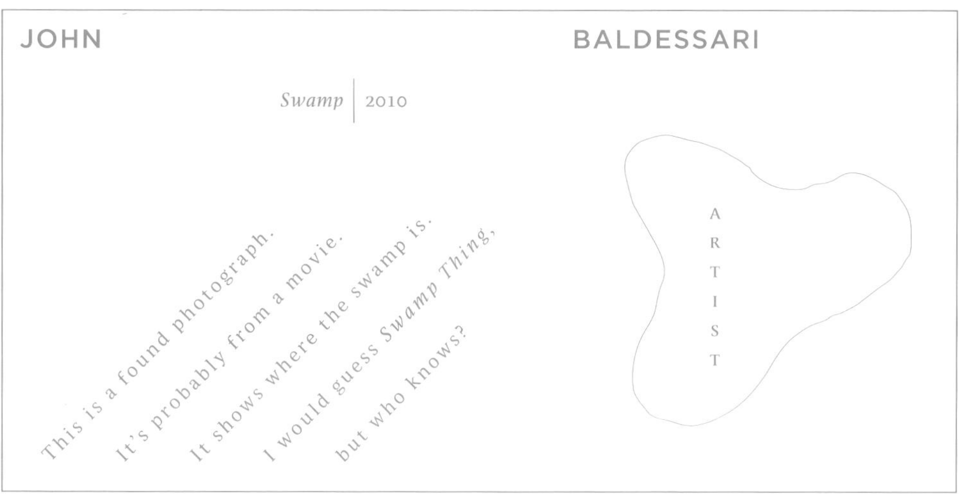
JOHN
BALDESSARI
Swamp | 2010
This is a found photograph.
It's probably from a movie.
It shows where the swamp is.
I would guess Swamp Thing,
but who knows?
ARTIST

YONA FRIEDMAN

A | R | T | I | S | T

A Map to the Future, 2010

06-JUI-09 08:22
33147346911
PAGE: 2
A MAP TO THE FUTURE
YOU ARE HERE
PRESENT
THE FOG OF THE FUTURE
THE FOG OF THE PAST
HISTORY DOES NOT KNOW THE STRAIGHT LINE

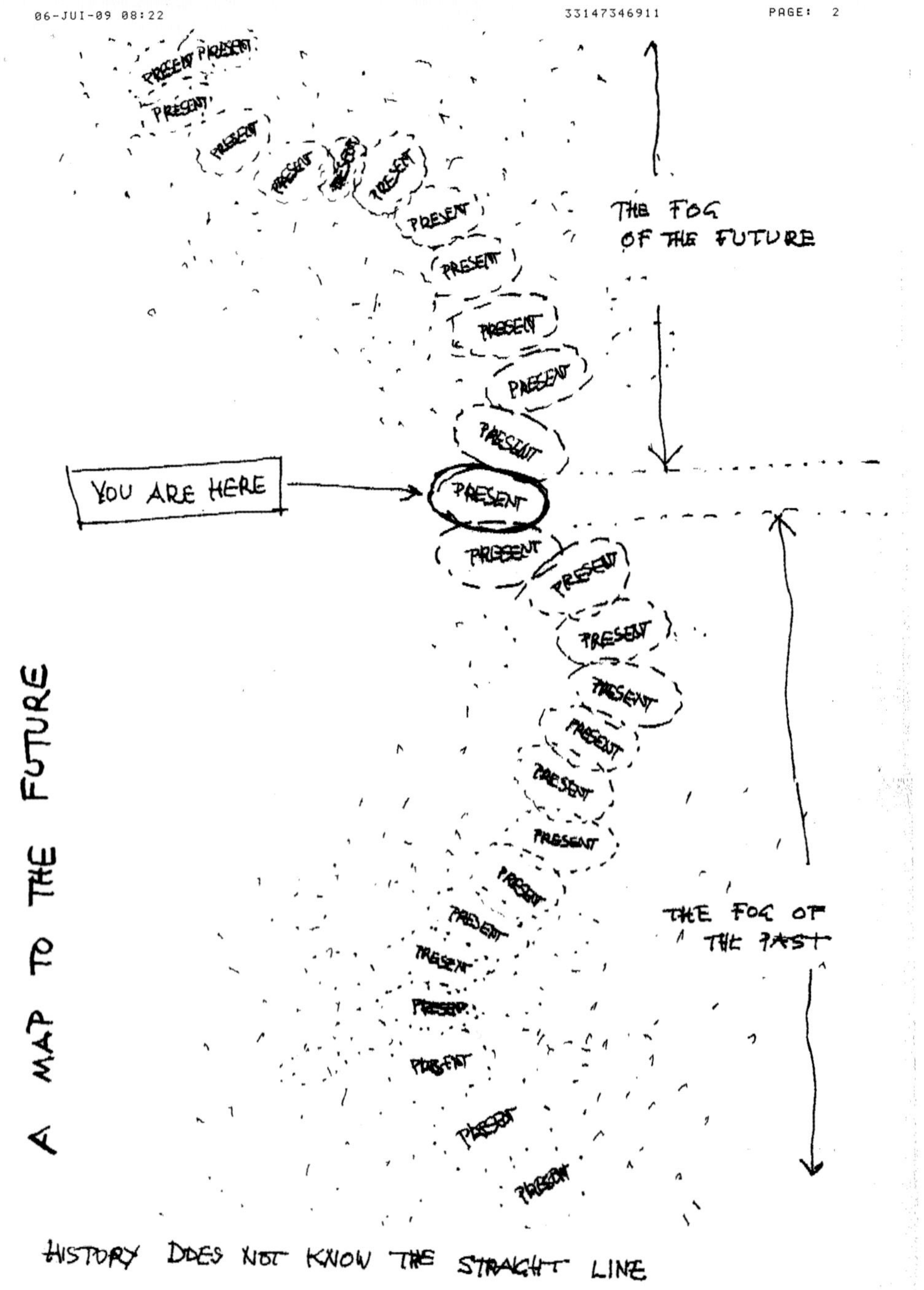

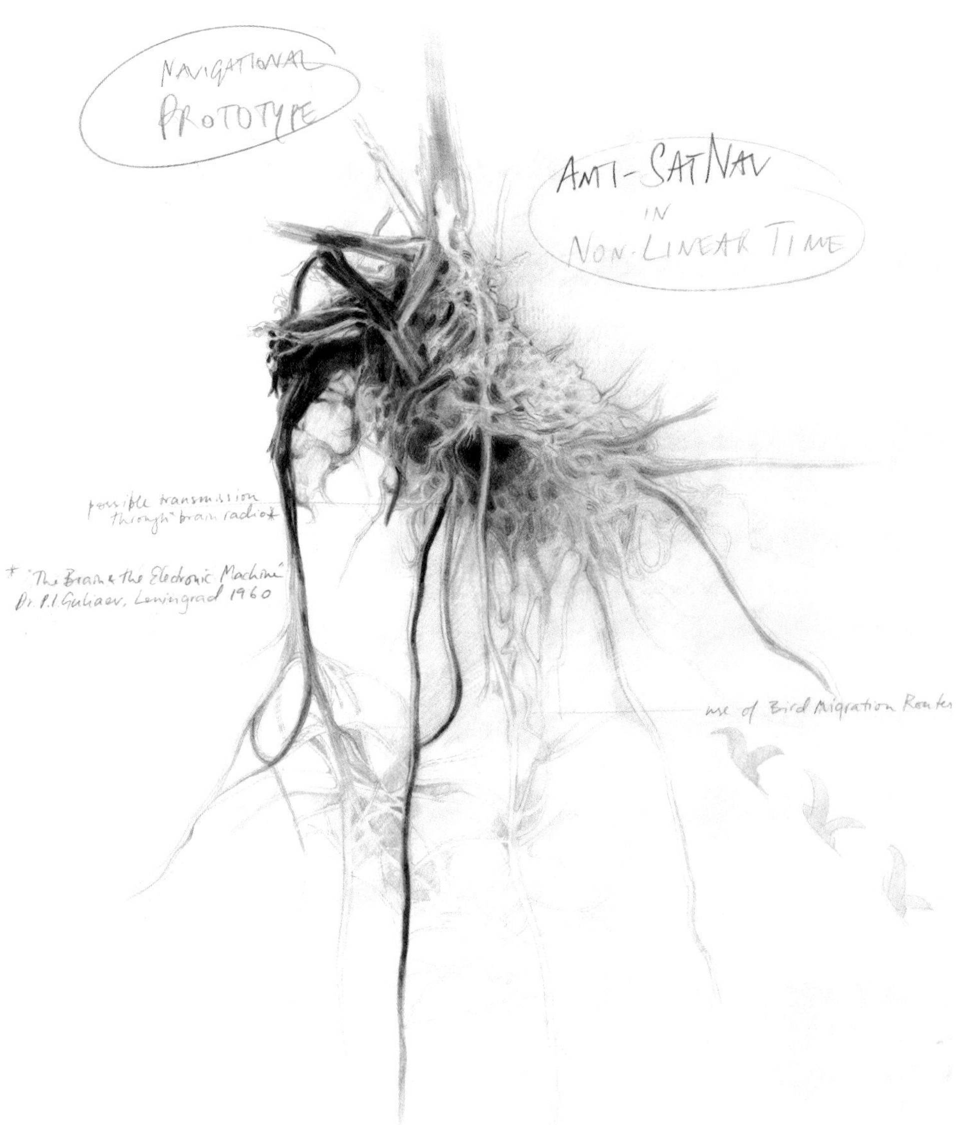

A—R—T—I—S—T

MARGARITA GLUZBERG

A Rhizomatic Navigational Device for the 21st Century, 2012

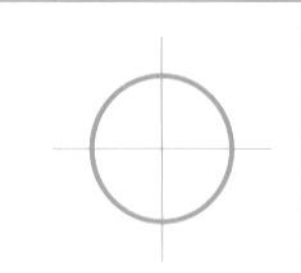

SIMON FUJIWARA

ARTIST

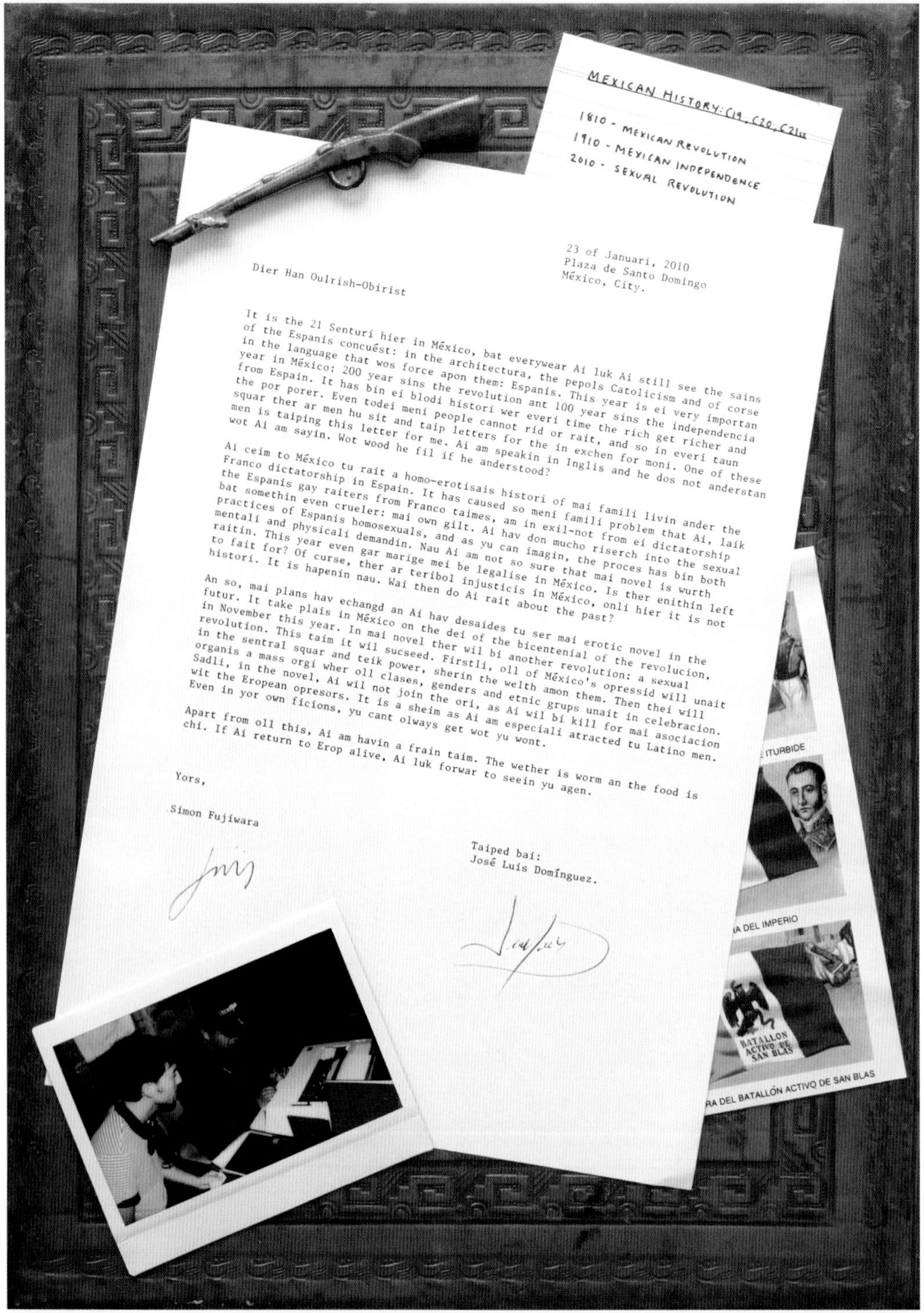

MEXICAN HISTORY: C19, C20, C21st

1810 - MEXICAN REVOLUTION
1910 - MEXICAN INDEPENDENCE
2010 - SEXUAL REVOLUTION

23 of Januari, 2010
Plaza de Santo Domingo
México, City.

Dier Han Oulrish-Obirist

It is the 21 Senturi hier in México, bat everywear Ai luk Ai still see the sains of the Espanis concuést: in the architectura, the pepols Catolicism and of corse in the language that wos force apon them: Espanis. This year is ei very importan year in México: 200 year sins the revolution ant 100 year sins the independencia from Espain. It has bin ei blodi histori wer everi time the rich get richer and the por porer. Even todei meni people cannot rid or rait, and so in everi taun squar ther ar men hu sit and taip letters for the in exchen for moni. One of these men is taiping this letter for me. Ai am speakin in Inglis and he dos not anderstan wot Ai am sayin. Wot wood he fil if he anderstood?

Ai ceim to México tu rait a homo-erotisais histori of mai famili livin ander the Franco dictatorship in Espain. It has caused so meni famili problem that Ai, laik the Espanis gay raiters from Franco taimes, am in exil-not from ei dictatorship bat somethin even crueler: mai own gilt. Ai hav don mucho riserch into the sexual practices of Espanis homosexuals, and as yu can imagin, the proces has bin both mentali and physicali demandin. Nau Ai am not so sure that mai novel is wurth raitin. This year even gar marige mei be legalise in México. Is ther enithin left to fait for? Of curse, ther ar teribol injusticis in México, onli hier it is not histori. It is hapenin nau. Wai then do Ai rait about the past?

An so, mai plans hav echangd an Ai hav desaides tu ser mai erotic novel in the futur. It take plais in México on the dei of the bicentenial of the revolucion, in November this year. In mai novel ther wil bi another revolution: a sexual revolution. This taim it wil sucseed. Firstli, oll of México's opressid will unait in the sentral squar and teik power, sherin the welth amon them. Then thei will organis a mass orgi wher oll clases, genders and etnic grups unait in celebracion. Sadli, in the novel, Ai wil not join the ori, as Ai wil bi kill for mai asociacion wit the Eropean opresors. It is a sheim as Ai am especiali atracted tu Latino men. Even in yor own ficions, yu cant olways get wot yu wont.

Apart from oll this, Ai am havin a frain taim. The wether is worm an the food is chi. If Ai return to Erop alive, Ai luk forwar to seein yu agen.

Yors,

Simon Fujiwara

Taiped bai:
José Luis Domínguez.

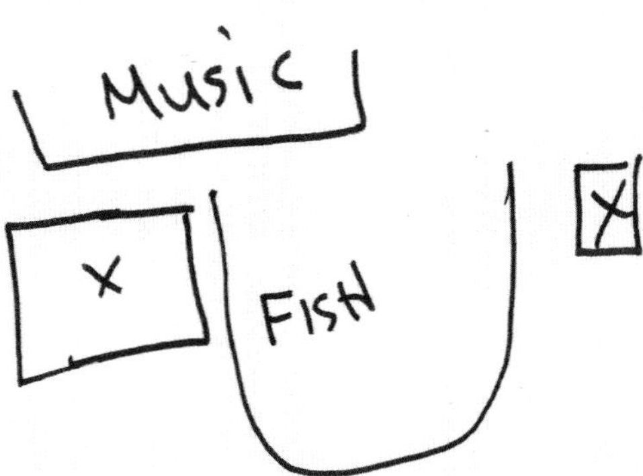

Joseph Grigely

ARTIST

Untitled Conversation

2010

Often, people will stop me and ask for directions, and sometimes I will do the same. An advantage in being deaf is that I usually have at hand paper and a pen. Everyday maps of everyday places can get pretty complicated when you draw them in the air. But when you draw them on paper, everything has a way of resolving itself into startling clarity. Usually, anyway.

LAURENCE C. SMITH

Earth Scientist

These maps illustrate my vision of 'the New North' – eight countries and surrounding seas in the planet's northern quarter of latitude – that will enter a period of rising biological productivity and global strategic value in the twenty-first century. The New North will emerge as a new geographic and economic region alongside the more familiar global North ('core') and global South ('periphery') in the next few decades. The first map shows 'the northern rim' as viewed from North America, and includes population density, human infrastructure, anticipated resource deposits, and a quiltwork of overlapping political claims to the Arctic Ocean seafloor. The second map illustrates the onslaught of shipping that invades the Arctic each summer, as the seasonal sea ice retreats. In the twenty-first century, with sea ice expected to disappear completely in summer, such human activity will likely intensify.

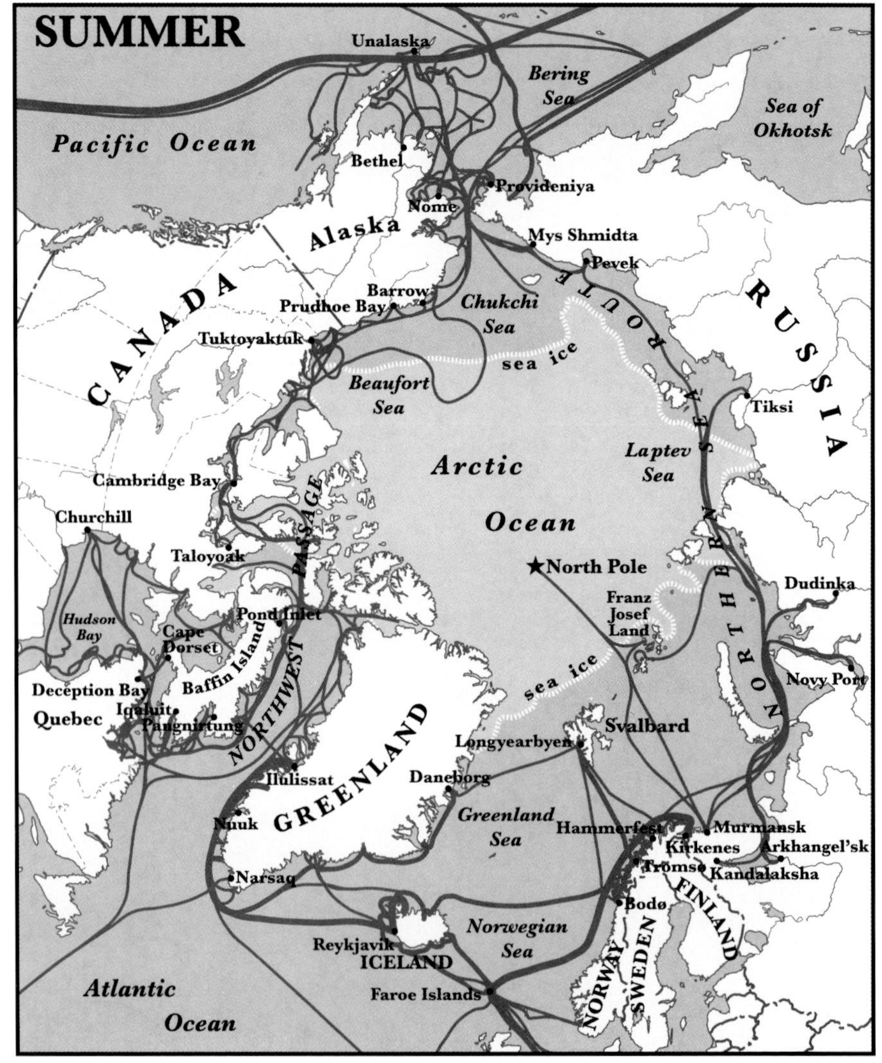

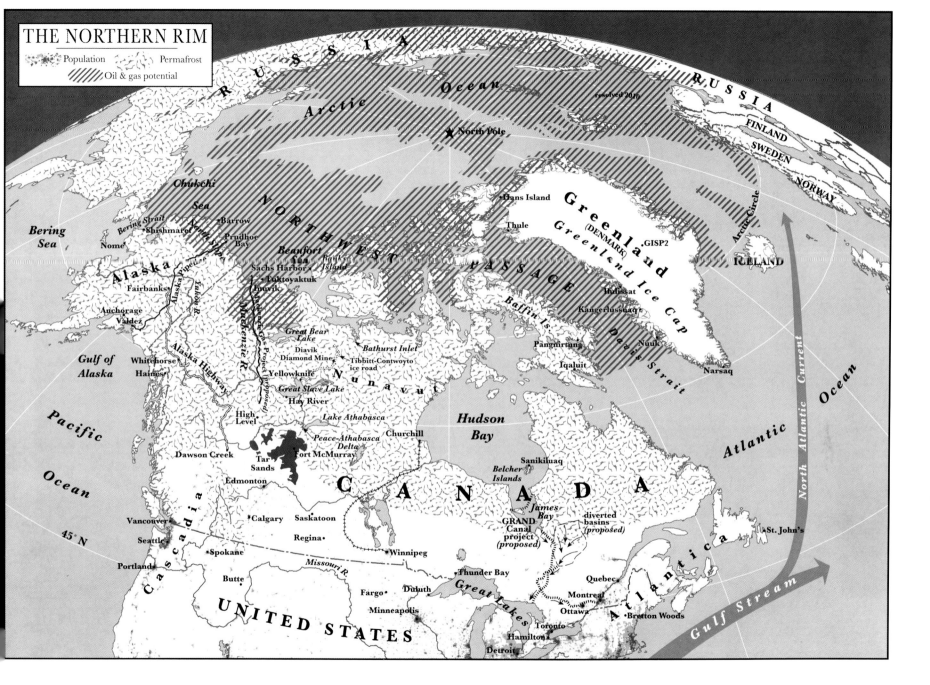

THE NORTHERN RIM

Population
Permafrost
Oil & gas potential

RUSSIA
Arctic Ocean
resolved 2010
RUSSIA
FINLAND
SWEDEN
NORWAY
North Pole
Chukchi Sea
NORTHWEST PASSAGE
Hans Island
Greenland (DENMARK)
Greenland Ice Cap
Thule
GISP2
Arctic Circle
ICELAND
Bering Sea
Bering Strait
Shishmaref
Barrow
Nome
North Slope
Prudhoe Bay
Beaufort Sea
Banks Island
Sachs Harbor
Tuktoyaktuk
Inuvik
Alaska
Alaska Pipeline
Yukon R.
Fairbanks
Anchorage
Valdez
Mackenzie R.
Mackenzie Gas Project (proposed)
Great Bear Lake
Bathurst Inlet
Diavik Diamond Mine
Tibbitt-Contwoyto ice road
Ilulissat
Kangerlussuaq
Baffin Is.
Pangnirtung
Iqaluit
Nuuk
Davis Strait
Narsaq
Gulf of Alaska
Whitehorse
Haines
Alaska Highway
Yellowknife
Nunavut
Great Slave Lake
Hay River
High Level
Lake Athabasca
Peace-Athabasca Delta
Churchill
Hudson Bay
Pacific Ocean
Dawson Creek
Tar Sands
Fort McMurray
Sanikiluaq
Belcher Islands
Atlantic Ocean
North Atlantic Current
Edmonton
CANADA
James Bay
GRAND Canal project (proposed)
diverted basins (proposed)
St. John's
Cascadia
Vancouver
Calgary
Saskatoon
45° N
Seattle
Regina
Spokane
Winnipeg
Missouri R.
Portland
Thunder Bay
Quebec
Butte
Fargo
Duluth
Great Lakes
Montreal
Ottawa
Atlantica
Minneapolis
Bretton Woods
UNITED STATES
Toronto
Hamilton
Detroit
Gulf Stream

A somewhat fanciful depiction of a multiverse consisting of a background empty space–time giving birth to baby universes, as proposed in my 2004 paper with Jennifer Chen (artwork by Jason Torchinsky).

MATTHEW BARNEY

ARTIST

Untitled, 2010

ARTIST

Textorama, 2011

DOMINIQUE GONZALEZ-FOERSTER

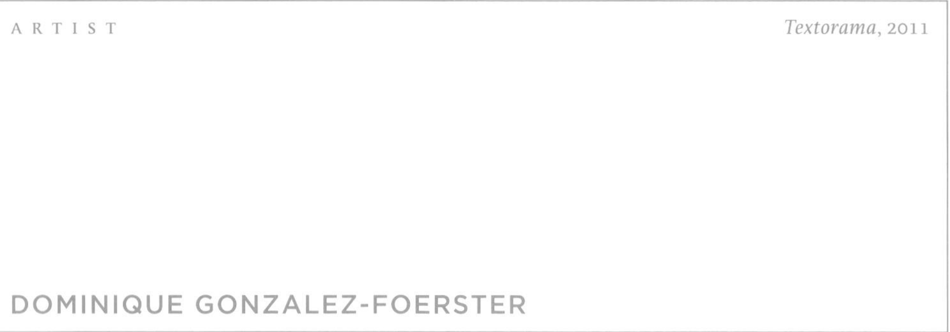

De ces villes ne restera que ce qui
un jour les traversa : le vent...

LA INVENCIÓN DE MOREL

Hoy,
en esta isla,
ha occurido
un milagro

THE EMIGRANTS

Creo que esta isla se llama Villings y que pertenece al archipiélago de Las Ellice.

America
is nothing
if not
spacious

W.G. SEBALD

Los desiertos de Sonora
(1976)

I carried the book
a hundred yards
into the desolation,
toward the southeast.
With all my might I threw it far out in the direction she had gone.
Then I got into the car, started the engine,
and drove back to Los Angeles.

SMOKE
RISING

En la biblioteca
municipal
de Hermosillo,
Belano,
Lima y yo
buscamos
el rastro
de Cesárea Tinajero.
No hallamos
nada.

¿Qué hay detrás de la ventana?

2666

ARTURO BELANO

ULISES LIMA

JOHN FANTE

The
ship
had
already
slowed.

Und morgens wie abends und in den Träumen der Nacht vollzog sich auf dieser Straße ein immer drängender Verkehr, der, von oben gesehen, sich als eine aus immer neuen Anfängen ineinandergestreute Mischung von verzerrten menschlichen Figuren und von Dächern der Fuhrwerke aller Art darstellte, von der aus sich noch eine neue, vervielfältigte, wildere Mischung von Lärm, Staub und Gerüchen erhob, und alles dieses wurde erfaßt und durchdrungen von einem mächtigen Licht, das immer wieder von der Menge der Gegenstände verstreut, fortgetragen und wieder eifrig herbeigebracht wurde und das dem betörten Auge so körperlich erschien, als werde über dieser Straße eine alles bedeckende Glasscheibe jeden Augenblick immer wieder mit aller Kraft zerschlagen.

Una tarde, se embarcó en Veracruz
en dirección a Nueva Orleans.
Embarcarse significó para
él renunciar a la poesía.

C'était si facile de rester. D'observer. De sentir.
De rester.

À
Buenos Aires,
les jours
rallongent
lorsque
arrive septembre.
Tu n'y as jamais pensé,
n'est-ce pas ?

Aujourd'hui, j'ai envie d'écrire sur Buenos Aires.

Tout le monde sait que ces villes
furent bâties pour être détruites.

April 7.
It is eighteen months since
M. first proposed coming
to America. Spring rains
are over, we are told. It will
be dry until November.

La Biblioteca Brautigan reúne exclusivamente
manuscritos que, habiendo sido rechazados por las editoriales
a las que fueron presentados, nunca llegaron a publicarse.
Esta biblioteca reúne sólo libros abortados.

Cambie
los discos;
las maquinas
proyectarán
la nueva semana,
eternamente.

The whole of the Lower East Side
was one huge dormitory.

Possessing things
was
a technique
of consolation.

ENRIQUE VILA-MATAS

VUDÚ URBANO

»Ich habe mich verirrt,« sagte Karl,
»Ich habe es während der Fahrt gar nicht so bemerkt,
aber es ist ein schrecklich großes Schiff.«

THE WAY THE WAVES ROSE UP FROM THE DEEP AND CAME ROLLING ON WAS TERRIFYING, HE SAID.

All
along
the coast,
in places
like Leonardo,
Atlantic Highlands
Little Silver,
Ocean Grove,
Neptune City,
Belmar
and Lake Como,
they built summer palaces
for their families
and villas for their women
and usually a church as well
and a little house for a chaplain.

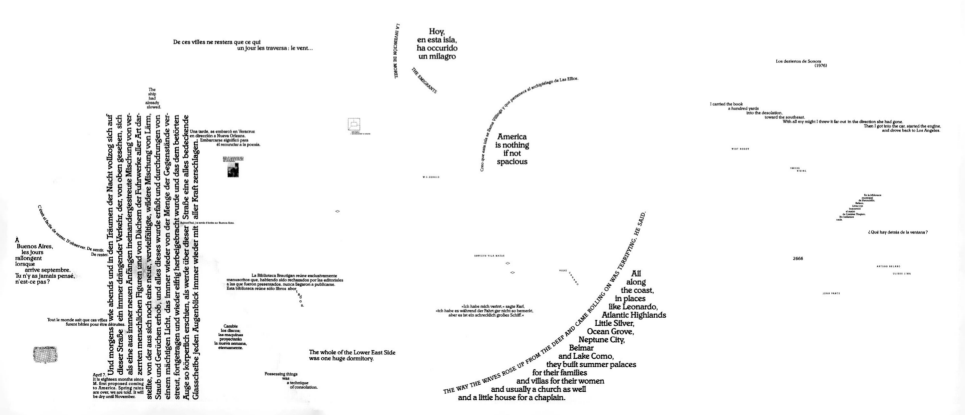

THE WIND
THE MARTIAN CHRONICLES
wind was the cause of it all. The sand, too, had a share in it, and human beings were involved, but the wind was the primal force, and but for it the whole series of events would not have happened.
LITTLE CROW
INDIAN COUNTRY

RICHARD BRAUTIGAN

Tupi or not Tupi, that is the question.

WILLIAM GADDIS

Foi porque nunca tivemos gramáticas, nem coleções de velhos vegetais. E nunca soubemos o que era urbano, suburbano, fronteiriço e continental. Preguiçosos no mapa-mundi do Brasil.

The time came when there was no occasion for geography

MANIFESTO ANTROPÓFAGO

O verdadeiro pensamento parece sem autor.

This was a red jungle. There were floor lamps and rugs in the clearings, and rows of books back in the shadows.

And all those flecks and blobs of land were covered with trees.

Ocean: forest.

CLARICE LISPECTOR

his eyes wide open in the rainy dark.

There came a moment when she found herself knowing it was daytime rather than night, and when she was aware of one hour following upon another. She was in the open air, lying in bed on a balcony.

A invenção

Agora te escreverei tudo o que me vier à mente com o menor policiamento possível.

"Don't you understand I loved him, I loved him. I loved him!"

Minimal incoherent fragments: the opposite of History, out of your ruins, creator of ruins, you have made creations.

PHILIP K. DICK

A nunca exportação de poesia. A poesia anda oculta nos cipós maliciosos da sabedoria. Nas lianas da saudade universitária.

CATITI CATITI

GEOGRAPHY AND PLAYS

ÁGUA VIVA

Os bichos me fantasticam

PAUL BOWLES

WILLIAM BURROUGHS

Contra as elites vegetais. Em comunicação com o solo.

THE WORD FOR WORLD IS FOREST

We penetrated deeper and deeper into the heart of darkness.

What is Geography?
A description of the earth's surface.

GERTRUDE STEIN

Contra as histórias do homem que começam no Cabo Finisterra. O mundo não datado. Não rubricado. Sem Napoleão. Sem César.

Só podemos atender ao mundo orecular.

JAMES G. BALLARD

O INSTINTO CARAÍBA

MARLOW

"Forget!" muttered Almayer, and that word started before him a sequence of events, a detailed programme of things to do.

Almayer's Folly

Such were Almayer's thoughts as, standing on the verandah of his new but already decaying house – that last failure of his life – he looked on the broad river.

A surpresa

JOSEPH CONRAD

Obuses de elevadores, cubos de arranha-céus e a sábia preguiça solar. A reza. O Carnaval. A energia íntima. O sabiá. A hospitalidade um pouco sensual, amorosa. A saudade dos pajés e os campos de aviação militar. Pau-Brasil.

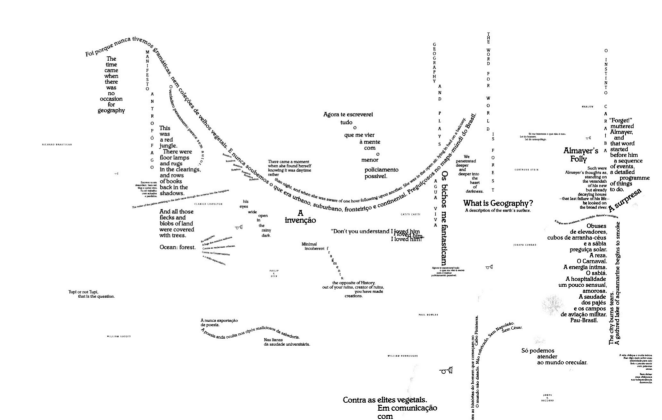

The city burns tears. A gathred lake of aquamarine begins to smoke

ROSA BARBA	ARTIST	Alkuna ('Nordic mythology') was built in the 1950s as a highly planned, climate-adapted model community on the fictionalized island of Forgotten, where building was successfully coordinated with terrain in order to mitigate the cold winds. North of the Arctic Circle, this city must be relocated due to ground instability caused by massive mining in the area. A large crack in the ground will overtake the community in fifteen years if the current rate of mining continues. ¶ While exploring the municipal archives there, I discovered documentation of another successful planning initiative: the Nordic shift from driving on the left to driving on the right-hand side of the road. Ostensibly a symbolic gesture of unity with the Common Market, I believe the initiative was a diversion technique by UFO-SD, the mining company that in many ways controls the fate of the area around Alkuna. Despite an obvious anachronism (the footage is from 1967), it was a well-orchestrated attempt to redirect local and international attention from the distressing task of relocating the city. As in any area where a single corporation dominates the local economy, it plays the roles of benefactor and potential foe simultaneously. ¶ The county named Forgotten reminds us of an era when habits as entrenched as driving on a certain side could be flawlessly changed with collective effort and comprehensive planning. In an era of cynical resignation to situations ranging from corrupt government to climate change, it seems like an idea, or an ideal, worth remembering.
Vertiginous Mapping	2008	

ARTIST

PROCESS 18

{ A rectangular surface filled with instances of Element 5, each with a different size and grey value. Draw a quadrilateral connecting the endpoints of each pair of Elements that are touching. Increase the opacity of the quadrilateral while the Elements are touching and decrease while they are not.
}

ELEMENT 5

{ Form 2: Line
Behaviour 1: Move in a straight line.
Behaviour 5: Enter from the opposite edge after moving off the surface.
Behaviour 6: Orient toward the direction of an Element that is touching.
Behaviour 7: Deviate from the current direction.
}

CASEY REAS

MARIANA CASTILLO DEBALL & AMALIA PICA

2012	*Figures don't lie but liars can figure*
	The poet asks the explorer to read his book on the journey and throw it into the heart of the desert upon arrival. The poet hears nothing else.
	Acoustic radars were early warning devices built with the aim of detecting airborne invasion. When made of cardboard one hears nothing.
	A desert island drawn in the snow.
	A monument reads: 65 million years ago, a meteorite impacted this place, finishing with the dinosaurs, and beginning the history of humanity.
	The astronomer confuses the reflection of his own eye with a distant galaxy.
	The elephant was shot in Congo, sent to England to be dissected and from there to Brussels for the world fair in '58. The elephant travelled in his own custom-made box.
	The artist disorients the taxi driver by drawing a plane that looks like a dolphin. He ends up at the aquarium and misses his flight.
	The hunter eats himself.

THE FIRST JIGSAW PUZZLES WERE MADE FROM MAPS

MAPPING THE 21ST CENTURY 2010

QIU ZHIJIE *artist*

MAPPING IS A PROCESS OF TRYING TO UNDERSTAND THE RELATIONSHIP BETWEEN THE WORLD AND ONESELF. TO MAP IS TO KNOW, AND TO DIRECT FUTURE ACTION. THE FIVE IMPORTANT SIDES BECOME FIVE AVENUES, SO WE HAVE THE POLITICAL AVENUE, ECONOMY AVENUE, ENERGY AVENUE, TECHNOLOGY AVENUE, AND THE ART AND CULTURE AVENUE. THEN FROM NORTH TO SOUTH, THE STREETS OF DIFFERENT YEARS. THE FUTURE IS NOT TOTALLY UNKNOWN, THERE ARE SOME CERTAIN POINTS WE ALREADY KNOW FROM RESEARCH. FOR EXAMPLE, IN THE YEAR 2025, WORLD POPULATION WILL REACH 8.2 BILLION AND INDIA WILL BECOME THE WORLD'S MOST POPULOUS COUNTRY, SURPASSING CHINA.... BUT STILL I HAVE ENOUGH EMPTY ROOM FOR IMAGINATION. IN 2025, WE HAVE THE USA MARS EXPLORATION BASE; THEN WE HAVE THE ASIAN DOLLAR MINT. IN 2045, WE HAVE AN OVERWHELMING MONUMENT, AND BECAUSE OF GLOBAL WARMING THE TWO MOST IMPORTANT DEPARTMENTS IN THE NEO-UN WILL BE FOOD STORAGE AND CLIMATOLOGY. AT THE SAME TIME, HERE IS TRANSGENE ZOO, AND I BELIEVE HOLLYWOOD WILL PRODUCE A PILL AS A KIND OF CHEMICAL MOVIE AT THIS TIME. IN 2080 STREET, WE HAVE THE UN COURT FOR THE PARTITIONING OF THE HIGH SEA. SO THERE WILL BE A REAL-ESTATE COMPANY AND THE PRIVATE SEA. IN 2090, WE HAVE THE NEO-COLD WAR BRIDGE BETWEEN DIFFERENT COUNTRIES WHO ALLOW OR ARE AGAINST POPULATION CONTROL AND GENE INTERVENTIONS. IN 2100, WE COME TO THE SQUARE OF GLOBALIZATION. HERE WE HAVE SENSORY PERCEPTION INTERNET. HOPEFULLY WE CAN HAVE AN EARTH ENVIRONMENTAL RESTORATION MEMORIAL PARK.

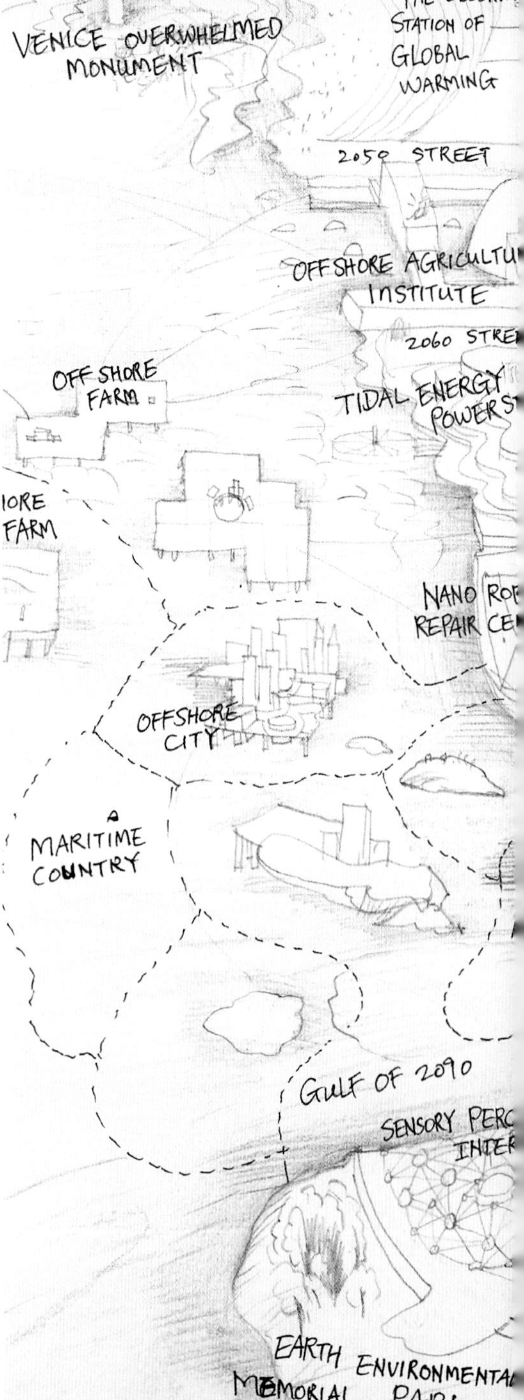

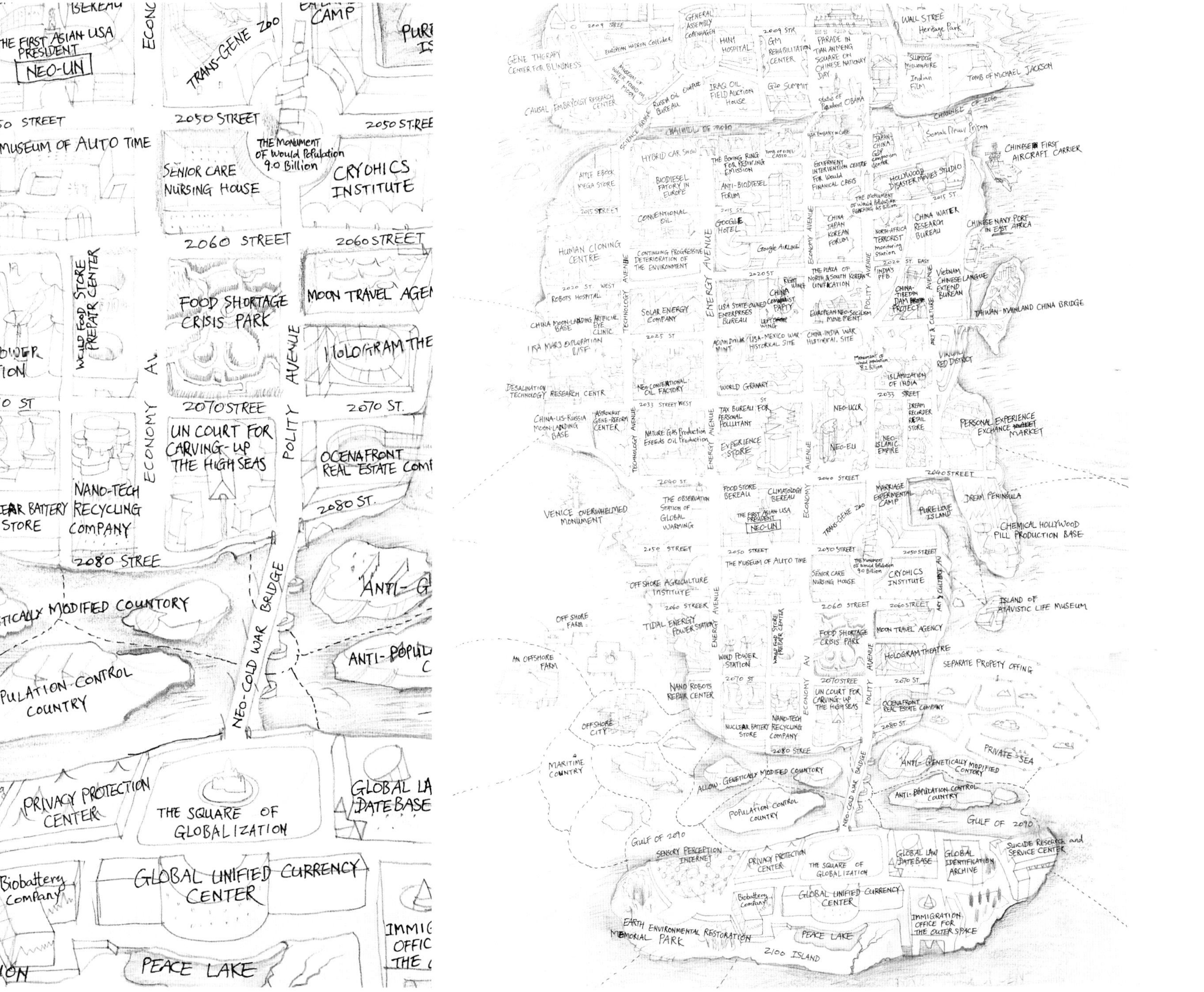

THE FIRST ASIAN USA PRESIDENT
NEO-UN
ECONOMY AV
TRANS-GENE ZOO
CAMP
2050 STREET
THE MUSEUM OF AUTO TIME
THE MONUMENT OF WOULD POPULATION 9.0 BILLION
SENIOR CARE NURSING HOUSE
CRYOHICS INSTITUTE
2060 STREET
WOULD FOOD STORE PREPAIR CENTER
FOOD SHORTAGE CRISIS PARK
MOON TRAVEL AGENCY
HOLOGRAM THEATRE
POLITY AVENUE
2070 STREET
2070 ST.
UN COURT FOR CARVING-UP THE HIGH SEAS
OCENAFRONT REAL ESTATE COMPANY
NANO-TECH RECYCLING COMPANY
NUCLEAR BATTERY STORE
2080 ST.
2080 STREET
NEO-COLD WAR BRIDGE
ALLOW-GENETICALLY MODIFIED COUNTORY
POPULATION CONTROL COUNTRY
ANTI-GENETICALLY MODIFIED CONTORY
ANTI-POPULATION CONTROL COUNTRY
PRIVACY PROTECTION CENTER
THE SQUARE OF GLOBALIZATION
GLOBAL LAW DATE BASE
GLOBAL UNIFIED CURRENCY CENTER
Biobattery Company
IMMIGRATION OFFICE FOR THE OUTER SPACE
PEACE LAKE
GENE THERAPY CENTER FOR BLINDNESS
GENERAL ASSEMBLY COPENHAGEN
H1N1 HOSPITAL
GM REHABILITATION CENTER
PARADE IN TIAN AN MENG SQUARE ON CHINESE NATIONAL DAY
WALL STREET Heritage Park
SLUMDOG MILLIONAIRE Indian Film
TOMB OF MICHAEL JACKSON
CAUSAL EMBRYOLOGY RESEARCH CENTER
IRAQ OIL FIELD AUCTION HOUSE
G20 SUMMIT
STATUE OF President OBAMA
CHANNEL OF 2010
Somali Pirates Prison
CHINESE FIRST AIRCRAFT CARRIER
HYBRID CAR SHOW
APPLE EBOOK MEGA STORE
BIODIESEL FATORY IN EUROPE
ANTI-BIODIESEL FORUM
HOLLYWOOD DISASTER MOVIES STUDIO
CONVENTIONAL OIL
GOOGLE HOTEL
Google AIRLINE
CHINA JAPAN KOREAN FORUM
CHINA WATER RESEARCH BUREAU
CHINESE NAVY PORT IN EAST AFRICA
HUMAN CLONING CENTRE
TECHNOLOGY AVENUE
ENERGY AVENUE
THE PLAZA OF NORTH & SOUTH KOREAN UNIFICATION
ROBOTS HOSPITAL
SOLAR ENERGY COMPANY
USA STATE-OWNED ENTERPRISES BUREAU
CHINA COMMUNIST PARTY
EUROPEAN NEO-SOCIALISM MOVEMENT
CHINA-TIBETAN DAM PROJECT
TAIWAN-MAINLAND CHINA BRIDGE
CHINA MOON-LANDING BASE
USA MARS EXPLORATION BASE
USA-MEXICO WAR HISTORICAL SITE
CHINA-INDIA WAR HISTORICAL SITE
ART & CULTURE AVENUE
VIRTUAL RED DISTRICT
DESALINATION TECHNOLOGY RESEARCH CENTR
NEO-CONVENTIONAL OIL FACTORY
WORLD GRANARY
ISLAMIZATION OF INDIA
CHINA-US-RUSSIA MOON-LANDING BASE
TAX BUREAU FOR PERSONAL POLLUTANT
NEO-UCCR
DREAM RECORDER RETAIL STORE
NATURE GAS Production Exceeds Oil Production
EXPERIENCE STORE
NEO-EU
NEO-ISLAMIC EMPIRE
PERSONAL EXPERIENCE EXCHANCE MARKET
VENICE OVERWHELMED MONUMENT
THE OBSERVATION STATION OF GLOBAL WARMING
CLIMATOLOGY BEREAU
MARRIAGE EXPERIMENTAL CAMP
PURE LOVE ISLAND
DREAM PENINSULA
CHEMICAL HOLLYWOOD PILL PRODUCTION BASE
OFFSHORE AGRICULTURE INSTITUTE
ISLAND OF ATAVISTIC LIFE MUSEUM
OFF SHORE FARM
TIDAL ENERGY POWER STATION
WIND POWER STATION
AN OFFSHORE FARM
SEPARATE PROPETY OFFING
NANO ROBOTS REPAIR CENTER
OFFSHORE CITY
MARITIME COUNTRY
PRIVATE SEA
GULF OF 2090
SENSORY PERCEPTION INTERNET
GLOBAL IDENTIFICATION ARCHIVE
SUICIDE Research and SERVICE CENTER
EARTH ENVIRONMENTAL RESTORATION MEMORIAL PARK
2100 ISLAND

Nas Ocsicnarf-Dnalkao Detinu Setats

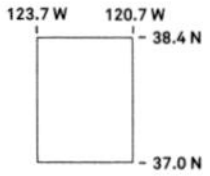

123.7 W 120.7 W 38.4 N 37.0 N

MET	CNT	OIL	DRY	PAX	CRG	MOV	TEL
35	14	8	14	14	24+27	26+28	5

Noitavele (m) 39

Noitalupop

Stnatibahni 2003	**7,154,000**

aihpargomed.moc

Natiloportem tnempoleved

	1965	2003
Raey	1965	2003
Latot natiloportem stnatibahni	3,730,000	7,154,000
Stnatibahni ni natiloportem eroc	1,128,000	1,160,000
Eroc erahs	**30.2%**	**16.2%**
Stnatibahni ni natiloportem yrehpirep	2,602,000	5,994,000
Yrehpirep erahs	69.8%	83.8%

aihpargomed.moc

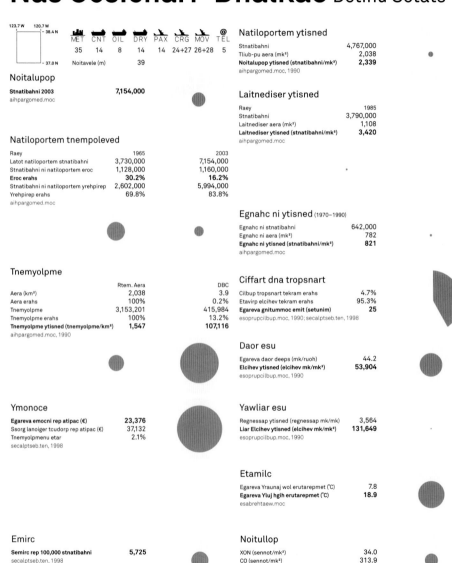

Tnemyolpme

	Rtem. Aera	DBC
Aera (km²)	2,038	3.9
Aera erahs	100%	0.2%
Tnemyolpme	3,153,201	415,984
Tnemyolpme erahs	100%	13.2%
Tnemyolpme ytisned (tnemyolpme/km²)	**1,547**	**107,116**

aihpargomed.moc, 1990

Ymonoce

Egareva emocni rep atipac (€)	**23,376**
Ssorg lanoiger tcudorp rep atipac (€)	37,132
Tnemyolpmenu etar	2.1%

secalptseb.ten, 1998

Emirc

Semirc rep 100,000 stnatibahni	**5,725**

secalptseb.ten, 1998

Natiloportem ytisned

Stnatibahni	4,767,000
Tliub-pu aera (mk²)	2,038
Noitalupop ytisned (stnatibahni/mk²)	**2,339**

aihpargomed.moc, 1990

Laitnediser ytisned

Raey	1985
Stnatibahni	3,790,000
Laitnediser aera (mk²)	1,108
Laitnediser ytisned (stnatibahni/mk²)	**3,420**

aihpargomed.moc

Egnahc ni ytisned (1970–1990)

Egnahc ni stnatibahni	642,000
Egnahc ni aera (mk²)	782
Egnahc ni ytisned (stnatibahni/mk²)	**821**

aihpargomed.moc

Ciffart dna tropsnart

Cilbup tropsnart tekram erahs	4.7%
Etavirp elcihev tekram erahs	95.3%
Egareva gnitummoc emit (setunim)	**25**

esoprupcilbup.moc, 1990; secalptseb.ten, 1998

Daor esu

Egareva daor deeps (mk/ruoh)	44.2
Elcihev ytisned (elcihev mk/mk²)	**53,904**

esoprupcilbup.moc, 1990

Yawliar esu

Regnessap ytisned (regnessap mk/mk)	3,564
Liar Elcihev ytisned (elcihev mk/mk²)	**131,649**

esoprupcilbup.moc, 1990

Etamilc

Egareva Yraunaj wol erutarepmet (°C)	7.8
Egareva Ylu hgih erutarepmet (°C)	**18.9**

esabrehtaew.moc

Noitullop

XON (sennot/mk²)	34.0
CO (sennot/mk²)	313.9
VOC (sennot/mk²)	34.7
Latot noitullop (sennot/mk²)	**382.6**

aihpargomed.moc, 1990

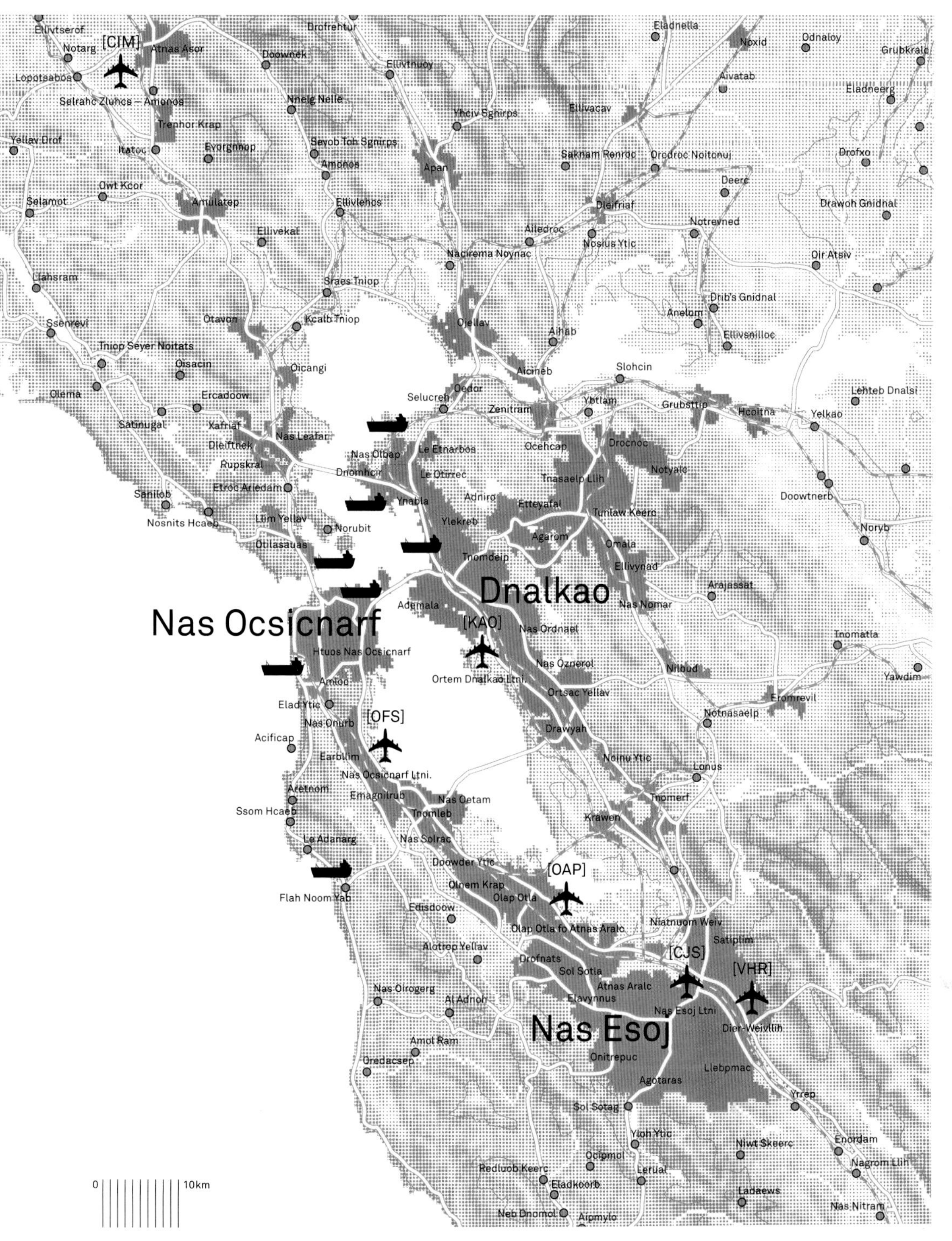

Ellivtserof
Drofrehtur
Eladnella
Noxid
Odnaloy
Grubkralc
[CIM]
Notarg
Atnas Asor
Doownek
Ellivtnuoy
Aivatab
Eladneerg
Selrahc Zluhcs – Amonos
Nnelg Nelle
Yhciv Sgnirps
Ellivacav
Trenhor Krap
Yellav Drof
Itatoc
Evorgnnop
Seyob Toh Sgnirps
Saknam Renroc
Drocroc Noitcnuj
Drofxo
Amonos
Apan
Deerc
Owt Kcor
Selamot
Amulatep
Ellivlehcs
Dleifriaf
Drawoh Gnidnal
Ellivekal
Allecroc
Notrevned
Nosius Ytic
Nacirema Noynac
Oir Atsiv
Llahsram
Sraes Tniop
Drib's Gnidnal
Anelom
Ssenrevi
Otavon
Kcalb Tniop
Ojellav
Ellivsnilloc
Tniop Seyer Noitats
Oisacin
Aicineb
Slohcin
Oicangi
Olema
Ercadoow
Selucreh
Oedor
Lehteb Dnalsi
Zenitram
Ybtlam
Grubsttip
Hcoitna
Yelkao
Satinugal
Xafriaf
Nas Leafar
Dleiftnek
Nas Olbap
Le Etnarbos
Ocehcap
Drocnoc
Rupskral
Dnomhcir
Le Otirrec
Tnasaelp Llih
Notyalc
Etroc Aredam
Adnirg
Sanilob
Etteyafal
Ynabla
Doowtnerb
Tunlaw Keerc
Nosnits Hcaeb
Llim Yellav
Ylekreb
Agarom
Norubit
Noryb
Omala
Tnomdeip
Ellivynad
Dnalkao
Arajassat
Nas Ocsicnarf
Ademala
Nas Nomar
[KAO]
Nas Ordnael
Inomatla
Htuos Nas Ocsicnarf
Nas Oznerol
Ortem Dnalkao Ltni.
Nilbud
Yawdim
Ortsac Yellav
Eromrevil
Elad Ytic
Notnasaelp
[OFS]
Nas Onurb
Drawyah
Acificap
Earbllim
Noinu Ytic
Lonus
Nas Ocsicnarf Ltni.
Aretnom
Emagnilrub
Nas Oetam
Tnomerf
Ssom Hcaeb
Tnomleb
Krawen
Le Adanarg
Nas Solrac
Doowder Ytic
[OAP]
Olnem Krap
Olap Otla
Flah Noom Yab
Edisdoow
Olap Otla fo Atnas Aralc
Niatnuom Weiv
Satiplim
Alotrop Yellav
Drofnats
[CJS]
Sol Sotla
[VHR]
Nas Oirogerg
Atnas Aralc
Al Adnoh
Elavynnus
Nas Esoj Ltni.
Nas Esoj
Dier-Weivllih
Amol Ram
Onitrepuc
Oredacsep
Llebpmac
Agotaras
Yrrep
Sol Sotag
Enordam
Niwt Skeerc
Ocipmol
Redluob Keerc
Lerual
Nagrom Llih
Eladkoorb
Nas Nitram
Neb Dnomol
Aipmylo
0
10km

DAVID ADJAYE

ARCHITECT

Europolis is a utopian vision of a city as a reduction. It is not a traditional city but an imagined, phenomenological city. European cities have evolved and emerged over time. They are the result of layers of history, development, destruction, mixing, migration and changing of populations. They are a collage of different profound ideas as well as superficial constructs. This map is the extraction of the essence of the European Union capital cities, which have been condensed into a single entity. Europolis has an organic plan and is the amalgamation of a concentrated urban form that relates to the density of European cities. It contains all of the information about material, texture, population, time, scale and occupation. ¶ The map explores the extremes of scale and the diversity of grain while proposing a distinct European DNA. It raises the question: if Europe were condensed into one piece and combined in one cell, what would result? The answer lies within the two extremes of Europolis: a very dense condition and a big void.

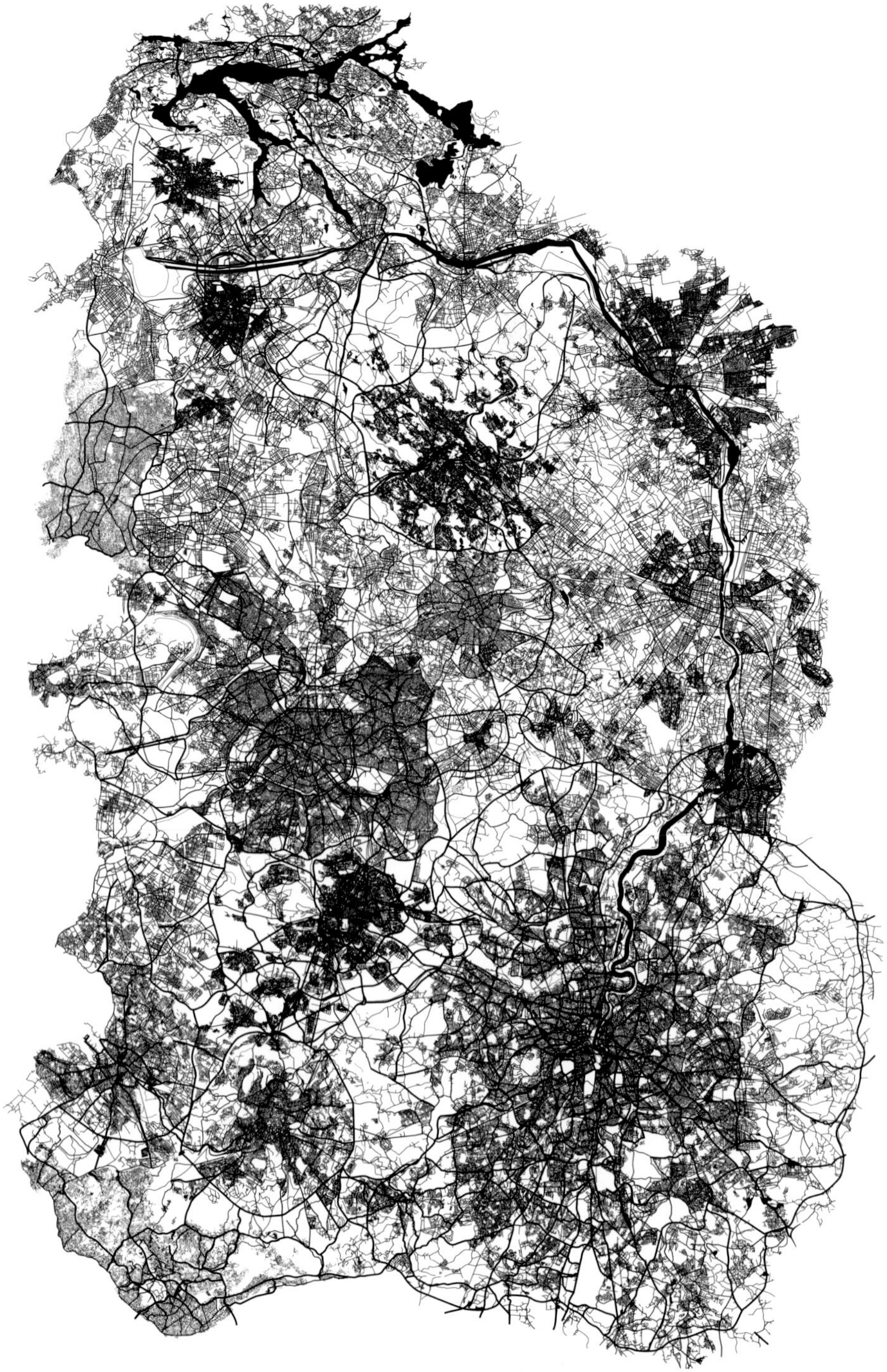

Classification of Air- Port-City - Genera Species and Varieties - Typical genera - High Air-Port-Cities, their base is above 6 KM: 1-Cirruscity, 2-Cirrocumuluscity, 3-Cirro
and 6 km: 4 Atocumuluscity, 5 Ltostratuscity, 6 Nimbostratuscity. Low Air-Port-Cities, their base is above 2 KM: 7 Stratocumuluscity, 8 Stratuscity, 9 Cumulus 10, Cumulon
Cities species, describing the shape and the structure of each type . Each specific term could in theory be applied to any one of the ten genera, but is practice they are u
Cirruscity Uncinus, comma or hook shaped – Cirruscity Spissatus dense and grey toward the sun - Cumuluscity Congestus, growing with cauliflower-shaped tops - Cu
bulges, Cumuluscity Humilis, flattened. / Varieties - The cloudscities variety defines either the transparency of the genera or species, or the particular arrangement of its e
Ac,As Variety Translucidus (tr) translucent, showing the sun or moon, Genera perlucidus (pe) allows sun or moon light to be seen./Accessory Air - Port - Cities - Certain f
appearances occurring only in association with one or two of the genera. They can often suggest physical processes occurring within a cloud. The nine Accessory Cloud
Air-Port-Cities 9) Virga, fall streaks; precipitation not reaching the surface. The invention and classification of Air-Port-Cities - As cloud ascend Stratus, are folded Cumulu

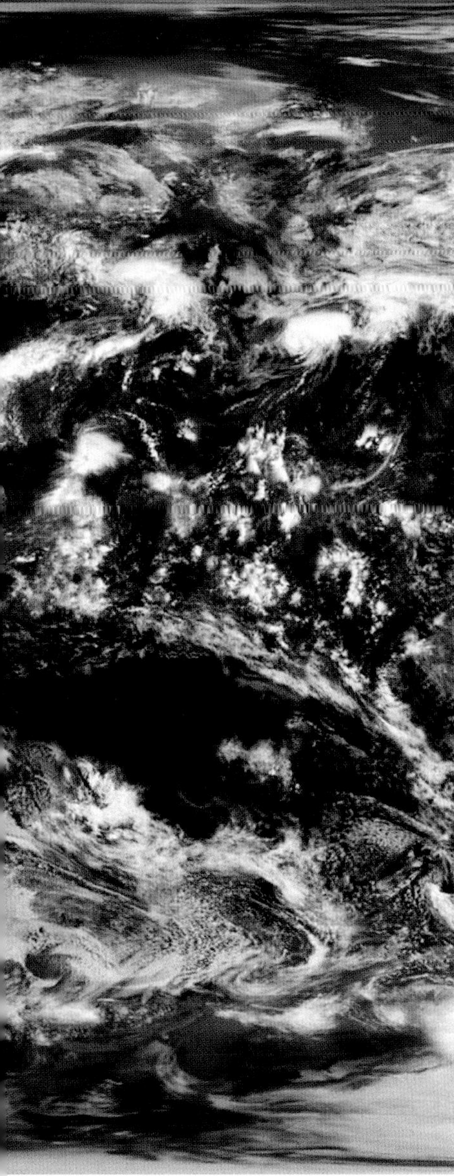

Middle Air-Port-Cities, their base between 2
y./ Species - There are fourteen Air - Port -
ed only to one or two. Here some of them:
Mediocris, moderate depth, tops with small
re some of them:Genera Air-Port-City St,Sc,
Port-Cities are not types in themselves, but
amma, pouches hanging down from upper
rrus, fall Nimbus.

TOMÁS SARACENO

Artist

Air Port City / Cloud Cities, 2010

My idea for an Air-Port-City is to create platforms or habitable cells made up of cities that float in the air. These change form and join together like clouds. This freedom of movement is borrowed from the orderly structure of airports, and it allows for the creation of the first international city. Airports are divided by 'air-side' and 'land-side'; on the 'air-side' you are under the jurisdiction of international law. Your every action is judged according to international norms. Air-Port-City is like a flying airport; you will be able to legally travel across the world while taking advantage of airport regulations. This structure seeks to challenge today's political, social, cultural and military restrictions in an attempt to re-establish new concepts of synergy. ¶ It will fly through the atmosphere pushed by the winds, both local and global, in an attempt to equalize the (social) temperature and differences in pressure. It will be a sustainable and mobile migration. These aerial cities will be in a permanent state of transformation, similar to nomadic cities.

CLASSIFICATION OF AIR-PORT-CITY / CLOUD CITIES

TYPICAL GENERA

High Cloud Cities
(base above 6 km)

1 Cirruscity
2 Cirrocumuluscity
3 Cirrostratuscity

Middle Cloud Cities
(base between 2 and 6 km)

4 Altocumuluscity
5 Altostratuscity
6 Nimbostratuscity

Low Cloud Cities
(base above 2 km)

7 Stratocumuluscity
8 Stratuscity
9 Cumuluscity
10 Cumulonimbusescity

SPECIES

There are fourteen Cloud Cities species describing the shape and the structure of each type of Cloud City. Each specific term could in theory be applied to any one of the ten genera, but in practice they are usually applied only to one or two. Here are some of them: *Cirruscity uncinus*, comma or hook shaped; *Cirruscity spissatus*, dense and grey toward the sun; *Cumuluscity congestus*, growing, with cauliflower-shaped tops; *Cumuluscity mediocris*, moderate depth, tops with small bulges; *Cumuluscity humilis*, flattened.

VARIETIES

The Cloud Cities variety defines either the transparency of the genera or species, or the particular arrangement of its elements: *Translucidus tr translucent*, showing the sun or moon; Genera *perlucidus pe* allows sun or moon light to be seen.

FRITZ HAEG

A – R – T – I – S – T

Edible Estates Street Map, 2010

This detailed neighbourhood map of a fantastical garden-lined street where each residence is hidden behind an exuberant, inviting, diverse, handmade, productive, edible, pleasure garden is also real – it is a mashup of maps of the first eight Edible Estate prototype gardens I planted from 2005 to 2010 in Salina, Kansas; Lakewood, California; Maplewood, New Jersey; London, England; Austin, Texas; Baltimore, Maryland; Los Angeles, California; and New York City. The continuing series has since established gardens in Ridgefield, Connecticut (2009); Rome, Italy (2010); Istanbul, Turkey (2011); and Budapest, Hungary (2012); Aarhus, Denmark (2013); Holon, Israel (2013); and the Twin Cities, Minnesota (2013).

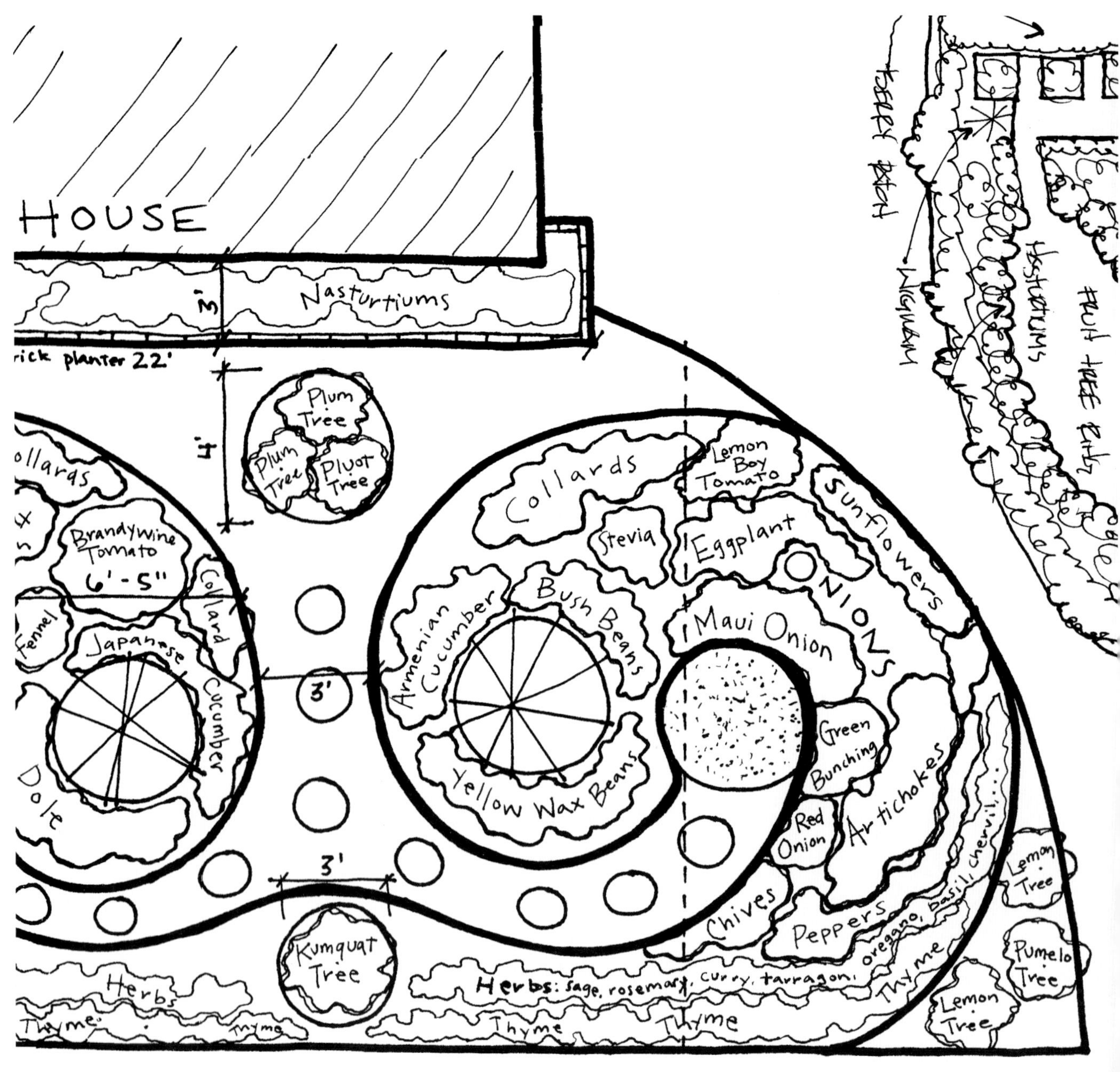

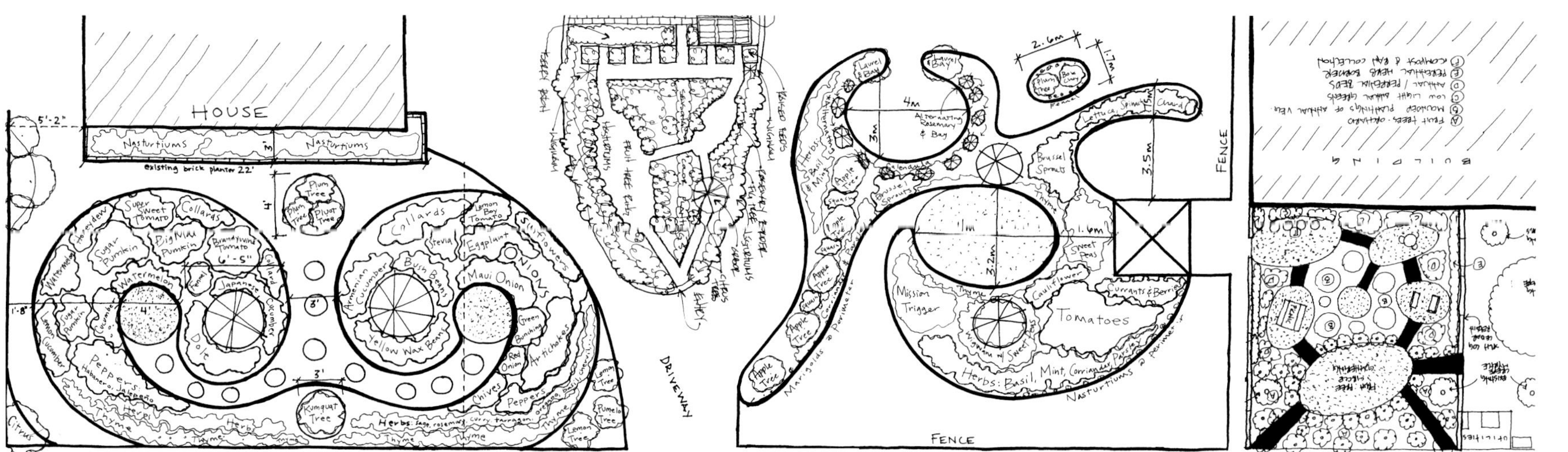
HOUSE
Nasturtiums
Nasturtiums
existing brick planter 22'
5'-2"
Plum Tree
Plum Tree
Pluot Tree
Collards
Super Sweet Tomato
Big Max Pumpkin
Sugar Pumpkin
Watermelon
Japanese
Cucumber
Collards
Stevia
Eggplant
Lemon Boy Tomato
Sunflowers
Onions
Maui Onion
Armenian Cucumber
Bush Beans
Yellow Wax Beans
Green Bunching
Red Onion
Artichokes
Peppers
Chives
Kumquat Tree
Herbs
Thyme
Lemon Tree
Pumelo Tree
Citrus
DRIVEWAY
FENCE
Laurel Bay
Bay
Plum Tree
Bay Tree
2.6m
1.7m
4m
3m
Alternating Rosemary & Bay
Lettuce
Spinach
Chard
Brussel Sprouts
3.5m
1.6m
3.2m
Sweet Peas
Cauliflower
Currants & Berries
Tomatoes
Mission Trigger
Apple Tree
Herbs: Basil, Mint, Corriander, Parsley
Nasturtiums @ perimeter
Marigolds @ perimeter
FENCE
BUILDING

STREET

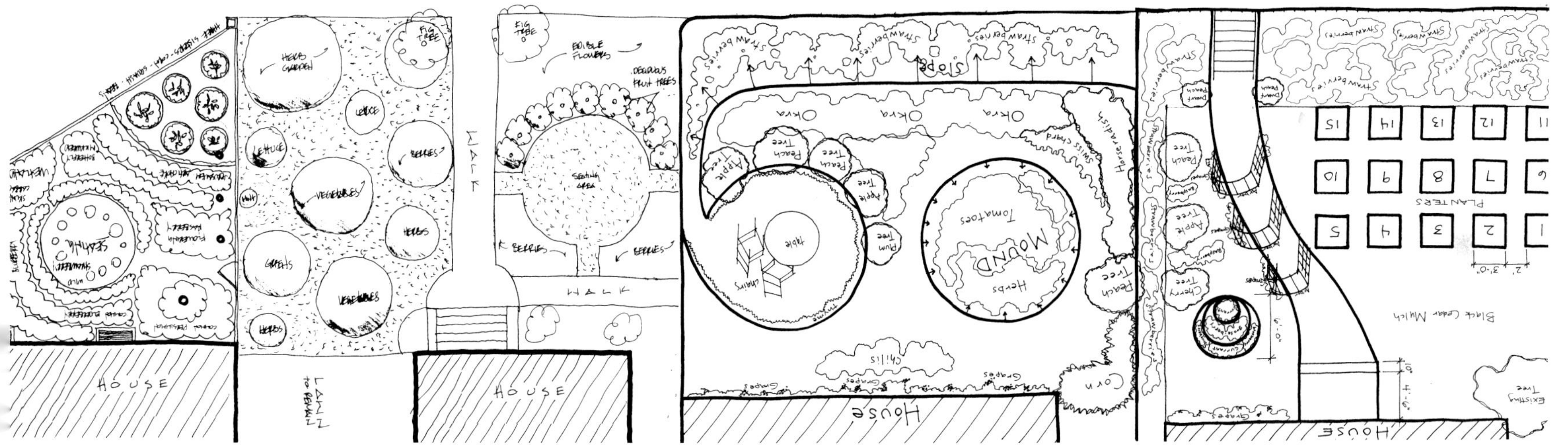
HOUSE
HOUSE
WALK
WALK
FIG TREE
EDIBLE FLOWERS
DECIDUOUS FRUIT TREES
SEATING AREA
BERRIES
BERRIES
HERBS GARDEN
LETTUCE
LETTUCE
BERRIES
VEGETABLES
HERBS
GREENS
VEGETABLES
HERBS
Strawberries
Slope
Okra
Okra
Okra
Apple
Peach Tree
Peach Tree
Apple Tree
Plum Tree
Table
Chairs
MOUND
Tomatoes
Tomatoes
Herbs
Swiss chard
Horseradish
Peach Tree
Chilis
Grapes
Corn
House
PLANTERS
Black Cedar Mulch
Existing Tree
HOUSE

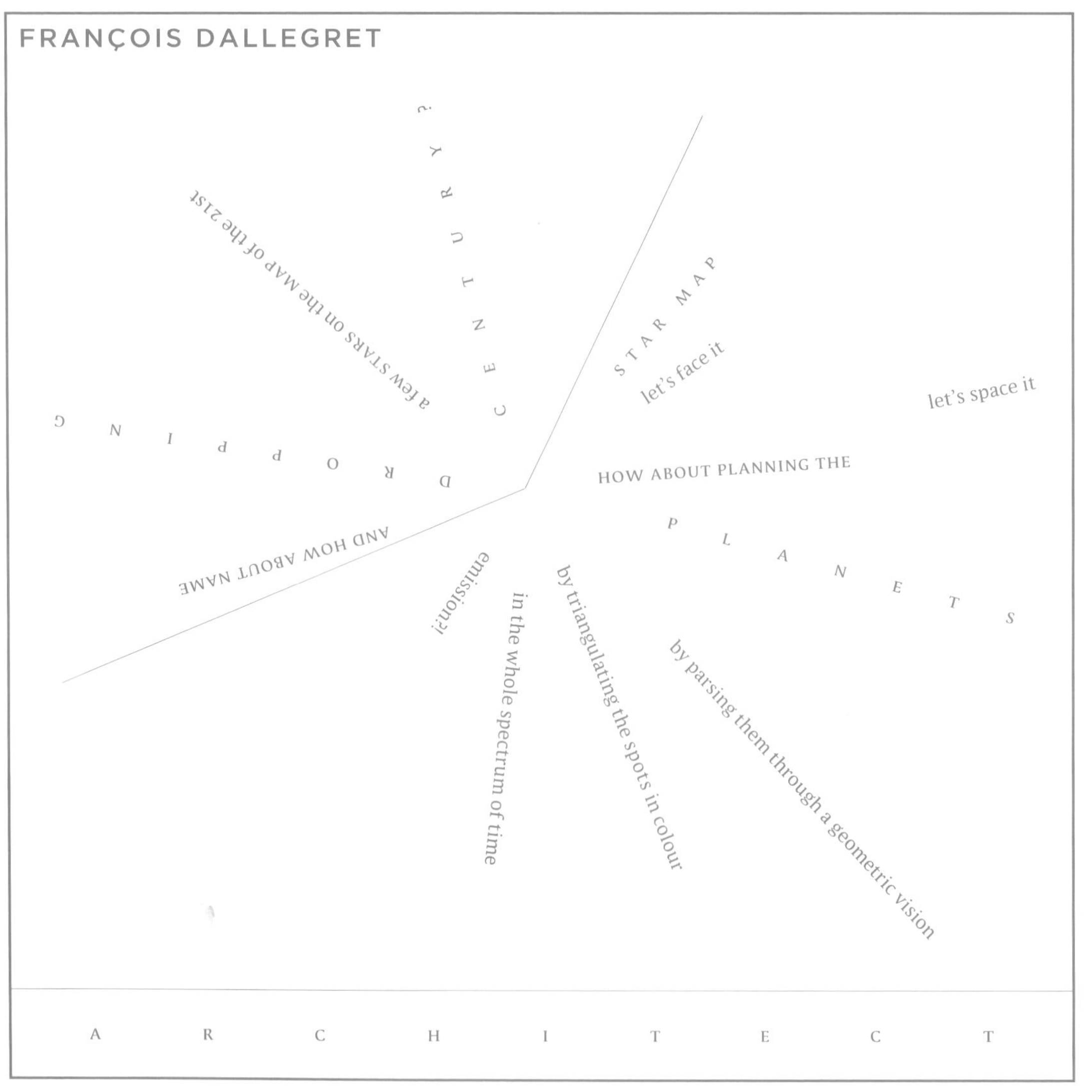
FRANÇOIS DALLEGRET
a few STARS on the MAP of the 21st
C E N T U R Y ?
D R O P P I N G
STAR MAP
let's face it
let's space it
HOW ABOUT PLANNING THE
P L A N E T S
AND HOW ABOUT NAME
emission?!
in the whole spectrum of time
by triangulating the spots in colour
by parsing them through a geometric vision
A R C H I T E C T

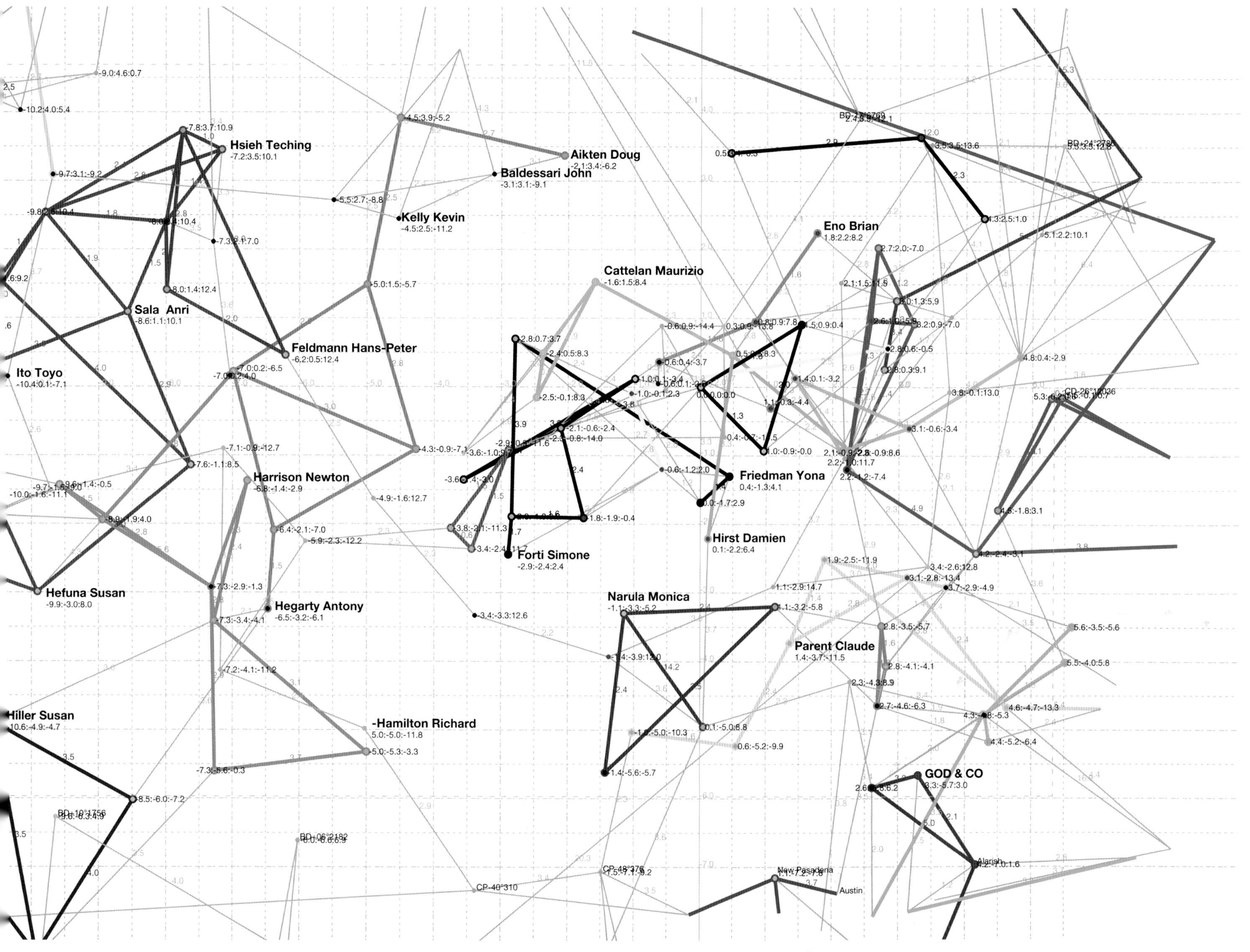

Hsieh Teching
-7.2:3.5:10.1
Aikten Doug
-2.1:3.4:-6.2
Baldessari John
-3.1:3.1:-9.1
Kelly Kevin
-4.5:2.5:-11.2
Eno Brian
1.8:2.2:8.2
Cattelan Maurizio
-1.6:1.5:8.4
Sala Anri
-8.6:1.1:10.1
Feldmann Hans-Peter
-6.2:0.5:12.4
Ito Toyo
-10.4:0.1:-7.1
Harrison Newton
-6.8:-1.4:-2.9
Friedman Yona
0.4:-1.3:4.1
Hirst Damien
0.1:-2.2:6.4
Forti Simone
-2.9:-2.4:2.4
Hefuna Susan
-9.9:-3.0:8.0
Hegarty Antony
-6.5:-3.2:-6.1
Narula Monica
-1.1:-3.3:-5.2
Parent Claude
1.4:-3.7:-11.5
Hiller Susan
10.6:-4.9:-4.7
-Hamilton Richard
5.0:-5.0:-11.8
GOD & CO
3.3:-5.7:3.0
CP-40°310
New Pasadena
Austin
Alarish

ETEL ADNAN

WRITER

MAPS ARE NOT ABOUT SHAPES BUT ABOUT ENERGIES FLOWING IN AND OUT OF PLACES. THEY ARE ABOUT DIRECTIONS AND OBSTACLES. THE CIRCULATION OF THE BLOOD. THE BLOOD OF CITIES. THE BLOOD OF A TERRITORY. ALL THIS AKIN TO THE INSTABILITY OF THE MIND. OF COURSE, MAPS ARE OBJECTS TO MAKE US DREAM, WHERE PLACES LOOK ALWAYS MYSTERIOUS. BUT I SEE THEM ALSO AS ENERGY FIELDS: STRUCTURES (OR CONTINENTS!) ARE FIXED, BUT LIFE CIRCULATES BETWEEN THEM. STREETS ARE DIRECTIONS, ARE SIGNS THAT ALLOW THE ONGOING FLOW OF LIFE.

SUSAN HILLER

Artist

Dream Mapping was an art event provocatively poised between an experiment (social or scientific) and a performance without an audience. Seven dreamers slept for three nights inside 'fairy rings' in an English meadow marked by an abundance of circles formed naturally by Marasmius oreades *mushrooms, a landscape feature that occurs in a number of British folk myths. The field became a site for dream experiences, which were discussed and mapped the following morning. The dream maps of each participant were collected and copied onto transparent paper, sandwiched together and traced to compile a composite group map for each night. A number of shared features were noted (see illustration).*

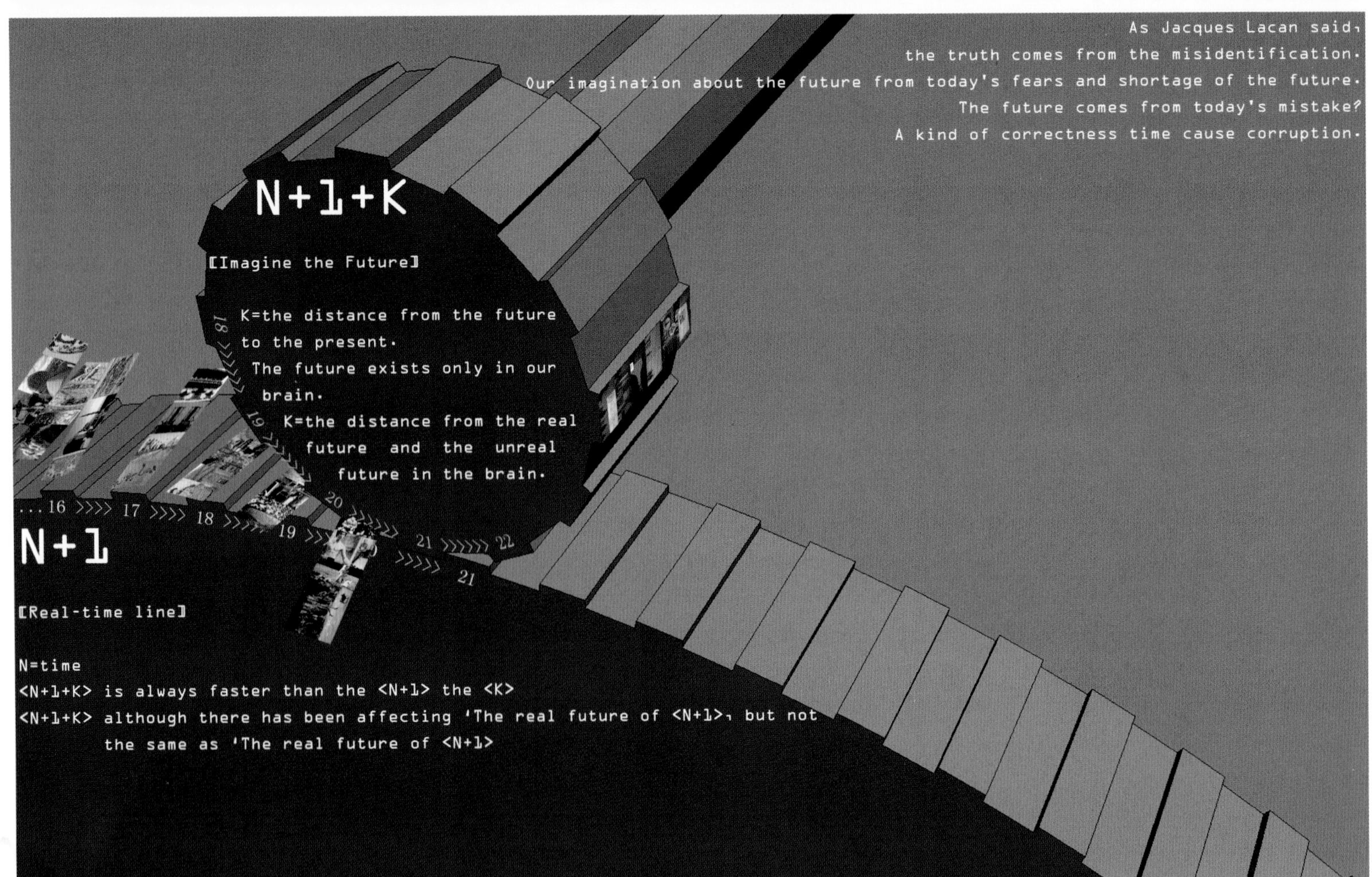

As Jacques Lacan said,
the truth comes from the misidentification.
Our imagination about the future from today's fears and shortage of the future.
The future comes from today's mistake?
A kind of correctness time cause corruption.
N+1+K
[Imagine the Future]
K=the distance from the future
to the present.
The future exists only in our
brain.
K=the distance from the real
future and the unreal
future in the brain.
18
19
20
...16 >>>> 17 >>>> 18 >>>> 19 >>
21 >>>>>> 22
>>>>> 21
N+1
[Real-time line]
N=time
<N+1+K> is always faster than the <N+1> the <K>
<N+1+K> although there has been affecting 'The real future of <N+1>, but not
the same as 'The real future of <N+1>

WANG
JIANWEI

ARTIST

NARCISSUS

QUEEQUEG

ORPHEUS

MONSTER

SNARK

Christ

Espaldas de Dios

horizon

Donald Campbell

M A T E R I A L I T Y

DANGER

tingle

CURDS

TOES

SPIDERS

MUD

Betty

Sally Hampson

Le Jété

Paul Perry

Marcel

Frankenstein

Dorian

Bonnet-maker etc.

Billiard-marker

Beaver

Boots

Banker

Broker

Baker

tingle

ermine

Stewart Home

Stewart Home

Stewart Home

Stewart Home

Stewart Home

Stewart Home

Stewart Home

Harry Kipper

Stewart Home

Stewart Home

Luther Blisset

Darko Maver

SACRIFICE

ORPHEUS

Ahab

QUEEQUEG

Ishmael

ZONE OF NO RISK

NARCISSUS

Will Self

Tonia Bern-Campbell

VENTURE

ping!

song

Robert Frost

Francis

SPONGE

Wallace Stevens

Rainer Maria Rilke

T. S. Eliot

P R O J E C T I O N

Orange

ping!

je repète

ping!

SPHERE

plane

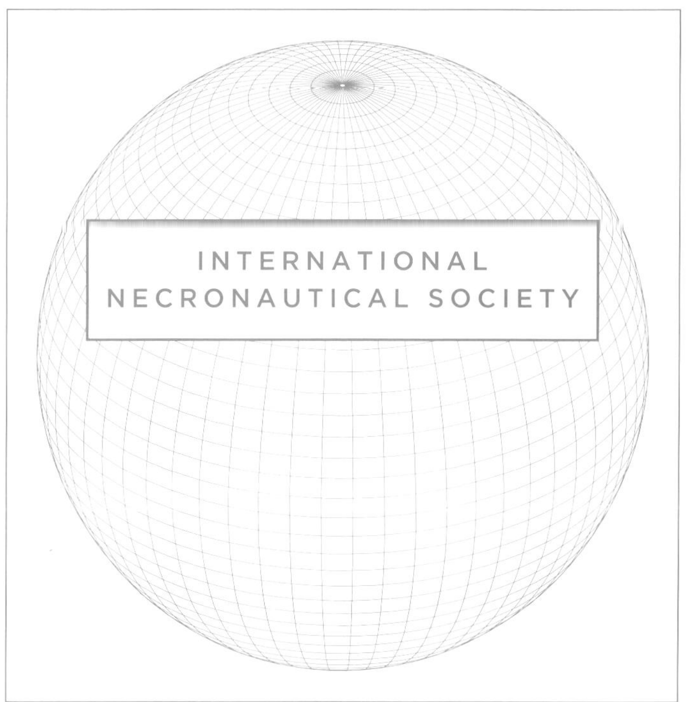

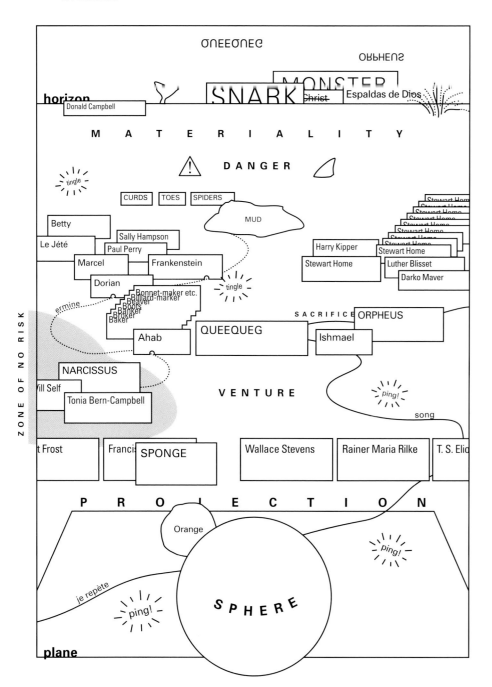

ERNESTO NETO	*A Seed of Brasília*	A frame of the meeting point between the small grid of streets and the large grid of avenues of the diagonally planned city of Belo Horizonte.

This pre-Mondrian plan, where a square becomes a lozenge, post-stardom Paris over a New York of squarely blocks, is the driving will of modernity of a Baroque colonial people, lodged on a soft-earthed valley, *cachaça*[1] in a streetlamp where vertical means downward, where hardness becomes crooked, leaving the *caboclo*[2] both rigorous and malicious, in the confusion of possibilities of a six-part crossroads.

ARTIST

[1] A Brazilian liquor produced from sugar cane

[2] A person of mixed of native Brazilian (Indian) and European (normally Portuguese) descent

Translated from the Portuguese by Renato Rezende

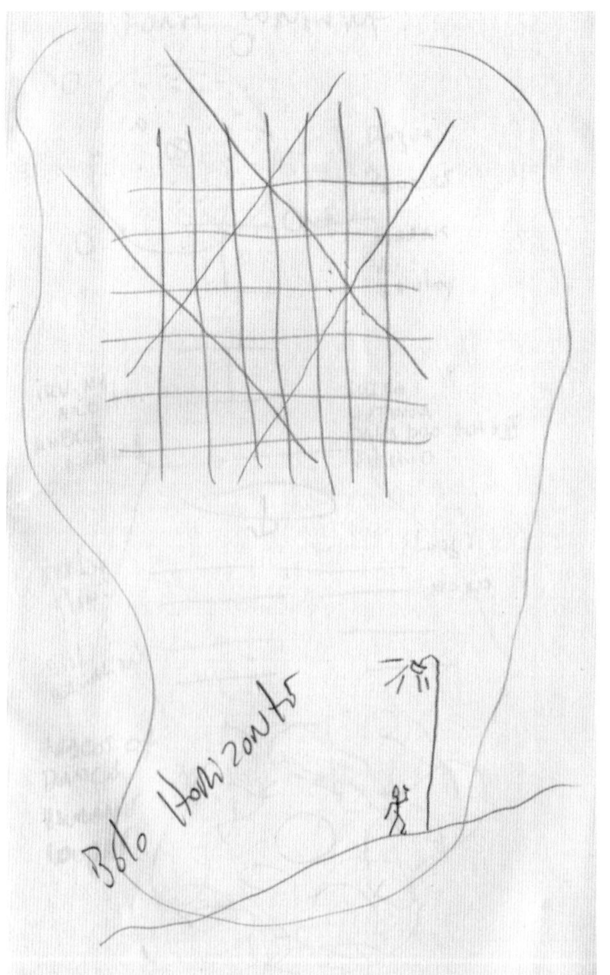

JULIETA ARANDA

ARTIST

The Unmappable: Breadcrumb Trails, 2010
∞° / ...° (from where to measure the ocean)

There is a valuable aspect to getting lost: the moment when the question 'Where am I?' breaks into my assigned set of tasks and trajectories, and impregnates my world for a second. A disruption is made and I have to establish myself in relationship to the objects that surround me: Where am I? Who am I? Who am I while I am here?

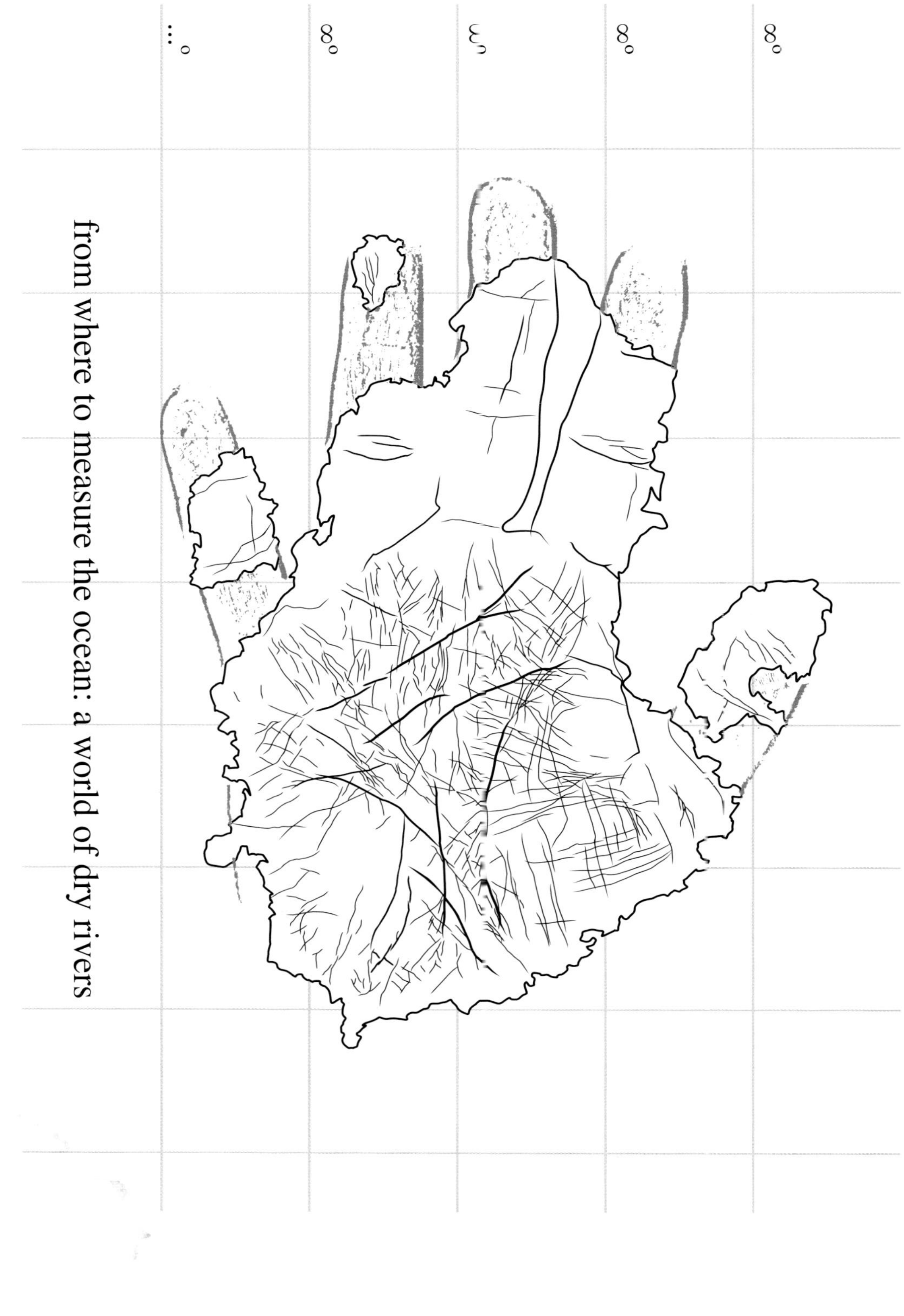

SANAA
(KAZUYO SEJIMA & RYUE NISHIZAWA)
ARCHITECTS AND URBAN PLANNERS

Ortofoto over Oslo

ØKERN-2

side 91

PLAN- OG BYGNINGSETATEN

Foto år 1997

OSLO KOMMUNE

Målestokk 1:5000

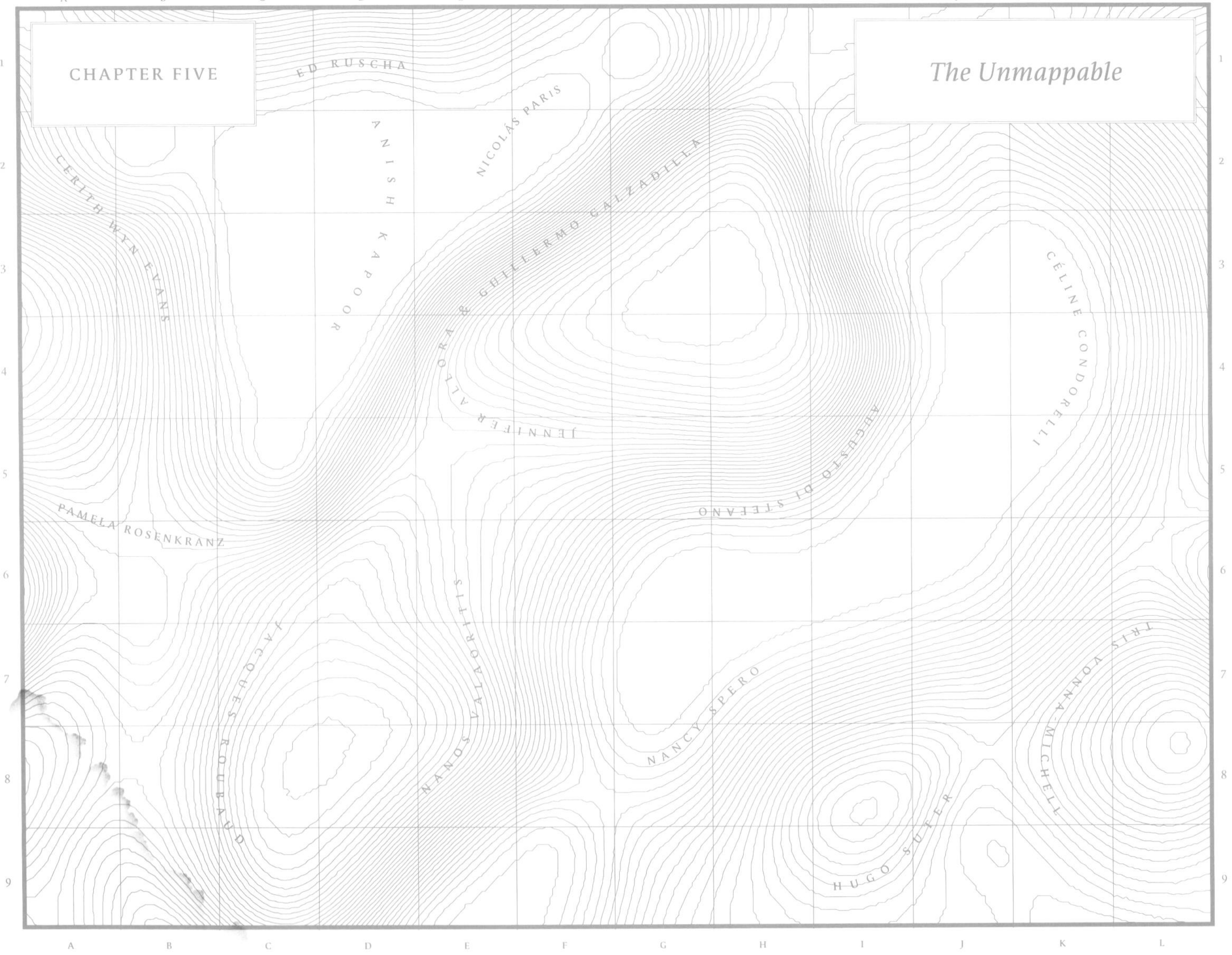
CHAPTER FIVE
The Unmappable
ED RUSCHA
ANISH KAPOOR
NICOLÁS PARIS
CERITH WYN EVANS
JENNIFER ALLORA & GUILLERMO CALZADILLA
CÉLINE CONDORELLI
AUGUSTO DI STEFANO
PAMELA ROSENKRANZ
JACQUES ROUBAUD
NANOS VALAORITIS
NANCY SPERO
HUGO SUTER
TRIS VONNA-MICHELL

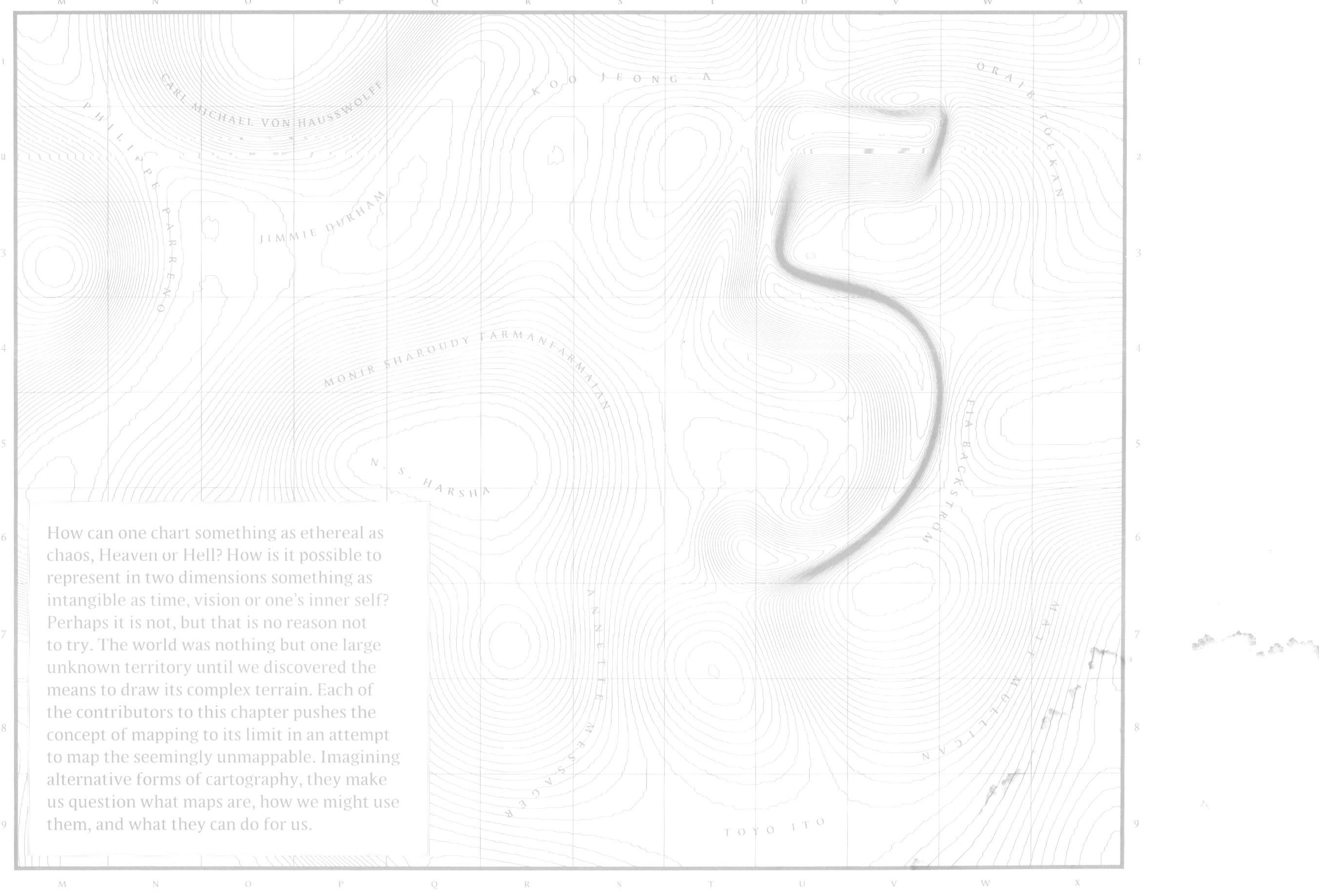

How can one chart something as ethereal as chaos, Heaven or Hell? How is it possible to represent in two dimensions something as intangible as time, vision or one's inner self? Perhaps it is not, but that is no reason not to try. The world was nothing but one large unknown territory until we discovered the means to draw its complex terrain. Each of the contributors to this chapter pushes the concept of mapping to its limit in an attempt to map the seemingly unmappable. Imagining alternative forms of cartography, they make us question what maps are, how we might use them, and what they can do for us.

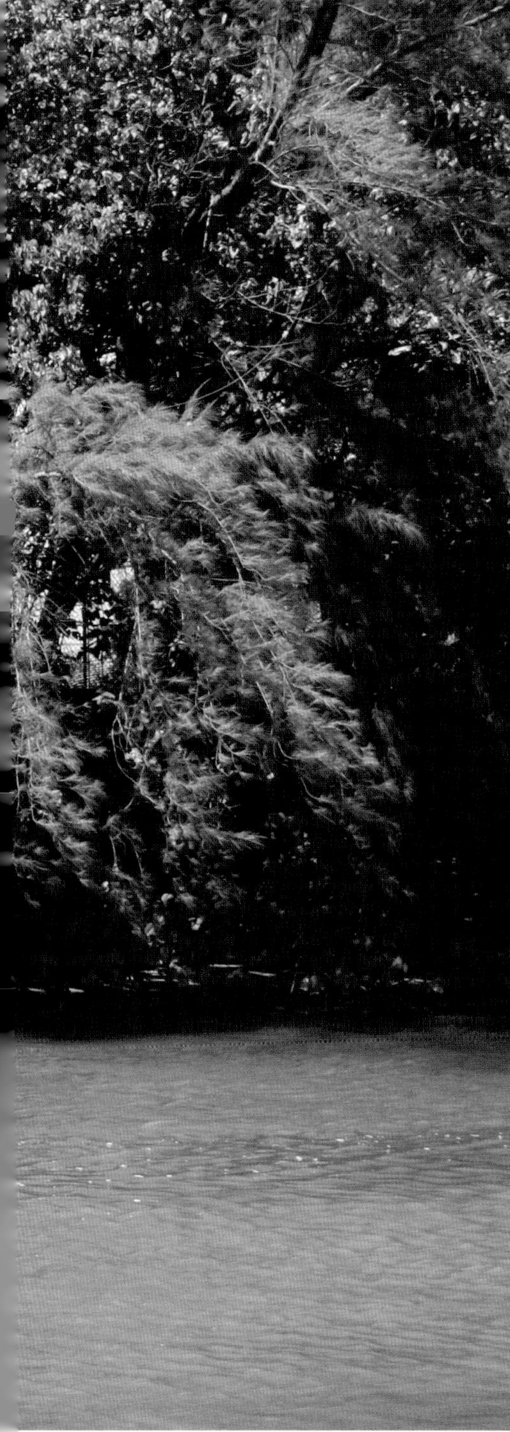

JENNIFER ALLORA & GUILLERMO CALZADILLA

f o r e c a s t

ARTISTS

Forecast uses the photographic apparatus to present the precise moment of formal stasis in the trajectory of a fishing net's casting into the water, where the lift of flight and the pull of gravity act equally upon its woven matrix of threads. ¶ The result is an amorphous shape that presents a possible form to come as well as its simultaneous disappearance. The collection of vertices, edges and faces that define the shape of this polyhedral object form a temporary map across physical, conceptual and poetic domains.

CÉLINE CONDORELLI

ARTIST

Terrain Vague, Persistent Images

2012 (detail)

series of levels, roughly by the scale of area involved, so that the observer moved as necessary from an image at street level to levels of a neighborhood, a city, or a metropolitan region.

This arrangement by levels is a necessity in a large and complex environment. Yet it imposes an extra burden of organization on the observer, especially if there is little relation between levels. If a tall building is unmistakable in the city-wide panorama yet unrecognizable from its base, then a chance has been lost to pin together the images at two different levels of organization. The State House on Beacon Hill, on the other hand, seems to pierce through several image levels. It holds a strategic place in the organization of the center.

Images may differ not only by the scale of area involved, but by viewpoint, time of day, or season. The image of Faneuil Hall as seen from the markets should be related to its image from a car on the Artery. Washington-Street-by-night should have some continuity, some element of invariance, with Washington-Street-by-day. In order to accomplish this continuity in the face of sensuous confusion, many observers drained their images of visual content, using abstractions such as "restaurant" or "second street." These will operate both day and night, driving or walking, rain or shine, albeit with some effort and loss.

The observer must also adjust his image to secular shifts in the physical reality around him. Los Angeles illustrated the practical and emotional strains induced as the image is confronted with constant physical changes. It would be important to know how to maintain continuity through these changes. Just as ties are needed between level and level of organization, so are continuities required which persist through a major change. This might be facilitated by the retention of an old tree, a path trace, or some regional character.

The sequence in which sketch maps were drawn seemed to indicate that the image develops, or grows, in different ways. This may perhaps have some relation to the way in which it first develops as an individual becomes familiar with his environment. Several types were apparent:

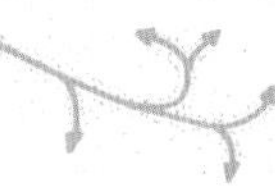

a. Quite frequently, images were developed along, and then outward from, familiar lines of movement. Thus a map might

be drawn as branching out from a point of entrance, or beginning from some base line such as Massachusetts Avenue.

b. Other maps were begun by the construction of an enclosing outline, such as the Boston peninsula, which was then filled in toward the center.

c. Still others, particularly in Los Angeles, began by laying down a basic repeating pattern (the path gridiron) and then adding detail.

d. Somewhat fewer maps started as a set of adjacent regions, which were then detailed as to connections and interiors.

e. A few Boston examples developed from a familiar kernel, a dense familiar element on which everything was ultimately hung.

The image itself was not a precise, miniaturized model of reality, reduced in scale and consistently abstracted. As a purposive simplification, it was made by reducing, eliminating, or even adding elements to reality, by fusion and distortion, by relating and structuring the parts. It was sufficient, perhaps better, for its purpose if rearranged, distorted, "illogical." It resembled that famous cartoon of the New Yorker's view of the United States.

However distorted, there was a strong element of topological invariance with respect to reality. It was as if the map were drawn on an infinitely flexible rubber sheet; directions were twisted, distances stretched or compressed, large forms so changed from their accurate scale projection as to be at first unrecognizable. But the sequence was usually correct, the map was rarely torn and sewn back together in another order. This continuity is necessary if the image is to be of any value.

Image Quality

Study of various individual images among the Bostonians revealed certain other distinctions between them. For example, images of an element differed between observers in terms of their relative density, i.e., the extent to which they were packed with detail. They might be relatively dense, as a picture of Newbury Street which identifies each building along its length, or relatively

plan (for a history), 2011

The work pairs two homes of the same individual, though from different times (in childhood … and as an adult) and at varying locations.

AUGUSTO DI STEFANO

ARTIST

JIMMIE
DURHAM

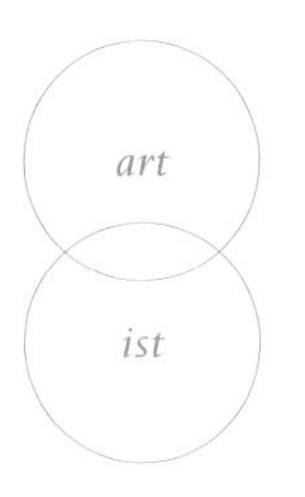

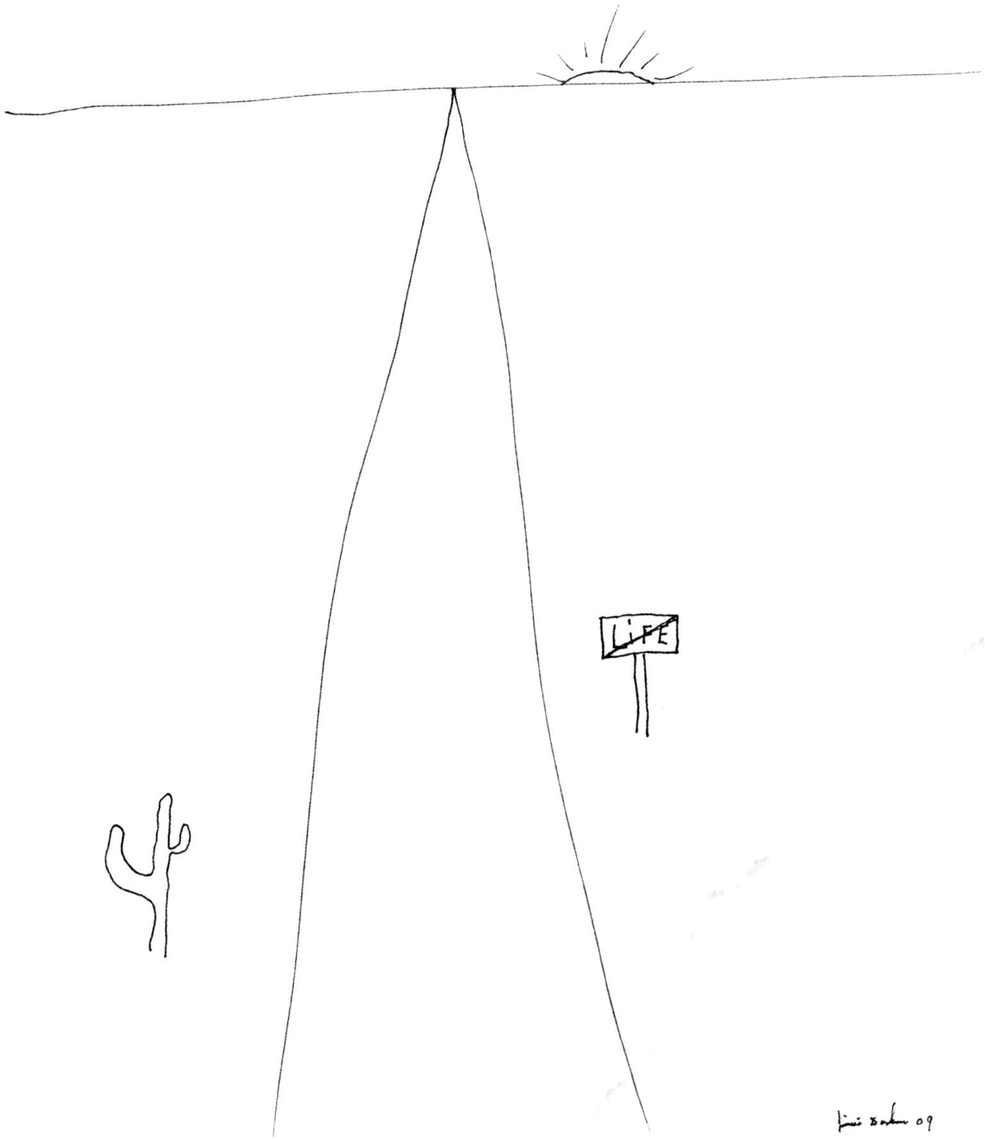

FIA BACKSTRÖM

ARTIST

A future where hazy lines and doped-up grids dissolve into limitless abstraction, a light blue fantasia of synthetic curaçao – an elixir to crack open corporate colour into fuzzy fuzzy flu-like fluzy.

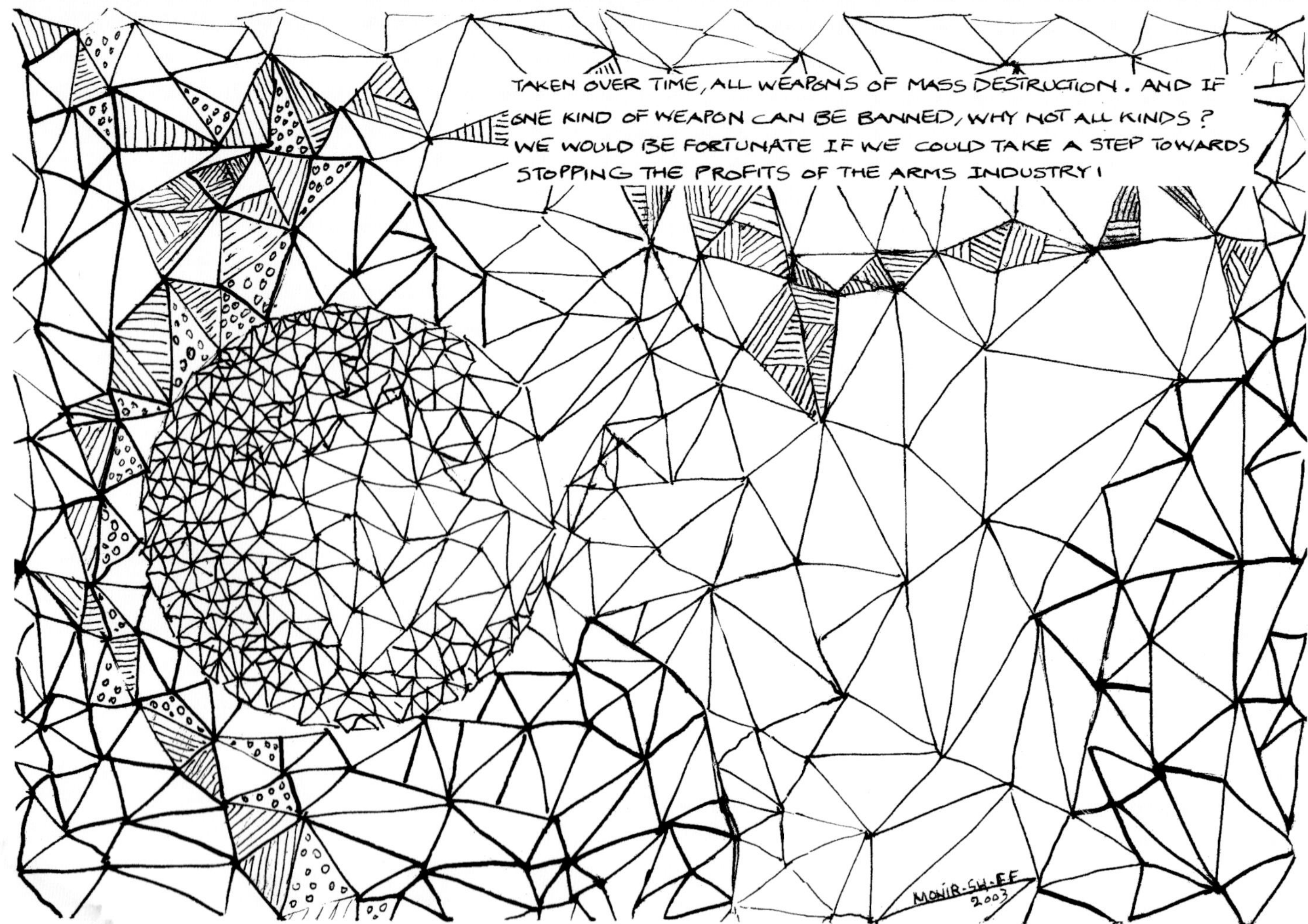

MONIR SHAROUDY FARMANFARMAIAN

ARTIST

As always, I feel the most interesting maps of the twenty-first century would be drawn from the internal journey that humans make into 'oneself'. These journeys would be fuelled by a 'thirst' to experience the cosmos that is 'within'. This will not be an easy terrain to venture into, with the present globalized situation, because humans are celebrating 'matter' on a global scale, which is resulting in a direct conflict with the 'natural order'.

N. S. HARSHA

A R T I S T

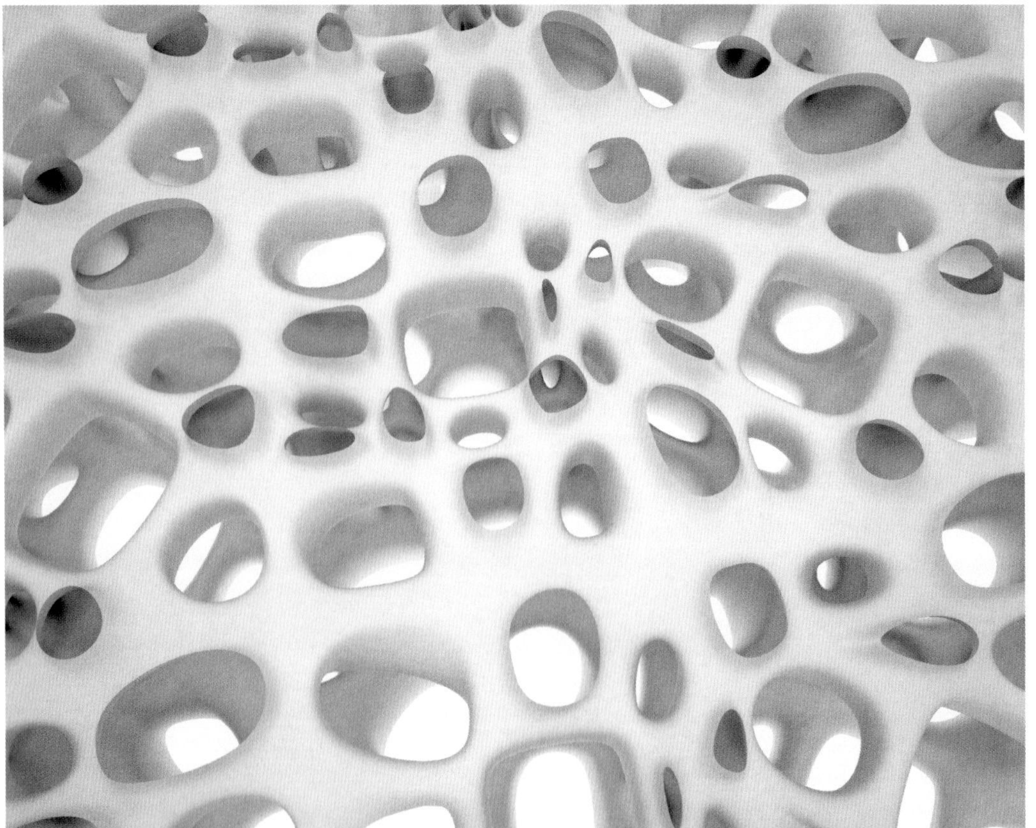

TOYO ITO

ARCHITECT

In the twentieth century, a city's map was drawn by means of linear grids seen vertically from above. We have, however, become weary of its simplicity, homogeneity and transparency. In the twenty-first century, we utilize instead the Emerging Grid to draw maps above and below ground, consequently generating a complex, diverse, and fractal labyrinth.

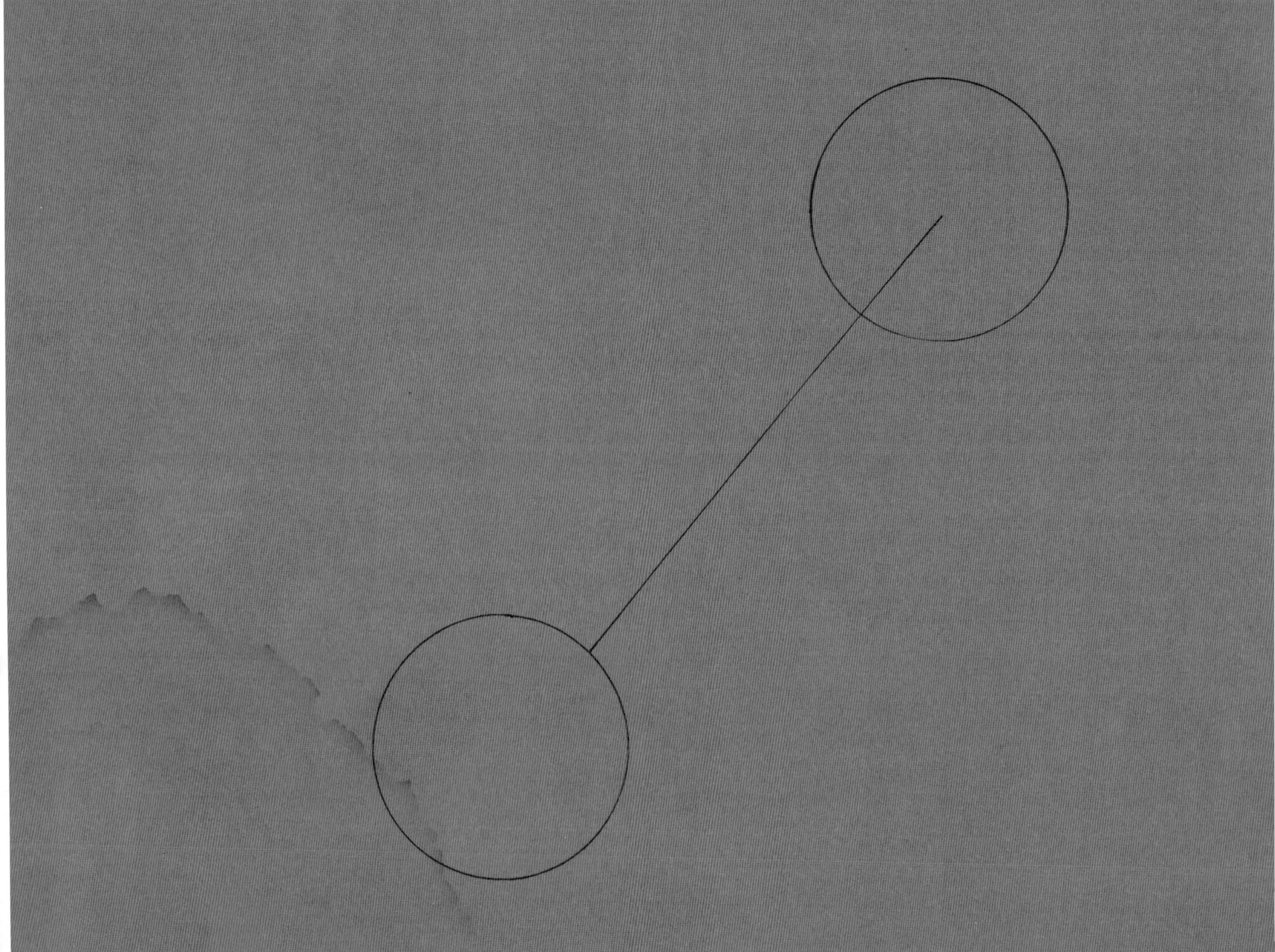

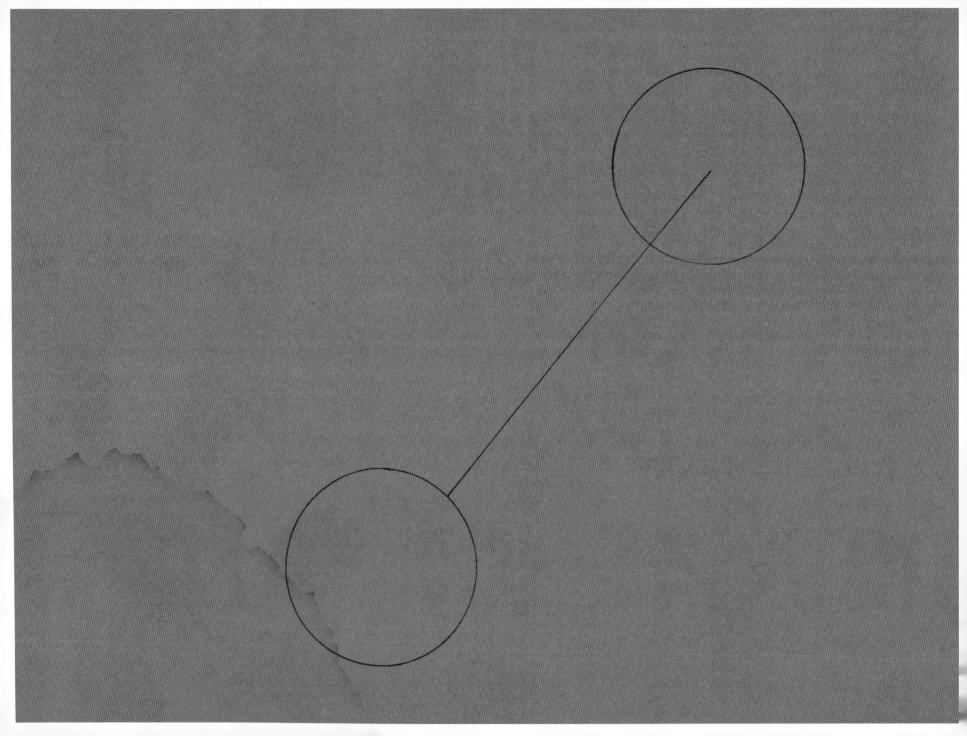

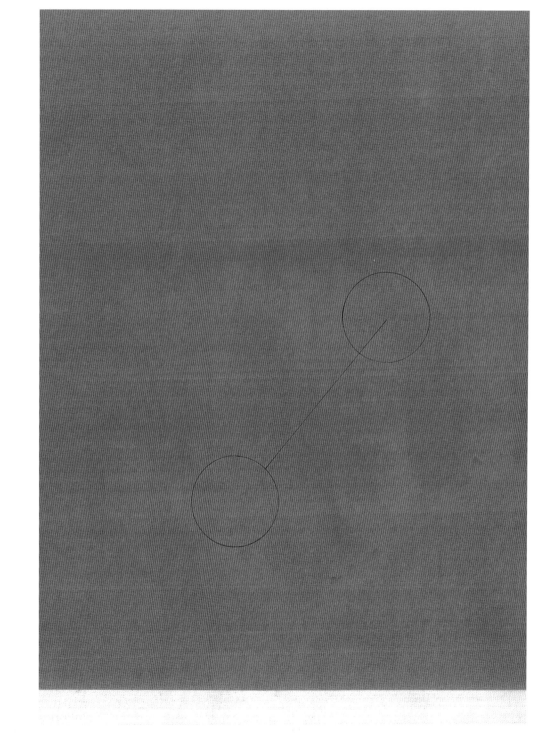
KOO JEONG-A
ARTIST
Map, 2010

ANNETTE MESSAGER
ARTIST
Worlds of dancing planets? Enemy worlds? Worlds of celestial bodies and words?
Garbage worlds? It is our war of the worlds ...

vertigo
futile

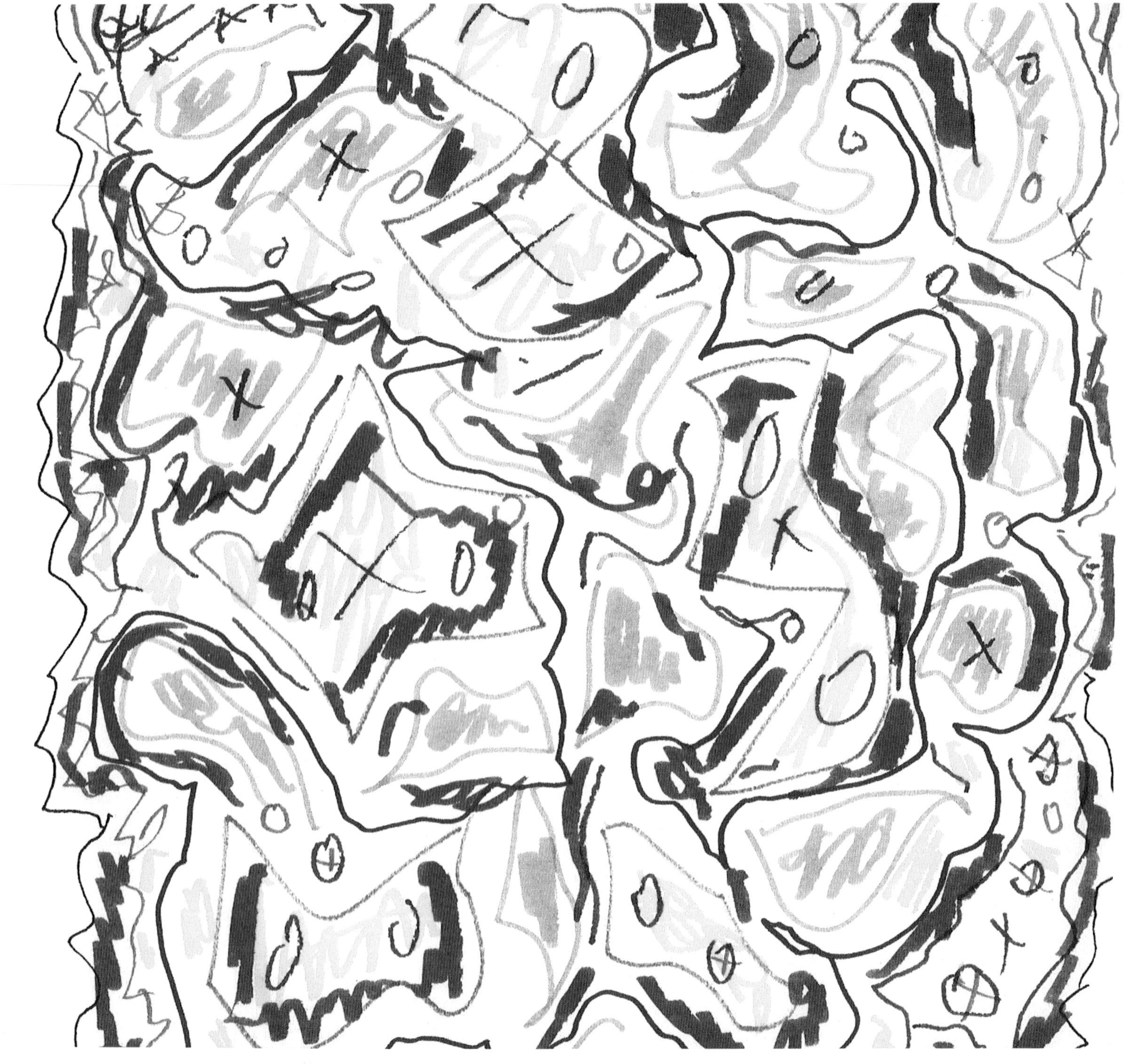

NANOS VALAORITIS

WRITER

Chaos, 2010

Chaos is the state of the Cosmos, in Greek/Orphic cosmogony. Out of Chaos the Universe was born, by the intervention of Eros, produced by an egg of Night, who mingled with Chaos and produced the race of the gods in Tartaros. Today the theory of Chaos has returned in science, so that we can envisage an image of things mingled with each other in the beginning. This does not differ so much from the soup of elementary particles in the early Universe as posited by some scientists. Nothing much has changed in theory since then. Only the particulars.

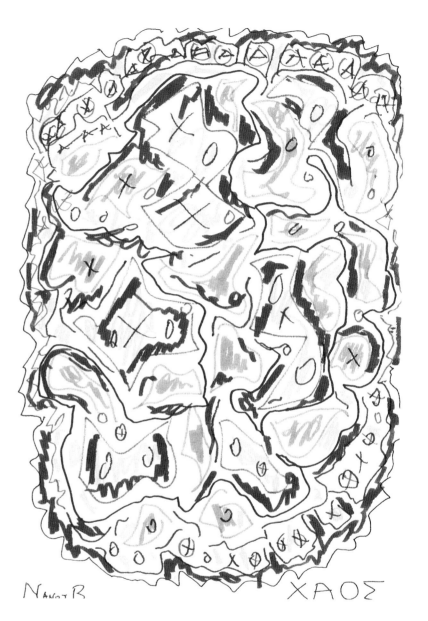

MATT MULLICAN | ARTIST

the year of the calendar

2001
2007
2012
2018
2029
2035
2040
2046
2057
2063
2068
2074
2085
2091
2096

A calendar is a map of the future. These are that person's drawings. That person loves calendars because they tell us when we have working days and holidays, and he loves holidays. In November we have Thanksgiving, which he likes because he likes the Macy's Thanksgiving Day Parade in particular ...

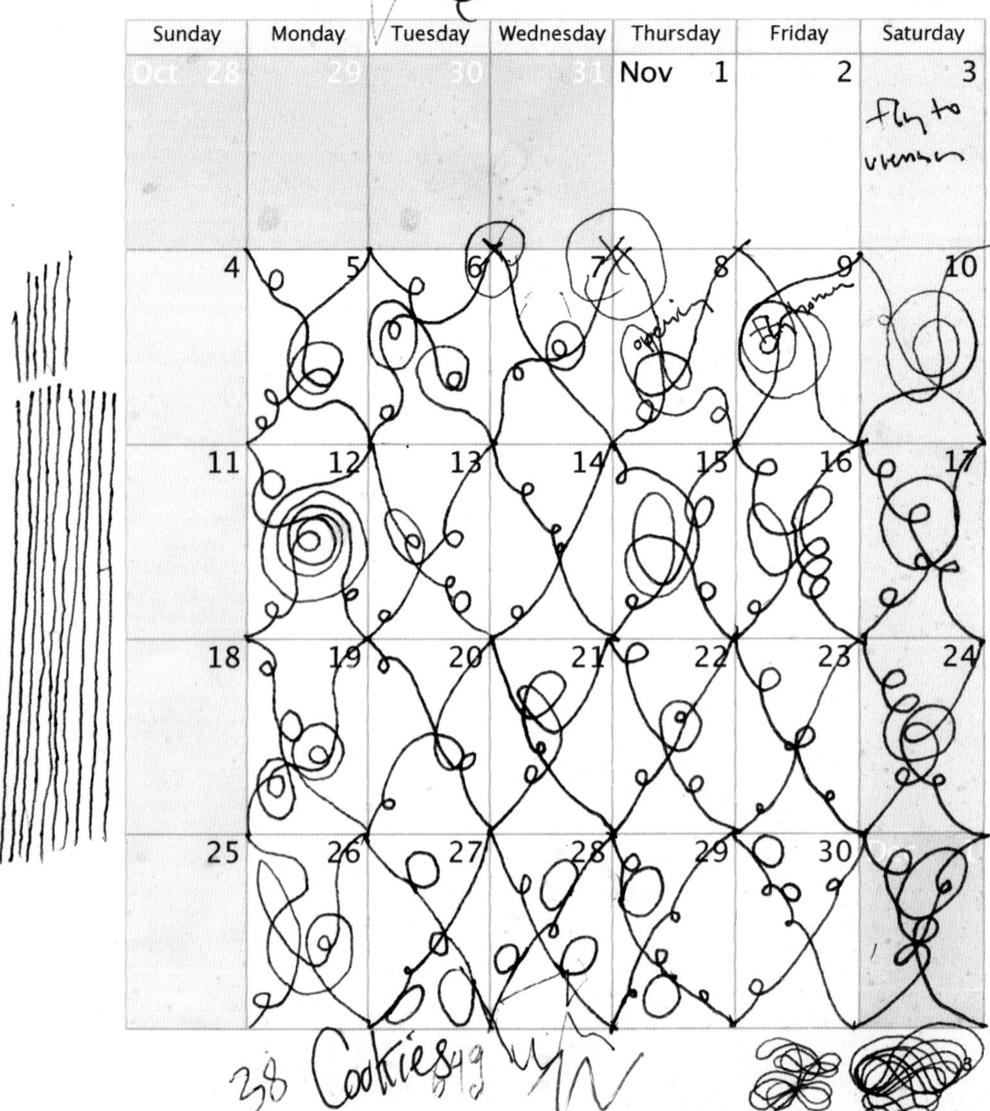

November 2007

December

S	M	T	W	T	F	S
						1
2	3	4	5	6	7	8
9	10	11	12	13	14	15
16	17	18	19	20	21	22
23	24	25	26	27	28	29
30	31					

ay	Tuesday	Wednesday	Thursday	Friday	Saturday
29	30	31	Nov 1	2	3 Fly to vienna
5	6	7	8	9	10

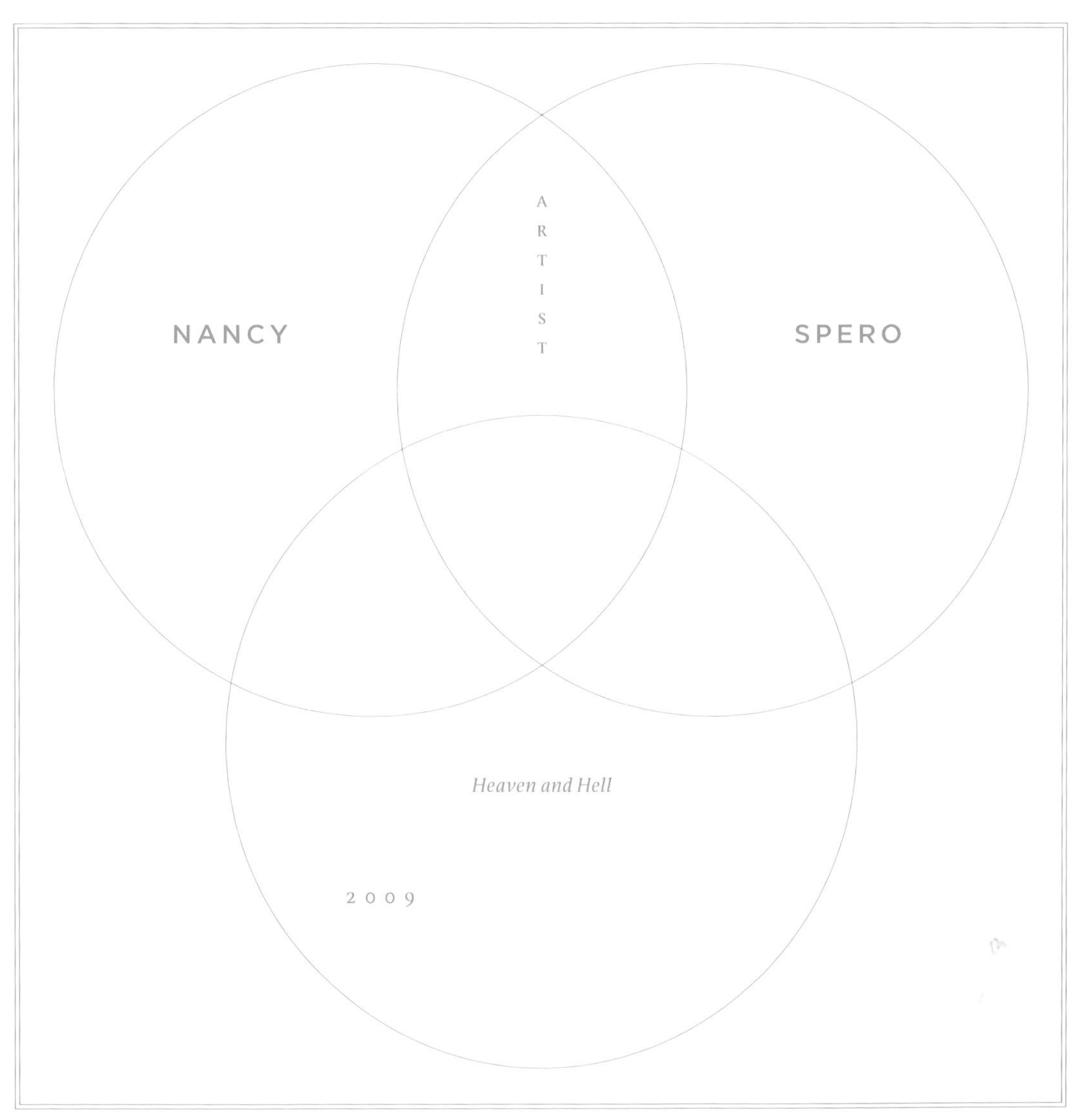
NANCY
A R T I S T
SPERO
Heaven and Hell
2009

HUGO SUTER

A R T I S T

Architecture (fluid/solid) Calming issues moving while moving does not issue calming, 2008

'Only he who lives for the day is present in alert calmness when the apparent matter of course turns into strangeness and when knowledge draws back into the fabric of premonition, the daily process with its colloidal phases of liquefaction and solidification, getting him lost in a swirl becoming a nest builder.'
'Flottierendes Material', 1998

'Movement does not emerge from stillness, stillness initially arises from movement.'

RUDOLF STEINER
24 June 1924

PAMELA ROSENKRANZ
A
R
T
I
S
T

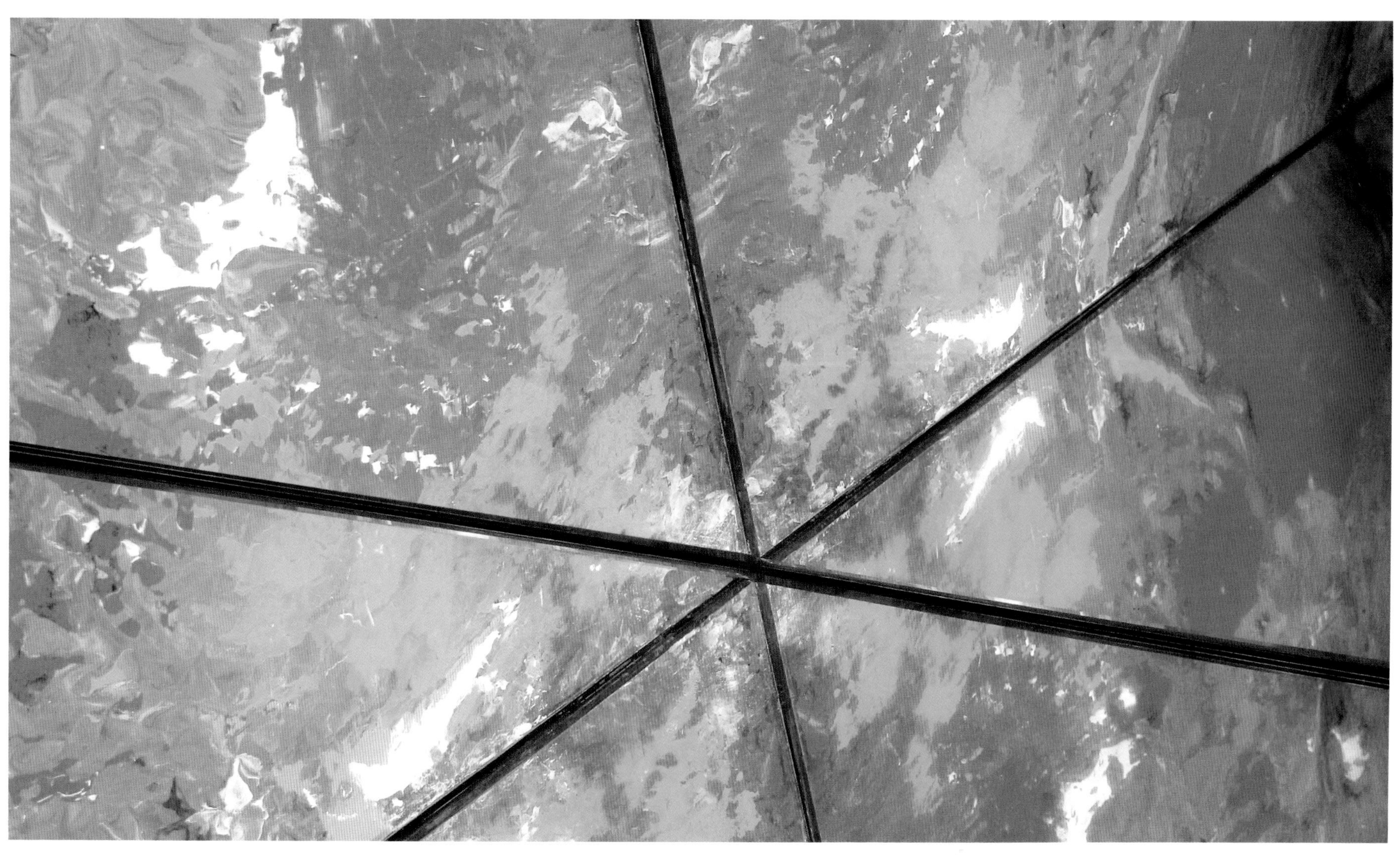

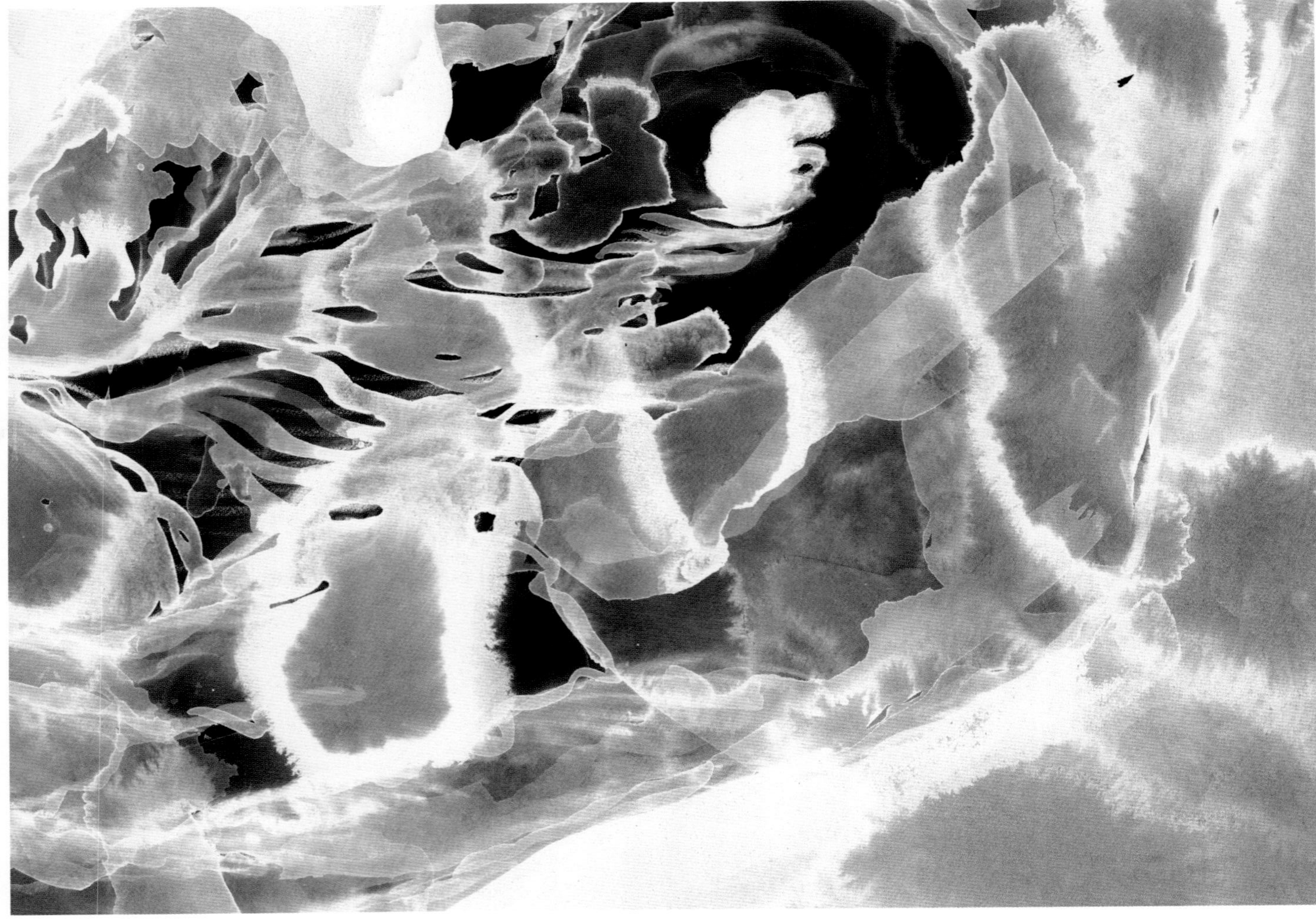

P H I L I P P E P A R R E N O

A – R – T – I – S – T

I did not know what to draw when I was asked to do a map, so I drew the skin of a cuttlefish. The reason why I did that was because I was kind of trying to be original, but also because I love this animal. A cuttlefish is a cephalopod, and most cephalopods have a skin that that contains chromatophores – that is, coloured pigments. Their colours can change in milliseconds; they adapt to their surrounding. They change colours to communicate in what my friend Jaron Lanier defined as being a post-symbolic form of communication. That is to say, in order to say 'crab' or 'algae', they turn into a crab or algae. But while drawing that creature, I was thinking that chromatophores also, and maybe mainly, provide those creatures with camouflage with their background, allowing them to disguise shadows from any predators by glowing.... When chromatophores glow on the skin, the shadow of the cuttlefish gets to be erased on the sand. So predators can't notice their presence. That is to say they become invisible. And I would like talk about mapping and invisibility. I would like to talk about transparent forms rather than communication forms. I would like to talk us out of the photo-logic in which we are. As Derrida wrote, that's what annihilates force and duration for the illusion of the simultaneous and the form. This obsession to mistake seeing with understanding, because at the end we all say 'I see' in order to say 'I understand'. To say it differently, what is real is not necessarily what is visible. You must remember the opening scene of *Un Chien andalou*, the Andalusian dog, when Buñuel cut the eye of the character with a razor in a famous close-up shot. I am just throwing some ideas here. Some notes. Nothing articulated really, just notes ... I guess there is here a paradox when an artist talks about invisibility. But I think maps should concern that. A map is something between a photograph and a painting. There's a strange process of creation where things are not created but where a frame is established that allows something to happen. We could call that a map – a map that produces a world. What a musician calls a score. A score that allow the instrumentalist to rearrange the music he is playing while playing it. This is what I we could call anarchic creation, a process of non-authoritarian creation. To track or trace particulars. To return authority from the artist as author to things in the happening of their truth. To return towards things in the happening of their truth is, to use another cinematic example, what Werner Herzog calls 'ecstatic truth'. One of the first things I did when I had my first exhibition was to organize a demonstration with kids in the street shouting 'No More Reality'. What does that mean, No More Reality? Isn't the case that there is no reality. It was an awareness that the condition of the image in the society in which we live is one of complete commodification, branding, surfaces, the magic of the commodity, as Marx would say. I am more concerned by what is not visible because I don't believe in resolution. That is the problem of Sony. I don't know much about maps and mapping, but I know that we have been using topological metaphors a lot during the different conversations I have had with Hans Ulrich Obrist over the last fifteen years. The metaphor consisted of taking *In search of lost time* as a great map, and the novelist is a great mapmaker. Recording what is not visible. And not recording with a media type of recorder. 'Invisibility' is thus the opposite of visibility, the other side of it within the ideological space. It is what has to remain invisible so that the visible may be visible. In the same way, the 'excluded' are, of course, visible, in the precise sense that, paradoxically, their exclusion itself is the mode of their inclusion: their 'proper place' in the social body is that of exclusion. I am now working on a feature film, called *Invisible Boy*. It is the portrait of an illegal Chinese child in New York, in Manhattan. It is a commercial film that tries to understand his anxiety through a series of creatures or monsters that incarnate his fears. So his paranoia gives me a way to map the city. I would like to end with a story that Hans knows really well because I have been talking about it a few times. I met Jean-François Lyotard after he did his famous exhibition called 'Les Immatériaux' (the Immaterials) in the late eighties in Paris. It was an important show for me. The catalogue was made of correspondences through time between the participants via an intranet system. The show was a great text by Lyotard, a show with no concept. The second show he wanted to do was supposed to be called 'Résistance'. It did not sound really sexy, but it's resistance in a way to try to address what theorems neglect. The force of resistance that heats up in a system throwing doubt into a theory.

NICOLÁS PARIS

ARTIST

DYnamic
MAXimum
tensION
MAP

Would you believe it if
Buckminster Fuller told you
that the continents are
but one single island?

Would you believe it if
Buckminster Fuller told you that
the continents are one system,
all connected to each other?

Would you believe it if
Buckminster Fuller told you
that even the farthest points
of a line stand side by side?

CUT OUT THE 'DYMAXION MAP' FOLLOWING THE BOLD DOTTED OUTLINE, THEN FOLD IT FOLLOWING THE DOTTED INSIDE LINES.

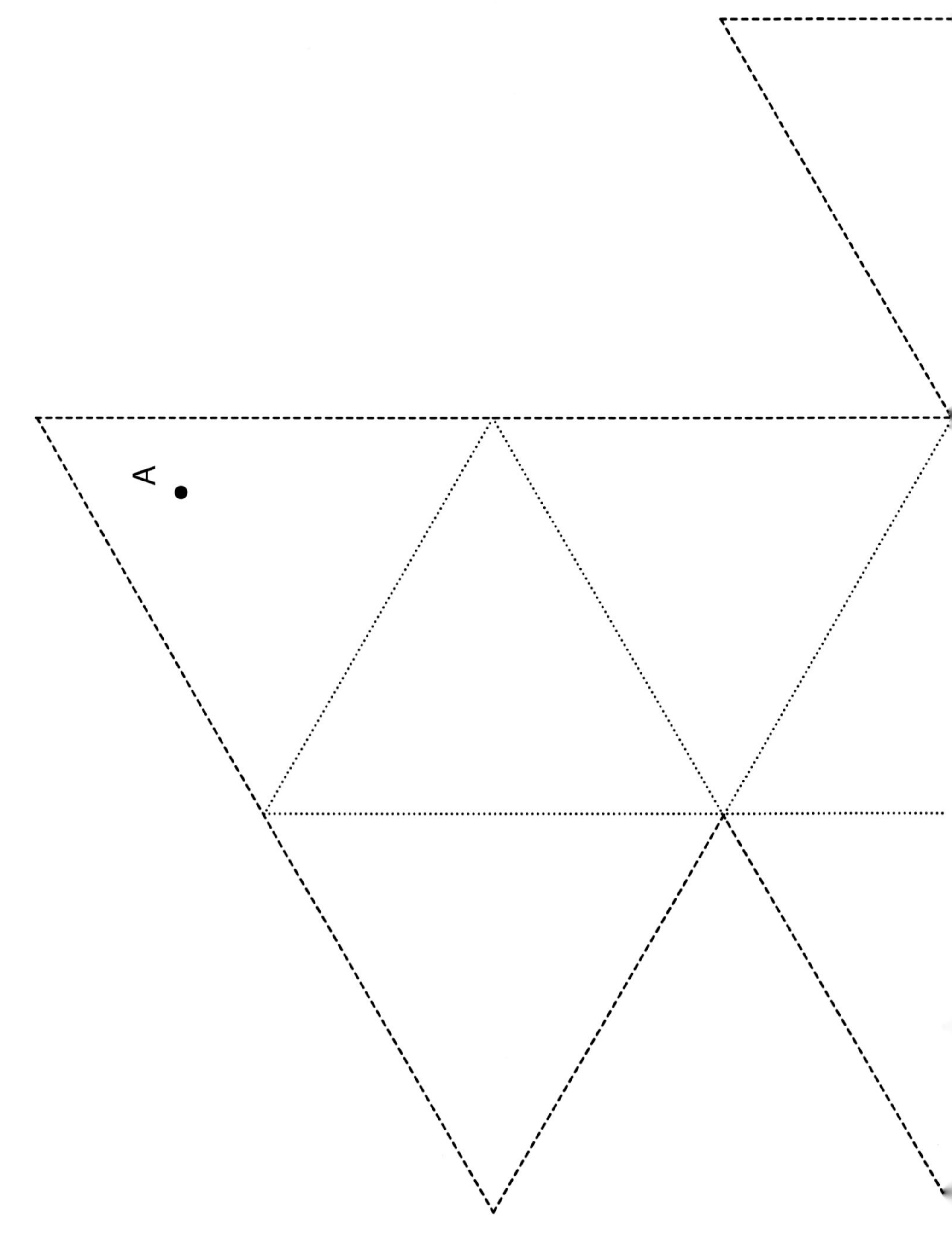

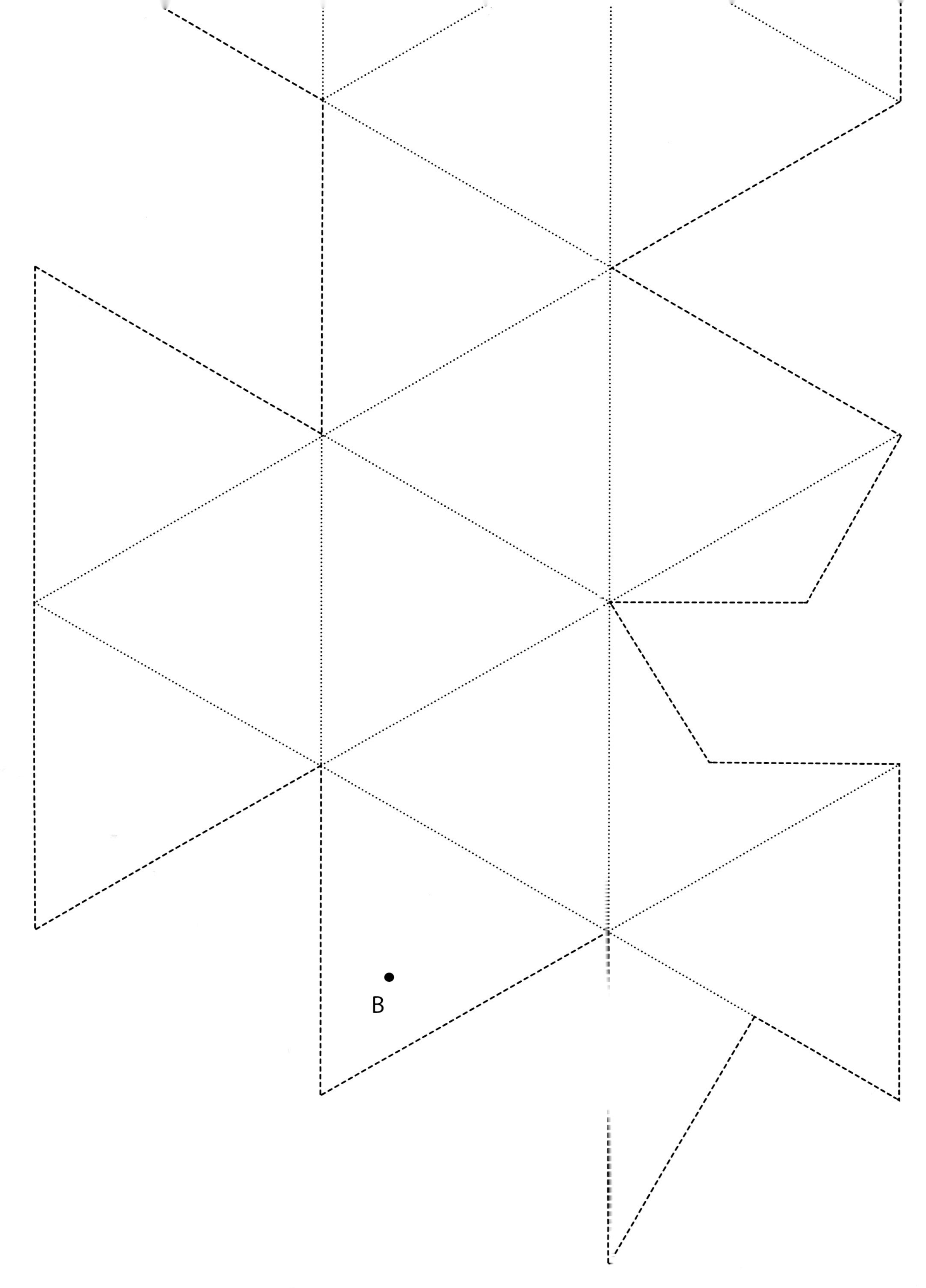
B

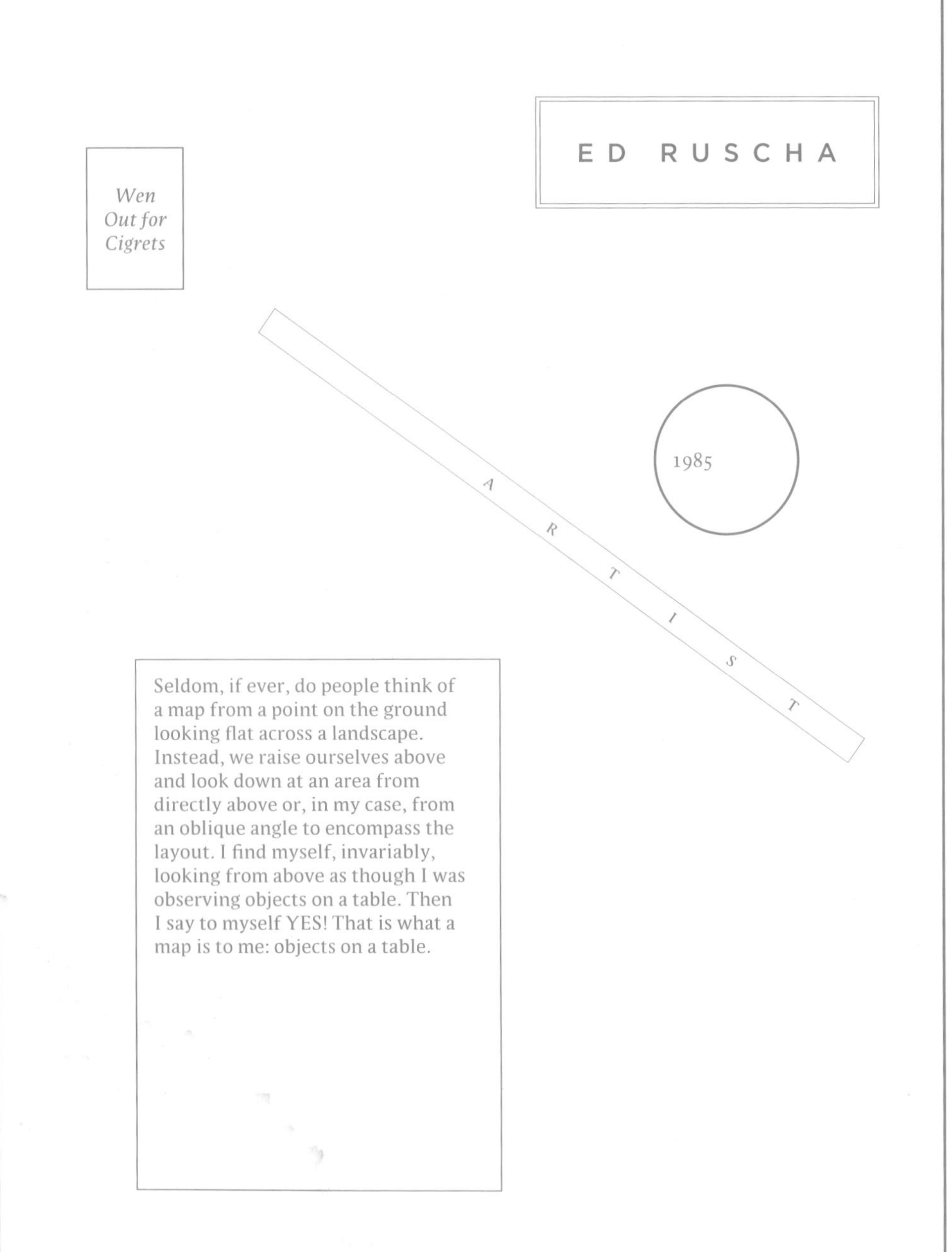
ED RUSCHA
Wen Out for Cigrets
A R T I S T
1985
Seldom, if ever, do people think of a map from a point on the ground looking flat across a landscape. Instead, we raise ourselves above and look down at an area from directly above or, in my case, from an oblique angle to encompass the layout. I find myself, invariably, looking from above as though I was observing objects on a table. Then I say to myself YES! That is what a map is to me: objects on a table.

WEN OUT
FOR CIGRETS
N NEVER
CAME BACK

THE RED MAP (scanned school world atlas symbol for 'City with More Than 1,000,000 inhabitants') | This map could be a version of Kasimir Malevich's *Red Square* (1915). It is the map of the world in a physical sense. The reddish surface represents the 'A-World' as we know it. All areas are either urban and hyper-developed or super-cultured and exploited. Humans have stepped on everything everywhere. There are no white spots left to explore. The black frame represents the border between being able and not being able – the black void stopping us from exploiting other worlds. The other worlds continue outside ...

THE WHITE MAP | (scanned part of an offset reproduction of Robert Rauschenberg's *White Painting (Two Panel)*, 1951) | This map could be a new version of one of the works from Rauschenberg's White Paintings series. It is the map of the world in a mental sense. The white surface represents the 'B-World' as we know it. All areas are subject to the mental capacity of all life forms where ideas, thoughts and feelings oscillate back and forth in a giving and taking mode. Apart from certain dusty areas, it can never be exploited and its omnipotence covers the entire system of universes.

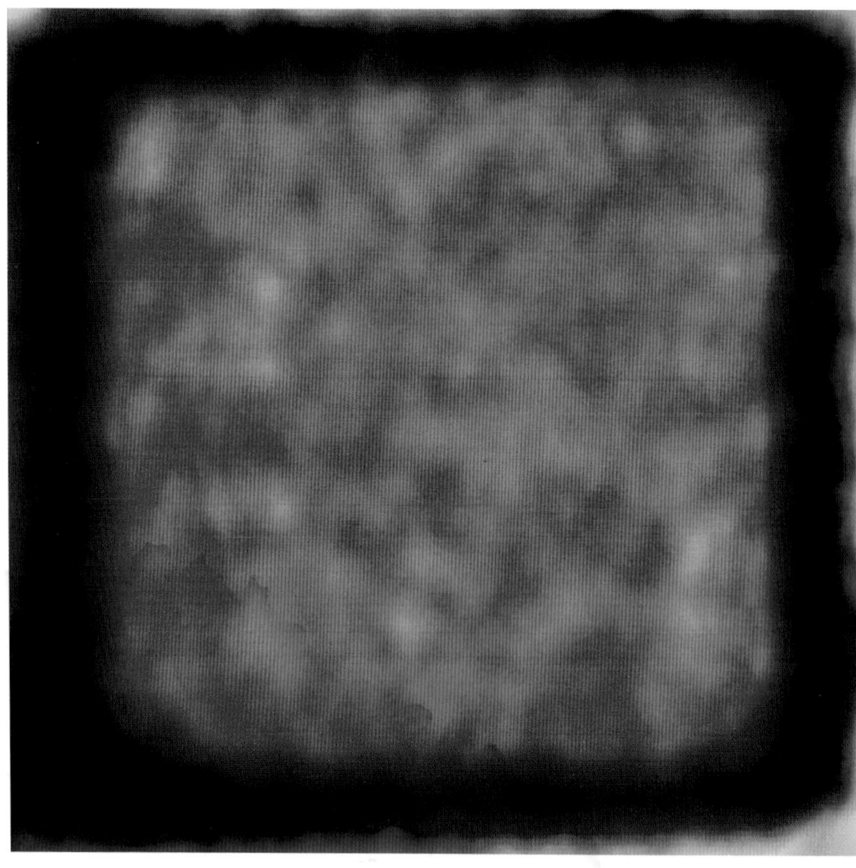

ORAIB TOUKAN

ARTIST 20/20

A
WOMAN
WITH
20/20
VISION
CAN
SEE
THE
SAME
DETAIL
FROM
20
FEET
AWAY
AS
ANOTHER
WOMAN
20
FEET
AWAY.
A
WOMAN
WITH
20/10
VISION
CAN
SEE
A
DETAIL
FROM
20
FEET
AWAY
AS
ANOTHER
WOMAN
CAN
SEE
IT
FROM
10
FEET
AWAY.
AND
SO
ON.

[crowd noises, sound of water being poured and drunk, inhales] so um good evening i actually just finished a performance about three minutes ago and i kind of er wasnt prepared to perform again in four minutes but nonetheless if i can fix this um i will try to continue from the first chapter [sound of egg timer being wound] chapter one and maybe even repeat the prelude [handling the egg timer] thats not working its its definitely not ticking ive got a spare one [sound of the bell of the egg timer] so [inhales deeply and exhales] there we go [sound of egg timer being wound] i spent most of the day today in this room and i paced up and down and i kind of believed that certain grid structures or curvatures or light fixtures or curtains or panels or pillars or anything in the space would help me find my place to stand to perform to start to orientate myself and work from to lose my orientation perhaps so i set up over here and then i set up over there and i set up in the corner over there and i drew the curtains back and forth and i had the lights on and off and basically i kind of paced around and believed that there was a right place to perform because acoustically sometimes it kind of projects and stops and kind of like halts here and theres a reverberation but then again i guess its difficult to actually control a space when people walk in and then you basically have to improvise on that occasion but then again i always derail and it always goes somewhere else ive got the egg timer to keep me on track because apparently this is meant to be act two or chapter two and its set well it was set for twelve minutes and one minute was lost just to introduce the story [drinks water] so i think now its probably about eight eight-fifty-two perhaps its supposed to end at er nine o clock and even though i have [single ring of a timer bell and the sound of the timer being wound] i am going to put this on eight minutes but its kind of to the point now where the first two years i was performing with an egg timer because i felt i needed that but now i just realise these things always break and my relationship to talking is always somehow with technology that always just fucks up so i think its apt that both times each act my egg timer experience hasnt been too fruitful and the other misendeavour is that as a kind of conclusion to act three is that the truth is when i arrived i had this idea that i wanted to tell a story

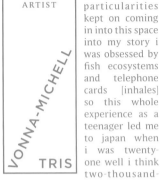

about berlin but when i came here i figured some of the fixtures here in this cylindrical space kind of reminded me of my obsessions as a teenager with telephone cards and i really wanted to return to that these kind of interferences almost like subjective fictional interferences actually truths somehow kept on coming in i know the egg timer is ticking and somehow i always need that but then again its irrelevant as well cos it may not ring but we are running out of time always but somehow these kind of of trajectories particularities kept on coming in into this space into my story i was obsessed by fish ecosystems and telephone cards [inhales] so this whole experience as a teenager led me to japan when i was twenty-one well i think two-thousand-and-one so as a teenager and and in a way somehow telephone cards and fish make sense in this space in this kind of cylindrical space and i did i did promise the third chapter but somehow thats all irrelevant now because i feel the story has come to a point where it only kind of goes around and around and around like a pond like a pond like clarity like in japan when i was in japan but now i am going back to cologne and hahnenstrasse and huhnstrasse and the same point in time the monument but i cant derail from it because when i came here i really wanted to say the story starts here in twothousand-and-one in nagasaki hiroshima hiroshima nagasaki because somehow i remember hiroshima a park bench marble marble and lattice structures and fish and i remember the park bench because toblerones like nori rice cakes or toblerones or lübeck lübeck marzipan or ferrero rocher i remember toblerones because they are triangular [inhales] i remember the toblerones because they had the passport and my clothes my camera my bulbous thirtyfive- mil or aps camera my bulbous large camera in two-thousand-and-one photographing sprockets and spools photographing clicking clicking clicking photographing verification of a journey but irrelevancies because i was in japan to collect telephone cards and to look for fish to marvel at fish to look at circular cylindrical systems like punctuations to look at fish and photograph fish because i love to watch fish and alignments and i wanted to feed the fish and i wanted to go and look at the fish from nagasaki to hiroshima from tokyo with the shinkansen bullet train or a bullet train or a bullet or a barbed wire but every time i wanted to say shinkansen bullet bullet and japan and exoticism and otherness i always went back to berlin and here and somehow i never wanted to talk about berlin but then again the train station was always there on my mind starts here or europe one facade north pole south pole asia africa four buses one tunnel stand back please s-bahn or u-bahn berlin dog walking wastelands bomb bomb bomb bang bang bang barbwire concrete americans communication again and again why are the russians in such a hurry to get beneath this one train station? its irrelevant one facade one monument one street sign i am failing like i always fail and i am running out of time why didnt you just go on google? youre mocking me bang reinhold hahn find out the cock reinhold huhn bingo nineteen-sixty-two twentysecond of june east to west my female chicken my family and the bullet the bullet now we have a man who dies for communism our female chicken who protects us ive got an image and the story ends and i realise its impossible to tell you this story in yes hmmm eight minutes or twelve in this space this city this place is always beyond me and every time i tried to capture something in this place he took me by the arm and said come with me your papers are wrong es stimmt nicht papiers papiers mind the gap please mind the gap please zurück bleiben zurück bleiben stand back an interrogation of a place a space capturing an image it took me elsewhere city time place and ending in berlin eighteen-eightyeight or eighteen-eighty-two the dates change repetition relocating crashing crashing

JACQUES ROUBAUD

MATHEMATICIAN (RETIRED) AND POET (NOT RETIRED, BUT TIRED)

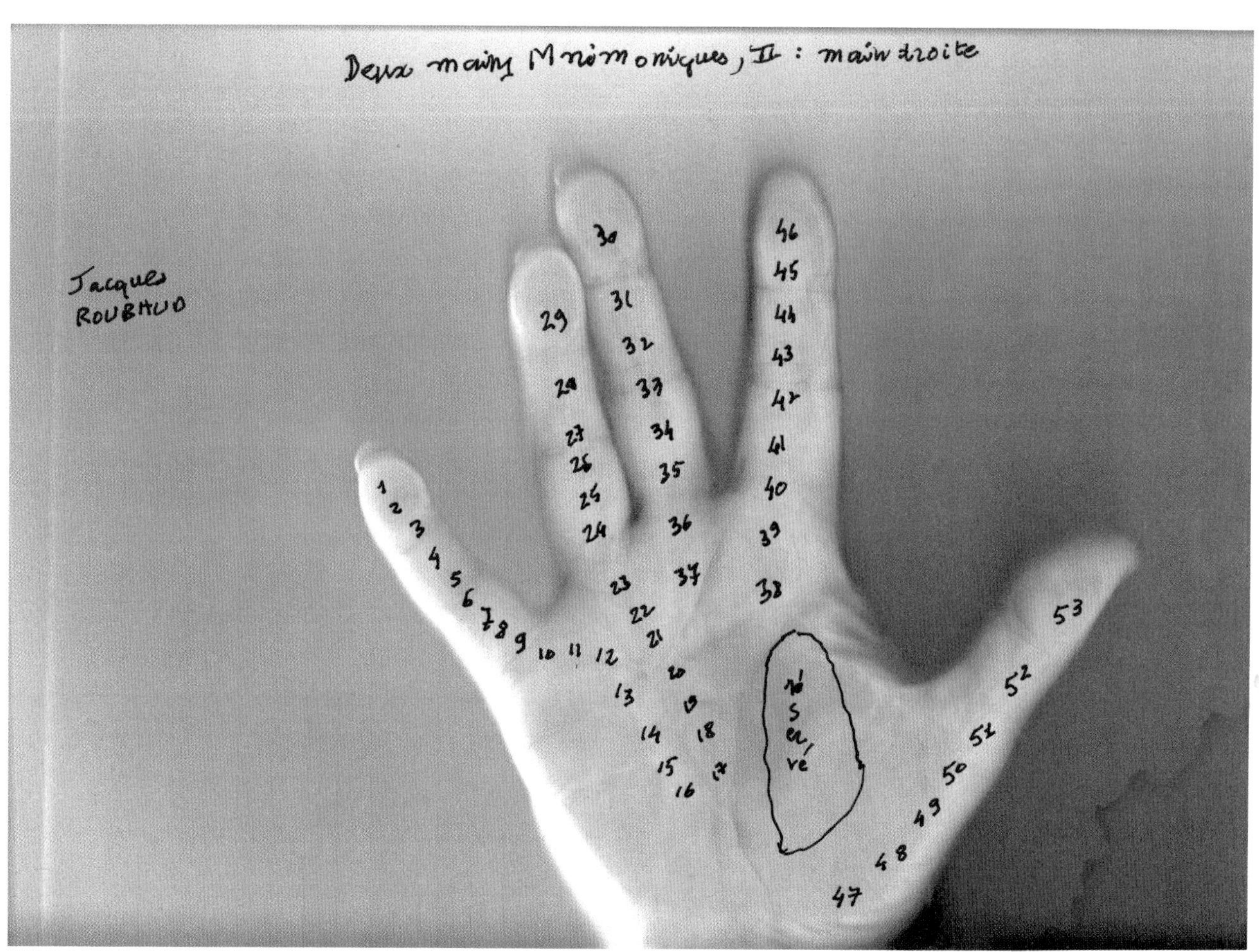

ARTIST

CERITH

WYN

EVANS

Unknown Territory, 2012

SCHOOL REVISITED.
BY G. D. LESLIE, A.R.A.
A Sketch from one of the Heads in the Picture in the Exhibition of the Royal Academy, 1875.

You are here ... and now

HANS ULRICH OBRIST

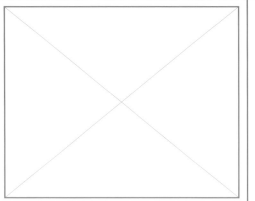

'The archipelago is a passage, not a wall.'[1]

'*Mondialité* is the extraordinary adventure whereby we all live today in a world which, for the first time, in real and in immediate, sudden ways, without wait, is simultaneously multiple and unique.'[2]

ÉDOUARD GLISSANT

My passion for maps began with Alighiero Boetti. When I was seventeen, I met this visionary artist and he changed my life in many ways. Crucially, he introduced me to ideas around map-making. It was Boetti who first told me about the work of Édouard Glissant and the implications of his concept of *mondialité*; through his mapping projects, the Italian artist assimilated Glissant's ideas into his own practice. Boetti's extraordinary collaborations in Afghanistan and, later, Pakistan, intertwined aesthetic and political concerns, craftsmanship and the artist's physical journey, as well as the negotiation of linguistic and physical borders. 'With the embroidered *Maps of the World*,' Boetti stated, 'I didn't invent anything, neither the shapes nor the colours.'[3] The contributors to this book might say the same thing.

This volume explores and interrogates the practices and potentials of mapping in the world today, and its relation to multiple disciplines: art, literature, architecture, science and film. In the words of Hungarian-born designer, educator and design theorist György Kepes, it is an attempt to go beyond the fear of pooling knowledge. Kepes had a holistic approach to knowledge, and the links he made between art, design and other disciplines, especially science, are more important now than ever. Dialogue, conversation and exchange between different fields is the only way we can chart a course through the increasingly complex terrain that is contemporary life. Indeed, as one of the book's contributors, Qiu Zhijie, puts it, 'To map is to know, and to direct future action.'

47°22'28" N 9°17'57" E

In May 1992, I founded the Robert Walser Museum in honour of the German-speaking Swiss writer, as a museum on the move, with its starting point at the Hotel Krone in Gais (Appenzell, Switzerland). At first, this migratory museum consisted of nothing but a small, movable vitrine, the idea being to create a non-monumental, modest and very discreet establishment, an elastic institution that could permanently question its own definitions and parameters. Walser's walking eye, or walking vision, mapped a presence for his subjects, which is perceived as an in-between space. Characters move between presence and absence, between experience and imagination.

> 'To me the Parisian papers are a substitute for the theatre. Also, not even the finest restaurants will I honour with my feet, so subtle have I become. Gulps of beer no longer pass my lips. My ear approves only the most melodiousness of the French language. Once I adored a lady, a true lady; today I find her most clumsy, since *Le Figaro* has spoiled me. Did *Le Matin* not drive me half-mad? While my colleagues write themselves sick in this modern time of crisis, I grow exuberant through my papers. A trip which I intended to take to Paris, I consider completed, I became acquainted with France's capital by way of reading.'[4]
> ROBERT WALSER

Walser spent the last twenty-seven years of his life in isolation, writing his microscripts and punctuating his days by taking long walks in the woods (where he eventually died in 1956 at the age of seventy-eight). His history in turn drifted into the writings of Catalan novelist Enrique Vila-Matas, whose *Doctor Posavento* (2005) imagines and fictionalizes the last years of Walser's life. Vila-Matas has spoken to me at length of his fascination with Walser and mapping and the importance of both on his own output, which is described as his 'literary geography'.

53°17'22" N 6°6'50" W

Maps produce new realities much as they seek to document current ones. Maps are always a going-beyond the space-time of the present. This is something that the Situationists understood well in their concept of the *dérive*. In a conversation I had with Raoul Vaneigem, he said:

> 'I hold Robert Walser in high regard, as many do. His lucidity and sense of *dérive* enchanted Kafka.... My psychogeographic *dérives* with Guy Debord in Paris, Barcelona, Brussels, Beersel and Antwerp were exceptional moments, combining theoretical speculation, sentient intelligence, the critical analysis of beings and places, and the pleasure of cheerful drinking. Our homeports were pleasant bistros with a warm atmosphere, havens where one was oneself because one felt in the air something of the authentic life, however fragile and short-lived. It was an identical mood that guided our wanderings through the streets, the lanes and the alleys, through the meanderings of a pleasure that our every step helped us gauge in terms of what it might take to expand and refine it just a little further.'

The *dérive* is not merely a spatio-temporal drift through urban landscapes, but a drift through the spaces of the imagination in order to arrive at an invention of reality. This is why Joyce's *Ulysses* takes the simultaneous form of a *dérive* through the environs of Dublin and a drift through the mind of Stephen Dedalus. Wandering and drifting can be a geographical and a psychological movement, a migration across borders. Maps are errors to arrive at truth. To paraphrase the words that Joyce gives to Dedalus, these 'errors are volitional and are the portals of discovery'.

51°30'19" N 0°10'31" W

A decade ago, the exhibition 'Live/Life' at the Musee d'art moderne de la ville de Paris/ARC, which I co-curated with Laurence Bossé, proposed a possible cartography of the London art scene. This was illustrated by David Shrigley's map of artist-run spaces, many of which no longer exist. Mapping was also at the core of the migratory exhibition 'Cities on the Move' that I curated with Hou Hanru in 1997–8. More recently, this interest has expanded through the years of the Serpentine Gallery Marathons, each of which has used mapping as a curatorial device. I conceived of the Marathon format in Stuttgart in 2005, as a transdisciplinary model that seeks to capture the present, creating a platform for the production of realities that contain the potential for further and future knowledge. The format was launched in 2006 with the Serpentine Gallery Interview Marathon, the fruit of a dialogue with gallery's director Julia Peyton-Jones and her extraordinary vision of the Serpentine Gallery Pavilion. During this twenty-four-hour event, Rem Koolhaas and I interviewed seventy-two leading cultural figures based in London, mapping the city through conversations with the protagonists who inhabit it. As Oskar Kokoschka said, it is very difficult to make a synthetic image of a city, because by the moment one has seized it, it has changed. The Interview Marathon aimed to formulate new ways of mapping or charting the activities of a city while acknowledging its perennial mutability. Similarly, the Experiment Marathon in the following year (organized with Olafur Eliasson) mapped the interface between art and science; while the 2008 Manifesto Marathon charted artists' relationships to politics, polemics and poetics, a theme that was further explored in the subsequent Poetry Marathon. For the 2010 iteration, the participants in the Map Marathon were invited to present elements of their current project or research that together created a fluid, multi-vocal 'map' of contemporary cartographic and mapping practices.

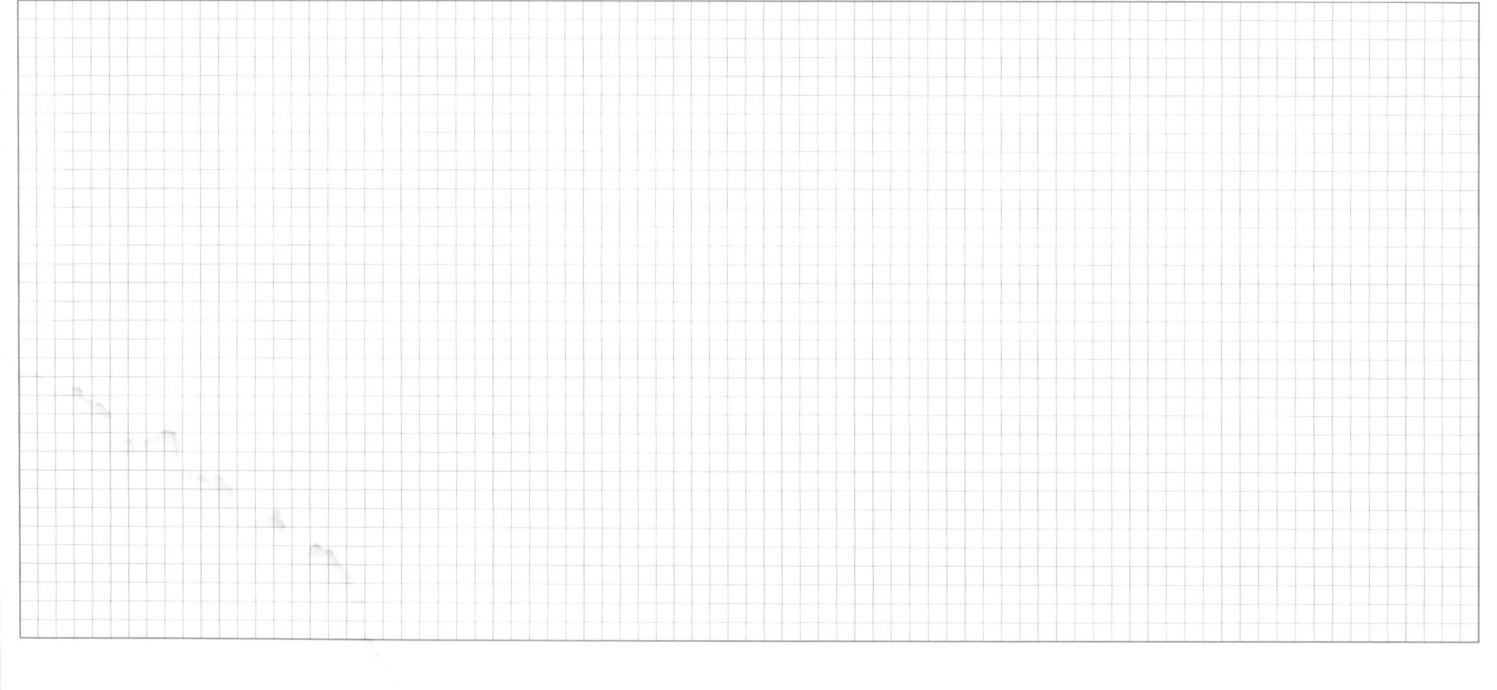

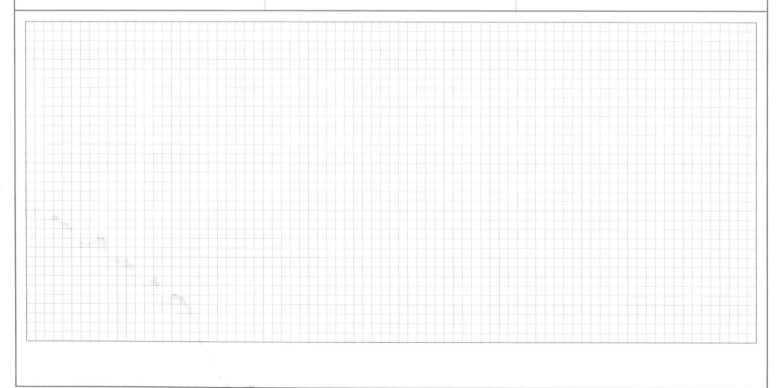

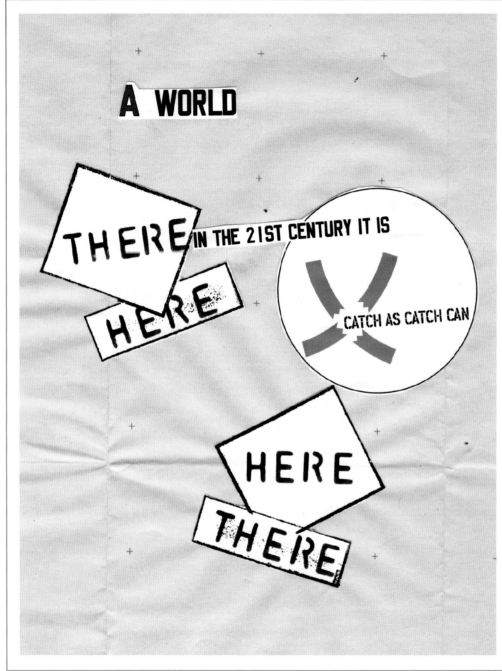

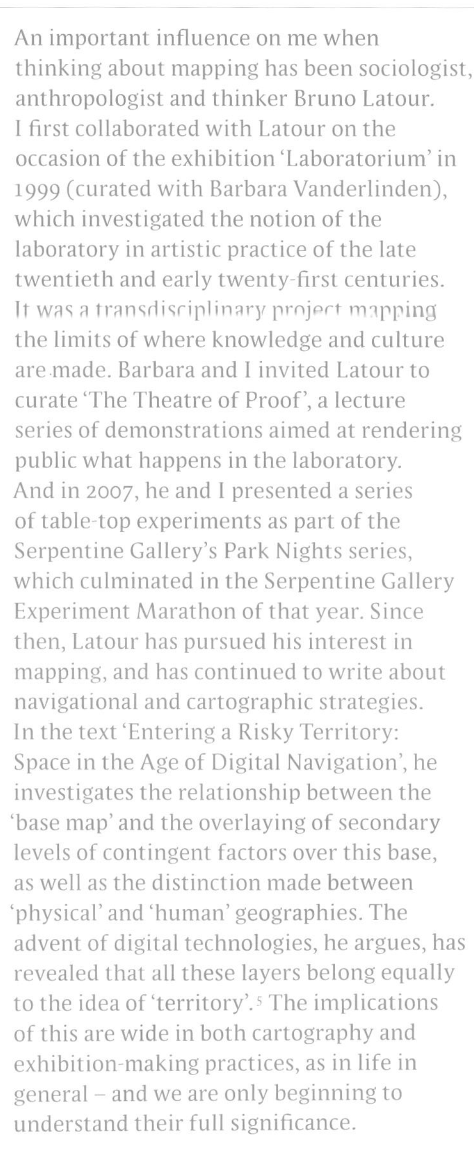

51°12'38" N 4°23'18" W

An important influence on me when thinking about mapping has been sociologist, anthropologist and thinker Bruno Latour. I first collaborated with Latour on the occasion of the exhibition 'Laboratorium' in 1999 (curated with Barbara Vanderlinden), which investigated the notion of the laboratory in artistic practice of the late twentieth and early twenty-first centuries. It was a transdisciplinary project mapping the limits of where knowledge and culture are made. Barbara and I invited Latour to curate 'The Theatre of Proof', a lecture series of demonstrations aimed at rendering public what happens in the laboratory. And in 2007, he and I presented a series of table-top experiments as part of the Serpentine Gallery's Park Nights series, which culminated in the Serpentine Gallery Experiment Marathon of that year. Since then, Latour has pursued his interest in mapping, and has continued to write about navigational and cartographic strategies. In the text 'Entering a Risky Territory: Space in the Age of Digital Navigation', he investigates the relationship between the 'base map' and the overlaying of secondary levels of contingent factors over this base, as well as the distinction made between 'physical' and 'human' geographies. The advent of digital technologies, he argues, has revealed that all these layers belong equally to the idea of 'territory'.[5] The implications of this are wide in both cartography and exhibition-making practices, as in life in general – and we are only beginning to understand their full significance.

29°46'8" N 95°22'12" W

With the Serpentine Gallery Map Marathon and now with this book we wish to remember the American artist Mark Lombardi (1951–2000), whose practice has been important for the youngest generation of artists trained in the abstraction of digital mapping. Between 1994 and 2000, Lombardi produced complex drawings, which he called 'narrative structures', charting and narrating international conspiracies and the web of invisible power relations between corporations and politics. It was his experience as a curator at the Contemporary Arts Museum in Houston and a reference librarian for the Fine Arts department in the Houston Public Library that gave him access to the information he would filter into his diagrams. 'I am pillaging the corporate vocabulary of diagrams and charts', Lombardi explained, 'rearranging information in a visual format that's interesting to me and mapping the political and social terrain in which I live.'[6] Although the information that is visualized on Lombardi's diagrammatic maps can be found in the public realm, it is the transmissible nature of map-making and the form of the chart that renders his work so radical. The active and political potential of maps is found not only in their content, but in the way in which information is communicated through them instantly. Lombardi's untimely death, 'still shrouded in mystery, occurred at the same time at which his art became visible to the broader audiences', said curator Carolyn Christov-Bakargiev. Other data visualizers, such as Benjamin Fry, have highlighted how Lombardi's data-charting and narrative-production through mapping has influenced design and contemporary forms of digital data visualization by maintaining a link to human experience and human history while successfully synthesizing information.[7]

90°0'0" S 0°0'0" W

There are no longer unknown countries on a map. There are no longer blank zones. *Terrae incognitae* no longer exist. We know all there is.[8] The twenty-first century, characterized by growing displacement, migration and globality, has inaugurated the age of the Internet. This book includes maps that first appeared as online digital visualizations, as well as real-time geolocating systems and satellite-guided navigation. Google Earth and the like challenge our conventional understanding that a map is a representation of a specific territory – an idea, Latour reminds us, that derives from an art-historical perspective on cartography.[9] Similarly, as this project of digital mapping develops, it will invite its own revising, and as it evolves, it will change. There is a point when everything could become a map. Maps can be totalizing visions, but they always invite their own revision. As another contributor to our volume, the eminent astronomer Dimitar Sasselov, suggested, it might be that the question we need to ask now is 'What is not a map?'

NOTES

1. 'L'archipel est un passage, et non pas un mur.' Édouard Glissant, inscription on a map drawing, 2010.
2. 'La mondialité, c'est l'aventure extraordinaire qui nous est donnée à tous de vivre aujourd'hui dans un monde qui, pour la premiere fois, *réellement* et de manière immédiate, foudroyante, sans attendre, se conçoit comme un monde à la fois multiple et unique.' Édouard Glissant interviewed by Yovan Gilles, *Les Périphériques vous parlent*, no. 14, Summer 2000.
3. Alighiero Boetti, quoted by Annemarie Sauzeau Boetti in *Alighiero e Boetti: Shaman-Showan* (Cologne: Verlag der Buchhandlung Walther Koenig, 2003), p. 150.
4. Robert Walser, 'Parisian Newspapers' (1925), trans. Tom Whalen and Carol Gehrig, from *Selected Stories* (New York: New York Review of Books, 1992), p. 144.
5. Bruno Latour, Valérie November and Eduardo Camacho-Hubner, 'Entering a Risky Territory: Space in the Age of Digital Navigation', *Environment and Planning D: Society and Space*, no. 28 (4), 2010, pp. 581–99.
6. Mark Lombardi, quoted by Frances Richards in 'Obsessive-Generous: Toward a Diagram of Mark Lombardi', *wburg.com/0202/arts/lombardi.html*
7. Benjamin Fry, 'Learning from Lombardi', *benfry.com/exd09*
8. Édouard Glissant, interviewed in 2002 by Landry-Wilfrid Miampika, *africultures.com/php/index.php?nav=article&no=2842*
9. Bruno Latour, Valérie November and Eduardo Camacho-Hubner, op. cit.

ILLUSTRATIONS

p.233 Jurg Lehni & Alex Rich, *Reminder*, 2010.
p.235 Lawrence Weiner, *There in the 21st century it is here*, 2010.

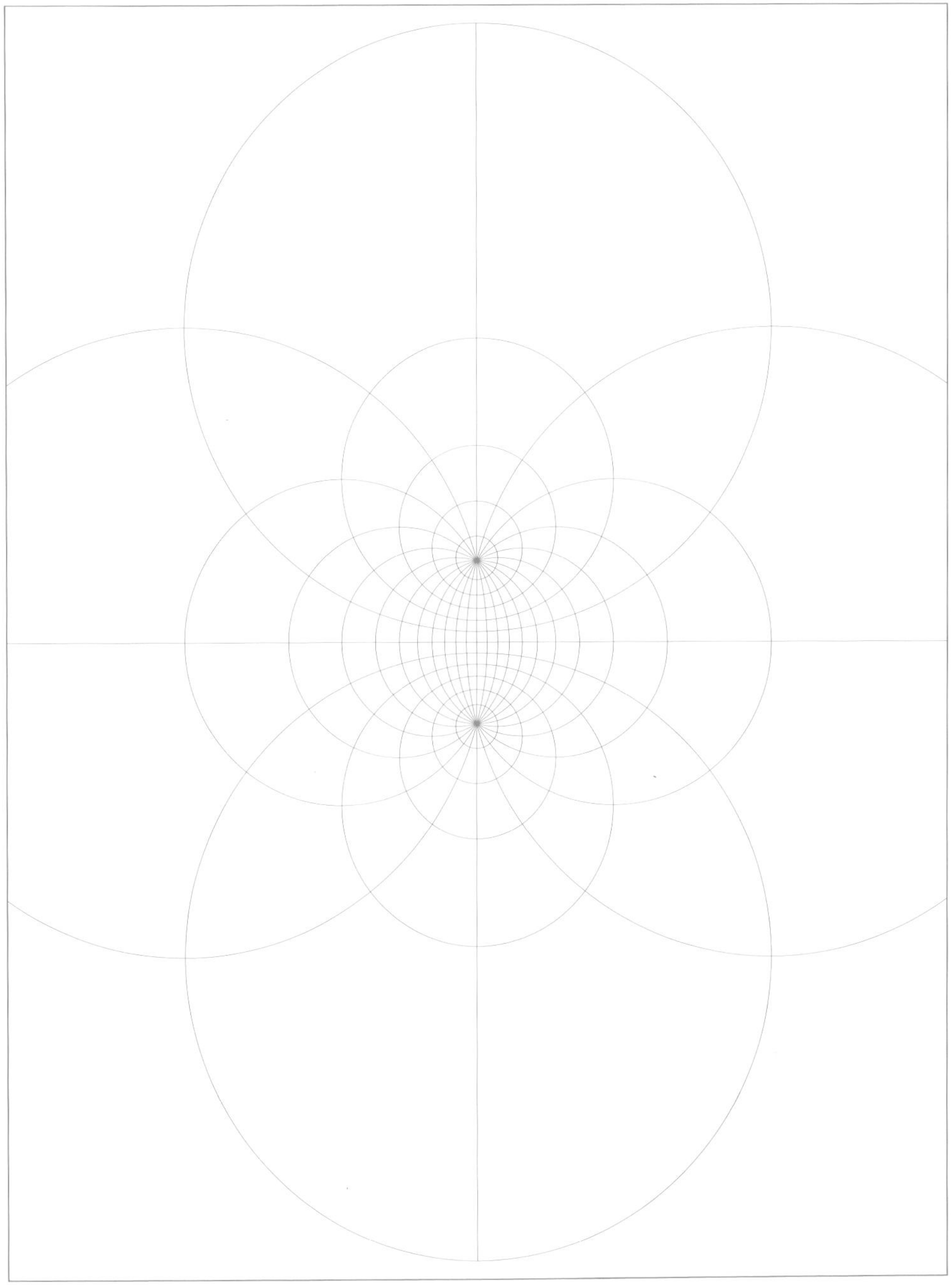

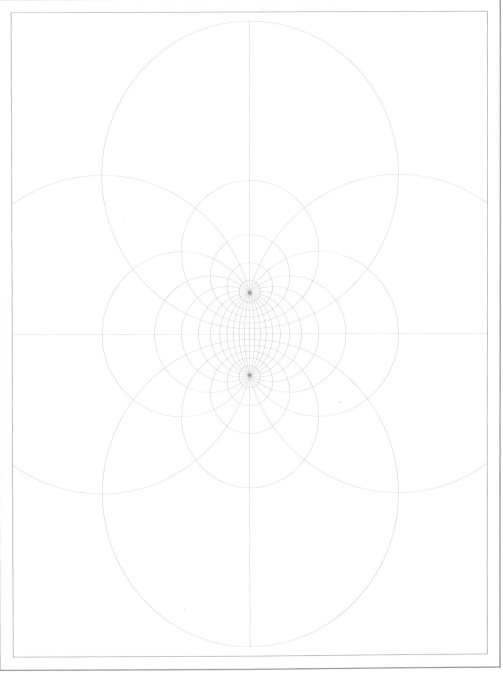

ACKNOWLEDGMENTS

This book grew out of the Map Marathon held at the Serpentine Gallery, London, in October 2010. The event was part of the Serpentine's Marathon series that began in 2006 and that is produced alongside the gallery's annual Pavilion Commission, conceived by Julia Peyton-Jones in 2000. A Marathon always hides within it another marathon. The Map Marathon was the product of several partnerships. John Brockman and the EDGE Foundation curated a special section of maps, and the editor of this volume is particularly grateful to John and the contributors to the website www.edge.org. The Marathon was also the continuation of an ongoing collaboration with DLD – Digital, Life, Design, which began with the panel 'Maps for the 21st Century' for the 2010 DLD conference (dld-conference.com). The editor continues to be very grateful to Steffi Czerny for this ongoing partnership.

The Map Marathon was curated by Hans Ulrich Obrist, Sally Tallant, Nicola Lees, Lucia Pietroiusti and Vanessa Boni. It was produced by Justin O'Shaughnessy with Marty Langthorne, Sarah-Jane Grimshaw, Allison Jeny and Jacob Patterson; and it was accompanied by a publication conceived and designed by CRASH! (Scott King and Matt Worley), with Régis Tosetti and Simon Palmieri. It was funded by Arts Council England and supported by the Annenberg Foundation, DLD – Digital, Life, Design and the Kensington Hotel, London, with kind assistance from the Royal Geographical Society (with the Institute of British Geographers) and additional support from the Luigi Ontani Performance Circle: Giulio Count of Gropello and Galleria Lorcan O'Neill, Rome. The Marathon's media partners were *Time Out* and *Wired*.

Hans Ulrich Obrist would like to thank all of the contributors to this book for their generous, imaginative and inspiring contributions.

PUBLISHERS' NOTE

The publishers wish to thank the director and staff of the Serpentine Gallery for their kind assistance and collaboration throughout the production of this book. In particular, we are grateful to Hans Ulrich Obrist for originally conceiving the whole venture and for having invited us to oversee its publication. Our gratitude also goes to Tom McCarthy for his insightful introduction, which so deftly maps out the terrain of the subject. Above all, we would like to thank all of the artists, scientists and thinkers who have so generously allowed their contributions to appear in the volume.